The Presidency and the Congress

A Shifting Balance of Power?

The Presidency and the Congress

Edited by William S. Livingston
Lawrence C. Dodd
Richard L. Schott

Lyndon B. Johnson School of Public Affairs
Lyndon Baines Johnson Library
1979

Copyright 1979 by Board of Regents
The University of Texas
L.C. Card Number: 79-88346
ISBN: 0-89940-407-3
Printed in the United States of America
Designed by Eje Wray

Contents

Foreword   ix
Introduction
  J.J. Pickle   xiii

I. The Imperial President and the Resurgent Congress: Myth or Reality?   1

Overview
  William S. Livingston   5
The Imperial Presidency Reexamined
  Thomas E. Cronin   7
Congress and the Cycles of Power
  Lawrence C. Dodd   46
Discussion   70
    Stephen Hess
    David R. Mayhew
    James L. Sundquist
    Tom Wicker
    Garry Wills

II. Points of Conflict Between Congress and the President 89

Overview
  Richard L. Schott   93
Whose Budget? It All Depends on Whether the
  President or Congress is Doing the Counting
  Allen Schick   97
Control of the Bureaucracy: A Mismatch
  of Incentives and Capabilities
  Morris P. Fiorina   124
Discussion   143
  Louis Fisher
  Francis E. Rourke
  James L. Sundquist

III. Congress and the President in the Making of Policy   159

Overview
  Bruce Miroff   163
Congress and the President: The Struggle
  Over Foreign Policy
  Robert A. Divine   166
Congress vs. President: The Myth and the Pendulum
  Sar A. Levitan   182
Discussion   197
  John Brademus
  Wilbur Cohen
  David E. Price
  Walt W. Rostow

IV. Johnson and Rayburn: The 1950s/An Era
  of Congressional Government   219

Overview
  Clarence G. Lasby   223
Sam Rayburn and the House of Representatives
  D.B. Hardeman   226

Lyndon B. Johnson and Senate Leadership
  R.K. Huitt   253
Discussion   265
    Alan Bible
    Lindy Boggs
    Harry McPherson
    J. William Theis

V. An Era of Presidential Government: The 1960s   279

Overview
  Horace Busby   283
Congressional-Executive Relations During the 1960s
  Barefoot Sanders   286
Discussion   300
    Wilbur Cohen
    Henry B. Gonzales
    Harry McPherson
    J.J. Pickle
    Margaret Chase Smith

VI. The Reorganization of Congress and the Executive   319

Overview
  Emmette S. Redford   323
Management as a Priority in Executive Branch
  Reorganization
  Alan K. Campbell   325
Our Changing Congress: the Inside (and Outside) Story
  Roger H. Davidson   341
Discussion   363
    Lawrence C. Dodd
    Herbert Kaufman
    Bruce I. Oppenheimer
    Harold Seidman

VII. Conflict and a Search for a New Balance: The 1970s 379

Overview
  Robert L. Hardesty 383
Discussion 387
  Carl Albert
  Graham T. Allison
  Bill Moyers
  Richard E. Neustadt
  Elspeth Rostow
  John Tower
  Nan Waterman

Participants 423

Foreword

The struggle between the President and Congress over the direction of American public policy is a familiar phenomenon—not new to this decade, or for that matter to this century. Its scope and intensity, however, have increased in recent years, and so has the rancor that it generates. This change can be seen in the conflict over foreign policy (Vietnam, Cambodia), over domestic policy (energy, social welfare), and over the relative power positions of the two institutions (Watergate, impoundment, the congressional budget, the War Powers Act). And the struggle goes on without regard to whether Congress and the Presidency are controlled by the same party.

To discuss and appraise the state of congressional-presidential relations, a symposium was organized at The University of Texas at Austin in November of 1977 under the title "The Presidency and the Congress: A Shifting Balance of Power?" It was sponsored by the Lyndon Baines Johnson Library and the Lyndon B. Johnson School of Public Affairs, in cooperation with the Department of Government. This volume reports the proceedings of that symposium.

Some sixty people gathered in Austin from various walks of life and various parts of the country to join in this reassessment of the Presidency and the Congress and of their relations with each other.

Foreword • x

It was a wide-ranging and sometimes wild-swinging discussion, animated by the change in the public mood that followed Watergate and Vietnam, and informed by the need to evaluate the institutional reforms in both Congress and the Presidency that have marked the decade of the seventies.

The outlook of the symposium was both retrospective and prospective, both descriptive and prescriptive, as is made clear by the titles of the individual sessions. The participants looked back to the 1950s when Congress was ascendant; they examined the 1960s when the President dominated the scene; they sought to appraise the new balance of power in the 1970s. They looked at the imperial Presidency and the resurgent Congress, and they examined the points of conflict and the mechanisms of cooperation between them.

There was considerable disagreement over the direction of congressional-presidential relations. Perspectives ranged from the viewpoint that the nation is experiencing a cyclical decline in the power of Congress, with a consequent destruction of the constitutional system, to the idea that the imperial Presidency has now given way to an imperial Congress, with Congress being the primary threat to constitutional government. Othe analysts stressed that less fundamental and more moderate changes are occurring in congressional-presidential relations, with primary developments including the emergence of a new non-imperial *style* of presidential behavior, and more responsible, effective policymaking within Congress.

The symposium was organized around seven sessions, each centered on a particular topic related to the conference theme. The book reflects that organization.* The papers were generally presented in summary form at the symposium to allow for fuller panel participation in the examination of the issues. The editors have attempted to preserve the character and pace of the interchange among panelists by including the transcribed comments after the formal papers. The discussions often provide entertaining reading and at the same time expand the scope and richness of the book.

The group that gathered for the symposium—paper givers, panelists, observers—was as notable for its diversity as for its competence. It included members of both houses of Congress, present and past; it

---

*An eighth session on the role of the press in executive-legislative relations carried a different format and does not appear here.

included members of the executive branch, both present and past; it included academic students of American governmental institutions; it included journalists, professional researchers, and the authors of some of the leading analyses of Congress and the Presidency. A glance at the *dramatis personae* will show scholars, observers, practitioners, savants, and eccentrics. It was a good group and a good symposium. And it was fun.

The symposium was planned and organized by a special committee drawn from the Library staff and the University faculty. It was jointly chaired by Elspeth D. Rostow, Dean of the Lyndon B. Johnson School of Public Affairs, and Harry J. Middleton, Director of the Lyndon Baines Johnson Library. Initially the task was shared by Alan Campbell, then Dean of the School and later Chairman of the Civil Service Commission. Other members of the committee included Charles Corkran and John Fawcett of the Library staff, Emmette Redford and Richard Schott of the faculty of the LBJ School, and Lawrence Dodd and William Livingston of the Department of Government. Funds for the enterprise were provided by the Moody Foundation and the Lyndon Baines Johnson Foundation, to both of which go our grateful thanks. Willa Beach helped with the typing. Virginia Sevier not only typed most of the manuscript but also managed the records and correspondence related to compiling the book.

         William S. Livingston
         Lawrence C. Dodd
         Richard L. Schott

Austin
March 1979

Introduction

The Honorable J.J. (Jake) Pickle

J.J. ("Jake") Pickle is a U.S. Congressman from Texas's Tenth District.

When Andy Jackson, that great early self-made man, was President, he stepped outside of the White House one morning onto the east grounds, stuck a shovel in the ground, and said, "Sot her here." With that order he decreed that the United States Treasury Building would be placed on the east side of the Capitol, out of line, out of place with all the buildings and drawings that were laid down by L'Enfant. And it juts out today on Pennsylvania Avenue as a reminder that a President can do pretty much what he wants to do. Jackson may well have been the first President to defy the established order and do it his way. But it is also significant that though he won that battle he lost the war, as many Presidents do. He built a building but the Congress prevailed with its policy.

I can speak as one who has had some first-hand knowledge of the President during the Lyndon B. Johnson Presidency. I was known then—and I still am, I'm glad to say—as the President's Congressman. Out of sheer vanity—usually when I came back to the district—I liked to say publicly that LBJ was my constituent. That little game always made me feel better, and it worked out pretty well until one day LBJ heard me use it. Right then that game stopped. He never did see the humor in my assertion that he was just a constituent.

Like most members of a political party, I would vote with the President and would try to help, and that was expected of me. On those infrequent occasions when I differed, there would be a cool draft of air from Pennsylvania Avenue, and the communications would be cut off for awhile. That was the beginning of a cold war. And it would stay that way until another important bill came up, and then things would warm up again, and there was a new ball game. That's the way the system works.

Nothing is more timely in the Capital these days than the topic of Congress and the Presidency. It is a hot item in Washington. It always is at the beginning of a new session or when any kind of trouble is brewing. Hardly a day goes by without some comment in the national news media on how President Carter is getting along with Congress. The *New York Times* data bank shows about five hundred news items written since January 1st of this year on presidential-congressional relations. Now that is not anything new; it has been pretty much the same since the Presidency of George Washington.

The same article in the *New York Times* said that President Jefferson once remarked, "The Senate is not supposed, by the Constitution, to be acquainted with the concerns of the Executive Department. It was not intended that these (materials) should be communicated to them."

Can you imagine what reaction there would have been in the Congress if one of our modern Presidents had said that? If President Eisenhower had said that to Majority Leader Lyndon Johnson, I have a feeling that Congressional World War III might have started very early. No doubt that is what President Jefferson really felt in those days, but of course the roles of the Congress and the Chief Executive have been the subject of much debate ever since the formation of the Constitution.

One of the things we have to ask ourselves is whether there really is anything new in the relative balance of power between the Congress and the Presidency. Anything new in the ways in which the President and the Congress interreact with each other and tackle what they consider to be major national problems. I suspect that not much has really changed fundamentally since the early days of the Republic.

On the other hand, it is quite clear to me that the relation between the Congress and the President is never quite the same. It has as much to do with the individuals involved as it does with the shifting strands of power or with the changing times and problems. No matter how many other factors remain the same, congressional relations with a Harry Truman are vastly different from those of a Jack Kennedy or a Lyndon Johnson.

Similarly, the task of the President in dealing with the Congress, as I have personally viewed it, changes dramatically with each change of congressional leadership. Men like Sam Rayburn, John McCormack, Carl Albert, Tip O'Neill, Mike Mansfield, Bob Byrd, Bob Taft, Everett Dirksen, Hugh Scott, Gerald Ford—all these men respond and react differently to a President, and that has to be one of the considerations when we talk about the Presidency and the Congress. There are several major factors involved here, and I should like to list some of them for you.

Presidential-congressional relations are shaped not only by the relations between the leaders and the President but also by the relations between the majority and the minority leaders; between the leaders and the general membership of the Congress; by the size of the majority party—because a narrow majority quite often necessitates a stronger loyalty—and by the age, the talents, and the general makeup of the membership itself.

When Lyndon Johnson was majority leader, he was able to work with President Eisenhower and with Minority Leader Dirksen to pass civil rights legislation and to shape foreign policy. Senators Mansfield and Scott ate breakfast together every morning and guided debate in the Senate with a minimum of party strife. Tip O'Neill and Gerald Ford used to play golf together, and did so off and on for twenty years, long before Ford became President.

It is worth noting that President Carter is the first modern President since Woodrow Wilson to have no Washington background. Whether the problems this poses will be as serious for him as they were for Wilson remains to be seen. But it does mean that he is having to build bridges that were already there for his predecessors. He seems to be attempting to build those bridges through frequent meetings with congressional leaders. He and Speaker O'Neill have apparently already built a close relationship. Probably that is the strongest thing going for the President today in Washington.

Politics is rife with personal stories and personal anecdotes, and for a reason. The individuals involved do play a tremendous role in the shaping of congressional-presidential relations, and for that matter in the shaping of almost anything political.

In the early post-Nixon days—and indeed in the last months of the Nixon Presidency—the Congress began to assert itself as a leading force in the political system. Now how did they do that?

First, by the passing of a Budget Act and the creation of a congressional budget; second, by the passage of the War Powers Act and a more aggressive and an outspoken Congress in foreign policy—without, I hope, its trying to play President in foreign affairs; and third, by the increasing use of the so-called veto power by the Congress as a weapon to combat the runaway growth of administrative rules and regulations.

But we must ask ourselves why Congress has begun to assert itself, to reclaim authority it willingly gave up over a fifty-year period, beginning with Woodrow Wilson and the creation of new regulatory agencies such as the Federal Reserve Board and the Federal Trade Commission.

Some observers build a cyclical theory showing power shifting back and forth among the various branches of government. Others point to the effects of particular major events such as the Great Depression, the Second World War, the Cold War, and the Vietnam War. It is no doubt true that the problems of the day contribute to shifts in power. But the temporary crisis, the temporary pressure of action and response, do not necessarily mandate permanent changes. This country went from Abraham Lincoln to Teddy Roosevelt, a period of over forty years, without a really strong President, unless you want to give honorable mention to Grover Cleveland. During that period the President and the executive departments were supposed to carry out the laws passed by the Congress—and otherwise to stay at home. And that's pretty much what they did. My belief is that if President Johnson had remained in office, or if Senator Humphrey had been elected in 1968—and assuming of course that the war had eventually been settled—the structure of presidential-congressional relations would have remained pretty much as before. At least, if Congress had begun to assert itself, its progress would have come far more slowly, would have been far less comprehensive, and would have commanded less support and acclaim.

Events, however, moved differently. The reawakening of Congress was prompted by the practices and events of the Nixon Administration—the impoundment of funds, Watergate and the cover-up, the abuses of power, and the arrogant and disdainful lack of consideration for Congress. All these combined to make Congress, which is normally a very slow and deliberate body (regardless of what the headlines in the daily papers may lead you to believe), rise up and reassert itself.

In spite of the revival of power in the Congress, however, only a small change has been made in the standard operating procedures of the past decades. For fifty years we have seen powers and responsibilities heaped upon the Executive. We have created agencies to regulate people and agencies to administer to people. If we have built up the Presidency too much, perhaps it will have to readjust itself downward just as the Congress must continue to build itself upward. At least that's the way one Congressman looks at it.

We must always remember that we are talking about two very different institutions. You can describe the President's actions on any one day in a three-minute television broadcast. That is impossible to do with 435 members of the House. And that is a fortunate thing. But it is a fact that they have two distinct roles and there is no way to describe them in comparable terms.

I think we can all agree that the power of the Presidency has grown and grown in the last forty years. And the Congress cannot complain, because Congress helped produce that growth. Every law we pass providing a new service has created another agency. And subsequently those agencies have to carry out the laws that the Congress passes. So while we focus here on the President and the Congress, I suggest that the real contest, if there is one, is not between the President and the Congress as much as it is between the Legislature and the people on the one hand, and the Executive with its vast bureaucracy on the other. It is the bureaus, which we have created and which the President must instruct to carry out the orders, the programs, the regulations, that are the core of our problem today.

I

The Imperial Presidency and the Resurgent Congress: Myth or Reality?

Overview: William S. Livingston
Papers: Thomas E. Cronin
Lawrence C. Dodd
Discussion: Stephen Hess
David R. Mayhew
James L. Sundquist
Tom Wicker
Garry Wills

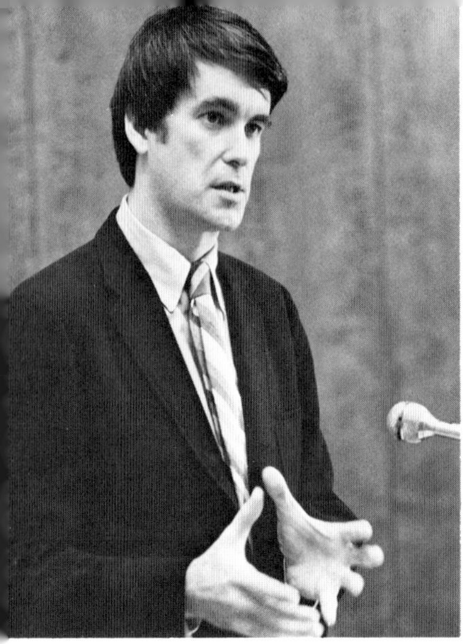

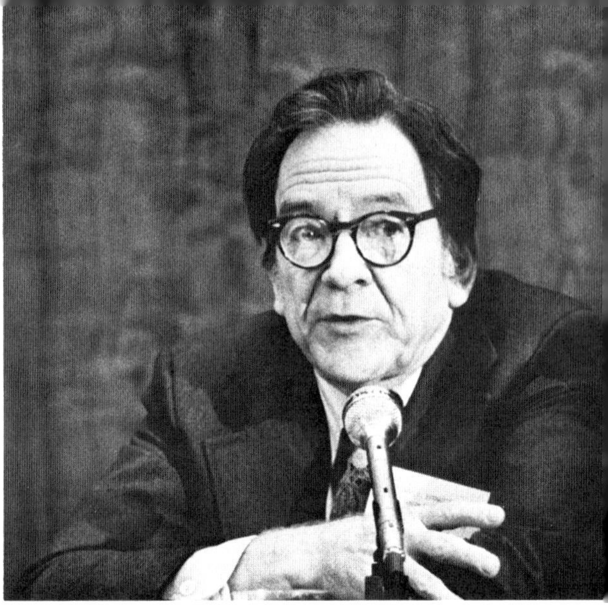

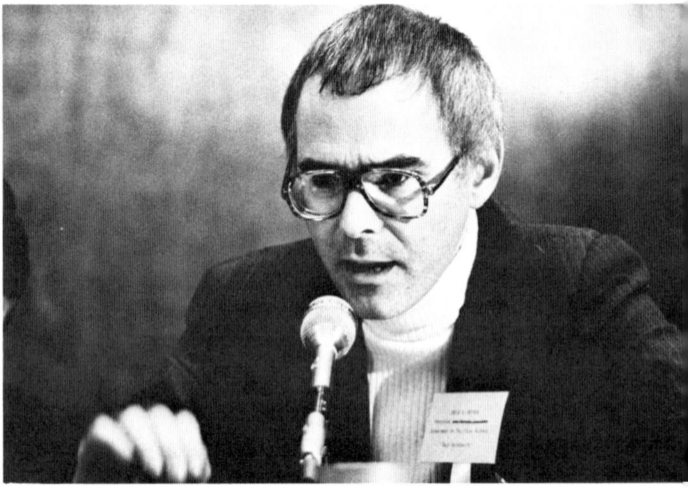

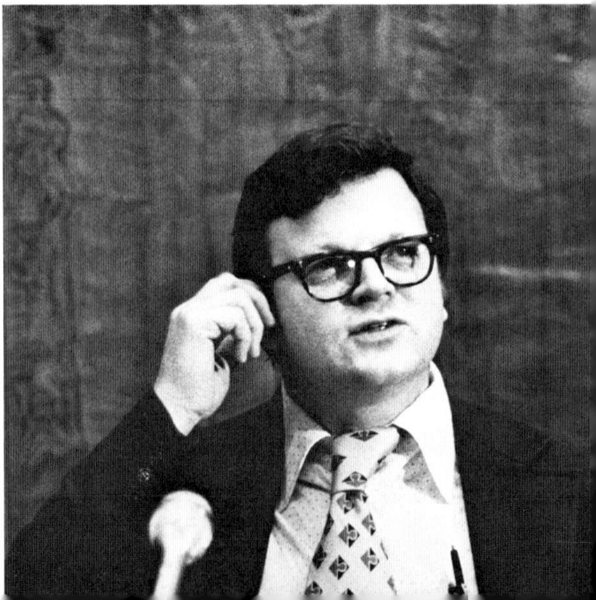

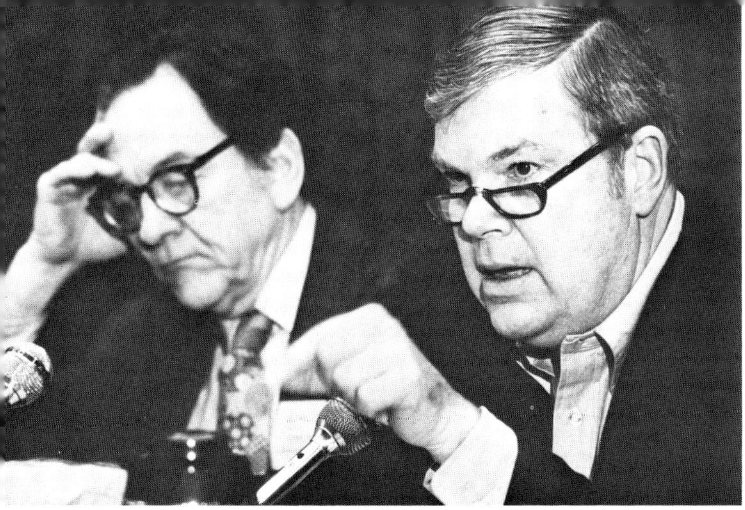

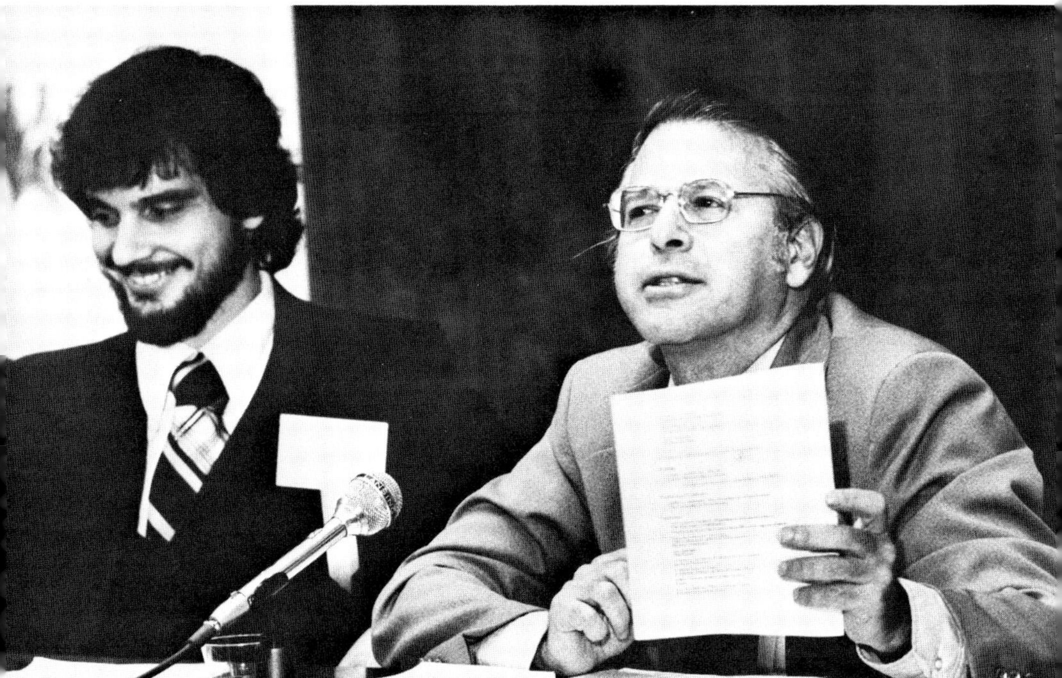

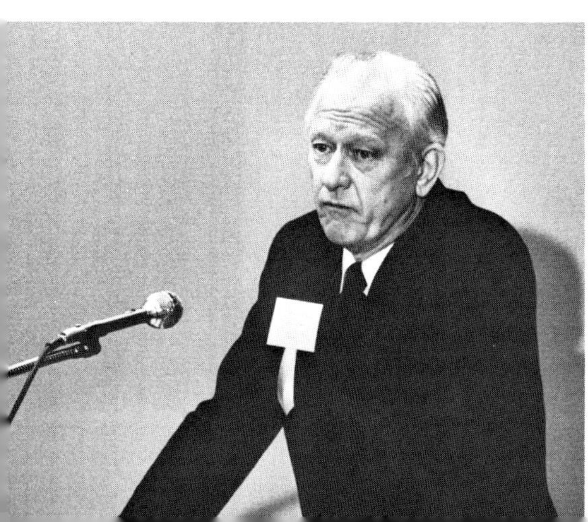

Overview

William S. Livingston

William S. Livingston is Professor of Government and Chairman of the Comparative Studies Program at The University of Texas at Austin.

In 1973 Arthur Schlesinger, Jr., wrote a very important book called *The Imperial Presidency*. In that book Schlesinger called attention to what he saw as a constitutional rather than a political shift of power, namely, "the appropriation by the Presidency of powers reserved by long historical practice to the Congress." Schlesinger saw this shift as a product of the changed circumstances of our domestic situation, especially of the economy; he saw it as a product of our newly broadened world position; and he saw it as a product of our particular foreign policies. But most significantly he also said, "It was as much a matter of congressional abdication as it was of presidential usurpation."

Now that was 1973. In the lamentations that followed the Watergate experience, in the multiple mea culpas of that age, yea even in the euphoria of the post-Watergate era, we have been exploring all sorts of ways of limiting the President, since we seem to believe that the lesson of Watergate was that the President was indeed too strong— even if we had not believed Schlesinger when he said it was imperial. Many of the proposals and speculations about the imperial and the too-strong President looked toward a strengthened Congress or a resurgent Congress.

Many of the participants in this symposium have taken part in this reassessment, or as practitioners have taken part in the actual

I/Imperial President and Resurgent Congress

realignment, of the Congress and its relations with the Presidency. Professor Dodd will suggest that there are cycles in congressional power. Are there, then, cycles in presidential power? Woodrow Wilson, who will be mentioned frequently in this section, is usually associated with the idea of a very strong Presidency. But it was that same Woodrow Wilson who a generation earlier wrote another book called *Congressional Government.*

The questions that are important for our concern tumble over one another in great profusion. Is the imperial Presidency a new or is it a recurrent phenomenon? To what extent was the imperial Presidency as perceived by Schlesinger a product of our own institutional system, and to what extent was it an aberration from that institutional system? Are there in the system built-in governing devices that keep the system running, and running right? Was the fall of Nixon an adequate answer to Schlesinger's imperial Presidency, or does Watergate tell us that it really is important after all that we elect good men to office?

To what extent was this imperial Presidency a product of forces in the external environment of the nation, and to what extent was it produced—deliberately or willy-nilly—by the men who held the presidential office?

To what extent are the rise and fall of presidential powers a product—or, if you prefer, a cause—of the fall and rise of congressional power? If Congress is, as some say, resurgent and ascendant—and one of the panelists has written a book with that very title—if Congress is resurgent and ascendant, are we due for an era of imperial Congresses?

If there is a cycle in all these relations, are we then destined to repeat ourselves haplessly in the future?

The Imperial Presidency Reexamined

Thomas E. Cronin

Thomas E. Cronin is Professor of Political Science at the University of Delaware.

We assemble to appraise the so-called "imperial Presidency," its meaning and its consequences for our ideals of separation of powers and for our governing practices. We shall also try to assess the current state of relations between Congress and the Presidency.

Symbolically we meet at a school and in a building dedicated to the memory of a man who devoted himself to making both of those institutions flourish and prosper. President Johnson was painfully aware of the limits of the Presidency and of the paradoxes of presidential power. He knew it was an institution that in some ways was too strong and in other ways too weak. His memoirs contain the acknowledgement that he had made mistakes. They contain as well a puzzlement about what should be done about the Presidency. He half-heartedly embraced the idea of a single six-year term for Presidents as one remedy. But he never had the time to offer a more detailed analysis of the Presidency as an institution. He would have welcomed an attempt to look critically and yet constructively at the powers of the Presidency and at the need to make it both more effective and more accountable. As a particularly practical man he would have urged us to be specific, to be concrete, and to focus on what we should do now and in the future rather than dwelling on the past. In that original LBJ School of Politics on Pennsylvania Avenue, he was forever asking of his advisers: "Okay, what do you think should be done next?" That pragmatic habit of saying let's get on with it should also guide our deliberations here.

The "imperial Presidency" means many things to many people. But it especially suggests the abuse and misuse of presidential powers. By the year 1973 it became an accepted term to describe presidential deceptions, lying, and transgressions against cherished notions of separation of powers. A deep-seated skepticism set in as an increasing number of Americans lost confidence in President Nixon.

As a general proposition, citizen trust in the President had been high during the New Deal and post New Deal periods. Historians, political scientists, and journalists had generally held that a strong Presidency was a necessity.[1] Indeed, many added that our leaders need a free hand. Too many checks and balances would paralyze Presidents. In a way, they were saying that the absence of power can also corrupt.

But then came Watergate. It was a subversion and corruption of the political process. Nixon did not invent the tactics so much as extend and refine them. For he inherited most of the short cuts, the growing reliance on secrecy and deceit, from several of his predecessors. But unlike them, he was caught. In the wake of Watergate we have witnessed the disappearance of the easy optimism that once characterized popular attitudes toward Presidents.

A disciple of Confucius once asked his master, "What are the basic ingredients of good government?" Confucius answered, "Weapons, food, and the confidence of the people."

"But," continued the disciple, "Suppose you had to dispense with one of these three things—which would you forego?"

"Weapons," replied the master.

The disciple persisted. "Suppose you were forced to choose between the two that are left. Which would you then forego?"

"Food," Confucius said. "From of old, death has been the lot of all men, but a people that no longer trusts its rulers is lost indeed."

These words of the ancient Chinese philosopher have a special meaning and a ring of wisdom in our day, all the more so because our republic was explicitly founded on the principle of the consent of the governed.

During the early and mid-1970s, the American public's attitudes toward the government took on a deep, almost estranged cynicism. This loss of faith was doubtless caused by a variety of events, among which were political assassinations, civil disorders, rising crime rates, racial strife, recession, soaring inflation, and high unemployment—and especially the deep divisions in the country over Vietnam and Watergate.

As one of my students very aptly put it:

> As one crisis has succeeded another, the wellsprings of American optimism have seemed to dry up, and the effervescent American spirit seemed to tire.
>
> Through all of this, political leaders appeared impotent at best and criminals at worst. People who had expected them to solve the nation's problems were sorely disappointed. People who had expected that they would listen to the popular will found they ignored it instead. It is therefore hardly surprising that the American people drew from the course of our times a simple lesson: they think their government is not to be trusted.

The Effect of Watergate

Reaction to Watergate and Vietnam took at least two forms. Critics said here was irrefutable evidence that the Presidency was isolated, autocratic, and imperial. They charged too that the deceptions during Vietnam and the corruptions of Watergate occurred because our checks and balances were inadequate and too much power had been given to the Presidency.

Defenders of the Presidency argued that Vietnam and Watergate exemplified not so much the *excess* of power as the *abuse* of power. Moreover, supporters of the American system of dispersed powers saw at least some evidence that the system was working—that is, they felt the courts, the press, and even Congress did assert themselves when put to a critical test.

The Watergate disclosures and the first forced resignation of a President in our history aroused public concern about the role of Congress. Certainly in the mid-1970s the public wanted Congress to become a more coequal branch of government, more assertive and alert, more jealous of its own powers.

The change in public attitudes is well documented by polls taken before and after Vietnam and Watergate. In 1959, social scientists at the University of Michigan asked: "Some people say the President is in the best position to see what the country needs. Other people think the President may have good ideas about what the country needs, but it is up to the Congress to decide what ought to be done. How do you feel about this?" Sixty-one percent chose the President and 17 percent chose Congress (the remainder said about equal, or were undecided).[2] In 1977 *The New York Times* asked virtually the same question: "In general, who do you think *should* have the most to say in the way our government is run, the Congress or the President?" Fifty-eight percent this time chose Congress and only 26 percent the President (the remainder said about equal or were undecided).[3]

What form has congressional reassertion taken? Has Congress effectively addressed the charges made against the "imperial Presidency"? Could a vast new array of checks and balances cripple the Presidency and undermine its potential for creative leadership?

The Imperial Presidency Argument

In his book *The Imperial Presidency*, historian Arthur M. Schlesinger, Jr., contends that presidential power became so expanded and abused by 1972 that it threatened our constitutional system. This imperial Presidency, he says, was created primarily as a result of America's wars, particularly Vietnam.[4] Schlesinger explores two critical instruments that gave rise to the abuse of power by Presidents: the war power and secrecy. In discussing the evolution of the war power, he points out the troubling constitutional ambiguity in the President's power as Commander-in-Chief: it is an undefined *office*, not a *function*, the only constitutional office a President is given. Schlesinger makes what he believes to be a critical distinction between the *abuse* and the *usurpation* of power. Abraham Lincoln, FDR, and Harry Truman temporarily *usurped* power in wartime, knowing they would be held accountable after the wartime emergency ended. Lyndon Johnson and Richard Nixon, however, *abused* power, even in peacetime, claiming a near absolute power to be the permanent prerogative of the Presidency.

Schlesinger's second central theme is the evolution of secrecy as a weapon to protect and preserve the President's national security power. He notes that until President Eisenhower, the presumption was that Congress would get the information it sought from the executive branch and that instances of secrecy were to be rare exceptions. Obviously, he adds, a Congress that knows only what the Executive wants it to know is not an independent body.

Schlesinger says that the notion of a bipartisan foreign policy was a bad one. It had the effect, the longer it ran, of stifling debate. "And it gave the Presidency a powerful new peacetime weapon by refurbishing the wartime theory of 'national security' as the end to which other values could be properly sacrificed in times of crisis."[5]

Schlesinger devotes much of his attention to the Nixon Presidency, arguing that under Nixon the office became not only fully imperial, but also revolutionary. That is, Nixon in effect tried to carry out a revolution against the separation of powers and the American Constitution. For instance, in authorizing the "plumbers" group, Nixon became the first President in our history to establish an extra-legal investigative force, subsidized by the taxpayers but unknown to Congress and accountable to no one but himself. Other misuses of intelligence agencies and authorized breaking and entering meant that Nixon became the only American President in peacetime who was publicly known to have supervised blatantly lawless actions. Moreover, the White House ignored, lied to, and spied on the Congress.

Schlesinger's book is a useful point of departure for a brief review of the general charges of a too-powerful presidency. Over the years, it had become obvious that the Presidency needed the power to respond to sudden attacks and to protect the rights and property of American citizens. But just how much power did a President have to conduct undeclared war?

The Department of State in a 1966 legal memorandum summed up some of this enlarged mandate this way:

> In the twentieth century the world has grown much smaller. An attack on a country far from its shores can impinge directly on the nation's security . . . . The Constitution leaves to the President the judgment to determine whether the circumstances of a particular armed attack are so urgent and the potential consequences so threatening to the security of the U.S. that he should act without formally consulting the Congress.[6]

Legal advisers to Presidents Johnson and Nixon insisted that while the framers of the Constitution rejected the traditional power of kings to commit unwilling nations to war, they recognized the

I/Imperial President and Resurgent Congress • 12

need for quick executive response to rapidly developing international situations. This apparently encouraged these Presidents to become exceedingly inventive in circumventing the congressional war-making power.

Congress became especially upset at President Johnson because in 1964 he succeeded in getting the Gulf of Tonkin Resolution passed on information that was later proved to be highly misleading. (Congress in 1971 repealed that resolution.) Later, a secret air war in Cambodia was waged in 1969 and 1970 with no formal congressional authorization or knowledge. Also, the U.S. military operated in Laos without anyone's formally notifying the Congress.

The framers of the Constitution, in giving to Congress, and not to the President, the power to declare war, intended to prevent just such occurrences as these. They sought to create a permanent institutional safeguard against unilateral presidential war-making. What happened in Indochina was the result, many members of Congress believed, of a disregard by the White House of the Constitution. But many members of Congress agreed too that presidential excess in these matters came about because Congress either agreed with presidential policies or silently did nothing to stop them.

Since the Depression in the early 1930s, Congress has passed about five hundred federal statutes that give a President extraordinary powers. Once a state of emergency is declared, for example, a President may seize property, organize and control the means of production, seize commodities, assign military forces abroad, institute martial law, control all transportation and communications, restrict travel, regulate the operations of private enterprise, call up all the military reserves, and in countless other ways control all aspects of our lives.[7]

Abuses of presidential power under these vast emergency laws included the detention of Japanese aliens and Americans of Japanese descent during the Second World War and the suspension of federal law requiring the publishing of official documents in the *Federal Register*. This latter practice allowed President Nixon to cover up the bombings in Cambodia, and also his directives to the FBI for domestic surveillance and intelligence work.

"If the President were to make use of all of the power available to him under the emergency statutes on the books, he could conduct a government without reference to usual constitutional processes," declared Senator Frank Church, D-Idaho. "These powers taken together could form a basis for one-man rule."[8] Congress in 1972 launched a drive to terminate and rewrite emergency law procedures.

Treaty ratification procedures require that diplomatic agreements receive the consent of two-thirds of the Senate, but executive agreements permit a President to enter into secret and highly sensitive arrangements with a foreign nation without congressional approval. Many members of Congress feel that the subversion of the treaty ratification process of the Constitution was an important element in the growth of the imperial Presidency.

Executive agreements have been recognized as distinct from treaties since George Washington's days, and their use by the Executive has been upheld by the courts. But what irked Congress in the 1960s and 1970s was that while the Senate was asked to ratify international accords on trivial matters, the White House arranged critically important mutual-aid and military-base agreements without even informing Congress. Walter F. Mondale, while still a Senator, put the complaint this way:

> During the 1960's and 1970's, the Senate disposed by treaty of such "crucial" issues as the preservation of archeological artifacts in Mexico, a protocol relating to an amendment to the International Civil Aviation agreement, the Locarno Agreement establishing an international classification of goods and services to which trademarks are applied, revisions of international radio regulations, and an international agreement regarding maintenance of certain lights in the Red Sea.
>
> Yet Congress was not informed about the secret agreements or understandings pledging American assistance that President Nixon apparently entered into with former South Vietnamese President Thieu in 1973, at the time of the signing of the Paris Peace Accords. And the Senate subcommittee involved with such matters had no knowledge of vital executive agreements in 1960 with Ethiopia, in 1963 with Laos, in 1964 with Thailand, in 1966 with Korea, and in 1967 with Thailand.[9]

It was argued that these practices were an insult to the Congress and a violation of the Constitution's clear intent that Congress share in the making of foreign policy. Members of Congress began to probe for ways to limit the President's authority to make executive agreements. "The executive branch should welcome this opportunity to share with the Congress the weighty responsibility of reaching agreements with other nations," said Senator Lloyd Bentsen (D-Texas), "agreements which reflect our national priorities and which lie at the very heart of the foreign policy process."[10]

The founding fathers did not intend that the President should decide what information the Congress and the American people needed to know. They were aware of the maxim that he who controls the flow of information rules our destinies. Moreover, without information, Congress cannot oversee the execution of its laws, and if it cannot do that, it is scarcely in a position to legislate at all.

The difficulty arises because constitutional scholars, the courts, and the Congress concede that a President does have the right to withhold certain diplomatic and military information when it is vital to the national security. Thus during the Second World War, the Executive properly kept secret the time and place of the Normandy Beach invasion.

Several Presidents have invoked a prerogative that has come to be called "executive privilege," a claim based on the constitutional separation of powers, to the effect that the executive branch may withhold information from Congress. It was invoked about thirty-four times prior to the Nixon Presidency. During Nixon's first term, executive privilege was invoked three times on matters that included military assistance and five-year plans and foreign aid for Cambodia.

It was only with the spectacular Watergate disclosures after the 1972 election, when the Senate investigating committee began to request documents, tapes, and testimony, that executive privilege became a really celebrated issue. It was then that Nixon and his lawyers, in a brief before Judge John Sirica, claimed that executive privilege is an inherent and absolute power and that while Congress and the courts may request information from a President, the separation of powers means that disclosure cannot be forced on him.[11]

Legal historian Raoul Berger, on the other hand, contends that executive privilege is "a myth, without constitutional basis, and the best evidence that can be mustered for it is a series of self-serving presidential assertions of power to withhold information."[12]

Most people, and most members of Congress, felt that the truth seemed to lie somewhere between the views of Richard Nixon and those of Raoul Berger. Senator Sam J. Ervin, Jr. accused the executive branch of "contempt of Congress" for refusing to cooperate by sharing information. In fact, Ervin supervised a study of refusals by the executive branch to provide information to Congress, and he found that there were nearly three hundred instances of withheld information during the 1964-1973 period. An exasperated Ervin complained:

> The actions of public officials whether elected or appointed to deny the Congress the information it requires in its legislative functions, or unilaterally to decide what information will be provided or which witnesses will appeal, are clear encroachments upon the powers of Congress. Yet a study of the findings of the survey will reveal a full range of devices, subterfuges, preposterous extensions and assumptions of authority, and outright evasiveness used by the bureaucracy to thwart the Congress in its legitimate inquiries.[13]

The extra-constitutional power of impoundment allows the Executive to refuse to spend funds that have been appropriated by Congress. Impoundment is a complicated practice because it can take—and has taken—so many forms. Refusals to spend have occurred in the past to effect savings either because of a change in events (e.g., a war is over and funds are no longer needed) or for managerial reasons (e.g., a project can be carried out in a more efficient way).

Before President Nixon, impoundments were rather infrequent, usually temporary, and generally involved insignificant amounts of money. Only occasionally were earlier impoundments controversial. Still, the precedent was set for the future. Nixon stretched the use of impoundment to limits previously not attained. Altogether he impounded about $18 billion of funds appropriated by Congress.

What bothered Congress about Nixon's impoundments of funds for water pollution control, urban aid, the emergency loan program of the Farmers Home Administration, and others, was that he used impoundment to set policy and reorder the nation's priorities. Congress felt it was one thing for a President to delay funds for purposes of efficiency, but quite another for him to engage in extensive policy-making or priority-setting by impoundment.

Congress responded to Nixon's frequent impoundment of its appropriations in a relatively united manner. Drawing strength from the Constitution's clause: "No money shall be drawn from the Treasury, but in consequence of appropriations made by law," Congress took this to mean it had the final voice in fiscal policy-making. Members of Congress complained that by refusing to spend appropriated funds the Executive was in effect exercising an *item veto* and destroying or delaying a program while avoiding the potential embarrassment of a public veto message and the risk of a congressional override. Nixon's impoundment practices, they added, were merely a means whereby the White House reallocated national resources in violation of congressional dictates. It was a question of which branch should decide how to allocate the public funds.[14]

Congress Tries to Reassert Itself: 1972-1977

The role of Congress in helping to end the war in Vietnam and then in the impeachment hearings against President Nixon gave the legislative branch some much-needed new vigor. The public looked to Congress for leadership. Congress set out to recover lost authority and discover new ways to participate more fully in national policymaking. In doing so it clearly tried to reassert itself. But even the most ardent supporter of Congress realizes that many of the so-called post-Watergate reforms are provisional. It is one thing to enact new curbs; it is quite another to put them into practice and enforce them rigorously. Moreover, it is not clear that presidential powers are really constrained very much by what has happened since 1973. A few examples of congressional reassertion are discussed below to illustrate the ambiguity of the enterprise.

In an attempt to redress the imbalance, Congress in 1973 took an unprecedented step when it enacted the War Powers Act. Nixon vetoed the act, calling it an unconstitutional intrusion into the President's constitutional authority and an action that seriously undermined the nation's ability to act decisively and convincingly in times of international crisis. Congress overrode the veto, however, and by law declared that henceforth the President could commit the armed forces of the United States only (1) pursuant to a declaration of war by Congress, (2) by specific statutory authorizations, or (3) in a national emergency created by an attack on the United States or its armed forces. After committing the armed forces under this third condition, the President must report immediately to Congress; and within sixty days, unless Congress has declared war, the troop commitment is to be terminated, with the proviso that the President may be allowed another thirty days if he certifies to Congress that unavoidable military necessity for the safety of U.S. forces requires their continued use. Ninety days having elapsed, the act then permits Congress, by concurrent resolution not subject to a presidential veto, to direct the President to disengage the troops. A President is also obligated by this resolution to consult Congress "in every possible instance" before committing troops to battle.

Not everyone was pleased by the passage of the War Powers Resolution. Some members of Congress supported President Nixon's stand. Still another group in Congress, and many scholars as well, felt that the act granted a President *more power* than he already had, perhaps even to the extent of encouraging short-term interventions. Whether or not this act will make any difference, it symbolizes a determination by the Congress in 1973 to try to control the President's formerly unlimited discretion to decide when and where and under what conditions American troops might be engaged. Any future President who remembers the reaction of Congress and the nation to Vietnam and who remembers the 1973 War Powers Resolution will know that a commitment of American troops to foreign combat is subject to the approval of Congress.

Whether the intensity of this reaction will last much longer than the disenchantment over Indochina remains an open question. Congress certainly has the constitutional authority to intervene whenever it has the will to do so. But will it have the courage to resist being stampeded into granting power whenever a President waves the flag and says there is urgent crisis? This emphasis on "will" or "courage" strikes some observers as naive or hazy. They feel that, under most circumstances, whenever a President takes a foreign policy initiative, he is likely to have most of the country behind him, including influential business leaders, the communications media, and the bulk of the public. The history of presidential actions in wartime suggests that Presidents in the future will not have much difficulty in doing pretty much what they please. The Constitution, as Chief Justice Hughes once said, is a "fighting Constitution." Nothing in it will ever be permitted to prevent a President from winning a war that is truly vital to our national survival. Legal niceties will be given little attention. The Lincoln example will doubtless be followed, for national survival will always be the ultimate value. Only after the initiative is shown "not to work"—that is, after the death tolls and inflation become unbearable—will popular support begin to flag and the Congress begin to reflect the popular feeling.

The National Emergencies Act of 1976 terminated, as of September 1978, the extensive powers and authorities possessed by the President as a result of the continuing state of emergency the nation has been in since the mid-1930s. It also established authority for the declaration of future emergencies in a manner that will clearly define the powers of the President and provide for regular congressional review.

The act also calls upon the President to inform Congress in advance and identify those laws he plans to use when he declares a national emergency. An emergency would automatically end after six months, although a President could then declare it again for another six months. But Congress is obligated to review the declaration of emergency powers at least every six months. A significant section of the new law states that a majority vote in both Senate and House can end the emergency at any time. President Ford called this section unconstitutional and hinted that future Presidents might go to court and fight this provision if Congress chose to act upon it.

Congress hopes that this legislation will insure that emergency powers can be utilized only when legitimate emergencies actually exist, and then only under safeguards of legislative review. As Senator Abraham Ribicoff (D-Conn.) reported to the Congress:

> Reliance on emergency authority, intended for use in crisis situations would no longer be available in non-crisis situations. At a time when governments throughout the world are turning with increasing desperation to an all-powerful executive, this legislation is designed to insure that the United States travels a road marked by carefully constructed legal safeguards.[15]

The Case Act of 1972, sponsored by Senator Clifford P. Case (R-N.J.), requires the Secretary of State to submit to the U.S. Senate within sixty days the final text of any international agreement made by executive agreement. Executive agreements having sensitive national security implications may be submitted to the Senate Foreign Relations Committee and the House International Relations Committee on a classified basis. Presidents still negotiate executive agreements, however, and sometimes fail to comply with the Case Act's relatively mild provisions.

Even when executive agreements are reported to the appropriate committees of Congress, there is no provision for any congressional response. Some efforts were made in the mid-1970s to enact a stronger law that would permit Congress an opportunity to review and disapprove executive agreements. In 1974 the Senate actually passed such a measure, but the House failed to act on it. Later attempts have also failed, but the following initiatives have won considerable congressional support.

- A Senate-sponsored bill requiring executive agreements to be submitted only to the Senate, such agreements to take effect at the end of sixty days unless the Senate disapproves them by simple resolution.
- A House-sponsored bill requiring executive agreements to be submitted to Congress, such agreements to take effect in sixty days unless both houses adopt a concurrent resolution disapproving them.
- Another Senate-sponsored bill providing that if either house decides that an international agreement is sufficiently important to require congressional approval, it must be approved through regular legislative procedures or as a treaty.[16]

Abuse of the intelligence and spying agencies was also a central contention of the imperial-presidency argument. The Central Intelligence Agency was established in 1947 at a time when the perceived threat of "world communism" encouraged a vast arsenal of national security instruments, including covert overseas political operations and espionage. When the CIA was established, Congress recognized the dangers to a free society inherent in a secret organizations not accountable in the ordinary way for what it does. Hence it was

I/Imperial President and Resurgent Congress • 20

stipulated that the CIA was *not to engage in any police work or to perform operations within the United States.*

Abuse of the intelligence and spying agencies was also a central contention of the imperial-presidency argument. The Central Intelligence Agency was established in 1947 at a time when the perceived threat of "world communism" encouraged a vast arsenal of national security instruments, including covert overseas political operations and espionage. When the CIA was established, Congress recognized the dangers to a free society inherent in a secret organization not accountable in the ordinary way for what it does. Hence it was stipulated that the CIA was *not to engage in any police work or to perform operations within the United States.*

But from 1947 to the mid-1970s, no aspect of national policymaking was more removed from congressional involvement than CIA operations. In many instances Congress acted as if it really didn't want to know what was going on. Said one Senator: "It is not a question of reluctance on the part of CIA officials to speak to us. Instead it is a question of our reluctance, if you will, to seek information and knowledge on subjects which I personally, as a Member of Congress and as a citizen, would rather not have."[17] The evidence is substantial that Congress declined to use its resources to participate in intelligence policymaking.

Congress has tried in recent years to amend this. In 1975 the Senate established a temporary committee of inquiry chaired by Senator Frank Church (D-Idaho). This committee found widespread abuses of power and violations of the rights of American citizens in the conduct of both foreign and domestic intelligence operations. The Church committee recommended that Congress bring all the intelligence operations within the framework of congressional oversight.

The Senate then voted to create a permanent Select Committee on Intelligence, with legislative and budgetary authority over the CIA and other intelligence agencies. Subsequently the House voted to set up a similar panel. But since we now know that even Presidents have had difficulty getting a handle on the CIA, there is some doubt about whether Congress will have any better luck. Yet in an unprecedented exercise of its power over the intelligence budget, Congress in 1976 amended the Defense Appropriations bill to terminate American covert intervention in Angola. "The inevitable public disclosure of a secret operation served, in this instance, the will of Congress; and in the short run the Angola controversy was a warning that the Executive should proceed with caution."[18]

How likely is it that Congress will be effective in regulating the CIA? People differ widely in their answers to this question. Halperin, Berman, Borosage, and Marwick conclude in their study, *The Lawless State: The Crimes of the U.S. Intelligence Agencies* (Penguin, 1976), by saying "To date, only a few patchwork elements of reform have been put into effect. At every turn the executive branch continues to fight any major changes and, instead, offers 'reforms' that end up authorizing for the future the abuses of the past." Some say the Senate committee should spell out a charter that would limit the CIA to foreign operations, severely restrict and control all covert activities, require written approval for any major field operations, and shut down the political intelligence work of the FBI. Others feel the full disclosure of the intelligence community's budget is necessary.

A longer-range view suggests that the intensity and direction of congressional interest in these matters depend on the movement of larger political forces. That is, when a national consensus supports a President and his foreign policy initiatives, as it plainly did in the early part of the Cold War, Congress is likely to go along. But in the absence of such a consensus, a more assertive Congress may try to find a more realistic system of accountability for the CIA and related activities as a substitute for the public scrutiny that normally is given major governmental operations. It is worth recalling that we have already had committees in the Congress to oversee the intelligence agencies, but those simply did not do their job.

"Congress has seen its control over the federal purse-strings ebb away over the past fifty years because of its inability to get a grip on the overall budget, while the Office of Management and Budget in the executive branch has increased its power and influence," said Senator Edmund S. Muskie (D-Maine) in 1974.[19]

Congress had become too dependent on the President's budget proposals and had no budget system of its own—only a lot of separate actions and decisions coming at various intervals throughout the year with little or no connection among them.

Muskie was one of the chief authors of the 1974 Congressional

Budget and Impoundment Control Act. That act was designed to encourage Congress to evaluate the nation's fiscal situation and program-spending priorities in a comprehensive way. It was also hoped that in a period of high inflation Congress could help put a lid on unnecessary spending.

The act creates a permanent budget committee for each chamber. In the House it is a twenty-five member committee: five members from the Ways and Means Committee, five from the Appropriations Committee, thirteen from remaining legislative committees, and one member each from the majority and minority leadership. The Senate committee is a sixteen-member committee picked in the regular fashion.

Under this law, Congress also established a Congressional Budget Office (CBO). It provides budgetary and fiscal experts and computer services, and gives Congress technical assistance on the President's budgetary proposals. Some members of Congress hoped CBO would provide hard, practical economic data to guide the drafting of spending legislation. Others viewed it as a potential "think tank" that might provide Congress a more philosophical approach to spending and help reorder national priorities. In fact, CBO is most frequently used to provide routine cost estimates for spending and tax bills and to keep track of the overall budget level.

Optimists feel that the budget reform act will force Congress into more systematic and timely action on budgetary legislation, tying its separate spending decisions together with fiscal policy objectives. Its new budgetary timetable gives Congress three additional months to consider the President's budget recommendations. By May 15 of each year, Congress, after receiving reports from its Budget Committees and its Budget Office, adopts an initial tentative budget that sets target totals for spending and taxes. This target is then broken down by categories and serves as a guide for the various committees and subcommittees considering detailed appropriation measures. By September 15, Congress is required to adopt a second concurrent resolution that will either affirm or revise the earlier targets. If necessary to attain compliance with the final budget resolution totals, this resolution must also dictate any required changes in expenditures and revenues.

How has it worked? The new budget process clearly has stimulated increased congressional participation in fiscal policymaking. Using these new powers of the purse, Congress seems better able to contribute significantly to budget making in the Carter area.

The budget resolutions provide a vehicle for debate in key macroeconomic issues, and the newly created House and Senate Committees are able to challenge the President's dominance in initiating fiscal proposals. The long-term success of the experiment will depend very much on whether the new committees are powerful enough to induce cooperation with their target and ceiling resolutions.

The impoundment control provisions of this new law have not worked out as well, but here again Congress has put the executive branch on the defensive. Presidents are obligated to report delays in spending to Congress; either house may veto presidential decisions to defer spending; and both the Senate and the House must approve any presidential request to eliminate a project that Congress has funded. If the Comptroller General finds in behalf of the Congress that impoundments have been made without proper reports to Congress, he may report these himself and Congress may act to force release of the funds. Should a President fail to comply with a congressional action overruling an impoundment, Congress may go to court for an order requiring the funds to be spent.

There have been many complaints about the new impoundment law. It is vague. It creates a vast amount of paperwork. Too many reports need to be sent to Congress—even when executive branch officials have saved a few thousand dollars simply for managerial and efficiency purposes. There will no doubt be further changes in the law designed to meet these and other objections.

Within recent years Congress has turned the so-called "legislative veto" into an instrument of policymaking. The Constitution stipulates that every bill, order, resolution, or vote to which the concurrence of the Senate and House may be necessary shall be presented to the President for his approval or veto. But "concurrent resolutions" in contrast to "joint resolutions" by convention do not have to be submitted to the President. In the past this made little difference, since concurrent resolutions were used merely to express congressional sentiments and had no force of law.

Then in 1932 Congress passed a joint resolution allowing President Hoover to reorganize the executive agencies but stipulated that his proposed reorganizations would not take effect for ninety days, during which time either house of Congress by a simple resolution could veto the regulation. Since then the legislative veto has come to be a frequently used statutory provision through which Congress authorizes a federal program to be administered by the executive branch but retains the authority to approve or disapprove part of the program before final implementation. Usually, Congress either may disapprove a measure by vetoing it, or must approve it by affirmative action. This must usually take place within a specified period of time, generally sixty or ninety days. The legislative veto may take the form of a concurrent resolution, a simple resolution passed by either house, or a committee veto.

Since 1932 more than three hundred pieces of legislation have carried some form of legislative veto; about half have been enacted since 1970, and most of those since 1974. Significant statutes with legislative veto provisions include the Budget and Impoundment Control Act of 1974, the Trade Act of 1974, and the Energy Policy and Conservation Act of 1975. In 1976 the House fell only two votes short of passing a bill that would have required federal agencies to submit all new regulations to Congress for sixty legislative days. If during that time either house acted to disapprove, the regulations would not go into effect unless the other house acted within thirty days to approve.

Congressional spokesmen favor the legislative veto and contend that it is the most effective device Congress has to insure that the President and the federal bureaucrats issue regulations that conform to the intent of Congress. They also argue that without the use of the veto, when Congress delegates powers to the President, he could use his veto to prevent Congress from terminating the delegation. Rep. Elliott Levitas (D-Georgia) reflects the sentiment in Congress in favor of a veto on administrative rules and regulations when he complains that the bureaucracy is infringing on Congress's right to make laws by putting out "a thick tangle of regulations that carry the force of law without benefit of legislative consideration." To back up his point he cites statistics showing that in 1974 Congress passed 404 public laws, while 67 agencies adopted 7,496 regulations.[20]

Most supporters of the Presidency consider the legislative veto a violation of the doctrine of separation of powers, and an unconstitutional intrusion into the executive branch.[21] They also argue that it gives lobbyists more influence on government. John Bolton, a Washington lawyer, writes that the legislative veto

> eliminates the president from the law-making function by not presenting him with "legislation" that he can veto. It allows Congress to change its mind an unlimited number of times about what a statute is intended to do after passage of the statute—in effect, amending the statute . . . . The President's administrative authority—his duty to "take care that the laws be faithfully executed"—is impinged (sic) because he is prevented from implementing regulations he deems suitable and consistent with the enabling legislation.[22]

Assistant Attorney General Antonin Scalia presented the executive branch brief in opposition to the expanded use of the legislative veto. Testifying before a congressional committee in late 1975 he argued:

> As our system operates Congress makes the laws, in as much detail as it desires; the President executes those laws, with due regard for the congressional intent; and the judiciary determines the President's execution, including issuance of regulations, to be of no effect when it is inconsistent with the laws or the Constitution.
> This rough division of government power is what the doctrine of separation of powers is all about.
> Both of the present bills (under discussion before the House Committee on the Judiciary) disrupt this system in one way or another, depending upon how the ambiguities discussed earlier are resolved. If they envision Congress setting regulations aside on the basis of its own notions as to what constitutes desirable enforcement policy, they intrude upon the executive's functions.
> If, on the other hand, they mean only to permit congressional review of the executive's compliance with statutory intent, they intrude upon the province of the judiciary. Either way, they carry Congress beyond its proper function of making laws under Article I of the Constitution.[23]

Whatever its merits, Congress has surely used the legislative veto to reassert itself, and it has become a new and significant feature of our constitutional system. Whether it will survive the test of its constitutionality is something the courts are likely to tell us during the coming years.

Congress has also become more involved in foreign policymaking, increasingly imposing its own goals on the Executive. Shaking off years of inertia, Congress imposed a cutoff of aid to Vietnam, called a halt to bombing in Cambodia, and restrained the Ford Administration from getting involved in Portugal and Angola. Led by Senator Henry Jackson (D-Wash.), Congress refused to permit the White House to grant the Soviet Union the "most-favored nation" treatment allowed for in the Trade Reform Act of 1974. Congress has also demanded and won a greater role in arms sales abroad and in determining U.S. aid to Turkey.[24]

The maintenance of democratic controls over foreign and military policy has become increasingly difficult in the Cold War and the nuclear age. Secrecy is at the heart of the problem. All of our recent Presidents have said that you cannot have successful diplomacy without secrecy. President Carter, for example, told members of Congress that he felt there were excessive restraints keeping him from reacting to a Cuban-assisted rebel invasion of Zaire.

But executive secrecy is subject to abuses, as Watergate has dramatically illustrated. People could understand, even if they might oppose, the use of secrecy in the President's negotiations with China or in his diplomatic initiatives with Middle Eastern nations. But most people found it difficult to understand the need for it in dealing with congressional leaders. Tapping telephones to prevent security leaks, breaking into offices—these are the tactics not of politics, but of war. These practices may be appropriate in dealing with enemies but they are not appropriate when dealing with domestic political opponents.

How to prevent the use of secrecy to cover up obstructions of justice while permitting its legitimate use for diplomatic purposes? Many Americans feel that even at the risk of a less effective foreign policy, what is needed is a greater power-sharing with Congress over foreign policy. And some indeed have doubts whether presidential exclusiveness is more likely than congressional sharing to produce good policy.

Some congressional reassertion proposals have failed of approval. Among them was former Senator Sam Ervin's suggestion that the Department of Justice be removed from the executive branch. He felt that was necessary to separate the vital justice and prosecution functions from the contamination of partisan politics and undue

White House influence; but he failed to persuade many members of Congress. Another variation of the Ervin proposal was to call for the establishment of a permanent office of special prosecutor—independent of the executive branch. Subsequently a proposed procedure that would establish an independent prosecutor in time of special need has won more substantial backing. Representative Henry Reuss (D-Wisc.) championed a constitutional amendment providing a vote of no-confidence that would permit Congress to call for new elections when it believed a President had become incompetent or had lost the support needed to govern effectively. Others proposed a constitutional amendment to limit the President to a single six-year term. Another proposal provided for an American "question hour" in which cabinet members or even the President would regularly go before the Congress to respond to questions and participate in a dialogue on major policy questions. Finally, some members of Congress wanted to establish ceilings on the number of White House aides and involve the Congress in overseeing the policymaking powers of the unconfirmed White House staff. None of these measures got beyond committee hearings.

"I do not want a honeymoon with you. I want a good marriage," said Ford to Congress as he started his Presidency. "As President I intend to listen . . . ." Ford said his relations with Congress would be characterized not by confrontation but by "communication, conciliation, compromise and cooperation." But his hoped-for holy wedlock soured and an unholy deadlock set in as he proceeded to veto sixty-nine legislative measures.

Congress did give Ford a hard time. Having shaken off years of inertia, Congress took advantage of an appointed President to regain some of its own lost authority. Thus they rejected some of his nominations; they took four months to confirm Nelson Rockefeller; they rejected his foreign aid bill, trimmed his defense appropriations, curtailed military aid to Turkey, denied him the means to conduct open or covert operations in Angola, and so on.

Some of Ford's aides warned of a new period of congressional government. Ford himself said:

> Frankly, I believe that Congress recently has gone too far in trying to take over the powers that belong to the President and the executive branch.

I / Imperial President and Resurgent Congress • 28

> This probably is a natural reaction to the steady growth of executive branch power over the past forty years. I'm sure it is a reaction to Watergate and Vietnam. And the fact that I came to this office through a Constitutional process and not by election also may have something to do with current efforts by the Democratic Congress to take away some of the power of the President.
>
> As a member of Congress for twenty-five years, I clearly understand the powers and obligations of the Senate and House under our Constitution. But as President for eighteen months, I also understand that Congress is trying to go too far in some areas.[25]

Why did Ford have such troubled relations with Congress? Reaction to Vietnam and Watergate obviously played a role in his difficulties. Congress had reorganized itself in several ways. It was a more democratic institution now, with power more noticeably dispersed among its members. It had streamlined some of its procedures, and it was more conscious of its responsibility to the people. But there were additional factors that help explain Ford's difficulties. Perhaps the major problem was that he was decidedly more conservative than Congress. That should have come as no surprise to those who had looked at his voting record in Congress. He had voted against Medicare, opposed the creation of the Office of Economic Opportunity, opposed aid to education, and opposed federal help for state water pollution control projects. He had, however, always been a strong supporter of Defense Department spending.

Moreover, he was an appointed President. As our first twenty-fifth-amendment President he also bore the stigma of illegitimacy. He had absolutely no mandate from the people. He had to deal with a Democrat-contolled Congress. He came to office right in the midst of a mid-term congressional election. At the State Department he had the always secretive Henry Kissinger who had by then acquired strong opponents in both parties. He had to contend with a strong attack from the right wing of his own already minority party. The Ford Presidency experienced additional troubles because it came during the seventh and eighth years of the Nixon-Ford Administrations. The top people were tired and had run out of imaginative ideas and solutions. And finally Ford suffered from the disillusionment that invariably sets in toward the end of an eight-year hold on the Presidency. The same thing had happened in 1960 and 1968.

In fact, the Ford Presidency was not as weak and constrained as it wanted people to believe. (The White House liked to convey the impression that the press, the courts, and the Congress were literally undermining presidential powers.) Ford himself may have been vulnerable, but the Presidency was not weakened during this period. The major powers of the office were still available to Presidents. Of course, the effective use of those powers required shrewd use and especially clear communication of intent.

President Carter and Congress

Carter's relations with Congress have been turbulent. He suffered setbacks on his energy package, election reform, his Korean strategy, the proposed consumer protection agency, and countless other measures. He scored victories, too (for example, on the B-1 bomber and the Panama Canal), but these often seemed to be the exception to the rule. And even the victories seemed to anger or at least divide the Congress.

Carter's initial difficulties with Congress were partially due to the post-Watergate efforts to constrain the American Presidency. But *only partially*. To be sure, Congress did not want to become a rubber stamp for a Democratic president. And Congress was enjoying its struggle to reassert itself. Also, the dispersion of influence (i.e., power to the subcommittees and subcommittee chairmen) in the House of Representatives made it more difficult for a President to deal with the Congress. Gone were the days when the White House could deal with a handful of "whales" who really ran the show. But Carter's difficulties stemmed from a number of other factors as well.

1. The Carter style was resented.

Carter ran for the White House as a Mr. Pure, a Mr. Integrity, and a Mr. Outsider. He sold himself almost like a detergent who would go to Washington and clean things up. That could only breed resentment. His campaign slogans were seen as a "put down" to

Congress. He talked too much of the mess in Washington to win friends there. He said Congress was "inherently incapable of leadership," and added that "In the absence of strong presidential leadership . . . there is no leadership."

His personal style of campaigning stressed confrontation more than negotiation. He seemed righteous and almost too good to be true. He implied that his administration would be guided by only the highest moral standards. So when the Bert Lance affair occurred, he was judged all the more critically. Congress resented his pious style and that plainly made the honeymoon shorter.

2. *Carter's base within the Democratic Party was weak from the outset.*

Much was made of the idea that most of the problems in presidential-congressional relations could be overcome if only both branches were held by the Democrats. That came to pass in January 1977, but the promised harmony never came about.

Part of the reason is that the Democratic Party is in many ways two parties in one. Any party with both a Ron Dellums and a James Eastland is a party either very split or very strange. Moreover, Carter really has no political base within the Democratic Party. He is not really a Southern old-boy conservative. Some have suggested that he is more of a Yankee puritan. In many ways, the mere fact that he is a Southerner in the White House makes him a novelty. Ironically, although Carter enjoys his highest popularity in the southeastern section of the nation, the members of Congress from that same region give him the lowest rates of support (about thirty percent) for his programs in Congress.

3. *Carter is an activist who wants to do many things but he has no mandate to do so from the 1976 election.*

Forty-seven percent of the voters stayed home. He lost nearly thirty points in the polls between August and election day as his election campaign stumbled hapahazardly to a narrow victory. White voters, and even white southerners, preferred Ford over Carter. The 1976 election was hardly an issues election the way 1936 and 1964 were.

Carter, moreover, ran well behind the Democrats running for Congress and for the state houses in 1976. His election seemed to be due more to the public's lack of confidence in Gerald Ford than to any program Carter put forth.

Yet Carter in office acts as if he has direct mandates to reshape domestic and foreign policy. While he may not be a populist, he tries nonetheless to be assertive, bold, and sometimes brash. He is clearly a Democrat in the activist tradition. He strives to be "a take-charge guy" who wants to set standards and establish policy guidelines. His statements on human rights, environmental protection, and energy conservation have often been unusually aggressive.

The Congress is not accustomed to handling so many initiatives at one time. The vast majority of its members weren't around for the 89th Congress. And even then most of Lyndon Johnson's programs had been incubating in the Congress for several years before they were passed. So, many of Carter's problems arise either because he is in advance of his times or because he is unable to communicate why his new policies are needed.

4. *Carter isn't political enough.*

Some of Carter's difficulties stem from the fact that he does not enjoy the politics of dealing with members of Congress. He gives the impression that he is the rational man and that Congress should deal with him and his programs completely on their merits. The idea that deals will be made and favors dispensed seems quite alien to Carter.

Reporters covering his trips around the country say he is almost incapable of saying nice things about members of Congress even as he travels among their constituents. One U.S. Senator's office had arranged for Carter to say a few words of endorsement for the Senator when Carter was recently in the Senator's home state. Elaborate and expensive television and video machinery had been rented and set up to capture Carter's few words of praise, hoping that they might be usable in the next year's election race. But Carter came and talked and went—and never uttered the expected words of praise. Washington is full of such anecdotes.

Members of Congress complain too that he does not consult them enough. Unlike Lyndon Johnson, he doesn't invite them in to go over the drafts of prospective bills; he often seems to prefer a government by surprise. He also has a penchant for bypassing Congress and going to the country. Of course, all Presidents do that, but his style of doing it coupled with his reputation as an "outsider" comes back to weaken his ties to Congress.

One scholar who has studied Carter's legislative-relations staffs offers the additional explanation that since Carter won the nomination and then the Presidency itself largely without having to build coalitions with the left, right, and center of the Democratic Party, so also his Congressional relations teams, both at the White House and in the departments, did not in the early period of the Administration build the coalitions needed to get things passed. Eric Davis puts it this way:

> Since they did not have to engage in bargaining to get the nomination or to win the election, they would not have to engage in bargaining or exchange to get their programs passed on Capitol Hill. Because they did not recognize the importance of coalition-building through brokerage, they did not, at the very outset of the Administration, make an effort to establish cooperative lobbying relationships with the other important participants in the legislative process . . . . Since these relationships were not established, the White House had to rely on its own resources to obtain legislative successes. Therefore, legislative defeats resulted. And these defeats fed upon themselves, creating the image of ineptitude on the part of the White House. This image of ineptitude, in turn, has led to members of Congress being less willing to rely on White House judgment and to accept White House analyses of issues.[26]

5. *The national climate of expectations has changed.*

In 1960 the mood of the country embodied a seemingly boundless confidence in itself and in what its government could achieve. We could go anywhere and do anything—from conquering outer space to effecting land reform in Latin America and political reforms in Indochina. Poverty in America could be ended once and for all. John Kennedy became our President during this era of good feelings, this era of confident adventuresomeness. Optimism and idealism aided both him and Lyndon Johnson in their efforts to deal with Congress.

But that era is over. Today we dwell on the scarcity of our

resources. We acknowledge that we overextended ourselves abroad. We salute the slogan "Small is Beautiful," and we read study after study predicting the limits to growth.

President Carter would like to provide leadership of the Roosevelt, Wilson, and Kennedy kind, but he doesn't have the appropriate climate of expectations. He can draw on neither the trauma of a depression nor the crusading spirit of a world war nor the buoyant national optimism of the early 1960s. The Presidency is obviously constrained by the national mood. Carter's difficulties with the Congress arise in no small measure from his desire to offer strong inspiring leadership to a nation that has turned inward, introspective, and self-centered as opposed to nation-centered. The people are acting as if this is a second Ford Administration while Carter is acting as if the year is 1933 or 1943 or 1963. In one sense, Carter's difficulty arises from the fact that he is an activist "doer" who came along at a time when many, and perhaps most, Americans want passivity and tax cuts.

So Carter is having problems with the Congress, but most of his problems are due to things other than the post-Vietnam, post-Watergate, anti-imperial-Presidency reforms.

A New Impatience: Restrengthen the Presidency

Even as the Presidency was being soundly criticized for abuses of power in the late 1960s and early 1970s, it was simultaneously portrayed by many people as alarmingly battered by Vietnam and Watergate. The ranks of the defenders of presidential government may have been temporarily thinned in 1973 and 1974, but at least by 1977 the cult of the Presidency was alive and well. As several analysts have observed, the Right worries about the imperial Presidency at home and the Left worries about the imperial Presidency abroad. What is not pointed out is that the Right doubtless wants a near-imperial Teddy Roosevelt kind of Presidency abroad and the Left often wants something approaching an imperial, super-planning Presidency at home.

The American public may have lost confidence in its leaders, but it has not lost hope in the efficacy of strong purposive leadership. The Gallup organization in 1976 asked a national sample: "Do you think what the country needs is really strong leadership that would try to solve problems directly without worrying about how Congress or the Supreme Court might feel or do you think that such leadership might be dangerous?" By a 49 percent to 44 percent margin the respondents indicated a preference for a strong government over a constitutional one.[27]

Fears of another Watergate Presidency are rapidly disappearing. Perhaps all the revelations about the crimes of Watergate and the dramatic resignation of a President have lulled most people into believing that "the system worked"—that the checks checked and the balances balanced. Perhaps the very cataloging of the misuses of presidential powers seemed to solve the problem. Obviously, it was not right, but the very revelations may have appeared the same as remedies.

Moreover, if the nation worried about an imperial Presidency, it worried also—alas even feared—an imperial Congress. Few could object to the efforts of streamlining, democratizing, or better staffing the Congress. But few informed people wished to rely only, or even primarily, on Congress for national leadership.

In the wake of the wounded or imperilled Presidency of the Watergate era, could Congress furnish the leadership necessary to govern the country? Most scholars and writers who comment on the Presidency have said no. The conventional answer heard in the late seventies is that "we will need a Presidency of substantial power" if we are to get on top of the energy problem and maintain our position in foreign affairs.

The President's primacy, they would add, has been founded in the necessities of the American condition. Today, the federal government has become committed to burdens of administration that demand vigorous, positive leadership. We live too in a continuous state of emergency, where instant nuclear warfare could destroy the country in a matter of minutes and where global competition of almost every sort highlights the need for swiftness, efficiency, and unity in our government. Further, today's social and urban and environmental problems require a persistent display of creative presidential leadership. Any reduction in the powers of the President might leave us naked to our enemies, to the forces of inflation and depression at home, and to the forces of unrest and aggression abroad.

Former President Gerald Ford scoffed in 1977 at the idea that

Congress had improved things in recent years. Speaking for the repeal of the War Powers Resolution of 1973, Ford said, "When a crisis breaks out, it is impossible to draw the Congress into the decisionmaking process in an effective way." Ford cited these reasons for this claim:

- Legislators have too many other concerns to be abreast of foreign policy situations.
- It is impossible to wait for a consensus among scattered and perhaps disagreeing congressional leaders.
- Sensitive information supplied to legislators, particularly via the telephone, might be disclosed.
- Waiting for consultation could risk penalties for the President "as severe as impeachment."
- Consultations with congressional leaders might not bind the rank and file, particularly independent younger members.[28]

Such defenders of a powerful Presidency as Samuel Huntington and columnist Robert Novak wondered how a government could conduct a coherent foreign policy if legislative ascendancy really meant the development of a Congress into a second United States government. Could the U.S. afford to have two foreign policies? A nation cannot long retain a leadership role in the world unless its own leadership is both clear and decisive. They argued, too, that congressional decisions—including foreign policy decisions—must be based almost entirely on domestic politics, which is why Congress cannot conduct foreign policy.

More specifically, Novak in 1976 charged: "Congress by its headline hunting investigations, has destroyed the Central Intelligence Agency as an effective means of national policy for the United States." Elsewhere he wrote: "In the . . . Angola episode . . . , Congress has served notice that the President of the United States cannot conduct the foreign policy of his country to confront brush fire occurrences, to confront Soviet expansionism."[29]

Political scientist Huntington, writing in 1975, urges readers to recognize the legitimacy and the necessity

> of hierarchy, coercion, discipline, secrecy, and deception—all of which are, in some measure, inescapable attributes of the process of government . . . . When the President is unable to exercise author-

ity, no one else has been able to supply comparable purpose and initiative. To the extent that the United States has been governed on a national basis, it has been governed by the President.[30]

The same verdict is heard from those who yearn for strong creative leadership in domestic or economic matters. Thus Arthur Schlesinger, Jr.—even as he condemns the imperial Presidency—says that "history has shown the presidency to be the most effective instrumentality for justice and progress."[31] Supporters of a strong, powerful Presidency worry that a President has too little power today to tackle economic and energy resource problems effectively. For example, he has very little influence over the Federal Reserve Board's policies on credit and money. He has few tools for effective, long-range economic planning. And, as President Carter learned in his first year of office, his authority over government reorganizations is puny compared to our expectations of him as the official "Chief Executive."

Without strong presidential leadership, the parochialism in Congress, they contend, is so profound and insidious and unremitting that Congress is not a good institution in which to place our hopes for the future. Advocates of national planning are especially fond of looking to the White House for leadership because they believe that only the President has the national perspective to plan coherently, to plan comprehensively. Sure, they say, Congress has its role. But Congress, rather than balancing presidential powers, has often simply blocked needed presidential actions because of localized self-interests.

Thus, as almost always during the twentieth century, advocates of a strong Presidency lament that presidential powers are not stronger. For the Presidency is America's strongest weapon against those banes of progress: sectionalism, selfish or over-concentrated corporate power, and totalitarianism abroad.

Americans still long for dynamic, reassuring, and strong leadership. Watergate notwithstanding, we still celebrate the gutsy, aggressive Presidents, even if many of them did violate the legal and constitutional niceties of the separation of powers. It is still the Jeffersons, Jacksons, Lincolns, and Roosevelts that get placed on the top of the lists of great Presidents. Time and again polls indicate that what the country wants most—more than laws and programs—is a few courageous, tireless, assertive leaders in whom the people can put their faith—the type, by the way, who will undoubtedly dominate Congress.

President Carter is also criticized for not having enough confidence in himself or his positions. He reverses himself frequently and is too diffident and humble. It is said, for example, that he has bent over too far to play down the arrogance of the White House. Thus, when he goes visiting around the country and says he has come to "learn from the people" the people may be momentarily flattered but soon begin to wonder about him. For if Carter has truly come to *them* to find the answers, then we may really be in trouble.

In sum, more and more people think the nation in the mid-1970s entered a period of overreaction to Watergate, Vietnam, and the Nixon Presidency. Some rebalancing was needed, but many in the Congress and elsewhere embarked upon a course that endangered the effectiveness of the Presidency. Those who hold to this overreaction thesis say the White House today is enmeshed in a complex web of constraints that hobbles Presidents and that would have prevented an FDR or a Lincoln from providing vital leadership. Fears of presidential dictatorship, they say, are much exaggerated. It is unfortunate that people dwell so much on Richard Nixon and his abuse of office. The Nixon Presidency, they contend, was one of a kind and it was dealt with effectively by the impeachment provisions of the Constitution. The central challenge, then, is not to reduce the President's power to lead, to govern, or to persuade, but to check the President's power to mislead and corrupt.

Counterpoint: The Case for An Even More Resurgent Congress

There are still many, though clearly a minority, who insist that the reassertion of congressional power is a much-needed corrective and that it hasn't gone far enough. Suporters of a truly strong and tenacious Congress question the depth, sincerity, and staying power of congressional assertiveness. They point to President Ford's failure to comply with the War Powers Resolution of 1973 when he ordered military action and bombings in connection with the 1975 rescue of the merchant ship Mayaguez. They note that the Defense Department's budgets continue to grow and to pass through the Congress with minimum changes. They point to President Carter's penchant for surprising the Congress or for bypassing it entirely with appeals to the public. They contend too that despite all the talk about more and better program oversight, most members of Congress find this type of work the least glamorous, least appealing, and least rewarding—especially in terms of winning reelection. Hence they wonder whether Congress will really maintain its interest in this vital work.

Those who want more reform point out that the imperial Presidency was at least as much the product of an unassertive Congress as it was of power-hungry Presidents. They argue, too, that although Congress may have asserted itself in response to the events of Watergate, the more distant those events become, the less motivated Congress will be to challenge the Presidency. This reasoning leads them to say: it is the Congress after Watergate that bears watching, and it is the Congress that needs to develop a leadership strength of its own.

There is also the view that the Presidency, as Watergate and the Ford Presidency have verified, is an indestructible office, tough and resilient. It readily survived, and Watergate may have actually strengthened it. That is, Watergate had a kind of purifying effect on the office, for after the trauma of 1973-1974, many people found a false comfort in the claim that "the system worked." Once Nixon was removed, the problems of the office were assumed to have been eliminated. But to those who still worry about a too-strong Presidency, this attitude is very dangerous. We should have been more alarmed than we were, or than we are. The seeds of the imperial Presidency are still there. The office still needs to be cut down to size.

But the period of post-Watergate reforming has just about run its course. Few new reform ideas are being heard these days. The call for strengthening the Presidency—or at least leaving the Presidency alone—is the dominant one these days and likely to be so for the next few years. Fears of another era of congressional government are unfounded. Plainly, the pendulum has already swung back in the other direction, although how far it will swing and what consequences will follow cannot yet be determined.

Conclusion

Congressional-presidential relations are not merely constitutional questions but also struggles for the support of public opinion. People may be more attentive to Presidents than to Congress, yet most Americans have reacted to Watergate and Vietnam by hoping that Congress will play a more significant role in shaping public policy. Americans cherish the ideal of separations of powers. But in practice the Presidency has become the dominant branch, especailly in foreign policy. The President must work with the Congress, but there is still ample latitude granted a President during emergency situations, in an era of emergencies. As Larry Tribe has put it, "We are, and must remain, a society led by three equal branches, with one permanently 'more equal' than the others: as the Supreme Court and Congress are preeminent in constitutional theory, so the President is preeminent in constitutional fact."[32]

Our system of checks and balances must be strong enough for effective leadership, while dispersing power enough to insure liberty. It is when the "national security" is at stake that uncertainties and confusion arise. Justice Jackson warned us that "security is like liberty in that many crimes are committed in its name." Certainly that was so in the recent past.

The balance is delicate, and rebalancing efforts such as the congressional reassertion of the 1970s will often be necessary. The reaction to the imperial or Watergate Presidency has been significant, though perhaps not lasting. There is a healthy skepticism toward Presidents. There is less glorification of Presidents and their policies. There is a new spirit of independence among members of the Congress. They say: "We want a strong and intelligent President, but he has to bear one thing in mind—we got elected, too." Or as former U.S. Senator Mike Mansfield put it, "The people have not chosen to be governed by one branch of government alone."[33]

There have been campaign finance reforms, open meeting laws, and a rash of congressional reorganization efforts. There is also a new emphasis on accountable and responsible leadership. We know now that a strong power-maximizing Presidency need not be an accountable one. Plainly, we also know now that a strong and responsible President is not one who holds himself above the law,

1/ Imperial President and Resurgent Congress • 40

who disregards the Constitution, who misuses the intelligence agencies, who intimidates the press. Strength in the White House these days is judged more on the quality of ideas, on the President's integrity, know-how, and negotiating skills, and on the quality of the staff he can assemble to help him.

Congress has most of the tools it needs to become a reasonably effective partner in shaping national policy. Whether it chooses to use them is another matter. The reassertion most needed in Washington is the reassertion by Congress of its traditional powers such as the power of the purse, and the powers to confirm, to investigate, and to oversee the implementation of national programs. Congress will probably achieve very little by passing symbolic "reform" measures such as the War Powers Resolution of 1973 or by writing countless legislative veto provisions into legislation that may make the implementation of some laws an administrative nightmare.

But however much the public may want Congress to be a major partner with the President and a major check on the President, the public's support for Congress will always be subject to deterioration. Power is much dispersed in Congress. Its deliberations and quarrels are very public. After a while, the public begins to view Congress as "the bickering branch" or the policy-thwarting branch, especially if there is a vigorous activist in the White House.

Polls show that people think Congress pays more attention to "their views" than does the President. Assuredly the Congress is a splendid forum that represents and registers the diversity of America. But that very virtue makes it difficult for Congress to provide leadership and difficult for it to challenge and bargain effectively with Presidents. Not surprisingly, a wary public, dissatisfied with programs that do not work and policies that do not measure up to the urgencies of the moment, will look somewhere else—and that somewhere else will usually be the President, or an aspiring presidential candidate offering himself as an alternative to the President.

How you stand on the question of a strong Presidency depends in part on what policies you favor and how those policies are advanced or hampered by the President or by Congress. It matters too, of course, whether you like the person in the White House. If you approve of the President and most of his policies, the tendency is to believe with Woodrow Wilson that the President should be "free to be as big a man as he can be."

The cycle theory of presidential-congressional relations has long been fashionable. It holds that there will be periods of presidential ascendancy followed by periods of congressional ascendancy. Usually these periods have been a decade or more, and sometimes a generation, in length. The analysis suggests that a moderate but brief congressional assertion has taken place in these immediate post-Watergate years. But the responsibilities of the Presidency in these days, coupled with the complexities of foreign and economic policy, do not really permit any serious weakening of the office. Congress has tried to curb the misuse and abuse of power—but it has not really weakened the Presidency.

The Presidency as an institution is still strong. Its powers are such that the country will rally behind a President if the nation's vital interests are threatened. A President has a greater obligation today to communicate more persuasively than in the past about when and why the national security of the nation is threatened. But Congress and the people will follow persuasive presidential leadership when it is linked with purpose.

Defenders of the Presidency argue that Congress and the reformers have overreacted to Watergate and they call for the repeal of the War Powers Resolution of 1973, restricting the use of legislative vetoes, restraints on the oversight of the intelligence agencies, independence for the Executive's use of executive agreements, and in general a word of caution to Congress not to interfere too much in executive branch negotiations in foreign policy and security matters.

Many will continue to worry about future imperial Presidents and about the possible alienation of the people from their leaders as complex issues continue to centralize responsibilities in the hands of the national government and in the Executive. Those who are concerned about these matters will not content themselves, nor should they, with the existing safeguards against the future misuse of presidential powers. The difficulty is that so few of the additional safeguards suggested seem to be politically or practically acceptable. It is not easy to contrive devices that will check the President who would misuse powers without hamstringing the President who would use those same powers for purposive and democratically acceptable ends.[34] There are some useful proposals heard nowadays, however, that might assist in achieving that goal. One example is a provision that either the Attorney General or a panel of designated federal judges could trigger the appointment of a special public prosecutor, outside of the executive branch, to investigate and prosecute alleged wrongdoing.

In the end, both the President and Congress have to recognize they are not two sides out to "win" but two parts of the same government, both elected to pursue together the interests of the American people. Too much has been made by too many Presidents and by too many scholars of that ancient but partial truth that only the President is the representative of all the people. Members of Congress do not represent the people exactly as a President does, but its two houses collectively represent them also and in ways a President cannot and does not.

Notes

[1] *See* Thomas E. Cronin, *The State of the Presidency* (Boston: Little, Brown and Co., 1975), chapter 2, pp. 23-52.

[2] Roberta S. Sigel, "Image of the American Presidency: Part II of an Exploration into Popular Views of Presidential Power," in *The Presidency*, ed. Aaron Wildavsky (Boston: Little, Brown and Co., 1969), p. 300.

[3] *New York Times*/CBS Poll, April 1977.

[4] Arthur M. Schlesinger, Jr., *The Imperial Presidency* (Boston: Houghton-Mifflin Co., 1973).

[5] Ibid., pp. 129-30.

[6] *See* Leonard C. Meeker, "The Legality of U.S. Participation in the Defense of Vietnam," *Department of State Bulletin* (March 28, 1966), pp. 484-85.

[7] *See* J. Malcolm Smith and Cornelius P. Cotter, *Powers of the President During Crisis* (Washington, D.C.: Public Affairs Press, 1960). *See also* Harold C. Relyea, "Declaring and Terminating A State of Emergency," *Presidential Studies Quarterly* (Fall 1976): 36-42.

[8] Quoted in "The President Versus Congress," *National Journal* (May 29, 1976): 736. *See also* U.S., Congress, Senate, *Emergency Powers Statutes, Report of the Special Committee on the Termination of the National Emergency*, 93rd Cong., 1st sess. (November 19, 1973).

[9] Walter F. Mondale, *The Accountability of Power* (New York: David McKay, 1975), pp. 114-15.

[10] Lloyd Bentsen, *Congressional Oversight of Executive Agreements—1975*, Testimony in Hearings Before the Subcommittee on Separation of Powers of the Committee on the Judiciary, U.S. Senate, 94th Cong., p. 79.

[11] *See* his own account in Richard Nixon, *RN: Memoirs of Richard Nixon* (New York: Grosset and Dunlap, 1978), pp. 896-910. See also Leon Jaworski, *The Right and the Power* (New York: Pocket Books, 1977), ch. 10.

[12] Raoul Berger, "The Grand Inquest of the Nation," *Harper's* (October 1973): 12. See also, by the same author, *Executive Privilege: A Constitutional Myth* (Cambridge, Mass.: Harvard University Press, 1974).

[13] Sam J. Ervin, Jr., quoted in *Separation of Powers Annual Report*, Report of the Committee on the Judiciary, U.S. Senate Subcommittee on Separation of Powers, 94th Cong., 2d sess. (July 19, 1976), p. 9. See also, *Refusals by the Executive Branch to Provide Information to the Congress, 1964-1973*, issued by the same committee, 93rd Congress, November 1974. Note that these instances of withheld information or refusals to share information with Congress are not the same as formal White House use of the "executive privilege" practice. More often than not these were delays and long and drawn-out instances of noncooperation, often by subcabinet or bureau chiefs or agency heads and not necessarily by cabinet officers or White House aides.

[14] The best source on impoundment is Louis Fisher, *Presidential Spending Power* (Princeton: Princeton University Press, 1975).

[15] Quoted in *National Emergencies Act*, Report of the Committee on Government Operations, U.S. Senate, 94th Cong., 2d. sess. (1976), p. 2.

[16] *See* U.S., Congress, Senate, *Congressional Oversight of Executive Agreements—1975*, Hearings before the Subcommittee on Separation of Powers of the Committee on the Judiciary, 94th Cong., 1st sess., 1975.

[17] Leverett Saltonstall (R.-Mass), quoted in Harry Howe Ransom, *The Intelligence Establishment* (Cambridge, Mass.: Harvard University Press, 1970), p. 169.

[18] John T. Elliff, "Congress and the Intelligence Community," in *Congress Reconsidered*, ed. Lawrence C. Dodd and Bruce I. Oppenheimer (New York: Praeger, 1977), pp. 193-206.

[19] Quoted in *National Journal*, May 29, 1976, p. 742.

I/Imperial President and Resurgent Congress • 44

[20] Quoted in Mary Russell, "Bill to Give Congress Veto Power is Defeated," *Washington Post*, September 22, 1976.

[21] For President Carter's message on his opposition to certain legislative vetoes, *see*, "Legislative Vetoes: Message to Congress, June 21, 1978" in *Weekly Compilation of Presidential Documents*, Week of June 26, 1978, p. 1146.

[22] John R. Bolton, *The Legislative Veto: Unseparating the Powers* (Washington, D.C.: American Enterprise Institute, 1977), pp. 31-32. For a different view, *see* Louis Fisher, "A Political Context for Legislative Vetoes," *Political Science Quarterly* (Summer 1978): 241-53.

[23] Antonin Scalia, Assistant Attorney General, Testimony in Hearings Before the Subcommittee on Administrative Law and Government Relations, U.S., House of Representatives, 94th Cong., 1st sess. (October and November 1975), p. 377.

[24] William J. Lanouette, "Who's Setting Foreign Policy—Carter or Congress?" *National Journal* (July 15, 1978): 1116-23.

[25] Ford, in a written reply to a *New York Times* query, quoted in Philip Shabecoff, "Appraising Presidential Power" in *The Presidency Reappraised*, 2d ed., ed. Thomas E. Cronin and Rexford G. Tugwell (New York: Praeger, 1977), p. 37.

[26] Eric L. Davis, "Legislative Liaison in the Carter Administration" (Paper delivered at the 1978 Annual Meetings of the Midwest Political Science Association, Chicago, Illinois, April 20-22, 1978), pp. 30-31.

[27] *Newsweek*, April 12, 1976, p. 31.

[28] Ford, quoted in Don Oberdorfer, "Ford: War Powers Act Not Practical," *Washington Post* (April 12, 1977), p. 8.

[29] John Hoy and Melvin Berstein, eds., *The Effective President* (Pacific Palisades, California: Palisades Press, 1976), essay by Robert Novak.

[30] Samuel Huntington, "The Democratic Distemper," in *The American Commonwealth*, ed. Natham Glazer and Irving Kristol (New York: Basic Books, 1976), p. 24.

[31] Arthur Schlesinger, *Imperial Presidency*, p. 404. *See also* a similar theme in Theodore Sorensen, *Watchmen in the Night: Presidential Accountability after Watergate* (Cambridge, Mass.: MIT Press, 1975). For a different view, however, *see* Philip B. Kurland, *Watergate and the Constitution* (Chicago: University of Chicago Press, 1978).

[32] Larry Tribe, *American Constitutional Law* (Mineola, New York: Foundation Press, 1978), p. 157.

[33] "The President Versus Congress: Special Report," *National Journal*, May 29, 1976, p. 730.

[34] For perceptive and sophisticated accounts of the debate over presidential accountability, *see* William S. Livingston, "Britain and America: The Institutionalization of Accountability," *Journal of Politics* 38 (1976): 879-94; Norman C. Thomas, "Presidential Accountability Since Watergate" (Paper delivered at the 1978 Annual Meetings of the Midwest Political Science Association, Chicago, Illinois, April 20-22, 1978); and Louis Fisher, *The Constitution Between Friends* (New York: St Martin's Press, 1978).

Congress and the Cycles of Power

Lawrence C. Dodd

Lawrence C. Dodd is Associate Professor of Government at The University of Texas at Austin.

Almost a century ago a young political science graduate student at Johns Hopkins wrote a provocative little book entitled *Congressional Government*.[1] The author's name was Woodrow Wilson. He argued that a two-fold power shift was occurring in American politics: (a) a shift of power from the state to the federal level; and (b) a shift of power at the national level from the Supreme Court and the Presidency to Congress. Wilson saw these shifts as historical necessities.

In the intervening century, *Congressional Government* has become one of the most influential studies of American politics. It was the first systematic and widely read book to argue that institutional politics in America is characterized by a shifting balance of power. In addition, Wilson's analysis was sufficiently cogent and provocative to provide a classic interpretation of American politics, an interpretation that political analysts continually restudy for its insight and method. For those of us who would attempt to assess the current shifting balance of power between Congress and the Presidency, Wilson's book provides three lessons.

The first lesson—one unique for Wilson's time though widely acknowledged today—is that power and power relations are not constant. They are not indelibly imprinted on institutions by a constitution. In Wilson's time political analysts assumed that the

Constitution guaranteed power to institutions. They assumed that a separation of powers/check and balance system of government would endure as written in the Constitution. They assumed that the chief threats to government were invasion from abroad or civil war at home. Political analysts in Wilson's day did not perceive that a slow transformation of power relations among American national institutions might substantially alter the government from within.

Wilson argued, in a dramatic departure from the legalistic mentality of his day, that the power of institutions rests not only on their constitutional mandate but also on the ability of institutions to organize themselves so as to utilize their power prerogatives. In order to use their constitutional power authoritatively, institutions must organize themselves in a cohesive manner that maintains their decisionmaking integrity. If an institution cannot organize effectively, its power will ebb away and other institutions will fill the void. In his own day Wilson saw the Presidency and the Supreme Court as less able to organize effectively, while Congress, through the expanded use of the committee system together with a strong Speaker, was organizing in a cohesive fashion. Thus the shift of power to Congress.

The second lesson of *Congressional Government* is that political analysts must be cautious and hardheaded in their interpretation of the shifting balance of institutional power. We must be careful not to extrapolate current patterns indefinitely. Short-term events and power shifts may well disguise the real nature of long-term power dynamics. Because we are all products of our time, we may be blinded by the nature of our time from seeing the real historical dynamics. We thus must seek historical interpretations of power relations that are as rigorously logical, empirically accurate, and broadly inclusive as possible.

Change is complex and interactive. At the time Wilson wrote he was basically correct in perceiving the existence of the two patterns he identified. Unfortunately, he relied too extensively on the immediate patterns as guides to long-term dynamics. Thus he saw Congress as becoming the supreme branch of American government because it seemed to be moving toward predominance during the Reconstruction era. Less than thirty years later he was to play a major role in creating the modern Presidency and setting it on its course toward predominance.

While Wilson was correct in his contention that power does shift between institutions, and that one institution may gain dominance over others, his long-term prognosis was incorrect. Ironically, Wilson's misinterpretation of the shifting balance between Congress and the Presidency occurred partly because of the accuracy of his forecast that power was shifting from the states to the national level. As will become evident later in this discussion, the rise of the national government played a major role in the decline of Congress, a decline that simply was not evident in Wilson's time.

Finally, the third lesson that Wilson taught us was that each generation must attempt to assess anew the shifting balance of institutional power. Every historical era has its own crisis and its own potential. The actors of each era can be so buffeted by change and so unaware of the character of change that crises overwhelm them and potential goes unfulfiled. Few generations will ever completely resolve their own problems or exploit their own opportunities. Nevertheless, the performance of a generation will improve significantly if it understands the historical forces that are operating.

Wilson was trying to make sense out of a world that had suffered a devastating Civil War, a debilitating Reconstruction, and a string of weak Presidents and strong-headed Congresses. By dropping the constitutional blinders that previous analysts had worn, Wilson accurately perceived the shift of power from the states to the national government; this perception was a major building block of the legislative programs of his Presidency. In addition, Wilson perceived that power relations do vary and that the way institutional actors behave within an institution influences the power of that institution. That insight led him to emphasize the potential importance of the congressional committee system, an organizational device that political analysts had not come to appreciate fully. In addition, Wilson's understanding of the importance for external power of an institution's internal behavior was critical to his own reinterpretation of the Presidency in later years and to his recognition that the behavior of a particular President can be critical for the power of the Presidency.

While the forecast of the young Woodrow Wilson concerning presidential-congressional relations was wrong, the intellectual style reflected in his early analysis later proved immeasurably useful to him and to other political analysts. Wison's example teaches us that to understand the nature of our time, to take short-term events and derive from them their underlying significance, to forecast the kinds of problems we are likely to face and thus to envision the kinds of responses likely to be required of us, we must actively and honestly seek to understand the broad historical dynamics that shape the power relations among our political institutions.

I

In our own time we have witnessed a series of events at least as dramatic as those of Wilson's time. In the sixty years since Wilson's Presidency, power has shifted from the Congress to the President. With this power shift the President has increasingly become the nation's chief legislator, chief budgetary officer, the primary overseer of the bureaucracy, the leader in foreign policy, the nation's chief tribune. For a generation at least the rise of the Presidency was often glorified as necessary to govern the country. During the 1950s and 1960s political analysts wrote that the Presidency was the nation's one truly democratic institution, the President the only officer elected by all the people. The Congress was seen as an outdated, obsolete institution elected to serve parochial rather than national interests. The interests of the Presidency were seen as essentially parallel to those of the nation at large, which meant that it was a safe, responsive, humane institution whose actions would necessarily be good for the whole country.[2]

In the last decade a series of events have led analysts to challenge both the benevolence of the Presidency and the historical necessity of its rise. The Vietnam War, Nixon's impoundment of duly appropriated funds, the credibility gap of the Johnson Administration, the Watergate crisis, the rise of a secrecy system which saw the executive branch supressing a wide range of information, presidential politicization of the FBI and CIA—all of these have led to a serious and widespread challenge to the desirability of presidential government.[3]

The 1970s have witnessed a new congressional resurgence, a new shift of power from the President to Congress. In this power shift, Congress has tried to regain its legislative power by strengthening the power of its party leaders. Congress has sought to regain control of the budget by creating a new congressional budget process. It has sought to regain control of the bureaucracy by reforming its oversight procedures. It has attempted to reassert its war-making prerogatives by passing a war powers act. And it hopes to improve its role as popular tribune by broadcasting its legislative sessions. These and other reforms, the most far-reaching congressional changes in sixty years, present a picture of a newly invigorated and assertive legislature that has retaken its place in the constitutional order.[4]

Political analysts today often worry less about presidential power and more about a return of congressional government. The short-term reforms and the congressional resurgence, extrapolated into long-term power shifts, fill many an observer with dread. It is not uncommon, in fact, to hear the assertion that the Presidency has been crippled and that the nation is moving pell mell into an era of congressional dominance. With the imperial Presidency still a warm memory, we are cautioned that the real problem we should fear is congressional government.

Thus the dilemma that we face in trying to understand the movement of events in our time. Do we extrapolate the long-term power shift, i.e., the rise of the Presidency, as the fundamental reality shaping our politics and our future? Do we highlight the short-term shift, i.e., the resurgence of Congress, as the new reality likely to persist? Do we simply throw up our hands and conclude that no sense can be made of these events? Or do we conclude that it simply doesn't matter what the balance of power really is or how it is shifting?

To take the last question first, it should be clear to us that the balance of power does matter, and that understanding it matters. The balance matters because the alternative is to leave decision-making power in the hands of one person—and that scheme is rejected by the full force of Western political thought. The difficulty is not merely that philosopher-kings are difficult to select it; it is also that the immense burdens of the Presidency itself may distort personality and make judgment unreliable.[5] Thus government by separate institutions sharing power, including a legislature composed of numerous elected representatives, commends itself to us today as it did to the framers of the Constitution.

Because we are committed to government by separate institutions sharing power, understanding the shifting balance of power among those institutions is critical. If, despite the recent resurgence of Congress, power is likely to continue shifting toward the Presidency over the long run, then the nation must consider new and more drastic ways to constrain executive power and revive Congress. If Congress now is overwhelming the Presidency and likely to increase its dominance during the coming decades, then the nation will need to adjust the institutional balance in the other direction so as to provide itself with a sufficiently strong executive. Finally, if the recent reforms have produced a roughly desirable balance between institutions, then, while keeping an eye on the balance of power, so as not to lose it, the country can turn its attention to other things.

So what sense do we make of the events of our day? What is the nature of the shifting balance of institutional power? What institutional problems are we likely to face in the coming decades for which we should now be preparing? A key to these questions lies, much as with Woodrow Wilson, in developing and discussing a broad historical interpretation within which to view and interpret the short-term events. The place to start an historical interpretation is at the beginning, with the Constitution itself.

II

The American Constitution was constructed on and justified by a particular theory of politics, a theory outlined by James Madison in the *Federalist Papers*.[6] That theory had three basic parts. First, it assumed that institutions act as they do and governments are governed as they are because of the motives of the politicians who exercise institutional power. The most basic motive is the quest for personal power. That quest may derive from any number of deeper motives: a desire for ego gratification or for prestige; a search for personal salvation through good works; a hope to construct a better world or to dominate the present one; or a preoccupation with status and self-love.

Whatever the source of the power motive, Madison assumed that politicians generally seek to attain power so as to control the policy decisions that impose the authority of the state on the citizenry at large. He also assumed that, at an individual level, the quest for power can become so all-consuming that an aspiring politican may well overlook the public interest or civil liberties in pursuit of power and privilege for himself and his supporters. Thus he saw the power quest as a potential threat to political freedom and stability.

Madison's second assumption was that a stable representative government protective of civil liberties and property can best be generated by a constitution that divides governmental power among institutions, letting institution check institution. With governmental power divided in this manner there exists no one pinnacle of power from which one individual or group can control all governmental power. Rather, with power divided among institutions, governmental action requires cooperation among institutions that share governmental power. In the act of cooperating, the actors within each institution will jealously guard the prerogatives of their institutions so as not to lose their personal power base through power usurpation by another institution. As Madison wrote, "Ambition must be made to counteract ambition. The interests of the man must be connected with the constitutional rights of the place."[7]

In the Madisonian scheme of constitution-making, then, the constitution was important because it could constrain and guide the power quest in ways that would protect civil liberties and secure freedom. Thus the separation of powers, checks and balances, federalism, and government based on representation rather than direct popular democracy. In addition, there was a fifth element of the Madison model of constitutionalism that he saw as critical to the successful operation of the government: "In order to lay a due foundation for that separate and distinct exercise of the different powers of government, which to a certain extent is admitted on all hands to be essential to the preservation of liberty, it is evident that each department must have a will of its own."[8] While modern political analysts have recognized the importance of such doctrines as separation of powers, checks and balances, and federalism, they have sorely overlooked the emphasis of the founding fathers on "institutional will." In point of fact, however, the entire logic of the Constitution depends on this critical variable. The basic idea of the Constitution, of course, was to divide national power among three institutions—the Congress, the Supreme Court, and the Presidency— and to give each branch checks to use in balancing the others and forcing cooperative governance. The assumption was that if one institution went beyond the bounds of constitutional comity and attempted to usurp the power of another institution, the other institution would use its constitutional checks to thwart the aggrandizing behavior and restore the constitutional balance.

The expectation that checks and balances would work rested on the very explicit assumption that each institution would be able to know its own will, that it would be a cohesive decisionmaking body capable of exercising its constitutional prerogatives and defending its institutional integrity. Of course, the founding fathers were not content to hope blindly that each institution would be capable of developing and sustaining an institutional will. They saw the Constitution as an instrument that could structure institutions, nurture cohesiveness, and generate an institutional purpose. And they tried to shape it toward those ends. Thus the single Executive and the power of the President to nominate department heads with whom he would work. Thus a single Supreme Court composed of members possessed of virtually lifetime tenure. These and other devices were expressly designed to nurture the cohesiveness of the Presidency and the Supreme Court, to help them sustain their institutional integrity.

When the founding fathers came to the Congress, however, they lost their fervor for institutional cohesiveness. The constitutional provisions for Congress—bicameralism, separate selection procedures for the House and Senate, unspecified powers for the Speaker of the House, the use of the Vice President as presiding officer of the Senate—seem to nurture internal conflict and weakness rather than cohesiveness. The founding fathers took this approach to Congress because of a third element of the Madisonian theory of politics.

Madison's third assumption was that the way politicians approach political institutions and seek power through them depends very much on the nature of the society and on the role of government within that society. In Madison's case, he clearly recognized that the Constitution was being written for an agrarian society in which political service at the national level would be physically and economically difficult. Moreover, because the role of the national government would be quite limited in an agrarian society isolated by the ocean from European wars, and based on a constitution devoted to federalism, Madison realized that long-term service at the national level would not be greatly attractive to politicians. Power could be pursued more easily and perhaps more effectively in local or state politics.[9]

Consequently, at the national level of government there would be a high turnover of elected officials. And those who did tend to stay on for long-term careers would acquire expertise and be relied upon as power wielders. In particular, Madison feared that the Congress would come to rely on a few leaders, particularly a presiding officer, to exercise its power.[10]

The experience of the colonial assemblies suggested that a legislature in control of the power of the purse and guided by a strong-willed leader could come to dominate governmental affairs. For this reason, Madison feared that in an agrarian and isolated society, Congress would be a cohesive institution that could use its taxing and spending power to overwhelm the other institutions. Hence, the best constitutional course was not to reinforce the natural cohesiveness that Congress would derive from high turnover and centralized power, but to offset that cohesiveness through such mechanisms as bicameralism, thus equalizing the balance of power between Congress, the Presidency, and the Court.

So the Madisonian theory of politics envisioned a constitutional system in which each branch of government would be sufficiently cohesive to have an institutional will, assert itself in its own area of governmental authority, and respond effectively to aggrandizing efforts by the other branches. The Madisonian model worked to a large extent as he had foreseen—so long as Madison's assumptions held. In particular, Congress did centralize power through party leadership and thus nurture its own institutional integrity. If anything, the nineteenth century served to justify Madison's fear of the legislature. Certainly the nineteenth century often saw Congress as the dominant institution of American national government.

But Madison's assumptions did not hold indefinitely. It was not that politicians ceased to seek power. It was not that the system of checks and balances or separation of powers was changed through constitutional alteration. Rather, it was the character and setting of the nation that changed—the assumptions about states' rights, the agrarian social and economic order, the low involvement of the nation in international affairs. As the environment of the constitutional system changed, the role and power of the national government increased, setting in motion events that were dramatically to alter Congress, congressional-executive relations, and ultimately the constitutional system itself.

III

In the nineteenth century, the national government was not immensely powerful. Most politicians were not drawn to long-term careers in Congress. Those who were, however, and were concerned with congressional power, did struggle for power positions, and that contest initially served to create a fledgling committee system.[11] The committee system was balanced by and guided by strong central leadership, particularly in the House of Representatives, where the Speakership offered a clear mechanism for focusing power.

The central leaders of Congress were able to maintain considerable authority because they offered services—such as selection of committee members and chairmen, policy development and guidance, mediation of parliamentary conflicts, and scheduling of legislation—that were necessary to avoid the chaos implicit in the high turnover of members throughout most of the nineteenth century. The leaders' authority was challenged occasionally by other members who wanted greater independence and more autonomy for themselves and their committees. These challenges led to "minicycles" in which forces of decentralization occasionally would assert themselves within Congress and attempt to disperse power.[12] Supporters of decentralization during the nineteenth century were never numerous enough to break the power of central leaders permanently, however, since the number of Congressmen committed to congressional careers of any significiant duration was quite low.

Events of the late nineteenth century altered dramatically the nature of national power. The Civil War ended the ambiguities about the supremacy of the national government over the states and clearly established the hegemony of the national government in political affairs. The Industrial Revolution, whose effects began to multiply in the late nineteenth century, helped create an interdependent economy based on interstate commerce, thus expanding the power potential of the national government by confronting it with social and economic decisions of considerable magnitude that lay within its constitutional mandate. The Industrial Revolution also provided America (as well as other nations) with the technical means to span the oceans, conquer far-off lands, and gain international markets for domestically produced goods. America thus discovered the world, the world rediscovered America, and the national government discovered anew its constitutional responsibility for foreign policy and the regulation of American involvement in foreign commerce.

These new obligations enhanced the power of the national government over the lives of individual citizens, and Congress *pari passu* became the center of national decisionmaking. The Constitution gave to it the delegated powers to regulate interstate and foreign commerce, to give advice and consent (on the part of the Senate) to treaties and ambassadorial nominations, to control defense authorizations and appropriations, and to declare war. Politicians who wanted to exercise these prerogatives had to go to Congress and stay there, which they did in ever-increasing numbers.[13] In the early nineteenth century approximateley 50 percent of the members of a Congress failed to return to the next Congress, much of the turnover being voluntary. Between 1870 and 1910 the turnover rate dropped from 50 to 20 percent. Thus in the twentieth century, 80 to 90 percent of the members of a Congress return to the next Congress. This decline in turnover fundamentally altered the setting in which Madison had anchored his assumptions about the proper operation of the constitutional system.

As power-oriented politicians came to stay in Congress for long-term careers, they no longer found that a centralized system of power within Congress served their personal interests. Rather than seeing strong party leaders as aiding members by reducing organizational chaos and providing needed policy guidance, legislators of the new Congress saw party leaders as arbitrary tyrants interfering with personal careers and policy specializations. Thus, in a quest for personal power, early twentieth century members of Congress moved dramatically against strong party leadership in Congress. The system of committee government that emerged was held together by institutional norms and rules that had been developing over the preceding decades as congressional turnover had decreased, and the most important of these norms was seniority.[14]

The move away from strong congressional leadership and toward committee government knocked out a major underpinning of the Madisonian system of government, namely the assumption that Congress would maintain its institutional will because it would be composed largely of nonprofessional politicians who would centralize congressional power. This major move was a qualitative change in Congress and a watershed occurrence for the relation between Congress and the Presidency.

IV

Committee government distributes policymaking responsibilities among a series of relatively autonomous committees and subcommittees, each having significant control over policy decisions in a specified jurisdictional area. Although this system denies every member the opportunity to control all policy decisions, it ensures that most members can hope to satisfy a portion of their power drive if they remain in Congress long enough to acquire a chairmanship.

Despite several advantages, committee government possesses serious flaws that undermine the ability of Congress to fulfill its constitutional responsibilities to make public policy and oversee its implementation.[15] Among these flaws, three stand out: 1. Committee government is without strong, centralized leadership, and thus lacks the ability to develop comprehensive programs that cut across committee jurisdictions; moreover it leaves Congress without an authoritative spokesman to justify its policies to the nation. 2. Committee government is without a mechanism to ensure that decisions of the authorization, appropriations, and review committees bear some reasonable relation to one another; lacking fiscal coordination, Congress finds it difficult to develop a rational national budget. 3. Committee government provides no safeguards against self-interested policymaking; the committees that create and fund programs also oversee program implementation; and because the creators and funders are normally the most visible supporters, they are loath to undertake critical investigations of a pet agency or program. In this manner committee government leads to a failure of congressional oversight of the Executive.

Committee government thus produces a paradox: the wide dispersal of power within Congress creates such immobilism that Congress is unable to play a strong role in national decisionmaking. Or, differently put, the desire for power by individual members creates an organizational disperson of power that undermines the ability of Congress to maintain its institutional cohesion and its constitutional power, and thus diminishes the long-term value of power within the institution.

The inherent tension between personal power and institutional power in the twentieth century Congress generates an explosive dynamic within Congress as an institution and between Congress and the Presidency. This dynamic is cyclical in nature, and follows a relatively clear long-term pattern.

In the short run, congressional members follow the immediate dictates of their personal power motive and support committee government. The longer committee government operates, the more severe its problems become, and the more dissatisfied the nation is with the inability of Congress to act decisively. In efforts to resolve the growing immobilism, political activists turn gradually to the President to provide leadership, budget coordination, and bureaucratic control. The President responds by asserting leadership, and eventually his role becomes so central that he feels free to ignore the wishes of members of Congress, even those who chair very important committees, and impose presidential policy on Congress and on the nation at large.

The coming of a strong, domineering, imperial President who ignores and frustrates Congress stimulates its members into action. They see that their individual positions of power within Congress are meaningless unless the institution can impose its legislative will on the nation. They search for ways to regain legislative preeminence and constrain the Executive.

Members identify part of the problem as an internal institutional one and seek to reform Congress. Such reform efforts come during or immediately following crises in which Presidents clearly and visibly threaten fundamental prerogatives of Congress. The reforms will include attempts to provide for more centralized congressional leadership, fiscal coordination, congressional openness, better oversight mechanisms, clarification of committee jurisdictions, procedures for policy coordination, and procedures to encourage committee accountability.

Because the quest for personal power continues as the underlying motivation of individual members, the reforms are basically attempts to strengthen the value of internal congressional power by increasing the power of Congress vis-à-vis the Executive. The reform efforts, however, are constrained by consideration of personal power prerogatives while centralizing power builds structural flaws into the centralization mechanism, flaws that would not be present were the significance of congressional structure for the national power of Congress itself the primary, overarching consideration. The existence of these flaws provides the openings through which centralization procedures are destroyed when institutional crises pass and members again feel free to emphasize personal power and personal careers. Because policy inaction within Congress often will be identified as the immediate cause of presidential power aggrandizement, and because policy immobilism may become identified with key individuals or committees that have obstructed particular legislation, reform efforts also may be directed toward breaking up the authority of these individuals or committees and dispersing it among individuals and committees who seem more amenable to activist policies.

As Congress moves to resolve internal structural problems and circumscribe presidential power, Presidents begin to cooperate with Congress. This cooperation stems from a desire to defuse the congressional counterattack and protect the power prerogatives of the Presidency. To do otherwise would open a Presidency to serious personal attack as anti-congressional and thus anti-democratic, tarnishing the legitimizing myth of the Presidency as a democratic institution representing all the people, and impugning presidential motivations as power aggrandizement rather than protection of the Republic.

The presidential effort to cooperate with Congress moves the nation into a quiescent era in which political conflict over constitutional prerogatives fades and conflict over policy takes center stage. In the quiescent period, Congress is resurgent. Yet, because Congress still lacks truly strong leadership and sound structural mechanisms suitable to assertive policymaking, Congress uses its resurgent authority primarily in a negative fashion, to stop Presidents from acting. Because the reform era failed to create a truly strong and durable system of congressional leadership, and because individual members continue in a quest for personal power, Congress is unable to generate a coherent, aggressive set of policy programs.

With the passing of time, new members enter Congress in a quest for power. Indeed, turnover is particularly high during the reform era because old members who benefited from the previous power structure leave, grumbling that Congress is just not as much fun as it used to be, and because the party of the President who ultimately activated the crisis suffers congressional losses as the public expresses its disapproval of the President's actions. The numerous new members are unaware of the lessons of the crisis era, or of the problems of decentralization. In addition, many of the older members never were really convinced that the crisis was congressional, choosing instead to see it as a result of the malevolence of a particular President.

Thus there is pressure to decentralize power anew, pressure that is reinforced by the inability of the Congress to act decisively and coherently, despite the centralizing reforms. Since the party leaders are unable to generate coherent policy—in part out of fear that a vigorous use of power will generate a revolt against them—the rank-and-file members determine that aggressive congressional action requires vigor. Vigor requires a larger number of activist members who can shape policy and push legislation. The rank and file thus move to restrain the power of the leaders and rely on the innovativeness and dynamism of congressional experts at a committee and subcommittee level. Thus they move to decentralize power once again, and are aided in the process by the structural flaws built into the centralizing mechanisms during the reform era.

And so the reforms ebb away. As decentralization returns, Congress becomes increasingly immobile and enfeebled, lacking confidence even in its negating powers. At first, the calls for presidential assertion are faint and muted. But as time passes and the government lacks clear direction, the clamor for presidential government grows, leading again to presidential dominance of policy processes and to yet another era of constitutional confrontation and congressional reform.

V

This conception of institutional politics assumes a fairly clear cyclical regularity, a regularity characterized by six stages and a number of empirically observable patterns. While the stages overlap, they fall roughly in the following sequence:

- congressional decentralization;
- congressional immobilism;
- the emergence of presidential government;
- constitutional crisis and confrontation;
- congressional reform and resurgence;
- the era of quiescence.

This cyclical pattern has occurred twice in the twentieth century.

The first power cycle occurred during the period from 1910 to 1915—when Congress moved to decentralized committee government—through the mid-1940s. The process of decentralization that started in 1910 proceeded throughout the era, the occasional logjams in the legislative process being broken by ever greater decentralization of power. With decentralization came immobilism, the 1920s and early 1930s being the great era of congressional unassertiveness.[16] In the 1930s, facing congressional immobilism, the country turned to strong presidential government. The era of constitutional confrontation began roughly with Roosevelt's Court-packing plan of 1937 and continued on into the 1940s, marked by his decisions to serve third and fourth terms, his forceful use of power as Commander-in-Chief, and executive preeminence in legislative policymaking. The era of reform came in the 1940s, highlighted by the 1946 Legislative Reorganization Act.

The transition to the second power cycle came in the late 1940s and 1950s as the nation moved to a second era of quiescence in which conflict centered over policy rather than constitutional power. In this quiescent era, the Presidency was less aggressive than in the Roosevelt era, and a new decentralization stage began to emerge. Congress ignored the centralized budget procedure established in the 1946 Act and in the 1950s it came to rely increasingly on subcommittees for legislative activity. The move toward decentralization was fueled by a high turnover in the late 1940s, particularly among Rooseveltian Democrats, a high turnover that brought Congress in 1946, 1948, and 1950 new members less sensitive to the dilemmas of decentralization.

Beginning in the early 1960s, congressional decentralization proceeded steadily toward ever greater reliance on subcommittees and a weakening of party leadership. With the growth of decentralization, Congress became increasingly immobile, and an era of congressional immobilism stretched on into the early 1970s. Facing congressional immobilism, the country turned away from the somnolent Presidency of Eisenhower, just as it had turned away from the passivity of Hoover, toward the activism of Kennedy, Johnson, and Nixon. The move to presidental government ended in the constitutional confrontations of the 1970s, confrontations over such issues as impoundment, war powers, and secrecy of information. In response to these confrontations came the congressional reforms and resurgence of the 1970s.

Today the nation is in a quiescent period. Constitutional confrontation between the President and Congress is behind us. The era of centralizing reform in Congress is over. Congress is somewhat resurgent, but its resurgence seems expressed more in its willingness to stall the President's programs than in an ability to offer clear alternatives to them. The President is cautious, uncertain, and ineffective in dealing with Congress. Presidents in such eras, after all, face the double standard of being expected to emulate the positive leadership of their immediate predecessors (without the resources of an imperial President) while facing a resurgent Congress that their predecessors were spared. Thus we hear faint calls for an activist Presidency while Congress stands ready in principle to cripple most presidential initiatives and the press stands ready to denounce any presidential activism that seems to portend a power aggrandizement.

The future today looks all too clear. With the continuance of the quiescent era we can expect renewed congressional decentralization—including circumvention of the power of party leaders and the budget committees, the strengthening of subcommittees, and proliferation of special committees and subcommittees. As decentralization proceeds, Congress should become increasingly immobile. In fact, because of the existence today of the strongest subcommittee system in congressional history—and thus a more potent decentralization of power as the centralizing mechanisms are crippled or ignored—we should expect far greater congressional immobilism in the coming decades than was experienced during the previous power cycles. With immobilism will come calls for presidential government. And with presidential government will come constitutional crisis.

Unfortunately, there is reason to expect that the next crisis era will be more devastating than the preceding ones. The power cycles of the twentieth century do not appear to be mild fluctuations around a constant balance point, as envisioned by Madison. Rather, the executive branch gains more authority and power with each cycle than it is forced to give up during congressional reform and resurgence. In each cycle, presidential roles and responsibilities are legitimized that previously were nonexistent or ambivalent, and the Presidency's power base is thus expanded. In the first cycle from 1910 to 1946, the Presidency gained a legitimate role as the chief legislative policymaker, as organizer and overseer of the bureaucracy, and as chief budget officer. In the second cycle the Presidency gained authority to make war without previous congressional consultation, the power to propose budgetary deferrals and recissions that virtually amount to line-item veto power, Supreme Court recognition of a degree of executive privilege, general control over a vast system of information secrecy, and general responsibility for an extensive secret-activity network of the FBI and CIA. While in each case the cycle ended with some restraint imposed on the particular role, if one takes a broad historical view each cycle is seen to have yielded the creation, expansion, and legitimation of a growing number of roles.

Moreover, with each cycle presidential transgressions of constitutional comity are more severe, because the Executive's power base is greater, because Congress is increasingly weaker as it is more decentralized, and because popular acceptance of presidential government increases with each cycle. Thus with impoundment or the invasion of Cambodia, Nixon clearly transgressed the Constitution while Roosevelt with the Court-packing plan or the third term merely violated the spirit of constitutional norms or conventions. In the next generation we can expect that a President or Presidents—building on the expanded power base of the office, facing an even weaker and more decentralized Congress, witnessing severe policy immobilism, and hearing desperate calls for action—will be lead to a still greater assertion of presidential power and still greater disdain for the constitutional division of power between Congress and the Presidency. These moves will probably not come soon. The legacy of the Nixon confrontation is too recent, and the resurgence of the Congress still too great. Yet within our lifetime, assuming that there are no fundamental changes in the systematic setting of national politics, we shall surely witness the further decline of Congress, the rebirth of the imperial Presidency, and a severe constitutional crisis surpassing any previous one of this century.

VI

What we are witnessing is the self-destruction of the Madisonian system of government. Short-term congressional reforms do not redress the long-term loss of power by Congress. This self-destruction is not the result of malevolence, evil motives, or evil people. After all, the quest for power by members of Congress may derive from the most noble and genuine desire to serve humanity. Likewise, presidential assertiveness may derive from a very real presidential concern for economic stability or national security, and from a very accurate perception that Congress cannot act.

Nevertheless, the self-destruction of the system is real. Because of the cyclical nature of the changes, the long-term weakening of Congress and the long-term rise of presidential government are not immediately clear. Its reassertiveness suggests that Congress is still viable. This viability, however, is an illusion. Short-term congressional resurgence simply diverts attention from the long-term momentum toward congressional impotence and greater presidential power.

So where does the problem lie and what is to be done? The problem lies in the Constitution, in its failure to provide constitutional provisions that can nurture the institutional cohesion of Congress in ways comparable to those that nurture the institutional cohesion of the judicial and executive branches. In retrospect it is understandable why the founding fathers failed to provide specific functions or organizational structure for Congress and to insure that cohesion. They were structuring a constitution for a very different world in which it could be realistically assumed that Congress would naturally maintain its organizational cohesion, in which indeed a strong Congress would be the chief threat to the other separated organs of government. But there have been many changes in the world since the age of the founding fathers, and those changes have altered significantly the way in which the provisions of the Constitution operate.

It is time to reconsider the appropriateness of our constitutional structure to the problems and realities of our age. In reassessing the Constitution we must, of course, be mindful of the lessons of Woodrow Wilson, particularly the possibility that we may fail to see changes occurring in our own age that negate the accuracy of our forecasts, even though we may accurately understand the dynamics of the past sixty years. It may be, for example, that dramatic though subtle moves toward regional or world government are occurring that will undermine the significance of national politics. Likewise, alterations may be occurring in the economic order that will transform politics as fundamentally in the next generation as the move toward industrialization did in the last. Both of these are real possibilities, but neither seems to me so imminent as to alter fundamentally the national politics of our generation. Rather, I suspect that the systematic setting of national institutional politics in the coming thirty years will be much as it has been in the past sixty years—only more so. If that is so, then the debilitative nature of the power cycle is likely to continue and worsen.

First, the domestic and international problems appear to be increasing in severity, rather than decreasing. The existence of these problems, and the necessity of national action to resolve them, will continue to draw politicians to Congress and sustain the power cycle. The severity of the problems, however, and the existence of congressional immobilism, will lead to a continuing and increasing reliance on the Executive.

This move toward executive power will be reinforced by a second trend: the electoral difficulties of becoming President, already very great, are increasing significantly with the well-intentioned reforms designed to purify presidential politics. The consequence is that the self-selection and weeding-out process is now so rigorous that the people who rise to the office are immensely power-driven and will be even more so in the future. Moreover, even if Presidents should be disposed to decline the proffered power, the structure of American politics and of the presidential office will offer them no real alternative to accepting it: faced with congressional immobilism and a surging economic and social crisis, it would be an act of high irresponsibility for a President not to act vigorously to meet a desperate situation.

A final reason why the momentum toward presidential power will continue and increase has to do with the internal power structure of the current Congress. Underlying the centralizing reforms of 1973-1976 are the decentralizing efforts of 1947-1973. These earlier reforms created a dispersion of power within Congress that is truly unprecedented in American history. As the centralizing mechanisms of the 1973-1976 era falter, congressional decisionmaking will depend on an institutionalized system of subcommittee government. Given the greater dispersion of power in that system, the problems of leadership, coordination, and oversight that face Congress will be of a magnitude beyond any we have witnessed thus far. The political immobilism implicit in this situation will be intolerable without a strong President. Presidents seeking to assert authority will face not the relatively strong committee chairmen such as Wilbur Mills, with authority over a considerable range of policy matters, but relatively weak and isolated subcommittee chairmen who can at best dominate a small policy domain and thus will have less maneuverability and fewer resources to use in a congressional-executive struggle. The fragmentation of Congress increasingly will be used as a primary justification for a strong Presidency, and Congress itself will become a less effective instrument for constraining presidential imperialism.

To end the debilitating cycles of the twentieth century will require that we direct attention not to internal congressional reform but to fundamental alterations of the constitutional system itself. We must create an incentive system within the Constitution which, while permitting enough congressional decentralization to encourage innovation and expertise, will lead members of Congress naturally to support centralizing mechanisms that can sustain institutional integrity. We also must reconsider the nature of the checks and balances system with the intent of strengthening the position of Congress.

It may be that the necessary changes can be accomplished within the confines of the current Constitution.[17] Perhaps a more competitive electoral system could be provided at the congressional level, which by encouraging higher turnover and generating a greater need for institutional leadership, would force a greater degree of centralization. Constitutional provisions giving greater authority to the Speaker of the House or the president pro tempore of the Senate might help them to create and maintain significant centralized policy organs in each house. The creation of a Congressional Security Council that could exercise congressional authority under specified emergency conditions might help Congress regain constitutional control of war making. Finally, a revision of the veto provision (making overrides easier or vetoes harder) would enhance congressional control over policymaking. While some of the above perhaps could be handled legislatively, it makes better sense to make the changes at the constitutional level if possible, the level most difficult for members of Congress to manipulate and undermine for personal advantage.

Finally, we must realize that the complex and demanding nature of contemporary life raises serious and fundamental questions as to the viability of Congress within a system of separation of powers and checks and balances. At the minimum we must consider how our constitutional system can be altered so as to discourage policy immobilism and institutional conflict. But constitution-making is serious and difficult business. It requires a realistic and hard-headed assessment of human nature, of the implications of different institutional arrangements, of the social conditions within which politics are to be conducted, and of the consequences that will derive from the interaction of these three elements of political life. In many ways Madison in the *Federalist Papers* is still the best guide to this type of undertaking. Yet we must unlock ourselves from the infatuating clarity and logic of Madison's arguments, which continue to exert a seductive hold on our imaginations long after the supporting conditions assumed by them have disappeared. The transformations of our society in the last century undercut the accuracy of his forecasts and we simply cannot afford *not* to take those changes into account. The only way to do that is to abandon our preoccupation with internal congressional reform and reconsider the constitutional structure that today necessarily consigns Congress—our most democratic institution—to an increasingly weakened political role in an ever more powerful national government.

Notes

[1] Woodrow Wilson, *Congressional Government* (Gloucester, Mass.: Peter Smith, 1885, 1973).

[2]Some of the major academic works that reflect these views are Richard Neustadt, *Presidential Power* (New York: John Wiley and Sons, 1960); Joseph Harris, *Congressional Control of Administration* (Washington, D.C.: Brookings Institution, 1964); James MacGregor Burns, *The Deadlock of Democracy* (Englewood Cliffs, N.J.: Prentice-Hall, 1963). The classic glorification of the twentieth-century Presidency is Clinton Rossiter, *The American Presidency* (New York: New American Library, 1956).

[3]*See* most particularly Arthur M. Schlesinger, Jr., *The Imperial Presidency* (New York: Popular Library, 1973).

[4]For a review of these reforms, and analyses of particular reforms, see the various essays in *Congress Reconsidered*, ed. Lawrence C. Dodd and Bruce I. Oppenheimer (New York: Praeger, 1977).

[5]The literature on presidential personality and its significance is growing rapidly. Several distinctive viewpoints are represented in George E. Reedy, *The Twilight of the Presidency* (Boston: Houghton-Mifflin Co., 1973); James D. Barber, *Presidential Character*, 2d ed. (Englewood Cliffs, N.J.: Prentice-Hall, 1977); Bruce Buchanan, *Presidential Experience* (Englewood Cliffs, N.J.: Prentice-Hall, 1978).

[6]*See* Alexander Hamilton, James Madison and John Jay, *The Federalist Papers*, ed. Clinton Rossiter (New York: New American Library, n.d.). Hereafter cited by author and paper number.

[7]Madison, *Federalist # 51*, pp. 321-22.

[8]Ibid.

[9]*Federalist # 53*, pp. 334-35.

[10]*Federalist # 48*, p. 309.

[11]Joseph Cooper, "The Origins of the Standing Committees and Development of the Modern House," *Rice University Studies* 56 (1970); Lauros G. McConachie, *Congressional Committees* (New York: Thomas Y. Crowell Co., 1898).

[12]The assertion as to a minicycle is based on a reading of George R. Brown, *The Leadership of Congress* (Indianapolis: Bobbs-Merrill, 1922); and Richard Bolling, *Power in the House* (New York: Capricorn, 1968).

[13]The literature demonstrating the decline in turnover includes H. Douglas Price, "Congress and the Evolution of Legislative 'Professionalism' "; and Morris P. Fiorina, David W. Rohde, and Peter Wissel, "Historical Change in House Turnover"; both in *Congress in Change*, ed. Norman J. Ornstein (New York:

Praeger, 1975); Nelson Polsby, "The Institutionalization of the House of Representatives," *American Political Science Review* 62 (1978): 144-69.

[14] For illustrative discussion of this era, see Kenneth W. Hechler, *Insurgency: Personalities and Politics of the Taft Era* (New York: Columbia University Press, 1940); Brown, *Leadership of Congress*; John D. Baker, "The Character of the Congressional Revolution of 1910," *Journal of American History* 60 (1973): 679-91.

[15] For a more extensive discussion of these and other flaws of committee government, *see* Lawrence C. Dodd, "Congress and the Quest for Power" in *Congress Reconsidered*, Dodd and Oppenheimer, pp. 227-83.

[16] Discussions of the problems in the 1920s are contained in Brown, *Leadership of Congress*; and Lindsay Rogers, *The American Senate* (New York: Alfred A. Knopf, 1926).

[17] For a most interesting dialogue on the Constitution and current problems, see Bob Eckhardt and Charles L. Black, Jr., *The Tides of Power: Conversations on American Constitution* (New Haven, Conn.: Yale University Press, 1976).

Discussion

JAMES SUNDQUIST: I have been listening carefully to find something to disagree with, but I haven't heard anything with which I fundamentally take issue. So instead of assessing these papers, I want to begin by disagreeing with a notion that seems to be very current—the notion that the imperial Presidency was created somehow by Presidents usurping powers. I rather agree with Arthur Schlesinger that it was as much congressional abdication as it was presidential usurpation. If you leave out what happened in 1972, when Richard Nixon went too far and did some unconstitutional things, you can come close to saying that it was a hundred percent congressional "abdication," and zero percent presidential usurpation.

The fact is that the accretion of presidential power was all done with the consent, and often with the leadership, of Congress. The Congress took its powers and deliberately handed them over to the President. To begin with, Congress made the President the general manager of the government. The principal act that started that off was the Budget and Accounting Act of 1921. Before 1921 if the government had a general manager it was the Congress; after 1921 it was the President. That transition was a congressional initiative. The President at the time, Woodrow Wilson, didn't even endorse the bill until, at the last moment, congressional leaders sent him a cable in Paris and asked him to endorse the bill to strengthen the chance of getting it passed. He gave it a routine, lukewarm endorsement. In fact he actually vetoed the first bill on technical grounds.

In 1946 in the Full Employment Act the Congress made the President the general manager of the economy. That act too was a congressional initiative. The President hadn't asked for it. Rather the Congress recognized that somebody had to stabilize the economy after the war. In the first draft of the bill, the Council of Economic Advisers was set up in the Legislature. That provision disappeared after the first draft, however, and Congress made the President the general manager, asking him to come up every year with an economic policy for them to consider. Before 1946 there was no requirement that the President have an economic policy and most of them didn't. After 1946 the President had to have an economic policy, so the economic leadership of the government was handed to the President by the Congress quite voluntarily.

Congress deliberately yielded supremacy in foreign policy after the Second World War. They recognized in the 1930s that when members of Congress tried to control foreign policy they made a mess of it. Now in this new interdependent world where the United States had to deal constantly with other countries through intermediate mechanisms like the United Nations, Congress recognized that foreign policy was beyond its capacity and that the President had to manage it.

Likewise, the Congress made the President the nation's legislative leader. When he began sending up legislative programs the Congress welcomed it. The Congress got in the habit of waiting for the President to initiate action before the Congress moved. They didn't have to do this. They did it voluntarily. They freely chose to let the President set the policy agenda, set the nation's priorities, force Congress to act. They could have put that power in the Speaker of the House and the majority leader of the Senate. They didn't. They chose to put it in the President.

Why did Congress create this imperial Presidency? Well, if you look to the literature surrounding these acts of Congress in transferring power to the President, three things stand out. First, Congress recognized its own weaknesses: it recognized that the Congress by its nature is a deliberative body; it has two houses; it has lots of committees; it is supposed to take its time—that's what it's set up for. So the Congress recognized over and over again that in areas in which rapid action is required, only the President can act. That is particularly important in foreign policy. It is also important much of the time in economic policy, where the government has to move fast to counter adverse economic trends.

Second, the Congress recognized that it really can't plan, for many of the reasons Professor Dodd talked about. Having chosen to decentralize itself into committees, it has no way of pulling its committees back together and developing a common strategy for attacking broad issues that cut across committee lines. It cannot do that unless it organizes itself in some kind of hierarchical, centralized fashion. But it is unwilling to do that. It is unwilling to set the Speaker or a policy committee up at the top with power to command and control the whole Congress. And why should it when the President is there, as the party leader, as the national leader in a perfect position to do that for it?

Third, Congress prefers to rely on the President for reasons on which Professor Mayhew is as much an authority as anyone alive: individual Senators and Congressmen are elected by states and districts. That's where their responsibility lies. As representatives of particularized interests, they feel uncomfortable trying to be the mediators of broad national issues. No Senator from Texas would want to be the one who came up with a national position on an energy plan. He has to represent the oil producers. And in the opposite sense the same thing is true of a Senator from New England. The person who can put together the national balance on this kind of question is the President of the United States and only the President of the United States. No Senator, no individual Congressman can do it.

What members of Congress are comfortable in doing, what they know how to do, is to take a broad presidential program and look at it from the standpoint of their segment of the national interest, their constituency, their local concerns. They do that well and in doing it they frequently improve presidential programs. But it is a responding kind of job, not an initiating kind of job.

So, as Tom Cronin suggested, we are back to the pre-1972 relationship. The Congress now is letting the President initiate, and is responding in the usual way. I don't believe Congress stepped out ahead of the President on any important subject in the past year.

Congress didn't start considering the energy program until the President's energy plan came up; and that was the way it was in field after field.

In virtually every aspect of the relations between Congress and the Presidency, the pendulum is swinging back. The Congress is settling back into its old comfortable habits, and when all the fuss and fury is over, and after the worst usurpations of 1972 have been corrected—as regards impoundment and executive secrecy—I think we will find that the relation and the balance of power between the branches will be just about what they were prior to Richard Nixon.

GARRY WILLS: I must confess I felt some misgivings about the topic today and they have grown as I listened to the papers. We heard first about cycles and then about a pendulum, and the whole discussion was shaped by a concern for determining which is up and which is down, President or Congress. Underlying the papers seems to be an assumption that if one branch goes up, the other goes down, and vice versa. I am always a little afraid of that way of looking at things.

Naturally, we are pattern-seeking animals, and recurrences are the things on which we build our knowledge. There is a great drive, in political science especially, to find patterns and cycles—and sure enough, people find them all the time. Yet none of the theories of the past has allowed people to predict accurately, and when predictions fail, the theorists always say, "Well, accidental factors enter in: wars, assassinations, depressions, whatever."

At the outset, then, I think we should be very cautious about assuming that there are going to be cycles, or for that matter that we can just pit President against Congress and say that if one is up the other must be down. It seems to me in some ways they can both gain power and in some ways they both should, and in some ways they could both lose power and in some ways they should.

It is also dangerous just to think in terms of quanta of power, and say that the President is losing a certain amount of power because of the War Powers Act or other reforms. It is not only a quantitative question, but a qualitative one. It seems to me the best critics of the President don't want to take away presidential power, or "x" amount of presidential power. They want to take away the illegal presidential power, the power of presidents to conduct their own private police force, to conduct their own private war, to impound money and therefore control public policy.

So cutting back certain kinds of presidential power seems to me a necessary thing. People who say we are weakening the Presidency too much are treating all restrictions on the Presidency as parts of a single quantum. Yet we must not rush pell-mell into curbing all kinds of presidential power.

We talk about institutions as if they had a certain momentum of their own, whether constitutionally mandated or contrived for more recent purposes. We assume that everything is supposed to be charted: Is that institution increasing in power or decreasing in power? We act as if institutions proceed on a grand power continuum, with sweeping, long-term historical changes along the continuum. But what we see is that an institution can fluctuate very rapidly and widely. The rebuke to Roosevelt over trying to pack the Supreme Court took away a great deal of the freedom of movement he thought he had. President Nixon was reelected by a landslide and stood in very strong position and thought he was going to reorganize government and do all sorts of grand things, and overnight his power disappeared.

Institutional power fluctuates rapidly because a great deal of the interplay between Congress and the President is really the power of the people, popularity power. Without it, a President can do very little, as Nixon proved. With it, he can do a great deal, even circumvent the law, even when his action is known. For example, Nixon indulged in certain constitutional breaches—the secret bombing of Cambodia, or impoundment, or the war on drugs, or the activities to suppress dissent—which were all known and were all popular at the time. When it came time to impeach the President, nobody could list those actions as bills of impeachment, because they were too popular.

And that brings me to a kind of power which is very important to consider here because it makes you look at cycles in a much more skeptical way. Essentially, I don't quite read Madison the way Professor Dodd does. I think everyone would agree that one of the great powers that Madison and the other constitutional framers envisaged was the power to impede, the power to slow down, the power to check transient moves among the populace and in the branches of government.

Professor Dodd laments congressional impotence during the time of the so-called imperial Presidency, yet if we look back to that period we will find people like James MacGregor Burns saying that Congress was much too powerful, much too powerful because it could deadlock the process. And Schlesinger in his book says that in a way it was okay for President Roosevelt to break the Constitution. He had to go outside the Constitution because the Congress was so powerful in checking him within the Constitution. So you have the oddity of the constitutional power of Congress driving a President, out of frustration with the constitutional process, to extra-constitutional acts. That he gets away with those acts is not surprising, because if the populace supports a move, there is no way for Congress to check it. If the people support a Mayaguez decision, there is not much Congress can do. But it can slow down presidential actions and I think that is a very valuable power. Think what a President could do with presidential power if there were no institution to frustrate his will.

Until recently few people cared about the rise of presidential power because there was a general consensus that Presidents had used their extra-constitutional powers in good ways. It took Nixon to suggest to us that it may be a bad idea most of the time for Presidents to go outside the Constitution. It took Nixon for us to realize that, if the Congress will just use its checking power, that power can be quite valuable.

There is still another valuable power that Congress has: power in reserve. As you know, Madison said that the Constitution rested on a system of legislative supremacy; in a showdown situation Congress can always win, pro forma, if it has popular support. And that's true. De jure sovereignty is with Congress; it can impeach a President it can impeach a judge, it can change the Constitution; it can change the structure of the Court. Ultimately Congress has a tremendous power—we saw it exercised in the impeachment of President Nixon. The fact that the power is not used very often doesn't mean it isn't there. Quite the opposite. In all human societies, the decision to use the ultimate power is always put off as long as possible. People don't want showdowns, *force majeure*, executions of all criminals. People don't want constitutional issues raised with every bill. The power of king and parliament, or the power of the head of the family, is often held in reserve. The reserve power of Congress does not disappear, even though it is not exercised with great frequency. As a matter of fact, some of its majesty might be dissipated if it were used too often.

So I think that probably what we need is more power in Congress and more power in the Presidency, but different in kind from what they have had in the past. I must say I do not conceive the two institutions as simply sitting at either end of a board going up and down like a see-saw. They are reacting in very complex ways, both of them, to exterior circumstance, to popular feeling, to the bureaucracy, to external threat, to economic hardship.

Moreover, Madison did not divide power in the Congress, as was suggested by Dodd, because Congress was not all that important in an age when the states were doing most of the legislative work. He thought Congress would be very powerful. That's why he deliberately divided it in every way he could think of. In *The Federalist* No. 51, Madison writes that in a republican government the legislative authority necessarily predominates. The remedy for this inconveniency is to divide the legislature into different branches and to render them, by different modes of inaction and different principles of action, as little connected with each other as the nature of their common function and common dependence on society will admit. The weight of the legislative authority requires that it should be thus divided.

I think Madison's words are still true. The power to impede highhanded executive action, even action of a good sort, together with the power to legitimize executive action, are kinds of power that are terribly important, even when inaction is the result. That's precisely what Madison wanted, and that's one of the things that will continue to serve us well in the future.

STEPHEN HESS: Early in 1965 I got a call from a Congressman named Jerry Ford, who had just been elected Republican leader in the House. He said he was going to Chicago to address an Israeli bond rally, and could I suggest an opening for his speech. I said sure, why don't you start by saying, "Fellow members of a brave, beleaguered, oppressed minority?"

As one of the very few card-carrying Republicans in this conference, I will talk about how Republicans affect the balance between the Congress and the President. We are trying to review all the factors that play a part in the shifting balances, and one of these factors is the opposition party. It is not necessarily a major factor, but in a few cases, such as treaty ratification or constitutional amendments, it can become a decisive one.

In assessing the role of the Republican Party, particularly in the current balance of power, I think the first fact to notice is that President Carter's relations with Republican leaders in the Congress is substantially different from the situation in the early sixties. Lyndon Johnson had the pleasurable experience of working with Everett Dirksen and the not-always-pleasurable experience of working with Charlie Halleck. L.B.J. was in a position to bargain with the Republicans because he had things the Republicans wanted: appointments, projects, and so forth. Now Mr. Carter, on the other hand, cannot offer the Republicans in this Congress the one thing that they want most, namely the Presidency.

As a result we are witnessing a very interesting role reversal. For the Democrats, from the 1950s through the 1970s, the Senate was the breeding place of potential presidential candidates: Kefauver, Kerr, L.B.J., Humphrey, Jack Kennedy, McCarthy, McGovern, Bob Kennedy, Bentsen, Jackson—the list is almost legion. But it hasn't been that way for the Republicans, though two exceptions would be Taft and Goldwater.

Today we have the presence of Jimmy Carter in the White House, which must act as a depressant on the ambitions of the Democratic Senators. That fact, in combination with the presence of a relatively young Democratic Vice-President, must be enough to turn an ambitious Democratic Senator into a manic depressive.

On the Republican side, however, we find at least three Senators today—and probably more than that—who are dreaming about having their own presidential library some day. One of these potential hopefuls for 1980 happens to be the Republican Senate leader. Their hopes are given added credence at the moment by the sharp reduction in the number of Republican governors, the traditional rivals for the nominations. There are only twelve in the whole country. Moreover, there is a very active attractive class of freshmen Republican Senators, all relatively young, who simply don't look like the sort of men who want to wait on a back bench until they acquire enough seniority to become powerhouses.

My point is that presidential Senators act very differently from senatorial Senators. They are less apt to bargain; they seek rewards that are measured in column inches in newspapers, rather than in cloakroom assignments; they seek issues to exploit and they often prefer isssues of a high emotional content. So for this reason alone, I would expect the division between the Congress and the President to widen in the next few years and for the Congress to remain more assertive in its dealings with the President than usual.

A second reason why I expect an assertive Congress, however—one more visible among House Republicans than their Senate counterparts—is an attitude of "I've been down so long that everything looks up to me." Simply stated, the House Republicans, it seems to me, feel so close to party annihilation that they are beginning to put aside the individualistic tendencies that usually distinguish politicians. I suspect that when *Congressional Quarterly* compiles its party unity percentages for this session, we're going to see that Republicans have voted as a block to an unusually high degree. I think this is also reflected in the number of alternative Republican proposals that have been issued, such as the one on social security.

These remarks are about the shifting balance between Congress and the President in the short run. They are not meant to be partisan. But I would close by saying that for a party that has the allegiance of about twenty percent of the electorate, Republicans are a pretty plucky bunch. I am not sure that anyone is going to allow them to govern, at least not for very long, but it strikes me that they sure can make a lot of trouble for those who do.

DAVID MAHEW: I am inclined to accept the major contentions of both papers. I take the major point of the Cronin paper to be that there has been a considerable demand among the public and in the Congress, during most of the twentieth century, for strong presidential management both of foreign policy and of the economy. Foreign policy management and economic management are the twin duties expected of the President, and unhappiness with the way the Presidents perform these managerial things does seem to come and go, as Larry Dodd suggests, in cycles or at least in episodes.

I think that congressional reactions to the Presidency come as much just after wars as at any other times. The creation of the Appropriations Committee in 1865 came right after the Civil War.

The creation of the Budget Bureau and the regathering together of the appropriations powers in one committee in each house came in 1921, just after the First World War. Then the passing of the LaFollette-Monroney Act came in 1946 following the Second World War. I suspect it is not a coincidence that all these followed pretty closely upon the waging of wars in which power lapsed over to the President and to the bureaucracy. Whether or not the reforms in Congress during the seventies are additionally the consequence of Vietnam is difficult to say. It may be squeezing things too much to try to make that case.

I think Larry Dodd is correct in suggesting that these congressional rearrangements almost never succeed in locating managerial competence in the Congress itself. I would say the congressional reforms of the seventies are really efforts to put constraints on the Presidency rather than efforts to locate managerial competence in the Congress. The incentive structure in the Congress is such that it is very difficult to locate managerial powers on the Hill. Doing so would require a substantial rearrangement of congressional activities, more so than any we have seen in the twentieth century.

So the demand for presidential management is there in the public. If it is not constant, it is at least persistent. It is also persistent on Capitol Hill. Congress expects the President to lead, as Congressman Pickle told us earlier. But while the demand is there, the supply in the White House is not necessarily there. In this perspective I go along with Garry Wills in his statements about the idiosyncrasy of the institutional power balance. Events can interrupt power, create and take away power; events can make Presidents and Congressmen helpless. President Carter is a case in point.

It seems to me, looking backwards on other Presidents and then watching President Carter, that different Presidents have used different strategies to meet the public and congressional demand for government management. I believe that identifying the different strategies that Presidents have used over the last couple of centuries in trying to achieve their goals in the Presidency, and determining how well the strategies can be used, will help us to understand the problem of supplying presidential management and give us a clearer perspective on presidential-congressional relations today.

One strategy is simply to radiate authority. George Washington, I suppose, is the prime instance; but there are others since him. I should think that Eisenhower's Presidency was much like that. Insofar as Eisenhower did accomplish things in office, he accomplished them by simply radiating authority. By this "strategy" what I suggest is a situation in which people are likely to accept what a President says, at least on some things, without even looking very closely at what he is saying, simply because of the personal attributes of the President. That was true of Washington on a broad range of things, of Eisenhower on defense and foreign policy matters. In both cases, the country was inclined to take what the President said as authoritative, without trying to unwrap his argument. It should be added, however, that Presidents seldom have authority of this sort inherent in their persons. It may come only with generals, and it may not work much on domestic matters.

A second strategy is the bargaining strategy. Here very clearly the best exemplar was Lyndon Johnson. In fact, nobody has been in shouting distance of him as presidential bargainer. By bargainer I mean someone who knows Capitol Hill well, knows its resources, knows its lovers, knows how to give Congressmen things and take things from them by bargaining, either in specific transactions or in anticipation of future transactions. It's an interesting and difficult way to run a Presidency, and it is a technique almost impossible for anyone coming in from the outside who has not had experience on Capitol Hill.

The third strategy by which to manage the Presidency is by persuasion: to adduce information, to set it out before the public and before the Congress, and to provide along with the information, arguments about what should be done. It is a problem-solving strategy, a strategy oriented toward achieving consensus. It comes easily to people with an engineering cast of mind, though I suppose the earliest instance of this strategy was a non-engineer, John Quincy Adams. This cast of mind also turns up in Hoover, the great engineer, and it also turns up in Carter. A persuasion strategy can be successful in a time of crisis, as in the first two years of Franklin Roosevelt's first term, when people could agree easily enough that there were troubles, could listen to his messages, accept his information, and act accordingly. His first two years were consensual in their nature, but in a time of noncrisis, it is very difficult to run the country by persuasion. Sadly, President Carter is now discovering that hard truth.

A fourth and last strategy is one that is peculiarly American—no, ostentatiously American. The President can generate or exacerbate conflict in the public and profit thereby. I mean by this that a President can create passionate friends and passionate enemies and reap benefits from the conflict between them, both for himself and for the White House. In so doing, he sets an agenda for Capitol Hill. This conflict-generating strategy was eventually the Jacksonian model of the Presidency. What a President who has no obvious other ways of governing can do is to find some nice enemies and attack them: the Bank of the United States served nicely. A President using this strategy must find enemies who are likely to draw only minority support in the country and on Capitol Hill. In addition, he must cultivate a receptive public and a receptive majority. Conflict generation can endow a President with power. It is very nice to have passionate friends, but in order to have passionate friends, one may have to have passionate enemies. One may have to attack in order to build a base of support of the kind that Jackson built. In fact it interests me, looking back, to speculate how much conflict has been spawned and exacerbated by politicians rather than springing naturally from the public.

After his first two years Franklin Roosevelt became a master at creating conflict in U.S. politics. He created and depicted his enemies with great political skill, and they then became the enemies of a good section of the populace for a long time thereafter.

I think the major successor to Roosevelt in developing a "friends-and-enemies" strategy is Nixon. By 1972 he had successfully created a considerable sense of antagonism in the electorate and bolstered his Presidency in the process. He profited greatly thereby, winning reelection by a 61 percent margin.

It may be that Carter is now attempting this strategy by attacking the oil companies and other groups. He may just be seeking a new set of enemies that most people can detest. But I don't think he's got the instinct for it. It seems to me Carter is by nature a persuader. There may be no other style that comes naturally to him. He's not much of a bargainer; he hasn't been on Capitol Hill so he doesn't know much about political bargaining; he doesn't radiate authority by his very being; and I don't think he's a conflict creator. Hence the problem: he has no crisis about which to persuade people.

To sum up, I think the demand for presidential management is persistent in the public and the strategy by which Nixon responded to that demand through conflict generation could become a recurrent one. The Nixon combination of managerialism, divisiveness, and a conservative cast of mind thus may crop up again in American politics. I think it has been largely accidental in the twentieth century that strong managerial presidents have been associated with the left rather than with the right. Nixonism strikes me as being a reasonable functional equivalent of Gaullism in France, which, in some fashion, has had something of the political structure and political problems that the United States has had.

Thus we could get more Nixonism. I think Cronin is correct that the desire is strong among the public for Presidents who can supply management. And one of the ways of achieving that is to provide management at the price of substantial conflict.

TOM WICKER: I have listened to this discussion with great interest because I am the only participant with no claim whatsoever to any academic expertise. No doubt my response is precisely conditioned by that lack, because, while I agree with virtually everything that's been said, I find much of it somehow lacking in dimension. I agree with Mr. Sundquist that the rise of the imperial Presidency was at root and at heart a relinquishment of power voluntarily and necessarily by Congress. Nevertheless I think it occurred because of additional circumstances that made the enhancement of the Presidency more important than a simple shift of congressional power to the Presidency would suggest.

I believe the real birth of what we call the imperial Presidency took place toward the end of the Second World War. It could be seen in those images that came back to us in the old newsreels of President Roosevelt in his black cape and his hat turned up, riding around in a jeep at the front and discussing world affairs with Churchill and Stalin. The President of the United States as leader of the free world was something that Americans had never seen before. At almost the same time the atomic bomb was dropped in Japan. Suddenly the President of the United States became the only person in the world who could wipe out the human race.

Half a decade later President Truman intervened in Korea in a way that Americans had almost never seen, certainly not on such a scale and with such an import; and all of a sudden the modern role of Commander-in-Chief was created.

Thus in that very short span of time, between the end of the Second World War and the beginning of the Korean War, the President became the leader of the free world, the man who could wipe out the human race, and the Commander-in-Chief in fact as well as in law. It was these events that created the modern imperial Presidency; they did it in a way that really had nothing to do with institutional processes or cycles.

I would suggest also that from the Second World War, with Roosevelt in his black cape, to John Kennedy during the Cuban Missile Crisis, the imperial Presidency was perceived as being highly successful—and that that is what sustained it. It was perceived as highly successful because it was fundamentally a foreign policy phenomenon; it didn't have much to do with domestic affairs. It was thus very congenial to the years of the fifties and the early sixties, when the Cold War, America's emergence in the world as a world power, and its possession of nuclear weapons made foreign policy rather than domestic policy the important center of things. It was only later in the mid-sixties that we began to realize that it had consequences here at home, too.

Another factor that was extremely important in the rise of the imperial Presidency was the concomitant rise of television as a means of communication with the American people. Television, I think you will agree, obviously favors the President over Congress, because he is a single individual and because he is endowed with those other, almost mystical qualities that emerged in the 1940s and early 1950s. Television carries him into the farthest reaches of the nation. The President has become a more familiar face than the mayor, and Congress simply can't compete. At the same time, he who lives by the sword dies by the sword; and he who lives by television can die by television. And that possibility became very important a bit later, for in my judgment the imperial Presidency was not successful after the Cuban Missile Crisis.

It is also important to recognize the role of the press in supporting or criticizing the President. From the end of the Second World War to the Cuban Missile Crisis, the press was generally supportive of the imperial Presidency. Although the Presidents in office in those years wouldn't have agreed, the press in general was not very critical of the Presidency. Nowadays it has become an article of faith that the press is very critical of the Presidency, and in some sense I think the press helped to bring down the imperial Presidency in the sixties and seventies. Now why did that happen? And why did the imperial Presidency not succeed after the missile crisis? I think the main reason was simply the lack of success.

Nothing succeeds with the press like success. And nothing draws the bloodhounds of the press more quickly than failure. When it began to appear in the late sixties that the imperial Presidency was no longer succeeding, the press began to get off the team, so to speak. Congress began to get off the team. And we began to have what could be seen in other circumstances as a cycle, and indeed was a cycle in a way, the result of determinate processes. But I think it was much more nearly a product of presidential failure than a failure of presidential power.

Now why did it fail? It failed because too much expectation had been poured into it. Not only did the public expect the President to be the leader of the free world and the Commander-in-Chief—and the man who could wipe out the human race; not only did the public expect that in foreign policy he would know exactly what he was doing and exactly how to remedy whatever was wrong; the public expected that he would succeed! This expectation was not only a factor in the public mind; it also became a very heavy factor in the presidential mind. The idea of failing as imperial President in the realm of foreign policy became something that the presidential mind was conditioned to avoid as being the one thing that could be most dangerous to the President's political, personal, and institutional existence.

In my judgment, the imperial Presidency—in the mid-sixties, and still more in the early seventies—began to overreach itself precisely to maintain the kind of success that was expected of it, not only externally but internally as well, from within the institution. When that success proved unattainable, the collapse of the imperial Presidency, or at least the diminution of it, followed inexorably. I am in sympathy with those who say that there is a resurgence of support for the Presidency. I think the main reason for that is that when we came to mistrust the imperial Presidency, when people generally did want an alternative, the only alternative available was Congress. But in the short years since then, we have seen quite clearly that Congress is no alternative at all in terms of modern government.

I am in sympathy furthermore with those who say that we must still be on our guard, that the imperial Presidency in its most malignant sense might return. I don't think that the impeachment and ultimate resignation of Mr. Nixon will guard us against the return of the imperial Presidency, because I don't think the imperial Presidency is a product of an institutional process so much as it is a product of what is happening in the world at large. When one looks to the future and sees that we are still a long way from dealing with the energy problem successfully; that we are still a long way from resolving our environmental problems; that we have yet to address the most fundamental economic issue of the next twenty-five years, namely the redistribution of income; and that we have not even begun to cope with the worst aspects of the racial problem, which underlies all our politics—when you think about these problems and realize that we are very far from solving any of them, you understand that in respect to no single one of them are people easily going to do what they ought to do. Consequently there is going to be a greater and greater demand for a very powerful Presidency, this time not only in foreign policy but in the domestic matters as well. The demand will come because the Presidency is the one national office that can seriously attempt persuasion.

So I think that it is wise that we should be aware of trends and be thinking ahead, as was suggested in Professor Dodd's presentation today. Perhaps it would be wise to consider restructuring our Constitution or at least some of our institutions, to cope with these pressures that we are going to have.

In considering the restructuring of institutions, I should like to throw out a pet idea of mine for what it may be worth. As we face these intensifying issues over the next few decades, I suggest it might be instructive to think of the President of the United States in British parliamentary terms, to think of the President of the United States as being "the government," and recognize that we need a very powerful government. We should also think of Congress, regardless of which party dominates it, in British parliamentary terms, as the loyal opposition, and recognize that we need a loyal opposition that is organized and empowered to oppose and to oppose courageously and intelligently. If we look at the structure of our government in those terms we may find help in doing what we need to do.

FROM THE FLOOR: Professor Dodd said that Congressmen are motivated primarily by a desire for power. Professor Mayhew, in *Congress: The Electoral Connection* you argued that they are motivated primarily by a desire to be reelected. Both you and Professor Dodd argue that Congress is organized to facilitate these respective motives. I am wondering to what extent they are mutually exclusive, and to what extent they can be reconciled.

DAVID MAYHEW: I think the reelection goal is a proximate goal of great importance for all members, and that insulation from the problems of getting reelected is never fully achieved by anybody, so that the reelection goal is there and worth looking at. One must see what it amounts to and what it achieves, what its effects are. But surely Congressmen are up to other things as well, and one of them is power-seeking within Congress, as Mr. Dodd suggests.

It can be argued that seeking power inhibits one's efforts to keep one's seat. That sometimes happens. Ordinarily, however, it doesn't work that way. Usually people who rise in the House and the Senate are able to keep things going back home well enough to retain their seats—though not always.

FROM THE FLOOR: As regards the constitutional changes that Professor Dodd proposed, it would seem doubtful to me that Congress is going to accept anything of the sort. Congress has just rejected more incremental changes, and with the decline of parties, both in the electorate and in the Legislature, there is no organization in Congress that might try to get the constitutional changes through. So we're left just with individuals and their own limited power bases. Is there another institution that can produce the changes?

LAWRENCE DODD: I take it that your basic question is what are the chances that we could move toward constitutional reform, inasmuch as Congress seems disinclined to do so, and the political parties seem too weak to lead us in that direction.

Well, first, one has to understand that I think about the future of American politics within my own model. Consequently what I see coming is that the current age of quiescence will be followed by another decentralization in Congress, a resurgence of the Presidency, stronger than in the past, and then I think another crisis period. Within this perspective we would not see Congress voluntarily move to effect reforms in the short run. I think that constitutional reforms are likely only in an even more severe crisis in the future— so long as that crisis is not so severe as to remove completely our chance to reform democratically. Thus I don't think another institution will do it; I think the dynamic process of history will do it.

And I should take this opportunity to say that I do disagree somewhat with some of the comments made by others. I think that after Nixon, the Presidency is stronger than it was after Roosevelt, that there is a progressive movement toward an even stronger Presidency, in regard to impoundment, the war-making power, and so forth.

So I do not see, as Jim Sundquist does, that we have moved to a balance much like that before 1972. I think we have moved farther away from a balance. The process is self-destructive; there will be a strong Presidency and a worse crisis in the future. Only then will we move to reform the Constitution.

FROM THE FLOOR: As regards President Carter's relations with the Congress, and particularly on his energy program, it seems that he has a very severe disability in that he lacks Washington rapport. His Georgia power base and his Georgia advisers don't seem equal to the task of meeting with the Congress and getting its support. Doesn't the executive branch need a sort of liaison, a person in the group who can work with the Washington scene if the President is really going to be effective with Congress?

THOMAS CRONIN: I'm not sure I can give a definitive answer on that, but I think you're right that Carter is floundering and needs better staff. I think the people here at the table are agreed that his staff operations have not been very impressive. I think the other point that you alluded to, however, is the more important one, that is, that he lacks a power base in the Democratic party.

One of the ironies of Carter, currently, is that his highest popularity in terms of the Gallup Poll is in the southeastern section of the United States. At the same time, his lowest support scores in the Congress have come from the congressional delegations from that same southeast. So, although his popularity is high in that area, he is not able at all to translate that popularity into any support in Congress; but more important than that, Carter really has no strong identification with any classic element within the Democratic Party.

FROM THE FLOOR: Would the panel agree with the notion that television has really created a demand for a kind of surface impression or image of what constitutes the good President? The reason I ask is that if you go back over the past few years, it appears that the ones who have really had trouble with the public have been those who have been perceived as not being—whatever the word may mean—"presidential." I'm thinking of Harry Truman, of Jerry Ford, and now perhaps of Carter. I think Ford, for example, was not successful in his two years as President, because he was widely perceived as not being of the "presidential type." I am wondering how much that may be a function of television. Maybe it has taught us to look for the charismatic leader. How much is image and how much is the public looking for substance in our Presidents?

TOM WICKER: I think that television, and the media generally, are very important here, because I think in order to play in electoral politics, that is, in order to get elected, the candidate must accept the fact that the media have become so nearly the arena of the whole thing. Assiduous poll takers can tell an assiduous candidate a lot of things that are on the public's mind. And the candidate can respond very widely and effectively through the press and television and be quite responsive to those concerns that are on people's minds.

But the way in which the public confronts a candidate, particularly in a primary when there are many candidates, is quite different from the way the public looks at that single man who is President. People may say to themselves during the campaign, "Well I'm going to vote for Carter because he's going to be the detergent in Washington." They may say that, but then when that man becomes President they really do expect a great deal more from him.

As I said earlier, I think that they who live by television ultimately will die by television, and by the other media. It may very well be that the very qualities which Carter brilliantly perceived would get him elected are precisely those qualities that in the final analysis mark his failure to live up to what the public demands of a President once in office.

II

Points of Conflict between the Congress and the President

Overview: Richard L. Schott
Papers: Allen Schick
Morris P. Fiorina
Discussion: Louis Fisher
Francis E. Rourke
James L. Sundquist

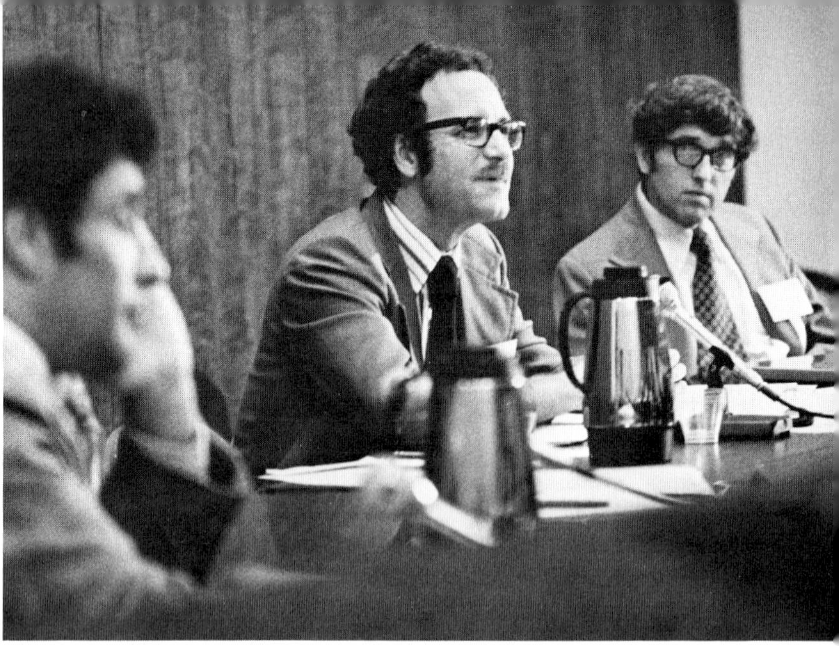

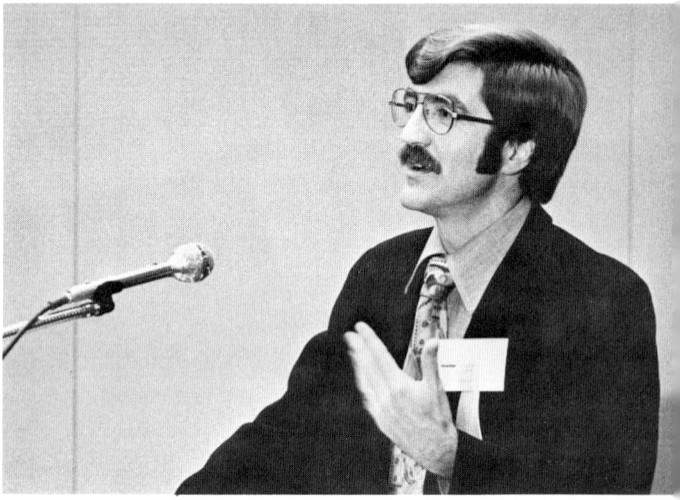

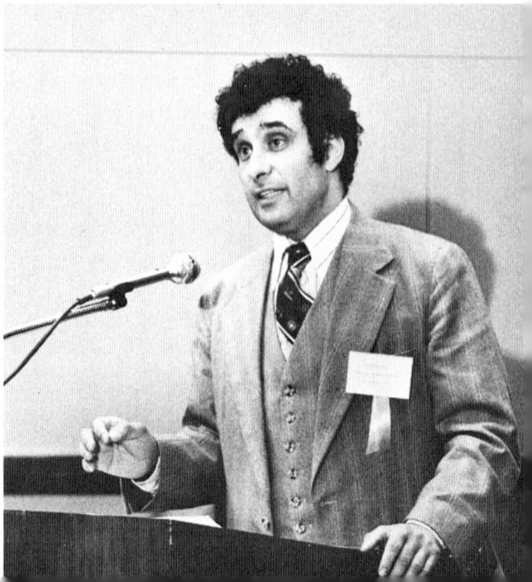

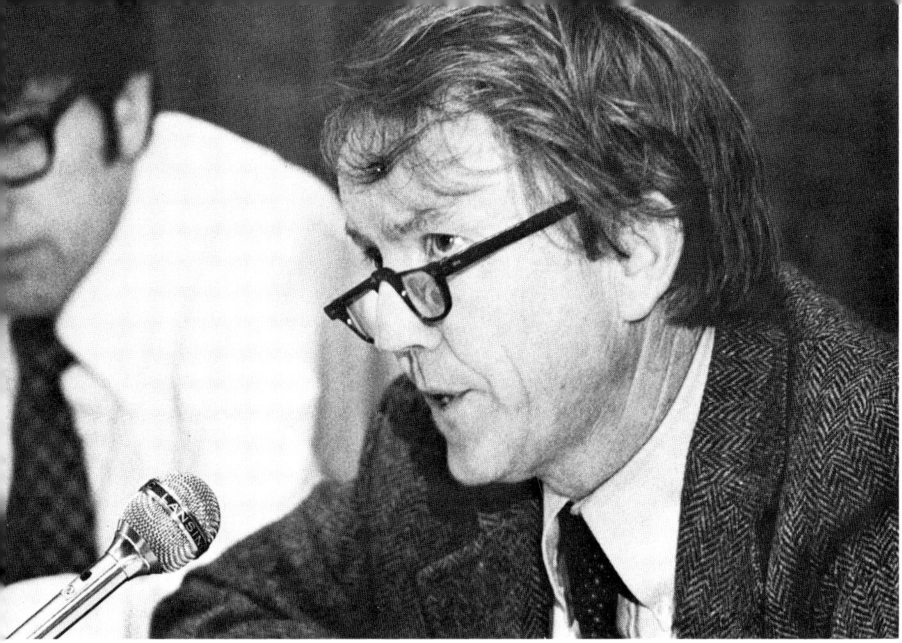

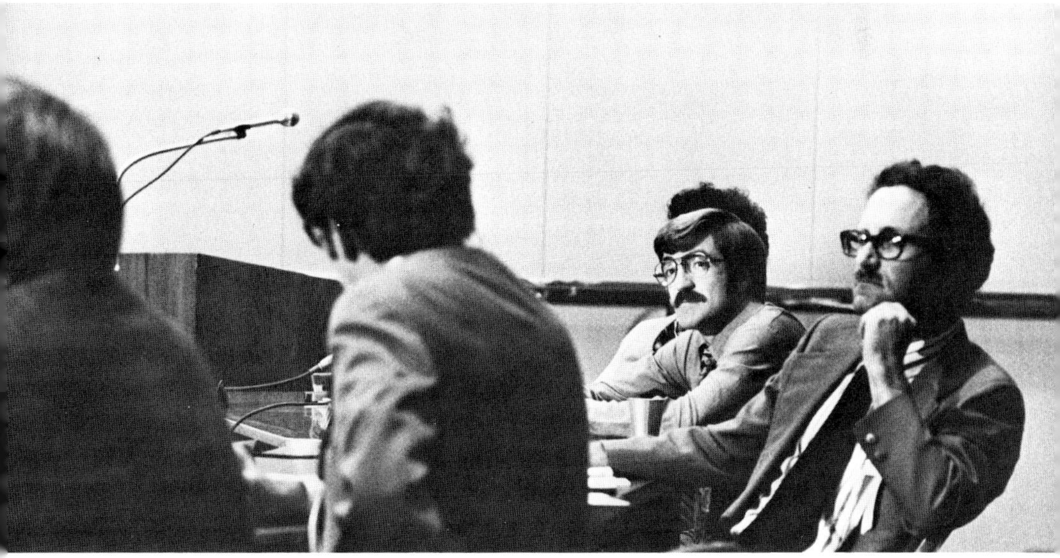

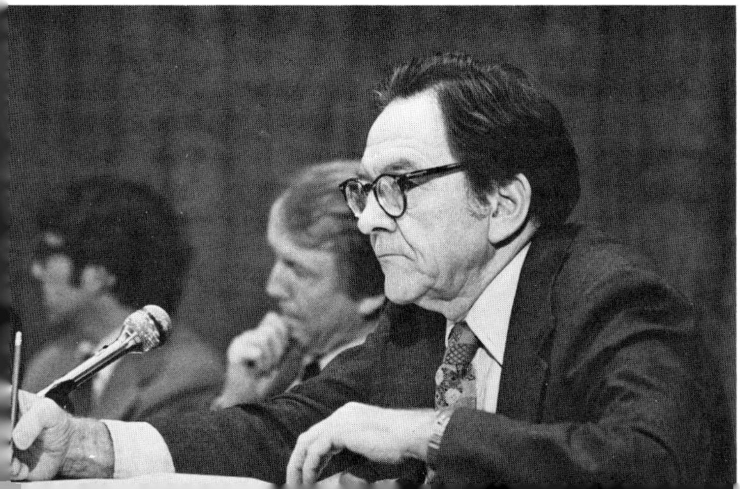

Overview

Richard L. Schott

Richard Schott is Associate Professor of Public Affairs at The University of Texas at Austin.

We now shift our focus from an historical and theoretical analysis of the relations between the President and Congress to several arenas in which the conflict between them is played out. One of these is the federal budget, especially the moves toward budgetary reform on the part of Congress and the effect of these moves on congressional-presidential relations.

The enactment of a new congressional budget, some observers feel, returns to the Congress a substantial portion of the budgetary powers which it gave to the President in the Budget and Accounting Act of 1921. The national budget process, as spelled out in that act, consisted of four distinct phases. The first phase, that of budget formulation, became the responsibility of the President, assisted by a new presidential staff agency, the Bureau of the Budget (BOB). The second phase, that of approval, remained and remains the province of Congress and especially of its appropriations committees, which examine presidential requests for spending. The third phase, that of actually administering the budget, became the responsibility of the President, assisted by the Bureau of the Budget and other units of the Treasury Department. The fourth and final phase, the audit, was reserved to the Congress and a newly created congressional staff agency, the General Accounting Office. The national budget process, shared by Congress and the Chief Executive, retained essentially this form until 1974, when Congress overhauled the process in the Congressional Budget Act of that year.

It should be noted, however, that in the decades between 1920 and 1974, relations between Congress and the President over the budget became increasingly strained. Congress—by creating trust funds, entitlement programs such as social security, and other forms of "backdoor spending"—placed ever-increasing portions of the federal budget beyond the President's reach and influence, so that by the early 1970s nearly three-quarters of the federal budget was, in the jargon of the BOB, "relatively uncontrollable." Presidents, for their part, moved to impound or refuse to spend monies that had been appropriated by Congress. This they did sometimes in the name of efficiency, but increasingly they did it for the purpose of redirecting, scaling down, or even gutting congressionally-mandated programs—a trend which reached its zenith in the impoundments of the Nixon Administration. Thus Congress, over the years, had invaded the prerogatives of the President in budget formulation, and the President had flouted the will of Congress in budget administration.

With the Budget Act of 1974, Congress attempted to put its own house in order by developing a "congressional" budget. Special mechanisms were designed to enable it to consider expenditures in the light of expected revenues and to manage the budget process more effectively. New entities were created to control budgetary priorities, which seriously limited the power of its appropriations committees. But the real effect of the new budget process is a matter of debate, and the extent to which it represents a victory for Congress in its budgetary struggles with the President is unclear. It is these issues that Allen Schick, a member of the Congressional Research Service and a leading scholar of the federal budget process, will examine.

A second arena in which Congress and the President often come to blows is the struggle for control of the "fourth branch" of government, the federal bureaucracy. Its growth has come in several waves—the first shortly before the turn of the century, a second during the New Deal and the Second World War, and a third during the New Frontier and Great Society days of the 1960s. The mushrooming of the bureaucracy brought with it some major problems of control and guidance. One response of the President was to ask

Congress for increased presidential staff and an Executive Office to help monitor the bureaucracy. That request Congress granted to President Franklin Roosevelt in the late 1930s. Congress, for its part, came to take more seriously the question of "oversight" of the executive branch, and beginning in the 1940s, took steps to improve its capacity to watch over the numerous federal agencies. In the eyes of many observers, however, neither Congress nor the President has succeeded in gaining effective control of the bureaucracy, and our fourth branch of government often seems to be beholden to neither of its putative masters. Indeed, the federal bureaucracy often seems to co-opt both political executives and the members of Congress, and to bend them to its views and positions.

These are among the problems and issues that will be addressed by Morris Fiorina, Professor of Political Science at the California Institute of Technology.

Whose Budget?

It All Depends on Whether the President or Congress is Doing the Counting

Allen Schick

Allen Schick, a Senior Specialist with the Congressional Research Service, has also served as a Senior Fellow at the Brookings Institution and a Research Associate with the Urban Institute.

For more than fifty years—from the Budget and Accounting Act of 1921 until the Congressional Budget and Impoundment Control Act of 1974—the President exercised virtual monopoly power in the preparation of the national budget. The 1921 act is justly regarded as one of the giant leaps in the buildup of presidential power during this century; the 1974 legislation has the potential of altering presidential-congressional relations and contributing to a resurgence of Congress. Our purpose here is to examine the first years under the Congressional Budget Act in order to assess its potential effect on the budgetary roles of the two branches and the relations between them.

A Half Century of Presidential Domain

The Budget and Accounting Act was the culmination of an executive budget movement that swept across the United States during the first decades of the twentieth century. Its purpose was to transfer the money power of government from legislative to executive hands. The early budget reformers looked covetously at the British system where the national legislature had neither initiative nor effective voice in the determination of spending policy. Influenced by Woodrow Wilson's commentaries on the ills of Congress, they viewed legislatures as congenitally incompetent to make budgetary decisions. A budget, in their view, required comprehensiveness, cohesion, consistency—the integration of government policy. These were virtues deemed to be associated with the executive branch, and so far from being concerned about the centralization of power inherent in an executive budget arrangement, they welcomed it. They wanted a budget process that would do away with the disorders and fragmentations of the legislative system that had prevailed through the nineteenth century.

Before 1921, the President had a limited and uncertain role in the making of budgetary decisions. He could bring his influence to bear on the amounts requested by federal agencies or appropriated by Congress, but he had no sure route to success. Some Presidents were more interventionist than others; after the Civil War and the expansion of government, none could completely remain on the sidelines while executive agencies transacted their money business with a diversity of congressional committees. But for a President to influence a particular year's outcomes he had to improvise ad hoc rules and roles.

The 1921 act gave the President an annual budget routine and an arsenal of executive weapons. Each year, as prescribed by the act, the President submitted a budget to Congress, in contrast to the prior arrangement under which agencies independently decided how much to campaign for on Capitol Hill. The budget and accounting law barred agencies from going directly to Congress with their budget claims; their requests were to be screened through a budget process operated by a presidential agency—known through most of its existence as the Bureau of the Budget and redesigned in 1970 as the Office of Management and Budget (OMB). Section 206 of the law relating to the submission of agency estimates to Congress was applied by the President's budget bureau in a way that kept Congress in the dark about raw agency estimates even after the President had submitted his budget.

The Budget and Accounting Act could not do away with the appropriations power vested in Congress by the Constitution. With presidential budgeting, Congress continued to make appropriations, but with the big difference that Congress now acted only after it was informed how much the President wanted to spend. The President's requests were only recommendations, but inevitably they became standards against which Congress could make its judgments. With few exceptions, the boundaries for congressional action were the amounts appropriated in the past year and the amounts requested by the President.

At the very outset, the President used his budget power to gain additional dominion over Congress and the federal agencies. In his account of the first year of the budget, Charles Dawes, the first budget director, described how Warren Harding—generally reckoned among the less potent Chief Executives—effectively used his brand-new budget authority to prevent agencies from spending funds appropriated to them as well as to deter them from going directly to Congress with their favorite legislative proposals. Using the authority granted in the new act, the President issued an executive order requiring agencies to clear all money legislation through the Budget Bureau.

If presidential power was enhanced by the budget process during a decade of limited government, it was stretched much farther during the next decade. The coming of the New Deal meant a major expansion of the Presidency and its budget functions. In 1939 Roosevelt shifted the Budget Bureau from the Treasury Department, where it had been lodged in the 1921 compromise, to his new Executive Office of the President, in which it rapidly gained stature as the management center of the federal government. He authorized a ten-fold increase in the Bureau's staff and armed it with an assortment of executive orders. Its jurisdiction was extended beyond the budget process to the supervision of the operations of government agencies.

The role of the budget agency and the use of the budget power necessarily have shifted over the years with changes in presidential leadership. Budgeting has become much too important to be divorced from the style and interests of the President. Yet through half a century of variation and flux in presidential fortunes, the budget process has been a constant source of presidential power. It is virtually axiomatic in our times that a President cannot command government if he doesn't control the budget. The budget is used by some Chief Executives to formulate a comprehensive program for presentation to Congress, by others as means to manage administrative functions. As the scale and sprawl of government have grown, so too has the President's reliance on the budget process. Even if there had been no 1921 act, the President today would necessarily be squarely in the business of preparing and defending budget recommendations.

Yet I shall argue in the concluding section of this paper that scholars and practitioners alike probably have had an exaggerated view of the budget's reach and potency. Perhaps we have tried to load too many extraneous functions upon it. Just in the space of a decade, successive Presidents have sought to convert the budget cycle into a system for planning the future course of government (Planning, Programming, Budgeting System, or PPBS), strengthening central managerial control over agencies (Management by Objectives, or MBO), and reexamining the past commitments of federal agencies (Zero-Base Budgeting, or ZBB). Judging from the fate of some of these efforts, the budget process seems to resist attempts to divert it from its basic functions. Not every good idea can be piggybacked onto the budget and carried to political and administrative success. Nevertheless, it is precisely because of the reputed leverage of the budget process that modern Presidents have sought to extend it to other purposes.

Congress began chipping away at the President's budget role during the early 1970s. One path of attack was to exempt various agencies from the 1921 requirement that their budgets pass through executive review before being sent to Congress. The Consumer Product Safety Commission, for example, was directed by its 1972 law to send its budget requests to the President and Congress at the same time. "Whenever the Commission submits any budget estimates or request to the President or the Office of Management and Budget, it shall concurrently transmit a copy of that estimate or request to the Congress." Financial estimates of the Postal Service are included in the President's budget "with his recommendation but without revision." The Legal Services Corporation, AMTRAK, and other corporate entities are permitted by law to take their budget cases directly to Congress and to ask for more than the President has requested for them.

These cracks in the executive budget tradition account for only a small portion—certainly not more than one-half of one percent at the most—of the federal budget. But they point to a much larger, though informal, breakthrough. In recent years, congressional committees, by sheer persistence, have managed to obtain the raw estimates, though usually not before the annual budget has been presented. Not every committee—or appropriations committee—avails itself of this advantage, but the important thing is that the President has been compelled to abandon his claim of budgetary privilege in the face of congressional threats to rewrite the 1921 law to clarify Congress's entitlement to the information. There is a good chance that within a few years a number of regulatory agencies will be required to give Congress budgetary parity with the President. Under threat to write a sterner congressional entitlement into law, President Carter in 1977 pledged to furnish committees with the zero-base budgets prepared by federal agencies for the 1979 fiscal year. Presidential willingness to part with once privileged information has been the minimum price necessary to deter further legislative encroachments on the President's budget-making prerogatives.

Another indication of slippage in the President's budget position was the 1974 law requiring Senate confirmation of the director and deputy director of the Office of Management and Budget. President Nixon vetoed the first version of that law because it would have applied the confirmation test retroactively to Roy Ash, incumbent OMB Director. But Nixon could not forestall the second version which applied the new requirement only to future appointments. This confirmation requirement contributed to the downfall of Bert Lance, President Carter's first budget director. Although the initial confirmation review for Lance was hurried and perfunctory, it did open the door to later revelations and proceedings. And in view of the embarrassment caused the Senate by its inadequate investigations of Lance's financial background, one can expect more careful scrutiny of OMB appointees in the future.

Legislative intrusions on the President's information advantage and appointment power were provoked both by the reassertion of congressional independence in the aftermath of Vietnam and Watergate, and by the reaction to the Nixon Administration's overstepping of the traditional "gray areas" between the two branches. The most portentious congressional reaction was the 1974 Budget Act, a law signed by Richard Nixon less than one month before he was driven from office. The law resulted from conflict within Congress as well as between the legislative and executive branches. We shall sketch two of those battles, both involving President Nixon: the first concerned a limitation on total federal expenditures; the second concerned the impoundment of funds appropriated by Congress.

Fighting Over Money: Nixon Versus Congress

On July 26, 1972, President Nixon challenged Congress to enact a $250 billion spending limit on the fiscal year (1973) that had just begun, and he threatened to take unilateral action to restrain spending if Congress failed to act. He coupled this demand with an attack on "the hoary and traditional procedure of the Congress, which now permits action on the various spending programs as if they were unrelated and independent actions." Although there was little public controversy over the $250 billion level (1972 was a presidential election year), there was deep conflict as to how the limitation should be enforced. The President wanted unrestricted discretion to reduce expenditures, and Administration spokesmen refused to specify in advance which programs might be cut. This position was upheld in a debt-ceiling bill reported by the House Ways and Means Committee on September 27, 1972. The bill would have authorized the President to withhold such amounts as might be necessary to maintain the $250 billion limit. When the bill was considered by the House, Representative George Mahon (Chairman of the Appropriations Committee) proposed a substitute which would have denied the discretionary authority sought by the President. Mahon argued that the measure approved by Ways and Means would be a dangerous transfer of legislative power to the executive branch. The Mahon substitute provided instead for the President to propose specific reductions which would take effect only if approved by Congress. But despite Mahon's vigorous plea, his substitute lost by a vote of 167-216. The House then passed the debt ceiling along with the limitation on expenditures.

The legislation moved to the Senate where it again emerged from committee with full authority for the President to curtail programs as he wished. The Senate, however, voting 46-28, added a floor amendment requiring the President to make proportional cuts in programs and prohibiting reductions of more than 10 percent in any activity or item. The amendment also exempted nine specified program categories from any presidential cuts. In conference, the

Senate requirement of proportionality was dropped in favor of presidential discretion to cut individual programs by as much as 20 percent. The House approved the conference report on October 17, 1972, but the Senate rejected it on the same day. With adjournment rapidly approaching, the two chambers resolved the impasse by writing contradictory provisions—one establishing and the other negating a ceiling on expenditures—in the same law.

The legislative-executive battle over spending totals was closely related to another dispute between Nixon and Congress over the authority of the President to impound (refuse to spend) appropriated funds. One reason why Congress was reluctant to enact a spending limit was its fear that the President would use it as authority to cancel or curtail—by means of impoundment—social programs enacted by Congress in excess of his budget request. When he demanded a $250 billion limitation in 1972, Nixon warned that he would not "sit by and silently watch" Congress raise spending above the level he wanted. Throughout the 1972 presidential campaign, Nixon openly attacked Congress for its "budget busting" actions. In a nationwide radio address less than one month before the election, he decried the lack of a budget process in Congress:

> . . . The Congress suffers from institutional faults when it comes to federal spending . . . . Congress not only does not consider the total financial picture when it votes on a particular spending bill, it does not even contain a mechanism to do so if it wished.

When Congress did not accede to Nixon's demands, he embarked on a "second line of defense"—widespread use of his veto power. Nixon vetoed the 1973 Labor-HEW Appropriations bill, charging that the $1.8 billion added by Congress "is a perfect example of that kind of reckless spending that just cannot be done without more taxes or more inflation." He also vetoed a second Labor-HEW bill, one of nine pocket vetoes packaged into a single presidential message. All told, Nixon vetoed sixteen bills during 1972, twelve of them after Congress had adjourned and thus too late for any override.

Rather than abating after the 1972 elections, conflict between the President and Congress intensified as Nixon withheld $6 billion in water pollution control funds, impounded more than $10 billion voted by Congress for other domestic programs, and took a variety of unilateral steps to prevent the expenditure of funds already appropriated. More than any other contemporary budget dispute, the impoundment battle prompted Congress to devise its own budget process.

Impoundments have had an uncertain history, and until 1974, when the Impoundment Control Act took effect, they also had an ambiguous legal status. While the first recorded impoundment dates back to the Presidency of Thomas Jefferson, it was not until the Second World War that the modern era of policy impoundments—in contrast to routine, noncontroversial impoundments—began. Not surprisingly, the first confrontation was over rivers and harbors, a matter over which Congress has exercised dominion for more than a century. During the war, FDR deferred various public-works projects on the ground that the resources were required for the war effort. Some members protested those impoundments, but Congress generally recognized the need to give priority to national defense. During the two decades following the war, successive Presidents refused to spend money for military weapons authorized by Congress. In 1966 President Johnson broadened the scope of policy impoundments to cover an array of federal programs, but when he contemplated impounding $5.3 billion, Johnson discussed his proposed actions with more than thirty members of Congress, including the principal members of the appropriations committees. Moreover, he regarded these as temporary deferrals, and expected to release the funds as economic conditions warranted. These pre-Nixon impoundments were different in purpose and scope from those practiced in the early 1970s.

Far from administrative routine, Nixon's wholesale impoundments in late 1972 and 1973 were intended to rewrite national priorities at the expense of congressional power and preferences. His aim was not merely to defer expenses; it was nothing less than the cancellation of unwanted programs. Although the Administration reported on $8.7 billion in "reserve"—the term it preferred to use—the real level of impoundment reached about $18 billion, far above the amounts withheld by any previous President.

Dollars, however, tell only a part of the Nixon story; another part relates to the purpose, duration, and distribution of the impoundments, and their effect on federal policies and priorities. The Nixon

Administration had no intention of spending most of the impounded funds, a large portion of which would have lapsed at the end of the fiscal year. While money was withdrawn from more than one hundred domestic programs, not a single dollar was taken from military programs, at least not for policy reasons. The full brunt of the President's policy impoundments fell upon civilian programs.

When Nixon impounded funds for policy reasons, he told Congress in effect,"I don't care what you appropriate; I will decide what will be spent." In the impoundment battles, the President had an important advantage vis-à-vis Congress: inaction meant that the President's priorities would prevail. The longer the dispute dragged on, the greater the loss of congressional control over the purse. Congress could not permit the impasse to continue on such unfavorable terms. Thus in 1973 Congress commenced work on designing both a budget process for its own decisions and an impoundment-control procedure to govern its relations with the executive branch. These efforts bore fruit in the Congressional Budget and Impoundment Control Act of 1974.

The Budget Act

Before the act was cast into its final form, it went through a series of legislative committees: a special committee (the Joint Study Committee on Budget Control); one House committee; two Senate committees; and a conference. What emerged from eighteen months of legislative deliberations was a "compromise" in the sense that it reconciled diverse legislative interests. It made little effort, however, to harmonize legislative and executive perspectives. Congress was creating a budget process for itself, to function in addition to the executive process set up in 1921. A few provisions of the 1974 act directly affected the executive budget process; for example, the requirement that the President prepare a "current services budget" each year, estimating the cost of continuing past programs and policies without change. In addition, the Impoundment Control Act deals directly with presidential impoundment of funds.

The act establishes budget committees in both houses, which are given jurisdiction over the congressional budget process and certain related matters. The committees have the duty to report at least two concurrent resolutions on the budget each year, to study the effects of existing and proposed legislation on federal expenditures, and to oversee the operations of the Congressional Budget Office (CBO). This process supplements—it does not supplant—the older tax, authorizations, and appropriations processes of Congress, each of which is maintained by its own committee structure.

CBO has been established as an information and analytic arm of Congress. While it is charged to serve all congressional committees, it must accord highest priority in the assessment of staff and other resources to the needs of the budget committees. In CBO, Congress has sought an independent source of budgetary data, an alternative to the President's Office of Management and Budget. CBO has a staff of about two hundred, over half of whom are program and budget analysts; it furnishes Congress with a stream of scorekeeping reports dealing with the status of money legislation; it prepares five-year budget and cost projections; and it conducts in-depth studies at the request of congressional committees.

The congressional budget process is the framework within which Congress each year determines total revenues, expenditures, and debt, and the budget priorities of the United States. The first stage in the new process is the adoption of a concurrent resolution on the budget by May 15. The allocations in this resolution guide Congress in its subsequent consideration of appropriations and other spending measures. After action has been completed on all money bills, Congress must adopt a second budget resolution and (if necessary) reconcile the determinations in this resolution with revenue, spending, and debt legislation. The calendar of the budget process is set forth in Table 1. It begins with the submission of a new document—the current services budget—to be followed by the President's own budget shortly after Congress convenes.

The first formal step within Congress is the preparation by each standing committee and joint committee of its views and estimates with respect to budget matters related to its jurisdiction. These are submitted to the budget committees by March 15, but no committee is restricted thereby as to the legislation (or amounts) that it may subsequently report. The sole purpose of these early submissions is to inform the budget committees of the views and interests of key legislative participants prior to their reporting of the first budget resolution.

The budget committees report the first resolution to their respec-

**Table 1
Congressional Budget Timetable**

On or before:	Action to be completed:
November 10	President submits current services budget.
15th day after Congress meets	President submits his budget.
March 15	Committees submit reports to budget committees.
April 1	Congressional Budget Office submits report to budget committees.
April 15	Budget committees report first concurrent resolution on the budget to their houses.
May 15	Committees report bills authorizing new budget authority.
May 15	Congress adopts first concurrent resolution on the budget.
7th day after Labor Day	Congress completes action on bills providing authority and spending authority.
September 15	Congress completes actions on second required concurrent resolution on the budget.
September 25	Congress completes reconciliation process, implementing second concurrent resolution.
October 1	Fiscal year begins.

tive houses by April 15 of each year, thus allowing a full month for floor action and any necessary conference before adoption. This resolution sets the levels of total new budget authority and budget outlays, the planned levels of revenues and public debt, and the appropriate budget surplus or deficit. Total new budget authority and outlays are allocated among major budget functions, of which there are currently fifteen. Additional subdivisions for each function (between existing and proposed programs; regular and permanent appropriations; and controllable and other amounts) are included either in the resolution itself or in the reports of the budget committees.

Because this and subsequent budget determinations are in the form of concurrent resolutions, they neither have the force of law nor will they directly limit actual federal expenditures. Their sole effect is to guide or restrain Congress in its own actions on revenue, spending, and debt legislation.

Final adoption of the first resolution is scheduled by May 15. In case of a deadlock in conference, House and Senate conferees are required (if seven days have elapsed) to report their agreements and disagreements to their respective houses. The adopted budget resolution must be mathematically consistent; that is, the sum of the functional allocations must equal the totals for new budget authority and outlays, and the difference between total outlays and revenue must equal the appropriate budget surplus or deficit.

May 15 is also the deadline for the reporting of authorizing legislation for the ensuing fiscal year by legislative committees. This schedule is intended to provide Congress with firm information on prospective authorizations, and more important, to enable it to proceed to the consideration of appropriations within a reasonable time after the budget resolution has been adopted. The act, however, established a procedure for the waiver of the reporting deadline by means of a simple resolution in either the House or the Senate.

There is a prohibition against considering revenue, debt, spending, or entitlement legislation prior to adoption of the first budget resolution. It is intended to insure that Congress considers such legislation in the light of the determinations made in the first resolution. The prohibition can be waived in the Senate, however, through a special procedure, and it does not apply to advance revenue or spending actions.

The levels specified in the first budget resolution serve as targets to guide Congress during its subsequent action on spending legislation. Congress is not restricted as to the amounts it appropriates, but it is aided by a scorekeeping process that compares the amounts in individual bills with the appropriate levels set forth in the budget resolution. That scorekeeping procedure is facilitated by a two-step allocation process involving the budget committees and all other committees with jurisdiction over spending legislation. First, the managers' statement accompanying a conference report on the budget resolution allocates the appropriate levels among committees having jurisdiction over budget-authority legislation. Second, each such committee subdivides its allocation among its subcommittees or programs and reports the amounts to the House and the Senate. These suballocations form the basis for comparing the amounts in spending bills with the levels in the budget resolution. As noted, however, Congress is not bound by its initial decisions and it may appropriate at higher levels if it desires.

President Versus Congress: Impoundment Control

Although most of the Budget Act was directed at congressional processes, it inevitably affects the Presidency as well, if only because Congress is now organized to make independent budgetary judgments. Congress can diverge from presidential budget preferences in two ways: first, when it adopts a budget resolution and makes revenue and spending decisions pursuant to the resolution; and second, when it monitors executive spending actions to ensure adherence to its budget choices. We shall begin with the second of these because thus far impoundment control provides a much clearer indication of the effect of the act on executive budgeting than does the core congressional budget process.

The budget of 1977 draws a distinction between two types of impoundment: *rescissions*, in which there is no expectation that appropriated funds will be spent in the future; and *deferrals*, in which the President wishes to delay the expenditure until some future time. In either case, however, the President must send a special message to Congress proposing that the expenditure be rescinded or deferred. Funds proposed to rescission must be made available for obligation if Congress does not adopt a rescission bill within forty-five days after receipt of the President's message. Funds proposed for deferral must be released if either the House or the Senate adopts a resolution of disapproval. The act provides that a deferral may not be proposed for a period beyond the end of the fiscal year or in instances where the President is required to submit a rescission message. The Comptroller-General is to report to Congress if it is found that the President has failed to submit a required rescission or deferral message or if an impoundment has been improperly classified as a rescission or deferral. Special procedures have been devised for floor consideration of rescission bills and impoundment resolutions, with time limits for debate and other expediting provisions.

While there was much confusion and controversy when the new process was initiated, impoundment control has settled into a three-stage process involving presidential recommendations and reports, review by the Comptroller-General, and congressional action. At each of these stages, Congress has been confronted with a great amount of documentation and paper work, much required by the law itself, and some growing out of the manner in which the law has been implemented. Each proposed rescission or deferral must be accompanied by a presidential explanation, and the Comptroller-General must review the proposal and inform Congress of his findings. In addition, many of the impoundment proposals have spurred the introduction of resolutions and other legislative measures. Thus far, hundreds of rescission and deferral messages have been submitted to Congress, the Comptroller-General has forwarded more than one hundred communications, a dozen rescission bills have been considered, and hundreds of impoundment resolutions have been introduced in the House and the Senate. Tens of billions of dollars have been proposed for rescission and deferral. A summary of the early action under the Impoundment Control Act is shown in Table 2.

In responding to rescission proposals, Congress appears to have drawn a fairly clear distinction between routine and policy impoundments. With few exceptions, Congress has approved routine rescissions involving no change in government policy—for example, when funds are no longer needed to accomplish the purposes for which they were appropriated. In cases of policy rescissions, when the President has sought to eliminate funds appropriated in excess of his budget requests, Congress generally has refused to approve the rescission. Congress has not wanted to give the President a second chance to accomplish by means of impoundment what it had

Table 2
Summary of Rescission and Deferral Actions

Rescissions

FY 1975	Number Proposed	Amount Proposed	Amount Rescinded
Presidential Message	87	$2,732,678,218	$391,295,074
GAP Reclassification	7	415,313,000	0
GAO Notification	2	1,144,500,000	0
FY 1976 (Through Dec. 31, 1975)			
Presidential Message	27	2,341,569,655	62,500,000

Deferrals

	Deferrals Reported	Resolution Introduced	Number of Deferrals Affected	Deferrals Disapproved	Amount Disapproved
FY 1975	161	82	30	16	$9,318,217,441
FY 1976	85	29	26	14	244,224,000

denied him only weeks or months earlier in the course of the appropriations process. The high rejection rate indicates that the President has been repeatedly rebuffed in his efforts to convert impoundment control into reordering the budget priorities established by Congress. However, the fact that 45 percent (39 out of 87) of the FY 1975 proposals eventuated in rescissions indicates that many of the rescissions did not involve substantial questions of policy. Most of the routine cases concerned comparatively small amounts of money while the policy impoundments often dealt with large amounts. The median amount proposed for rescission in the approved cases was less than $3 million; in the rejected rescissions the median was $14 million.

The distinction between routine and policy impoundments applies to deferrals as well. In his various reports to Congress, the Comptroller-General has identified almost half of the deferrals as being authorized by the Antideficiency Act and a dozen other deferrals as actions not requiring the submission of a special message under the Impoundment Control Act.

Congressional activity in the form of impoundment resolutions has been concentrated on policy deferrals. The eighty-two resolutions filed during fiscal 1975 related to only thirty impoundments, almost half of which attracted resolutions in both the House and the Senate. In virtually every instance when impoundment resolutions were introduced in both the House and Senate, the deferral was disapproved.

With regard to deferrals during fiscal 1976, twenty-nine resolutions were introduced and more than half were adopted. (In two cases, both the House and Senate adopted impoundment resolutions even though action by a single house suffices to disapprove a deferral.) These thirty-nine resolutions pertained to twenty-six deferrals. Thus, only about 20 percent of the 1975 deferrals and 30 percent of the 1976 deferrals led to the introduction of impoundment resolutions. The vast majority of deferrals did not generate any congressional action because they were routine financial transactions involving no change in government policy.

The Impoundment Control Act (Title X) has established a workable, if cumbersome, procedure for congressional review of presidential impoundments. It does not reach to the ultimate constitutional issues of legislative-executive relations and presidential powers, but it does offer a method of settling impoundment disputes without raising those more portentious questions. Congress has been able to prevent the President from unilaterally withholding funds, and the President has been able to manage the financial affairs of the government prudently. The impoundment battles of the early 1970s have not been ended by Title X, but they are now being fought through agreed-upon means. Compared with the contests of the Nixon era, Title X provides for limited warfare, and in most cases for resolution of differences within a limited period of time.

Yet Title X has raised a number of problems of its own, and at least four merit brief consideration: differences between rescissions and deferrals; the paper-work burden; delays in the availability of funds; and congressional knowledge of executive actions.

Deferrals Versus Rescissions

There is a marked difference in the effects of Title X procedures on proposed rescissions and deferrals. Almost every rescission proposed by the President is overturned by congressional inaction; almost every deferral proposed is sustained by congressional inaction.

Part of this remarkable difference is due to the greater likelihood that rescissions represent policy changes, while deferrals often are routine financial moves. Part is also due to the logic of Title X, namely, that if the intent of the impoundment is to preserve the ultimate availability of the funds, a deferral is used, while rescissions are to be used when the impoundment is intended to terminate all use of the funds. Nevertheless, the difference between the two classes of impoundments reserves to the President a considerable measure of policy discretion vis-à-vis Congress. Except for misclassifications detected by the Comptroller-General, it is the President, not the Congress, who determines which impoundment procedure is to apply.

Paper-work Burden

The surprising number of messages and documents generated by Title X has burdened the Appropriations Committee. The volume of paper is due primarily to three factors: (1) the number of impoundments proposed by the President; (2) the comprehensive definition of impoundment in Title X; and (3) the backup protection provided by the Comptroller-General in monitoring presidential actions.

The effects of this burden on Title X outcomes are difficult to assess, but they probably include the following: (1) Congress is deterred from approving some routine rescissions proposed by the President; and (2) the President is given an advantage in proposing deferrals, for their large number undermines Congress's ability to detect all the policy implications. In other words, the paper-work burden has contributed to congressional inaction, which favors the President in deferrals and penalizes him in rescissions.

Delays in Funding

This surely is the most difficult problem. The President has achieved months of delay through the impoundment-control procedures. He has exploited the procedures to give himself a "second crack" at programs funded in excess of his budget recommendations. He has been able to put those programs in cold storage for most of the fiscal year, thereby frustrating congressional intent and impairing program effectiveness. Delay has been sought for its own sake and possibly for political advantage as well. Whatever the motive, Congress thus far has been virtually helpless when the President has manipulated the rescission rules to hold up programs. The forty-five day period for rescission has been especially troublesome: in several instances, a rescission bill was passed after the expiration of this period; in others, the *sine die* adjournment of Congress had the effect of prolonging the waiting period substantially beyond forty-five calendar days. When the forty-five days were added to late enactment of appropriation bills, the effect was to prolong the period of uncertainty about how much money would be available for expenditure through much of the fiscal year. Because of these problems a number of bills have been introduced to provide that no rescission shall take effect unless explicitly approved by Congress.

Congressional Knowledge of Executive Actions

Title X provides Congress with only an imperfect monitoring capacity. Presidential messages do not—and probably cannot—provide every relevant bit of information. The Comptroller-General cannot inspect every administrative action affecting the availability of funds. Congress cannot always distinguish between a delay legitimately caused by prudent management and a delay prompted by policy motives. Inadequate information leads to under-reporting and delayed reporting of impoundments and to the kind of congressional inactions discussed above.

President Versus Congress: Tax Policy

The first three years of the budget process saw an extraordinary amount of tax action on Capitol Hill, including seven major revenue bills. In terms of executive-legislative relations, the most contentious have had to do with revenue policy. Let us examine two of these in an effort to assess the consequences of the Budget Act.

II/Points of Conflict • 114

The ones selected are both now complete, so we can observe the full effect: the first is President Ford's effort to link a tax cut with a spending reduction, and the second is President Carter's 1977 tax-rebate proposal.

(1) In 1975 Congress passed the Tax Reduction Act, a temporary measure effective only for that year. Unless the reductions it provided were extended, most taxpayers would have faced an automatic increase in the amounts withheld from their earnings at the start of the following year. In order to avoid that, the second budget resolution for FY 1976 directed the Ways and Means and Finance Committees to report legislation extending the tax cuts. Those committees readily complied: Ways and Means incorporated the extension in a tax-reform bill, but that approach was dropped in favor of a six-month extension reported by Finance. That extension, Senator Muskie explained, was "a result of a deliberate, rational process of discussion which has included the Finance Committee, the Ways and Means Committee, [and] the Budget Committees of both Houses." It seemed to be a straightforward, noncontroversial continuation of a law already in effect.

But that was not the case. Before Congress completed action on the temporary legislation, President Ford dropped a political bombshell into the new budget process. On October 6, 1975, Ford demanded that Congress enact a $28 billion tax cut together with a $395 billion ceiling on expenditures for fiscal 1975. On the basis of OMB's current estimates, that limitation would have required a $28 billion reduction in federal spending. Ford threatened to veto any tax cut that was not matched dollar-for-dollar by a spending reduction. He wanted Congress to bypass completely its new budget process, to revert to the ad hoc procedures used during the years 1967 to 1972, and to impose arbitrary ceilings without prior consideration of their fiscal or programmatic consequences. The call for a spending limit came almost a full year before the start of the fiscal year to which it would apply and more than seven months before the deadline for adoption of the first budget resolution.

Ford's intervention converted the extension from a tax issue into a fight over budget procedures, and it moved the budget committees from the periphery of legislative action to the center of the battle. These committees quickly gained recognition within Congress as the guardians of the new procedure, and they understandably saw the President's action as a direct challenge to their position. The conflict was waged over the proposed linking of taxing and spending, virtually all attention being directed toward the spending side of the issue. Most congressional Democrats viewed the President's move as a bid to gain political advantage for his forthcoming election campaign, and they found the budget process a convenient means of thwarting his demands. Republicans were cross-pressured, wanting to support their President's political and economic objectives, but without subverting the new budget procedure.

The controversy raged for several months—until the last day of the legislative session. House Republicans tried to attach a spending limit to both a debt-ceiling bill and tax reform legislation but were rebuffed both times. Senate rejection of the President's proposal was bipartisan, with Senator Bellmon, the ranking Republican on the Budget Committee, joining his Democratic colleagues in defense of the budget process:

> We pleaded with President Ford to accept the fact that we now have a better system than the arbitrary ceiling he has asked us to accept. I personally seriously doubt that President Ford understands the changes that have been made since he was a Member of Congress . . . . I believe it would be a mistake for us to abandon the budget process in the first year of its infancy and agree upon an arbitrary spending limitation without prior judgment as to its effects and method of enforcement.

Congress ultimately prevailed in this executive-legislative contest, though not because of its budget process. The President found himself at a serious political disadvantage. When Congress refused to link tax and spending reductions and instead passed a six-month extension of the tax cuts, the President vetoed the bill. The veto came near the close of the legislative session, barely two weeks before withholding rates were scheduled to rise. Cast in the unfavorable position of promoting a tax increase, the White House (after the House sustained the veto) embraced a face-saving compromise. With Republican approval, the Senate passed a new six-month extension along with a "sense of the Congress" resolution which endorsed the principle of dollar-for-dollar tax and spending cuts but asserted the right of Congress to adopt whatever spending level it deemed suitable. The House modified the resolution by insisting that future decisions about spending levels would be made through the congressional budget process. Months later, after the issue had abated, Congress ignored the linking of tax and spending reductions and passed a budget resolution for fiscal 1977 that set spending at more than $15 billion above the President's budget and called for $17 billion in tax reductions.

(2) In January 1977 the incoming Carter Administration proposed tax relief as part of an economic stimulus program worked out in preinauguration conferences with congressional leaders. Legislative interest was clearly on the spending side, since Congress enacted more costly job and public works programs than the new Administration had initially proposed.

The stimulus package necessitated a third resolution for fiscal 1977; both its revenue and spending components were at variance with the second resolution adopted before the presidential election. As presented to the House Budget Committee (HBC) on January 27, 1977, the plan called for $13.8 billion of tax reductions during the fiscal year, consisting of $11.4 billion for one-shot rebates and payments and $2.4 billion in other cuts. HBC chairman Giaimo expressed concern "as to the adequacy and sufficiency" of the program, but the committee opted for additional expenditures rather than deeper tax cuts. The Committee acknowledged "widespread skepticism that rebates and reductions can spur sufficient economic activity" to reduce unemployment, and it had reservations about the inequities of the President's program and its expanded use of tax credits. Nevertheless, the HBC went along with the Administration's tax package, though it left the components to be decided by the Ways and Means Committee. Ways and Means (acting before the third resolution was adopted) recommended tax reductions somewhat at variance with those of the Administration, so HBC offered a floor amendment to make its revenue figure conform to the amount reported by the tax committee.

The Senate Budget Committee (SBC) also had doubts about the Administration's approach, but it too fell into line. During its markup of the third resolution, Committee Republicans strongly attacked the temporary rebates and called for permanent tax cuts instead. Senator Muskie, however, took the position that the SBC should specify only total revenues and not decide whether the tax cuts should be temporary or permanent. Muskie wanted to avoid offending either the Administration (which wanted temporary cuts) or the Finance Committee (which wanted the SBC to deal only with total revenues). The SBC thus straddled the issue in its report on the third resolution, recommending an amount that would permit either "the tax relief as proposed by the Carter Administration, or enactment of permanent tax rate reductions or other forms of temporary tax relief of comparable amount."

Having dutifully complied with the Administration's tax preferences, the budget committees had the rug pulled out from under them in April 1977 when President Carter withdrew the rebate proposal. This action could not have come at a more embarassing time for the budget committees. The third resolution for fiscal 1977 (which had been developed primarily to accommodate the rebates) had already been passed by Congress, while the first resolution for fiscal 1978 (whose economic assumptions were predicated on the tax stimulus) had been reported by both budget committees and was scheduled for floor action in the near future. Neither budget committee chairman had been consulted or informed of the decision in advance of the public pronouncement; and both had to reconvene their committees at once to decide what to do about the Administration's reversal. They might have opted to do nothing, but that would have left the revenue floor for fiscal 1977 billions of dollars below estimated receipts. Not only would that have spotlighted the irrelevance of the budget resolutions for tax policy; it might also have prompted the tax committees to produce their own versions of tax cuts.

The HBC threw in the towel with a retroactive adjustment (appended to the first FY 78 resolution) to the revenue level for fiscal 1977. Chairman Giaimo conceded that "it was not the desire of the committee to eliminate the $50 payment . . . but we are now faced with the realities of life in that the President has said he is not going to pursue the rebate. The other body (the Senate) obviously is not going to implement it."

The Senate Budget Committee decided to stick with the rebates, reaffirming "its judgment about the advisability of tax stimulus in some form in 1977 . . . . The committee is not persuaded that significant changes in economic prospects for 1977 and 1978 have taken place since adoption of the third budget resolution for fiscal 1977." Muskie, who only weeks earlier had been the most vigorous congressional advocate of rebates at a time when the scheme was losing favor on Capitol Hill, accused the Administration of undermining the credibility of the budget process. But in conference, he recognized the futility of fighting for the abandoned rebates and the third resolution was modified to delete them.

In these two tax battles, the outcome favored the President in one instance and the budget committees in the other. One might be tempted to attribute the presidential success in the one to the fact that both branches were controlled by the same party, in contrast with the earlier presidential failure when the two major parties divided political control. Yet there is a deeper explanation: one was a contest over the substance of tax policy, the other over the budgetary procedures for the making of tax policies. Congress has been a vigilant guardian of its budget process against executive encroachment. The issue in 1975 was not merely one over tax rates or levels but over the prerogative of Congress to use and protect its new budgetary procedures. That was not the case in 1977; then the President did not challenge the legislative process but sought a substantive outcome in line with his own policies.

President Versus Congress: Spending Priorities

One of the main purposes of the congressional budget process is to enable Congress to determine its own budget priorities. That does not mean, of course, that Congress is totally free of presidential influence. The President's budget still is the benchmark with which much congressional action is compared. In its markup of budget resolutions, for example, the House Budget Committee constantly measures its actions by their deviation from the President's recommendations. Both appropriations committees have continued their traditional practice of line-by-line comparisons of appropriations accounts with the presidential estimates. Moreover, to a large extent, these committees still reckon their fiscal effectiveness and responsibility by the extent to which they have cut or increased the budget. But there are signs that the executive budget is losing some of its importance. The Senate Budget Committee, for example, conducts its markup using current service estimates as its starting point. This "neutral" yardstick enables the SBC to take action more independently of White House preferences.

Perhaps of even greater signficance is that when the CBO issues its scorekeeping reports, it shows the appropriations and other spending decisions in comparison with the congressional budget figures. In somewhat simpler form, those reports predated the 1974 Budget Act; they were initiated in the late 1960s by the appropriations committees as a means of demonstrating their budgetary responsibility. It was a wrenching experience for the scorekeepers to convert from a presidential to a congressional data base, but that has now been accomplished and the new reports supply Congress with up-to-date information on the budget.

Under the Budget Act, Congress makes priority decisions by setting spending levels (in terms of both budget authority and outlays) for each of the functions in the budget. The sixteen functions are listed in Table 3, which also shows the deviation of the congressional budget from the President's recommendations during each of the first three years of the new process. The comparisons are based on the first (May 15) budget resolution each year because that is probably a more valid indicator of the differences between the two branches' priorities than is the second resolution. The data in Table 3 make clear that for some functions there is no signficant difference between the presidential and congressional budgets. That is true of law enforcement, general government, and revenue sharing. Most controversy is concentrated in a few functions. Thus Congress usually cuts the President's defense request, while it votes more money than was proposed for education and social services—though the amounts of the reduction or increase vary sharply from year to year. In fiscal 1976, Congress pruned the national defense estimtes by $7 billion in budget authority, but the very next year it took less than one billion dollars from that function. This year-to-year swing represented not a shift from congressional to presidential priorities but a shift in national attitudes (as perceived by members of Congress) concerning the security needs of the United States.

Not surprisingly, the differences tended to be greater in the 1976 and 1977 budgets when a Republican President vied with a Democratic Congress on budgetary issues. President Ford's failure to lock Congress into a $28 billion budget cut for fiscal 1977 is reflected in the statistics for that year. Congress added $22 billion in budget

II/Points of Conflict • 120

Table 3
Difference Between the First Budget Resolutions and the President's Budget Request for FY 1976, FY 1977, and FY 1978*

Function	1976 BA	1976 Outlays	1977 BA	1977 Outlays	1978 BA	1978 Outlays
National defense	-$7.0	-3.3†	-.8	-.3	-1.6	-.9
International affairs	-7.7	-1.5†	-.6	-.3	-1.0	-.5
General science, space, and technology	—	—	—	—	—	—
Natural resource, environment, and energy	1.6	1.5†	7.3	1.9	.2	-.5
Agriculture	—	—	—	.1	-.5	2.1
Commerce and transportation	4.0†	2.0†	.3	1.3	.5	-.7
Community and regional development	5.8	2.8†	1.5	2.1	-1.2	.7
Education, training, employment, and social services	5.3	3.4†	8.6	5.4	.1	.7
Health	2.1	2.6†	1.3	2.4	.1	-.2
Income security	-5.4†	4.7†	1.0	2.2	.1	.2
Veterans' benefits and services	1.2	1.3	2.4	2.3	1.2	1.1
Law enforcement and justice	.1	.1	.1	.1	-.1	—
General government	—	.1	.1	.1	—	.1
Revenue sharing and general purpose assistance	—	— †	.1	—	-.9	—
Interest	.6	.6	-.9	-.9	1.2	1.2
Allowances	-6.9	-6.9	1.3	-.3	-2.1	-1.8
Undistributed offsetting receipts	— †	— †	1.4	1.4	.4	.4
Total	-7.3	7.4	23.1	17.5	-3.6	1.9

*In billions of dollars
†President's budget adjusted by the House Budget Committee

authority and $17.4 billion in outlays to the budget totals. In fact, fiscal 1977 was the first year in more than a generation that total appropriations exceeded the total requested by the President. One can properly conclude that it was the new budget process that emboldened Congress to deviate so markedly from the presidential course.

The Budget is Not the Only Fight in Washington

It is easy to understand why budgetary conflicts between the President and Congress attract so much notice. The stakes are astronomically high; federal spending will reach the half-trillion dollar mark in another year or two. As the budget has grown, we have come to regard it as the prime instrument for deciding America's priorities. The budget appears to hold a life-or-death outcome for the diversity of interests, programs, and agencies contending for public funds. To be in the budget is to possess status and resources; to be outside the budget is to be beyond the pale of public recognition.

The great wonder, therefore, is not why the President and Congress fight over budgetary issues, but rather why they seem to fight so little. Why do budgets get so easily settled, often with little more than posturing for political and programmatic advantage? The protracted disputes between Nixon and Congress over spending ceilings and impoundments were an aberration from the normal, but they were so disruptive and unsettling that Congress was prompted to establish a new budgetary mechanism. We should not, of course, take the Nixon years as the norm, though even during that period there was much more conflict resolution than stalemate. The federal government and its agencies were not closed down by a cut-off of funds or a failure of the two branches to settle their financial differences.

Sometimes government does verge close to breakdown as a consequence of budgetary strife. That was so in the fall of 1977 when two major federal departments—Labor and HEW—started the fiscal year without any legal authority to spend money. They put a hold on equipment purchases and travel and informed their workers that they might not be paid on the next regular payday. Then at the eleventh hour Congress enacted a continuing resolution extending funds to both agencies for a brief period. When the extension proved too short, Congress once again came through with a continuing appropriation. The battle was not merely a fight over money; it was an ideological struggle between supporters and opponents of abortion. Had the issue merely been one of dollars, it surely would have settled long before the contestants went to the brink. In fact, House and Senate conferees had reconciled all their differences about the level of appropriations for Labor and HEW programs. Abortion was the sole unresolved issue.

The key to the taming of budgetary conflict is to regard it as a money matter and little more. The complainant ripped off by a shyster will cut his losses if he perceives the dispute as one over dollars and cents. When he rants and raves about "the principle of the thing," the prospect for conflict grows. Because budgets are decided as financial issues, a versatile array of conflict-resolving strategies are available; hold the appropriation to last year's level, to last year's level plus inflation, to last year's minus a disputed item, divide the differences between the two parties, and so on.

But all this is also a way of saying that the budget excels as a process for making financial decisions, not as a process for making program or substantive choices. It is a mistake—one of the overblown conceptions of public administration—to regard the budget as the primary device for making $450 billion of program decisions each year. A task of that magnitude—or even a fraction of it—would overburden the federal government's capacities for bridging political differences. The budget must be seen as only one—and not necessarily the most important or decisive—arena for public choice. Congressional committees make budget decisions by developing legislation; administrators make budget decisions when they promulgate regulations; the President drives the budget when he hits the campaign trail. For a good part of federal government activity—much more than half—the budget is the place where decisions are recorded, not where they are made. Legislation mandating the payment of black-lung benefits will be entered into the budget, but the real choice was made at the legislative stage. As a comprehensive statement of the financial transactions of government, the budget displays the costs and records the decisions made elsewhere. It is easy to be deceived into thinking that the budget is the place where the decisions are made.

It would be astonishing if the United States practiced pluralist politics but monolithic budgeting. If the budget process were the all-reaching, consistent, critical process we often credit it with being, command over the budget process would bring command over the political system as well. OMB in the executive branch and the budget committees in Congress would have extraordinary leverage over all the other participants in the political process.

It might be said that the federal government has two budget processes, or that the budget process serves two rather different functions. Some program decisions are made in the budget; others are merely translated into dollar terms when budgets are assembled. Perhaps the best indication of this dual process is the budget's recognition that most expenditures are "uncontrollable under existing law." In the budget for fiscal 1978, $330 billion in expenditures—75 percent of the total—is reported to be uncontrollable. In one sense, nothing really is uncontrollable because Congress can revoke or revise the law mandating the expenditures. But that is precisely the point. For three-quarters of federal outlays, the budget is not the point of decision. Regardless of the amount estimated in the budget, actual expenditures will be determined by decisions made through other processes. "Uncontrollables" is a way of indicating that the budget is not the process by which such expenditures are decided.

Even with regard to the remaining 25 percent, the budget does not really provide a free choice each year. If it did, the amount of budgetary conflict would soar far beyond the capacity of government to resolve. Those making budget decisions follow—as Aaron Wildavsky has insisted—incremental norms to narrow the scope of budget conflict. The price we pay is a narrowing as well of the options open to government in a particular year. The benefits are in the form of budgetary peace, governmental stability, and administrative regularity. We trade away an awful lot to get those benefits, but the alternative might be warfare and a potential breakdown of government.

When the President and Congress fight over the budget, we should recognize that they are fighting over the margins. In a half-trillion dollar budget, they might fight over hundreds of millions or a few billions, rarely over more than one half of one percent of the total. Of course, this is margin enough to stir both combatants to battle, but fortunately it is sufficiently manageable to enable them to negotiate budgetary accord as well.

Control of the Bureaucracy

A Mismatch of Incentives and Capabilities

Morris P. Fiorina

Morris P. Fiorina is Associate Professor of Political Science at the California Institute of Technology.

The task of this essay is to explore the problem of "controlling the bureaucracy." By itself the phrase is neutral, but presumably it would not have been selected unless many political observers considered it a problem. In the popular press, of course, one frequently finds allusions to out-of-control or runaway bureaucracy. And academics, too, remark that the bureaucracy is not well controlled, perhaps that it cannot be well controlled. In a widely read recent book on the Presidency, for example, Stephen Hess contends that it is a mistake for modern Presidents even to attempt to manage the bureaucracy, in the sense of overseeing day-to-day bureaucratic operations.[1] Instead Hess advocates a presidential role of agenda setting and policy (not managerial) decisionmaking. Peter Woll writes that the emergence of the federal bureaucracy adds a fourth dimension to the constitutional separation of powers.[2] His work attempts to come to grips with the bureaucracy's place in that system. Samuel Huntington writes gloomily of the future of democratic assemblies in a world of inevitably larger and more powerful bureaucratic establishments.[3] Well-meaning reformers often construe such discussions as justifications for institutional panaceas: sunset and sunshine laws, zero-based budgeting, executive-branch reorganization, and so on. But I doubt that the authors just cited view their work as justifications for reform movements. It is one thing to note that the bureaucracy is an important branch of the federal government, that it can develop and use political resources, and that its expertise gives it an advantage in dealing with other branches of the government; it is quite another thing to claim that the bureaucracy is out of control. In one sense that claim is true, but in another sense it is simply false; too often observers confuse themselves and others by shifting too easily between the two meanings.

The bureaucracy is not out of control. The Congress controls the bureaucracy, and Congress gives us the kind of bureaucracy it wants. If some modern-day Madison were to formulate a plan that would guarantee an efficient, centrally-directed bureaucracy, Congress would react with fear and loathing. To be sure, particular members of Congress may wish to do away with particular agencies, but if the choice were between the existing bureaucratic world and the utopian bureaucratic world conjured up above, Congress would cast a nearly unanimous vote for the present scheme. The parent loves the child despite its warts.

Obviously I am playing on ambiguities in the concept of "control." In the first place many observers would distinguish between theoretical (i.e., formal or legal) control, and actual (i.e., politically feasible) control. As usual, the Constitution divides formal control over bureaucracy between the President and Congress (and the courts play a more important role than we often recognize). While the President is nominally the head of a large part of the federal apparatus, his actual authority is rather modest. Civil Service and advice-and-consent requirements circumscribe his appointment powers. His personal agency, the Office of Management and Budget, is indisputably powerful, but once matters escape its clutches and get into the congressional arena, the President may appear to be a pitiful, helpless giant when confronted by renegade agencies. Lacking the rifle of the item veto, the President can threaten only with the cannon of the general veto—and denizens of Washington can judge when he does not dare fire that cannon. Congress, on the other hand, has the formal power of life and death over the bureaucracy. Congress can abolish an agency or reorganize it, change its jurisdiction or allow its program authority to lapse entirely, cut its appropriations, or conduct embarrassing investigations. A hostile Congress unconcerned about the consequences of its action could wreck the federal establishment.

Of course, Congress seldom exercises its formal powers. Ideas such as sunset laws and zero-based budgeting are little more than attempts to insure that existing congressional powers are used more frequently, or at least that their use is contemplated more frequently. Procedural changes alone are insufficient to increase control over the bureaucracy; to achieve their purpose, such changes must also provide incentives to exercise that control.[4]

There is a second, more important ambiguity in the notion of "control." What kind of control do we want? Control for what? Imagine a naval fleet in which each vessel is under the absolute control of a chief officer. But suppose that these captains themselves are responsible to no higher authority, and moreover that they have no particular interest in communicating with one another. Well-meaning observers watching such a fleet maneuver might understandably judge it to be out of control. They might even recommend various measures intended to enhance control of the fleet's operation. Yet each commanding officer would greet such recommendations with skepticism; looking about his ship he sees no evidence of lack of control.

Like the individual ships in the preceding analogy the parts of the federal bureaucracy typically are well-behaved in the sense that they are responsive to the captains in the congressional committees and subcommittees which determine their fates. But the whole of the bureaucracy is out of control, as is Congress.[5]

Thus, the second distinction is that between coordinated and uncoordinated control, or less pejoratively, centralized and decentralized control. When I state that the Congress controls the bureaucracy, I use the term in the second sense. Parts of Congress control parts of the bureaucracy, but there is little coordination in such control. Particular congressional committees control the agencies they want to control and in the manner they prefer. Those who view "control of the bureaucracy" as a problem, however, have centralized or coordinated control in mind: how can the disparate parts of the bureaucracy be integrated; how can they be made to work in harness to achieve major policy goals?

That question is at the heart of our concern. What I now propose to do is to consider the degree to which the bureaucracy is out of control, and ask what can be done about it. Central to such a discussion is a consideration of the incentives of the interested parties: the Congress, the President, the bureaucrats, and the electorate. Who can exert influence? To what end do they wish to do so? What kind of control will result? Answers to these questions will provide a basis for speculating about the value of various suggested reforms. In a nutshell, I shall argue that the Congress has the power but not the incentive for coordinated control of the bureaucracy, while the President has the incentive but not the power. This mismatch between the incentives and capabilities of the important political actors is at least as important as the informational overload, the imbalance in expertise, and the internal processes of bureaucracies, in explaining the absence of coordinated control of the federal bureaucracy.

I am skeptical about the necessity of new procedures for achieving coordinated control over the bureaucracy. All necessary powers presently exist. That is not a novel contention, but it is an important one and it deserves explanation. Simple models or idealizations of our political order will serve as the vehicle.

Assume that a new President takes office with a large and reliable congressional majority, a majority that he can depend upon to rubber stamp his legislative program and budget. That President would first appoint his people to every political executive post not covered by Civil Service. With few exceptions agencies must clear proposed legislation with OMB. There, the President's people can make sure that all new proposals are consistent with the Administration's grand design. With these steps the future operation of the bureaucracy is brought under some control. Meanwhile, in formulating the budget, OMB can bring existing programs under presidential control by starving those found to be inconsistent with his program, or in extreme cases by having Congress abolish agencies or programs. We assume the Congress will approve all such requests as well as the budget and proposed legislation.[6]

In this simple world the bureaucracy could be out of control only because mistakes are made—mistakes of program conception or mistakes in administration. Perhaps there is simply too much proposed new legislation, or too little time to review existing programs. Even so, such mistakes would be unlikely to persist for very long; rather, old mistakes would be remedied and new ones would become apparent. There would be no chronic cases of out-of-control programs or agencies. For in such a world any outright opposition could be broken. Programs could be abolished, agencies reorganized, executives fired, and civil servants transferred. All this from the assumption of a cooperative compliant Congress.

Ah, you may say, Congress is not a rubber stamp. Congress makes more than marginal adjustments in the President's program and budget. So, let us posit a more active legislative body. Rather than assuming that the President's requests are rubber stamped, we now assume that the President's program is submitted to powerful legislative committees, and that his budget is submitted to a powerful Appropriations Committee. Let us assume moreover that the authorizing committees have jurisdiction over all aspects of his policies (other than appropriations), that such committees are representative of the membership of the whole chamber, and that the members who serve on such committees have as their primary goal the formulation of efficiently administered, effective national policy. For good measure let us also assume that a powerful party leadership consciously coordinates the work of the authorizing, appropriating, and revenue-raising committees, and that individual members heed the party position because they believe in it and because their fortunes are tied to it.

In this more complicated world I submit that again there would be little or no problem with out-of-control bureaucracy. The President and the Congress would each formulate coherent programs. Undoubtedly, those programs would differ in some respects, and in compromising the two, some incoherence might result. But the assumption of common party affiliation should afford a reasonably good insurance against too much irrationality in the end product.

Ah, you may say again, but that is just not the U.S. Congress you are describing. Committee jurisdictions are a "crazy quilt." Congress is no place for the compulsively neat person. The recently passed energy policy, for example, was worked over by five different House standing committees, and then run through an unprecedented ad hoc committee. Moreover, congressional committees are anything but representative. The westerners head for Interior, farm-district representatives for Agriculture, and so on.[7] This self-selection bias is then exacerbated by the observance of reciprocity: the country boys on Interior will keep their noses out of housing matters, if the city boys on Banking and Currency will do the same for public lands.[8] Suddenly, even common party membership is not sufficient to insure reasonable agreement between the program of the President and the programs of the congressional committees. And the worst is yet to come.

Implicit in the notion of reciprocity is the admission that Congressmen do not have as their primary goal the formulation of good national policy; that is a secondary goal. Policy that benefits the district (and thereby enhances reelection prospects) is the primary goal. Consider two policy alternatives in some particular area. Policy X provides $100 in net benefits to each of districts 1 to 400, and costs districts 401-435 $1,000 each. Policy Y provides districts 401-435 with net benefits of $1,000 each but costs districts 1-400 $100 each. In terms of national net benefits the policies rank as follows:

Policy X: (400 x $100) - (35 x $1,000) = $5,000

Policy Y: (35 x $1,000) - (400 x $100) = -$5,000

A President might understandably support policy alternatives like X; if you want to make an omelet, you've got to break some eggs. And Congress? Typically the representatives of districts 401-435 control the committee that chooses between X and Y. By enabling special-interest Congressmen to gain control of the subjects of special interest, reciprocity insures that more policies like Y will be chosen than would otherwise be the case. And given that we are a large, heterogeneous country, all Congressmen are special-interest Congressmen in some matters. Thus, reciprocity makes it possible for a relatively greater number of policies like Y to defeat policies like X than would be the case under simple majority rule.

When we see a public agency spending inordinate amounts of public funds to benefit certain congressional districts, we are not observing an out-of-control agency. We are observing an agency that is paying off the Congressmen who nurture it. The federal agencies exist in a symbiotic relation with the congressional committees and subcommittees to which they report. Of course, not everything an agency does is of concern to its "own" group of

Congressmen. It purchases its freedom on those things by playing ball on the things that *are* of concern. So, part of the agency's activities are typically out of control, but Congress wants it that way. It is a necessary cost of maintaining a bureaucracy sufficiently unconstrained (in law and by its nominal leaders) that it is susceptible to congressional influence.

What do sunset laws and zero-based budgeting do in such a case? Little, really. Occasionally they may force consideration of some overlooked program which no longer has any conceivable justification. But basically, such procedural innovations only shift more of the burden of proof from Congress to the bureaucracy, and thus make it easier for Congressmen to extort favors from the bureaucracy. If that's what you mean by control of the bureaucracy, fine.

Now, all this constitutes a rather forceful statement, a statement subject to many qualifications. But in broad outline I believe it is fair and accurate. If one is concerned about control of the bureaucracy, the critical questions do not revolve around the legal instruments of control. Those exist and are used regularly. The critical questions revolve around the fact that the Congress and the President do not want to control the bureaucracy for the same ends. The goals of the typical President and the goals of the typical Congressman differ considerably. In consequence, what they want from the bureaucracy differs. And therein lies the problem. Put most simply, the goals of the President lead him to prefer centralized or coordinated control of the bureaucracy, while the goals of Congressmen lead them to favor decentralized or uncoordinated control. And given that the Congress is in a somewhat stronger position than the President vis-à-vis the instruments of control, decentralized control will prevail.

What are the goals of the typical President? Reelection comes most immediately to mind, at least to the cynical mind. But place in history is a close second. The incumbent has already achieved the highest office possible; the only thing left is retirement as a revered elder statesman. Fortunately for analytical purposes the two goals often appear to be consistent. The President is the nation's chief official and responsible for major policy directions. He will presumably attain reelection as well as a prominent place in the history books by successfully solving important national problems: attaining peace with honor; stoking up a sluggish economy and reducing unemployment; cooling down a runaway economy and curbing inflation; ending crime in the streets; or achieving racial equality. Naturally there are times (as President Nixon so often reminded us) when the short-run bullet must be bitten to achieve long-run goals, times when reelection and place in history pull the President in opposite directions (e.g., energy policy, circa 1977). But even when his goals are not completely consistent, the President will still want to do something to accomplish broad policy ends. He will not be content to sit in his office and react to each problem or situation that arises. And in order to accomplish broad policy goals the President must control the executive branch. Many of the Nixon Administration's more original shenanigans were at least in part attempts to harness elements of the federal bureaucracy that were not under control of the Administration. As the representative of all the people, the President desires centralized control of the bureaucracy, whether to construct the national coalition he needs to win reelection or to make the major policy initiatives that will insure his place in history.

Congressmen are in a different situation. Most of them simply wish to stay where they are, although House members are always on the lookout for a stray Senate seat, and increasing numbers of Senators find personally compelling reasons to offer themselves as presidential candidates. With a few exceptions, place in history is an unrealistic goal for members of Congress. Each Representative is a paltry one vote of 435. Unlike the President, he or she cannot credibly claim responsibility for putting the economy back on its feet or healing the wounds of the civil war. At best, several generations may remember him or her as the person who brought many sewage-treatment plants to the district. Senators are in a somewhat better position, but even they have merely one vote of a hundred, and how many twentieth-century Senators can plausibly be said to have achieved a prominent place in history?[9] No, for members of Congress life is in the here and now. Especially for Representatives, "now" is literally "now"—their lives are organized into two-year cycles. The primary goal is figuring out how to survive the next election.

And survive they do! Since the Second World War about 90 percent of all incumbents have chosen to run for reelection and an average 90 percent of those have succeeded. Moreover, they have been getting still more successful in recent years.[10] How have they managed that, given the erosion of traditional partisan sources of support and the increasing public cynicism toward government institutions and incumbents? Elsewhere I have argued that the key to this puzzle is a mid-century change in the congressional role.[11] As the scope of the federal government has expanded, the federal bureaucracy has enjoyed a concomitant expansion. Citizens in turn "enjoy" increasingly more opportunities to interact with their federal public servants, whether in an effort to take advantage of various federal programs or to evade various federal regulations. The Congressman finds himself ideally situated. Traditionally, if one is having problems with the bureaucracy one writes one's Congressman. Congressmen have a long history of intevening in bureaucratic decisionmaking for the benefit of constituents. With the expansion of the federal bureaucracy the Congressman's role as an intervenor—an ombudsman—has become more important. Objectively there is a greater demand for his services, and sensible incumbents have done little or nothing to stem that demand. In fact, some representatives, particularly the more junior ones, have actually stimulated the demand for ombudsman services, seeing such activities as a means to reach those voters in their districts who would otherwise opposed them on policy, ideological, or party grounds. In short, Congressmen are increasingly deemphasizing their role as formulators of national policies, which are after all controversial, and emphasizing their role as ombudsmen who strike fear in the hearts of incompetent or arbitrary bureaucrats. Citizens in turn increasingly ignore the Congressman's position on major national policies. What does it matter if he's a conservative or liberal, Republican or Democrat? He can't make much of a difference given that he holds only one vote out of 535. But as subcommittee chairman or ranking minority member of such and such, he has been a whiz at helping us get sewage treatment plants, mass-transit feasibility studies, or whatever. Moreover, he kept the old coke ovens from being shut down by EPA and tracked down umpteen hundred lost social-security checks. Why give up the seniority and experience he has built up just because you disagree with him on the B-1 bomber or revision of the Hatch Act?

How have Congressmen managed to carry out ombudsman

activities so successfully? Simple. Congress has powerful instruments of control over the bureaucracy, and there is ample evidence that the threat of those instruments is seldom far from bureaucratic minds.[12] The effectiveness of the instrument is made all the more real by the establishment and maintenance of the elaborate committee-reciprocity system already mentioned. Each Congressman is given the opportunity to exercise disproportionate influence over the segments of the federal bureaucracy that are of special concern to him. If an agency is causing particular problems for his constituents, a Congressman need not organize a coalition of 51 or 218 members to discipline that agency. He need only get four or five subcommittee colleagues to see things his way. And given those facts, one can hardly blame an agency for paying special attention to "suggestions" from an interested Congressman.

The Congress has had a standing committee system for quite some time (upwards of 150 years), but the major trend of the twentieth century has been a decentralizing one.[13] First the party leadership lost power to the committee leadership, then more recently the committee leadership lost power to the subcommittee leadership. All of this has occurred, to be sure, under the guise of democratic "reforms." But we should not forget that the effect has been the ever-increasing dispersion of the power to control the bureaucracy. The House under Czar Reed could and probably did exert coordinated control over a small federal executive. The House under Tip O'Neill and 175 subcommittee chairmen still can coordinate the activities of a much larger bureaucratic establishment, but it won't. Reed was willing to lose back-benchers who were forced to support locally unpopular party positions—the breaks of the game. Today there are no back-benchers.

The situation in the last quarter of the twentieth century is not comforting. The citizen increasingly finds himself in contact with a bureaucratic establishment, usually federal, or at least federally stimulated. That bureaucratic establishment may be unresponsive, slow-moving, and at times downright capricious. And every day it seems to extend a little farther into the citizen's life. But whether he's in the right or the wrong, the citizen knows that he can count on one powerful ally in his attempts to triumph over bureaucratic procedures or dictates: his Congressman. Increasingly the citizen views the Congressman as a powerful, benevolent friend in an ever more threatening, impersonal world. Citizens get favors, Congressmen get votes.

Meanwhile, down in Washington, Congress maintains a federal bureaucracy deliberately organized to be susceptible to congressional intervention, not only to the chamber as a whole, but to subgroups and even individual members. So long as an agency cooperates when Congressmen make specific requests, it is unlikely to suffer long-term losses no matter how poor its performance. In fact, the more inefficient or unreasonable its performance the greater the political resource it constitutes. Not completely tongue in cheek, one could say that if the Occupational Safety and Health Administration (OSHA) did not exist, Congress might find it necessary to invent it.

And the President? He is largely left out of these important exchanges. His personal appointees become the captives of the subgovernments they were appointed to control.[14] He finds himself circumscribed at every step. In the first flush of victory, throwing a net around "runaway" agencies seems like a fine idea. But then Congress tells him that he can forget about a national energy policy if he doesn't learn to keep his nose out of where it doesn't belong. To achieve his goals the President must actively use a coordinated bureaucracy to achieve some positive purpose. But to achieve their goals Congressmen can increasingly do no more than fend off perceived bureaucratic assaults on their constituents. This asymmetry would put the President in a weaker position than Congress even if his formal powers were comparable.[15]

This state of affairs has several important consequences for the operation of the federal government in the foreseeable future. First, *in terms of organization and administration* we can expect still more inefficient, "out of control" bureaucracy. For Congress has no electoral incentive to work toward coordinated control. Quite the opposite. Congress is making increasing use of instruments that keep the bureaucracy more closely tied to increasingly decentralized congressional control: the legislative veto, "come into agreement" requirements, and sunset provisions. I think it is probably accurate to say that we are currently experiencing an increase in uncoordinated control and a decrease in coordinated control. Moreover, the dynamics of the current trends have a self-perpetuating aspect. The more Congressmen are perceived and elected as ombudsmen, the greater their incentive to maintain the current system, and the greater their reluctance to agree to proposals looking toward coordinated control.

Second, *in terms of policy*, we can identify certain biases that arise from conflicting presidential and congressional goals. A President may look fondly on proposals to replace the jerry-built structure of income-security programs with a guaranteed annual income accomplished entirely through the tax laws. Or perhaps he may contemplate razing the educational grant structure and substituting a voucher system. In theory such programs carry the promise of closing gaps and alleviating conflicts in existing programs while reducing the number of administrative personnel and allowing greater freedom of choice. They are naturals for Presidents on the prowl for places in history. Congressmen have a different bias. Even if such massive program shifts resulted in no net changes in their constituents' welfare (admittedly an unlikely possibility), they would decrease the political resource base of Congressmen. If benefits are distributed automatically, constituents will expect them as their due rather than something owed to benevolent Congressmen. And if costs are imposed automatically, as with the collection of taxes, fewer citizens will seek the aid of the Congressman to avoid those costs.

In essence, congressional goals encourage programs with a New Deal cast. Use the bureaucracy to regulate and subsidize and deliberately leave room for arbitrary (i.e., politically determined) decisions. Avoid general income redistribution; permit it to happen only as a by-product of a congeries of federal programs. If at all possible avoid revenue sharing; it's too easy for the locals to forget who gives them the money. Of course, we should consider the possibility that the congressional biases are preferable to the presidential biases. Those interests vested in existing programs think so.[16]

Finally, *in terms of political responsibility*, we can expect the continued abdication of that responsibility by the Congress. Theodore Lowi has provided a compelling analysis of the problem.[17] Elected officialdom delegates power to the bureaucracy and provides vague or nonexistent standards for the exercise of that power. Again the persistent theme appears. The bureaucracy can be out of control only because those charged with the responsibility to control it choose not to do so. Why do they so choose? Lowi sees the explanation in the acceptance of a public philosophy that holds that every problem should be bargained and brokered rather than settled according to a fixed rule of law. Perhaps. But why should this philosophy have such a hold on our decisionmakers? Lowi blames a generation of pluralist social scientists who laid the intellectual groundwork in the classrooms of academia. That is rather heavy stuff for a discipline that has been remarkably unconcerned with the conduct of political affairs. Still, ideas may take hold where we least expect.

Again, I think a more satisfactory explanation lies in the aims of individual Congressmen. They adopt (or appear to adopt) a public philosophy based on pluralist tenets simply because it rationalizes what their political self-interest dictates. Peter Woll makes the case nicely:

> A major reason for the power of the bureaucracy in policy formulation is the frequent lack of congressional incentives to adhere to the Schechter rule and establish explicit standards for administrative action. This is particularly true in the regulatory realm, an area involving political conflict that legislators often wish to avoid. Congress is always willing to deal *rhetorically* with problems requiring regulation and with the area of regulatory reform, but real decision on the part of the legislature will undoubtedly raise the ire of powerful pressure groups on one side or the other that are affected by government regulation.[18]

Why take political chances by setting detailed regulations that are sure to antagonize some political actor or another? Why not require an agency to do the dirty work and then step in to redress the grievances that result from its activities? Let the agency take the blame and the Congressman the credit. In the end everybody benefits. Congressmen successfully wage their campaigns for reelection. And while popularly vilified, bureaucrats get their rewards in the committee rooms of Congress.

To grant the bureaucracy the flexibility to deal with complex issues may seem to be the best way for an assembly of generalists to make public policy in a post-industrial society. But the entire justification of the committee-reciprocity system rests on the specialized expertise it purportedly fosters. Can we have it both ways? Can we afford to have it both ways?

Postwar political science has been slow to embrace proposals for change in our federal institutions. For example, prior to the internal fracturing of the congressional seniority system in the early 1970s, professional students of Congress were probably more united in defense of that system than any other group in the population, save perhaps old Congressmen. And today, campaign "reform" proposals are far more controversial within our ranks than among the informed public. Radicals in our midst charge us with reactionary defense of the existing system, whether as an unconscious by-product of concern with scientific standards, or as a conscious result of more sinister motives. Such theories are hardly necessary to explain the anti-reform bias of our discipline. History provides us with a distressingly long list of reforms that have failed to solve the intended problems, created new ones, and produced unanticipated side effects. Our hesitancy to support reform reflects our uncertainty about the eventual consequences; perhaps the devil that we know is better than the one we don't know.

Earlier I expressed some skepticism about the likely consequences of such currently fashionable proposals as zero-based budgeting and sunset laws. My skepticism in no way implies approval of the existing situation. In fact, I rather like both ideas; surely they are better than nothing. My doubts have to do with their probable effects, which I suspect will be marginal rather than major.

If we really want to work for coordinated control of the bureaucracy, we should be prepared to think big. For example, if it were possible to make one change in our federal institutions I would suggest that we consider replacing the single-member district system with a list system of proportional representation, treating the entire country as a single district. In every election each party would put up a list with a presidential and vice-presidential candidate, 100 senatorial candidates and 435 candidates for the House. Citizens would cast a single vote for the party of their choice. If one party got 55 percent of the vote, it would get the Presidency, the first 55 candidates on its senatorial list, and the first 229 candidates on its House list. One effect of such a reform, of course, would be to being the goals of Presidents and Congressmen into closer agreement. To a much greater extent than now, both presidential and congressional candidates would depend for election and reelection on the party's national record compiled over the same period of time.

Of course, so major a change in the electoral rule is politically improbable and constitutionally almost impossible. Additionally, it might create a multiparty system and numerous other by-products. Changing the electoral system is probably the least likely and most risky of the conceivable alternatives.

A less radical means of bringing congressional and presidential incentives into closer agreement would be to superimpose a responsible party system on the existing electoral structure. I am familiar with the reasons why such a system would not be "good" for the United States.[19] I only remind the doubters that we approximated such a system in the last years of the nineteenth century and first years of the twentieth. Can it be demonstrated that the country is governed better today than it was then?

I do not have the slightest hope that we could bring about a resurgence of responsible party government. Party bonds in the electorate are progressively weakening, an irreversible trend in the view of some scholars.[20] And candidates increasingly have divorced themselves from party organizations, an option that owes its attractiveness at least in part to the existence of decentralized control of the bureaucracy.[21] Advocating a responsible party system at this time is akin to advocating a strengthening of the Presidency—which is another possibility we might consider.

Who has the incentives to exercise coordinated control of the bureaucracy? The President. Ergo, to increase such control we should consider ways to strengthen his hand vis-à-vis the Congress. Scholars of the Presidency are much like French generals in their capacity to overlearn the lessons of history. After working under Franklin Roosevelt they spent two decades expounding the virtues of strengthening the Presidency. Now, following the tragedy of Vietnam, the revelations of Watergate, and precedents for those excesses, everyone sees great danger in a strong Presidency.[22] A bit more intellectual even-handedness would be desirable.

At any rate, given recent history and the attitudes formed in reaction to it, advocates of a stronger Presidency are unlikely to meet with much success. I find it difficult even to sketch the lines along which the Presidency might be strengthened. Congress will not give up its existing powers. Thus, if we strengthen the ties between the Presidency and the bureaucracy, we are more likely to produce stalemate than coordinated control. Recall, too, the fundamental asymmetry: to achieve his goals the President must take positive action, whereas Congressmen can do well enough by reacting and blocking.

Finally, we have the unlikely alternative of strengthening the Congress, strengthening it as an insitution, not as an agglomeration of four hundred odd subcommittees and committees, amorphous parties, and weak institutional leaders. The bureaucracy is subject to decentralized control because the Congress itself is so decentralized. Increasingly, the individual members can achieve their primary goals independently of, even in opposition to, the ends for which the institution was created. As Richard Fenno wryly notes, we see candidates running for Congress by running against Congress.[23] What can we do to harmonize the desires of the individual members for reelection and the integrity of the institution as a democratic, policymaking assembly?

The trick involves making the fate of individual members more dependent on institutional performance and less dependent on their personal efforts.[24] One possible change would be to assign members to committees randomly, for a maximum tenure of four years.[25] Such an innovation would curb the present practice of allowing Congressmen proportionately greater influence in matters of special concern to their own districts. It should reduce the number of policies and programs that exploit a large part of the country (consumers, for example) for the benefit of narrowly based interests (shoe manufacturers, for example). Less able to play the role of district ombudsman, the Congressman would have little alternative to playing the role of national legislator. He could only hope that if his colleagues did the same, they all might come out all right. Of course, we would have to sacrifice the system of specialization that now exists, but I regard that as a fair price to pay.

In the past a great deal of imagination has gone into proposals for the reform of Congress. I hope that imagination still exists. For in the final analysis an out-of-control bureaucracy reflects an out-of-control Congress. We might just as well avoid preoccupation with the symptoms and focus directly on the cause.

II/Points of Conflict • 140

Notes

[1] Stephen Hess, *Organizing the Presidency* (Washington, D.C.: Brookings Institution, 1976).

[2] Peter Woll, *American Bureaucracy*, 2nd ed. (New York: W.W. Norton, 1977).

[3] Samuel Huntington, "Congressional Responses to the Twentieth Century," in *The Congress and America's Future*, ed. David Truman (Englewood Cliffs, N.J.: Prentice-Hall, 1965), pp. 5-31.

[4] Woll (*American Bureaucracy*) makes this point very cogently in chapter 4 and passim.

[5] This conclusion is the basic thrust of Harold Seidman's analysis in *Politics, Position, and Power: The Dynamics of Federal Organization* (New York: Oxford University Press, 1975).

[6] Presumably, too, the serious President would instruct his people to look very hard at entitlement programs, existing and proposed. An uncontrollable budget is hardly a necessary feature of reality.

[7] Kenneth Shepsle, *The Giant Jigsaw Puzzle: Democratic Committee Assignments in the House of Representatives* (Chicago: University of Chicago Press, 1978).

[8] Classic discussions of reciprocity are found in Donald Matthews, *U.S. Senators and Their World* (Chapel Hill: University of North Carolina Press, 1960), pp. 99-101; and Richard Fenno, *The Power of the Purse* (Boston: Little, Brown and Co., 1966), chapter 4.

[9] No lover of Senators, Woodrow Wilson once remarked that "The Senators of the United States have no use for their heads except as a knot to keep their bodies from unraveling." Ironically, Wilson's nemesis, Henry Cabot Lodge, is one of the few twentieth-century Senators whose names are relatively familiar outside the ranks of professional historians.

[10] Albert Cover and David Mayhew, "Congressional Dynamics and the Decline of Competitive Congressional Elections," in *Congress Reconsidered*, ed. Lawrence Dodd and Bruce Oppenheimer (New York: Praeger, 1977).

[11] Morris P. Fiorina, *Congress—Keystone of the Washington Establishment* (New Haven: Yale University Press, 1977).

[12] Fenno, *Power of the Purse*; Aaron Wildavsky, *The Politics of the Budgetary Process*, 2nd ed. (Boston: Little, Brown and Co., 1974).

[13] This statement should be understood as an interpretation, not an uncontested fact. For an elaboration of the interpretation see Fiorina, *op. cit.*, chapters 1 and 7. For a more comprehensive interpretation see Lawrence Dodd, "Congress and the Quest for Power," in *Congress Reconsidered*, ed. Dodd and Oppenheimer.

[14] Thomas Cronin, *The State of the Presidency* (Boston: Little, Brown and Co., 1975), chapter 7.

[15] I am not really contradicting Huntington with this argument. Huntington claims that in a world in which the legislative initiative has passed to the President, Congress can show its power as an *institution* only by acting negatively—by frustrating presidential proposals. In contrast I am claiming that Congressmen can achieve their *personal* goals by acting negatively. The crucial point is that the personal goals of Congressmen bear a rather tenuous relation to the constitutional purpose of Congress. In this connection see also Dodd, "Congress and the Quest for Power."

[16] Perhaps it is time to reexamine the prevailing view of the 1960s that the President was the representative of all the people, the sole custodian of the national interest. Congress on the other hand was considered the stronghold of declining interests: small towns, rural backwaters, the South. For this reason, we were told, the Presidency was a more liberal institution than the Congress (*cf.* James MacGregor Burns, *The Deadlock of Democracy* [Englewood Cliffs, N.J.: Prentice-Hall, 1963], *passim*).

Today one could write that the President remains the sole representative of the national interest, and that the Congress remains the stronghold of declining interests: the cities, the Northeast, and so on. That is why the Presidency is a more conservative institution than the Congress. The point is fairly obvious. One must be exceedingly careful when talking about the policy biases of the President and the Congress: institutional biases must be distinguished from those that arise from ephemeral constellations of political forces.

[17] Theodore Lowi, *The End of Liberalism* (New York: W.W. Norton, 1969).

[18] Woll, *American Bureaucracy*, p. 173.

[19] For example, Julius Turner, "Responsible Parties: A Dissent from the Floor," *American Political Science Review* 45 (1951): 143-52.

[20] Walter Dean Burnham, "Revitalization and Decay: Looking Toward the Third Century of American Electoral Politics," *Journal of Politics* 38 (1976): 146-72.

[21] Fiorina, *Washington Establishment, passim.*

[22] For a critical analysis of scholarly writing, see William G. Andrews, "The Presidency, Congress and Constitutional Theory" (Unpublished paper delivered at

II/Points of Conflict • 142

the American Political Science Association, Chicago, 1971). Andrews takes note of the intellectual about-faces occurring even before Watergate. Since then, Watergate recantations have been running at flood tide.

[23] Richard Fenno, "If, As Ralph Nader Says, Congress Is 'The Broken Branch,' How Come We Love Congressmen so Much?" in *Congress in Change*, ed. Norman Ornstein (New York: Praeger, 1975), pp. 277-87.

[24] Recall that national surveys typically find that one-half to two-thirds of the population approve of the performance of their Congressmen, whereas only one-fifth to one-third approve of the performance of Congress. The perception of a divergence between individual and collective performance is precisely the problem, although incumbent Congressmen understandably wish to maintain that divergent perception.

[25] *See* Michael Nelson, "How to Break the Ties that Bind Congress to the Lobbyists and Agencies," *Washington Monthly* (December 1976): 36-38.

Discussion

LOUIS FISHER: I don't know whether Allen Schick would agree, but I find the new budget process, which was supposed to encourage Congress to involve itself more, to give more legislators an opportunity to participate, and thus to open up the budget process, a lot harder to follow than the old one. I find the opportunity for misconceptions greater. I find the physical burden of following it much heavier. There are many new actors and many new committees, and one needs sophistication to understand it.

From my own observations, however, I would credit the process with better educating the members to understand the relations between the budget and the economy, the relation between budget deficits and inflation, and the relations among unemployment, inflation, and the credit market. To give an example, several years ago, Secretary of the Treasury Simon, concerned that Congress was voting large budget deficits, came up with a "crowding out" thesis: if Congress tried to borrow too much from the Treasury, the effect would be to crowd out corporations wanting to invest or private individuals wanting to buy homes; the private credit market would be thrown into chaos and a strain would be put on it that it could not bear.

Here the process came into play quite well. The budget committees held hearings. They had bankers come in, economists come in, various people come in testifying that there would not be any crowding out. Indeed there was not. And the Congress—facing the Administration on a very technical topic, where expertise was at a premium—had the day. After a year the Congress could say that its prediction and understanding of the budget and economy were superior to those of the Administration.

On the other hand, the debate on priorities which was promised by the Budget Act has not materialized. Moreover, I find that Congress still exhibits some of its traditional weaknesses—that is, lack of an economic game plan, lack of will, lack of an institutional purpose.

Mr. Schick states that the 1921 Budget and Accounting Act's "open purpose was to transfer the money power of government from legislative to executive hands." I have a different impression of that history. I think those who looked to the British system failed in 1921; Congress decisively rejected that model. What the 1921 Act did was not to transfer the money power from legislative to executive hands, but to place upon the President the responsibility of submitting a budget. In that sense, and in that sense only, did it create an executive budget, for after the submission of the budget by the President, it became a legislative budget. Congress was free to amend that budget in committee or on the floor, up or down, exactly as it wanted to. Thus, I don't think the 1921 Act envisioned any particular transfer of money power from legislative to executive hands. The President's budget from 1921 on has been simply a recommendation and has no legal status at all. Congress, through its actions in voting funds and making bills into public law, has the final voice.

I agree with Allen Schick that Congress, in passing the Impoundment Act, did not want to give the President a "second chance." He could veto an appropriation if he wanted to—that is a constitutional option; but once an appropriation became public law, the assumption was that Congress had made up its mind on priorities and that the administrators were supposed to carry it out.

As impoundment provisions worked out, however—particularly under President Ford—the President and his staff regularly looked at the amount Congress had added to the President's budget— the so-called "add-on" amount—and instead of administering it and

Discussion • 145

executing it they sent it back to Congress the second time in the form of a deferral or a rescission. Therefore, the Impoundment Act, supposedly a restriction on presidential power, actually conferred on the President a power he never had before, which is certainly not what was intended. Everyone, at this point, is too scared to open up the package, worrying that what might come out of amendments would be worse that what we have now. It is not a happy situation.

Let me turn now to the paper by Morris Fiorina. It is possible to misread it, but I do find throughout the paper an anti-Congress bias, which I don't think stands up very well. Let me point to some specifics. First, there is a statement that "Congressmen are increasingly deemphasizing their role as formulators of national policies." Other political scientists I read say that members, particularly newer ones, are *more* interested in national policy and big questions. I don't know what the answer is, but this seems to be one of several assertions without any supporting evidence.

In the previous session several people talked about the probable return of a strong Presidency. I too think we are going in that direction, and I think we are tempted to turn back to the views we had in the 1950s and 1960s about the incompetent Congress. But I don't think those evaluations and criticisms of the 1950s and 1960s hold up well today. Congress, with all its shortcomings, can point to improvements.

Mr. Fiorina's paper, I think, presumes that the President supports efficient, "less bureaucratic" efforts that will allow greater individual freedom of choice, while Congress supports inefficiency, heavy-handed bureaucracy, and governmental intrusion into the lives of citizens. That, I think, comes closer to Huntington's thesis of the mid-1960s. To me, the evidence since then doesn't support such a contention. I find that the description Huntington gave of Congress applies a lot better to the executive branch, particularly after the years of LBJ and Nixon.

Mr. Fiorina concedes that we should consider the possibility that congressional biases are preferable to presidential biases. Well and good. But I myself am more inclined to support Congress and its policymaking efforts, not at all because they are preferable—they may or may not be—but because I think congressional policymaking comes a lot closer to satisfying the constitutional system.

II/Points of Conflict

JAMES SUNDQUIST: The subject of this session and the two to come are points of conflict between the Congress and the Executive. I was reflecting on that, and it seems to me useful at this point to try to figure out why these points of conflict are so endemic in the system, why we've always had them, and why, it seems, nothing can be done about them.

As we were waiting to begin, I jotted down in a sentence or so what seemed to me the basic reason for the whole thing. But as I was listening to Professor Fiorina, I realized that he had stolen my point and made it; so what I am going to do is underline something he said and perhaps expand on it a bit.

The point is the simple but significant one that there is always going to be conflict because the President and the Congress are elected from different constituencies and hence are pulled in different directions. You may think it's the same constituency at first blush because they are both elected from the nation at large. But from the standpoint of the individual voter, when he votes for the President, that vote gives his view as to the direction the national policy ought to go.

Then he comes down to the Senator and the Congressman. There he is really voting for an ambassador and giving the ambassador instructions. He is not voting on how the Congress as a whole shall behave; he is voting on how one or two people, at most, shall behave.

When the election is over, the President, with a mandate from sixty million people, is going to be pointed in one direction, and the members of the Congress, when they arrive in Washington, are going to be pointed in 468 different directions, by that many different constituencies. Some of them take the same general direction as the President, but most of them, on most matters, will not.

None of them has been sent there to follow a leader; none of them has campaigned on the platform, "Send me to Washington, and I will support the President." Instead it's "I am going to Washington to be my own man or woman; I'm going to vote my convictions; I take pride in my independence; I am going to vote for the President when he's right and against him when he's wrong." That's the way the people want their Senators and Congressmen to behave. Since that's what they want, that's what they get, and the consequence is that there is always going to be conflict between the branches.

There are times, of course, when the President has such prestige in the country, that whether a Senator or Congressman supports a President actually does become an election issue. That was the case back in the 1930s when Roosevelt was riding high; if you were anti-New Deal, or if you hadn't supported the President, you could be made to suffer.

But those occasions are vary rare, and it really hasn't happened since that time. Even when Eisenhower was at the height of his popularity, there were no Republicans, to my recollection, who ran on the ground that they would support the President, right or wrong. The customary situation is a kind of double mandate. The Congress and the President are judged differently and are elected by different constituencies.

When I was listening to Allen Schick, I was thinking back to when the Budget and Accounting Act was passed in 1921. The sponsors of that Act used two arguments. One was quite explicit; it said, "we have to cut the government back down to size." We had the first billion-dollar budget, which was a shocker, and Congress was nervous about it. The sponsors of the act argued on the floor, "If we pass this act, the heat will be off us; we'll put it on the President; it will be up to him to come up with a budget, and he's the one who will have to cut it."

The other side of the question was a concern that Congress was giving up the power of the purse, a power that was fundamentally its responsibility. The response to that was, "Well, we'll still be ultimately responsible because we do have the last word; we'll take what the President sends up and then we'll act on it."

So, they were making dual arguments, which are, obviously, quite contradictory. One said the President would be responsible, and one said the Congress would be responsible. And yet, that's the way they were able to present the act when they got back home, and that's the way Congress has handled the budget ever since. The individual Senator or Congressman can be against the budget that emerges from the Congress in the aggregate; he can denounce it with scorn and vigor. At the same time he can be for the particulars that are in it—every one of them.

You can call it "buck passing," you can call it a "double standard," you can call it "irresponsibility," you can say the Congress is "trying to have it both ways"—and all of those terms are fairly accurate.

The President can't get away with that. He has to take a stand; he has to have his name on a budget; but the individual Congressman, when he goes home, doesn't have his name on that budget.

And they do get away with it. The polls have consistently shown that the people have a pretty low respect for Congress as a whole, less than they do for the President. On one poll the prestige of the Congress was down to 26 percent. On that basis, they should have all been turned out, or most of them. If the President were down to 26 percent, you can be sure that he wouldn't be reelected, but at the time when the Congress, as a whole, has a favorable image of 26 percent, the members all get reelected! What it shows, as Mr. Fiorina said, is that the people exempt their own Senator or Congressman from the judgment that they pass on the institution as a whole.

We heard Congressman Pickle say, "The people want less government." If the people really do want less government, then the Congressmen that have given them more government ought to be penalized, but you can be sure they won't be. Presidents may be penalized for that sort of thing, but Congressmen are not. I haven't looked at Congressman Pickle's record, but he's been there quite a long time, and I wonder how he explains what's been going on while he's been there. Clearly he's been able to dissociate himself in some manner from the record of the institution of which he's a part.

There's another closely related phenomenon. The President is judged by the behavior of Congress more than the members of Congress are judged by that behavior, because the President is held responsible for the ultimate outcome. The President is thus held responsible for what the Congress does. He is expected to manage and control Congress. Our strong and successful Presidents are indeed those who succeeded in managing and controlling the Congress; but if he fails to manage the Congress, the President is penalized while the members of Congress who were unmanageable and caused him the trouble are rewarded for having done so.

You can contrast this with parliamentary government, where the members of parliament run on the record of the government, which is their government. They are sent to parliament not as ambassadors, but to be part of the government.

Here our members of Congress can run against the record of their own party, their own President, their own government, and they do get away with it. It is this double standard of conduct, it seems to me, that lies at the root of the conflict. These are the tendencies that pull the Congress and the President constantly apart, that encourage each to be independent of the other. Thus we have a very fragmented, centrifugal system that we then criticize for not coming out with a coherent and unified product, even though it is exactly the kind of representation that we as voters want and vote for.

FRANCIS ROURKE: My comments will be addressed mainly to Professor Fiorina's paper because I am bored and intimidated by everything that Allen Schick says about budgeting, and I would not have the audacity to challenge what he says.

I agree with Professor Fiorina that the problem of controlling bureaucracy is not simply that bureaucracy is out of control. I think that during most of our experience bureaucracy has been, as he says, very much under control. I am inclined to disagree, however, with his assertion that the chief or sole source of control over bureaucracy is Congress. As we view the development and operation of bureaucratic organizations in America, we can see in both past and present three alternative kinds of control to which any particular bureaucracy may be subject.

The first kind of control, which good-government people and reformers of various stripes advocate, is what we may call *public control* of bureaucratic behavior. Now, the crucial word here is "public"—ambiguous though we all understand it to be. By public control over bureaucracy, what reformers have usually meant are institutional arrangements calculated to produce policies consistent with some widely held definition of the public interest, at least as that interest is construed by reform groups. Often these are policies that serve the long-run as opposed to the short-run interest of the community. Or they may be the policies that reflect the interest of all those affected enough or resourceful enough to have their interest taken into account when policy decisions are made.

Historically, efforts to establish this kind of reform-oriented public control over bureaucracy have met strong and obstinate resistance from two other kinds of control to which bureaucratic organizations can also be subject. One is the kind that Morris Fiorina has described in his paper. Here the powers of executive agencies are held hostage by some "outside" party—private organizations, business organizations, perhaps a congressional committee or a congressional committee chairman—on which or on whom the agency is dependent for the flow of resources necessary to sustain it. Agencies falling in this category can best be described as subject to *constituency control.* Such control is common in areas of domestic policy where agencies have discretionary authority over the disposition of benefits or resources that are important to powerful outside groups.

There are three kinds of agencies, I think, that are especially subject to such constituency capture. First are the clientele agencies like the Veterans' Administration or the Departments of Commerce and Labor, agencies that were intended at the very outset to be subservient to some outside constituency or clientele. Their subservience has been legitimated by the statutes under which they operate.

The second kind of entity subject to constituency control is the regulatory agency —the ICC, the FTC, etc.—whose tendency to be captured by the groups it is presumably created to regulate is legendary. Preventing such agencies from begin captured, I should note, is a primary and enduring problem of American public administration.

A third kind of agency subject to constituency control is that which deals with public works, such as the Corps of Engineers and the Bureau of Reclamation. Those agencies make decisions that are particularly important to politicians, including Congressmen, and to well-entrenched community interests. Flood control projects, public works facilities, dams, and so on have a direct influence on the reelection prospects of Congressmen.

All these agencies subject to constituency control are highly politicized. The technical standards by which the law assumes their decisions are guided are very difficult to maintain or enforce. Those standards are usually on the defensive in the operation of the agency, and the alliances and partnerships that can develop between agencies and outside constituencies sometimes attain the status of a covenant.

From the point of view of its critics, an agency falling within this constituency control category—a clientele, a regulatory, or a public works agency—is clearly not out of control. Indeed, its problem is that it is too well controlled by the groups that it serves or regulates—the partners with which it is joined. What reformers usually hope to do with agencies of this sort is to liberate them from the control or capture to which they are subject.

A third distinct category of agencies that must be taken into account in analyzing the problem of controlling bureaucracy are those that are essentially autonomous in character. Their policies are largely directed and determined by the bureaucrats themselves—the professional career officials who man the agency. They are, in a sense, subject only to a system of *self-control* and self-direction.

This kind of agency has become increasingly prominent in the twentieth century and perhaps particularly since the Second World War. Its appearance reflects the development in post-industrial culture of forms of expertise that laymen have great difficulty understanding and to which, traditionally at least, they have been willing to defer. Whereas constituency bureaucracies tend to be captured by the groups they serve, autonomous bureaucracies, on the other hand, tend to capture their constituencies, to hold them in some kind of servitude, largely because they are highly professionalized and they tend to deal with largely defenseless or dependent clientele groups in society.

Three principal kinds of agencies seem to me to fall within this third category of the autonomous bureaucracy. First, there are the charismatic institutions that deal with national security, the CIA being the most notable example. They see themselves as immune from the ordinary processes of political control and subject only to the requirements of national security, as they interpret them. Richard Helms, the former CIA director, is a case in point. He felt privileged to lie in testifying before Congress—an instrument of political control to which the CIA is nominally a subject—because he obeyed a "higher" authority.

In the second category are the law enforcement agencies like the FBI and, to a lesser extent, the Drug Enforcement Administration. The FBI's harassment of Martin Luther King during the reign of J. Edgar Hoover is perhaps the prime example of the sort of independence an autonomous bureaucracy can acquire. That was an agency responsive, in its heyday, only to the idiosyncrasies of its director.

A third and very important category of autonomous organizations includes the scientific and technical agencies of government:

the National Science Foundation, the National Institute of Health, or the Federal Reserve Board. Such agencies are essentially insulated from effective outside control by the arcane nature of the disciplines of their professional employees.

In sum, I suggest, we have three alternative systems of control to which various sectors of American bureaucracy in different times and places are subject: first, a system of public control; second, a system of constituency control; and third, a system of self control on the part of autonomous organizations.

Much of the reform effort in recent times has been directed at increasing the scope and the strength of public control over bureaucracy, at least as the reformers have defined it. There are two important underlying trends in society that are helping to produce this pressure toward more public control and away from either constituency control or self-control on the part of autonomous bureaucracies. One is the increased ease with which citizens can be mobilized. Publics that were once thought to be phantom publics—like the consumer public, or the civil rights public, or the feminist public, or the environmental public—can now be quite effectively mobilized. One reason for this is that the expanded media of communications afford a means by which citizens can identify and share concern over issues. Some groups can now be mobilized for political action that were once thought impossible to mobilize. It can no longer be easily assumed that a citizens' group will be defeated in an eyeball-to-eyeball confrontation with a powerful producer interest. It is no longer certain, as it once was, that the oil lobby can necessarily impose its will on energy policy in the face of determined opposition by public-interest groups.

A second trend that strengthens the movement toward public control over bureaucracy is the erosion of faith in professional expertise, an erosion manifested in many ways, including the growth of malpractice suits in various fields like medicine, law, and—heaven forbid—even teaching. The loss of faith in expertise has many effects, but one of them is to weaken the position of autonomous bureaucracies dealing with scientific, technical, and national security matters, bureaucracies that have long traded on their positions as expert organizations.

My conclusion is that in assessing the strength of the three kinds of control over bureaucracy in American society—public control, constituency control, and self control—there is strong evidence that public control is today in a period of ascendency. The change is explained in part by certain reforms that have taken place in Congress, in part by the rise of public-interest groups, and in part by the growing role of new communications media in the American political system. The result is that the other two forms of control, namely constituency control and bureaucratic self-control, find themselves increasingly on the defensive.

ALLEN SCHICK: I want to begin with a comment by Mr. Sundquist. He spoke about Congress's hypocrisy in arranging for the President to bear the onus of the budget, while reserving for itself the final responsibility. Indeed that was the argument used by the Great Britainists—Woodrow Wilson, A.L. Lowell, Frank Goodnow, and others—in favor of a budget process. Congress adopted that argument lock, stock, and barrel. After all, that is what it means to have both an appropriations and a budget process, rather than one alone.

In spite of what Sundquist says, however, and in spite of a few contrary examples like the Clinch River and the Panama Canal, Presidents and Congress hardly ever fight. In fact, they get along amazingly well. It would seem to me they ought to fight more. They are set on two different electoral paths constitutionally, and the division of political labors deriving from those two different paths is such that one tends to see policy in the whole and the other seems to see it as specialized. I cannot escape the conclusion that those who think that Congress is in default in not controlling the bureaucracy are either ignoring or condemning the forms of specialized control, such as the legislative veto, which have been developed by Congress. It seems to me that if Congress and the President fight less, rather than more, it is because Congress is less specialized and more whole than we think it ought to be, and the Presidency is more specialized than it is credited with being.

Now a brief remark about Frank Rourke's typology. Frank made a very important point with regard to the topic for today. The same institutions that escape legislative control also escape executive control. The same institutions that seem to be successfully reined in by Congress are brought under executive restraint as well. There have to be factors and forces independent of the behavior of either

Congress or the Presidency to explain this parallelism.

One of those factors may be that the President is more specialized than we credit him with being and the Congress is more universalistic than we think. A second may well be the influence of interest groups. That would help explain the constituency rather than the presidential or legislative control, but if in fact we live in an interest-group society, then both Congress and the President are influenced and compromised by them.

Still a third factor may be the play of ideology upon the participants. You recall that Frank talked about three kinds of agencies. The public ones seem to be successfully controlled by Congress and the President; the constituency ones are controlled by the interest groups; and the bureaucratic ones are self-controlled. Those that are self-controlled are in possession of ideological benefits or advantages—the ideology of the "Fed," the ideology of the NSF, the ideology of J. Edgar Hoover. I've used the term "ideology," but we could use "mythology" equally well.

MORRIS FIORINA: I agree with and have little to say about the remarks by Mr. Sundquist and Mr. Rourke. I should like to take a few minutes, however, to respond to some of the things Louis Fisher said. First, I am accused of having an anti-Congress bias. Now, that obviously puts the audience on edge. Here is someone who is not an objective, dispassionate, open-minded social scientist; somebody we should thus be suspicious of. But, that is a game that anybody can play. I can just as easily accuse someone like Louis of being an apologist for the status quo any time I am accused of having an anti-Congress bias.

In fact, Louis comments that he really appreciates congressional policymaking because it is closer to the constitutional system than the kind of policymaking I envisaged. Larry Dodd has suggested that what exists today is not really what the founders had in mind when they set up the constitutional system. Whether that is right or wrong, one can still ask the question, "What is so sacred about that constitutional system?" Jefferson himself, in a line we often like to quote, talked about the necessity of changing our institutions to fit the requirements of our times.

Several of my observations were said to be contradictory, indeed more contradictory than they really are. For instance, take the question whether Congressmen are more interested in national issues and policy or in their ombudsman activities. It is perfectly possible for a Congressman within Congress to have a greater interest in national policy and yet in his election campaigns de-emphasize those interests and emphasize his ombudsman activities, "pork barrel" success, and so on. In fact, we could argue that the more Congressmen can run as ombudsmen, run on nonprogrammatic bases, the more flexibility they have in taking policy stands within the Congress. This increasing return to the ombudsman role is weakening the links of electoral accountability which bind Congressmen to their constituencies. But there is no necessary contradiction here; there is merely another disturbing development.

My remark that Congress generally supports programs of a New Deal cast, programs that emphasize bureaucratic growth, whereas Presidents emphasize more "efficient" kinds of policies, is, I think, perfectly valid. Mr. Fisher says he sees just the opposite. To use his terminology, I would say there is a strong tendency in the Congress to take programs that are redistributive or regulatory in nature and transform them into programs that are distributive. The model cities program is an example. The problem is that you often can't get purely redistributive programs through Congress because there aren't enough of them; they aren't located in enough congressional districts. So, you end by perverting the purpose of the program, dissipating the money by scattering the benefits around in enough districts so you can get the votes to pass it.

A President will support, say, a family assistance plan. Congressmen will have a tendency to favor something like a categorical grant from which they can get a little more credit out of the disbursement of funds. That's what I meant by the argument that Congress supports programs that are apparently more "bureaucratic."

FRANCIS ROURKE: I should like to ask Allen Shick and Louis Fisher whether they agree with Morris Fiorina when he says in his paper: "I think it is probably accurate to say that we are currently experiencing an increase in uncoordinated control and a decrease in coordinated control, as far as Congress is concerned."

My own argument or intuition on this would tend to be otherwise. I should think the creation of the Congressional Budget Office, the more vigorous performance by the General Accounting

Office of its oversight role, the new rules with respect to the selection of committee chairmen, and so forth—all those things would lead Congress in the opposite direction, toward more coordinated and less uncoordinated control.

ALLEN SCHICK: It seems to me that two things are happening simultaneously. Congress is tearing itself apart, and Congress is putting itself together. In my judgment, if one looked at the full sweep of the last decade, the tearing apart has been a much more powerful force than the putting together. Congress has torn down virtually every preexisting leadership structure—chairmanships, subcommittee chairmanships, closed meetings, and closed rules. Congress is more exposed than ever before to the play of interest groups.

There are a few ways in which Congress is trying to paste itself together, and the budget process is one. But I would say that over the last decade Congress has tried to perfect what Fiorina calls "uncoordinated forms of control." One such control is the legislative veto. It is a discrete action, limited to a particular sale of arms abroad, to a particular impoundment action, to a particular action or ruling of the Federal Election Commission, and so on. The weight of action thus far has been in favor of uncoordinated control rather than more coordinated control.

But what is most interesting is that both of these opposite tendencies are occurring simultaneously on the Hill.

MORRIS FIORINA: Since we have brought up the topic of the legislative veto and Congress's encroachment upon the Executive, I should like to draw some distinctions. One type of legislative veto pertains to agency rules and regulations. That type impinges upon the administrative rule-making process, which has a very elaborate hearing stage and notice stage, and falls under the Administrative Procedure Act. What I'm afraid of is that a handful of congressional staff people are going to make determinations on national policy matters. I see that as a poor development.

On the other hand, consider the legislative veto provisions of the War Powers Act, for example. If we didn't have in the War Powers Act a provision for a congressional resolution not subject to veto, then I think we would be back where we were in 1973, when each house had to muster a majority against the bombing in Cambodia. Even though there was a majority in each house, it wasn't enough because Nixon could veto the measure, and then you would need a two-thirds majority in each house to stop a presidential war. I don't think that fits any design in the Constitution. But the legislative veto of rules and regulations raises questions of the administrative process that do not arise with legislative vetoes in either the War Powers Act or the Impoundment Act.

FROM THE FLOOR: I am a little curious that you are so ready, if I understand you correctly, to accept the notion of a public interest, as somehow distinguished from a constituent interest.

Isn't it possible that these special public constituencies are really means by which the agency can insulate itself still further from Congress? That is, the agency cultivates those constituencies and then parades the constituency interests as the public interest?

FRANCIS ROURKE: Clearly the rise of public-interest groups and the role they play in the administrative process are not without their problems. When they are controlled by a narrow group, they can become special interests of their own.

But it is not necessarily true that every time an agency is captured by a particular constituency the result is bad. We expect certain specialized groups to receive the continuing and close concern of the government and to have an agency especially devoted to promoting their interest. The agencies, for example, that deal with handicapped persons are largely under the control of organizations representing those groups, and no one would argue that that is necessarily against the public interest. Certain kinds of interest representation in society are desirable, and democratic, and should not be disparaged or interfered with.

I would also argue that not all autonomous administrative organizations are bad. In some fields of activity it's important for government to have reliable data and statistics, so I approve the independence of the Bureau of Labor Statistics and the Bureau of the Census and the Bureau of Standards. Autonomy for agencies of that sort, I think, is quite desirable.

ALLEN SCHICK: When we speak here of public interests—as if they were different from constituency interests—we are making a very profound judgment about the kind of political system we have. It seems to me that if we put these public interests under the microscope, we find only two or perhaps three characteristics that distinguish them from the others.

First, they tend to be third parties. Consumers are a constituency. People concerned about the environment are a constituency. They are—in the sense in which the term is used in law and elsewhere—third parties. They are the parties adversely affected by the government's policies; they are the disadvantaged parties. So, when we speak of endowing these groups with an ability to influence the public policy process, including the agency decisions, we are simply giving them the capability that other constituencies have.

The second difference is that some of the public-interest organizations happen to be state and local governments. One of the truly significant changes in the course of a very short period of time is that state and local governments—counties, cities, regional governments and the like—have taken on virtually all the patterns of behavior which, in the past, we associated with clientele interest groups.

To vest them with this positive-sounding label "public interest," it seems to me, obscures the problem. If these governments now behave like constituency interests, what does it mean for federalism, what does it mean for representative government, what does it mean for local control, what does it mean for national control? These are profound questions.

III

Congress and the President in the Making of Policy

Overview: Bruce Miroff
   Papers: Robert A. Divine
          Sar A. Levitan
Discussion: John Brademus
          Wilbur Cohen
          David E. Price
         Walt W. Rostow

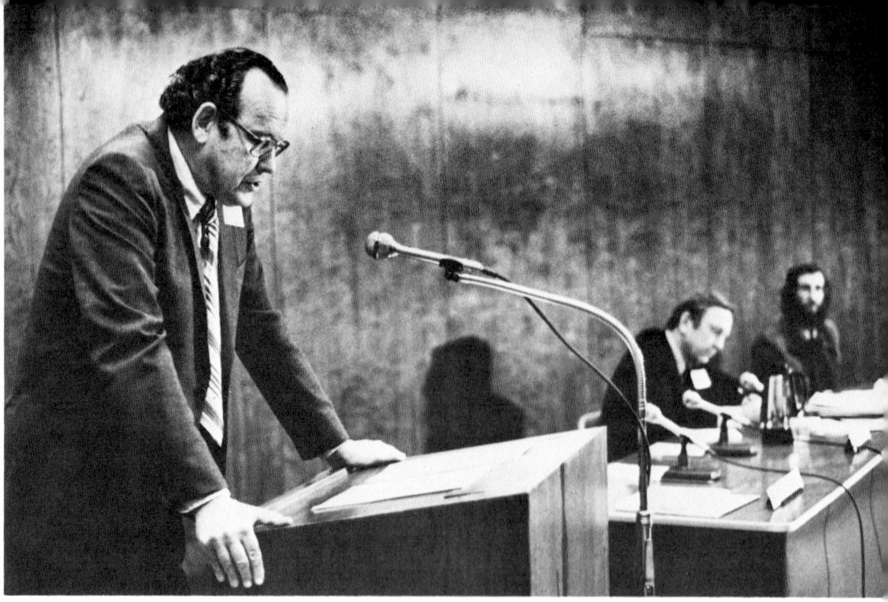
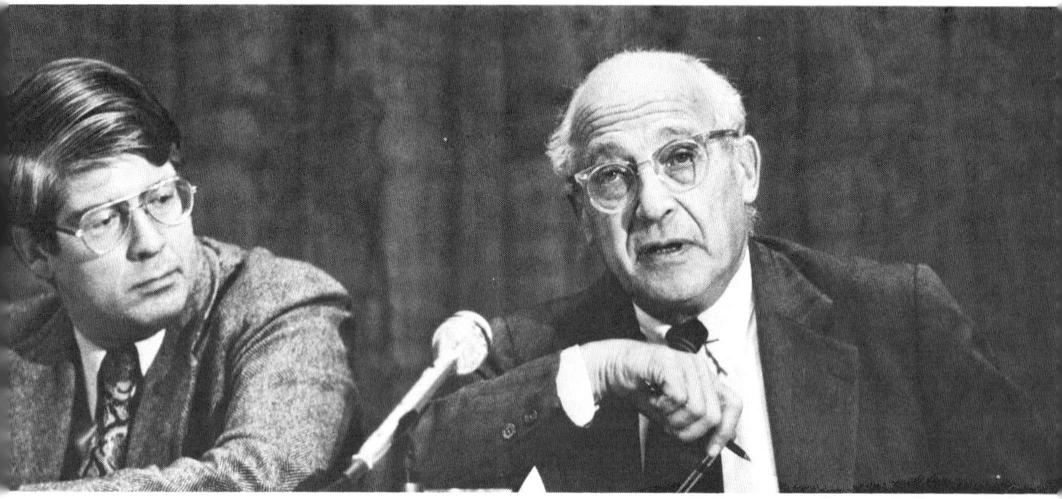
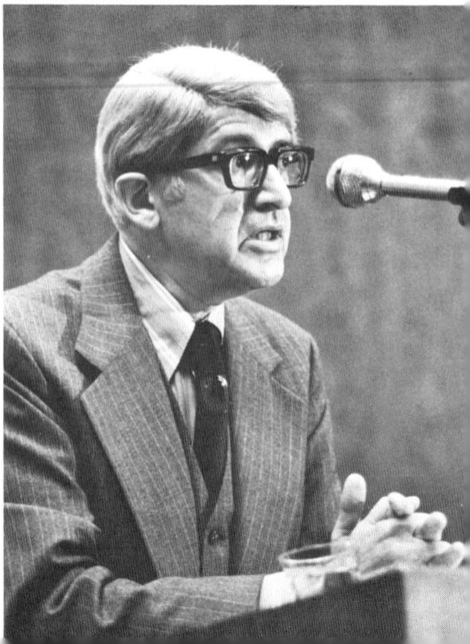

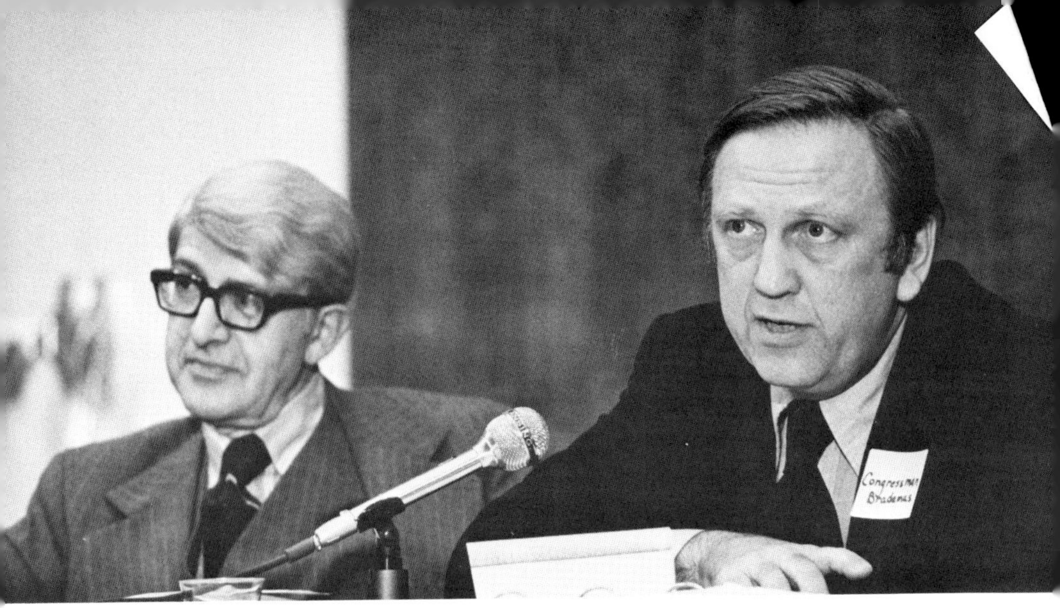
Congressman
Brademas

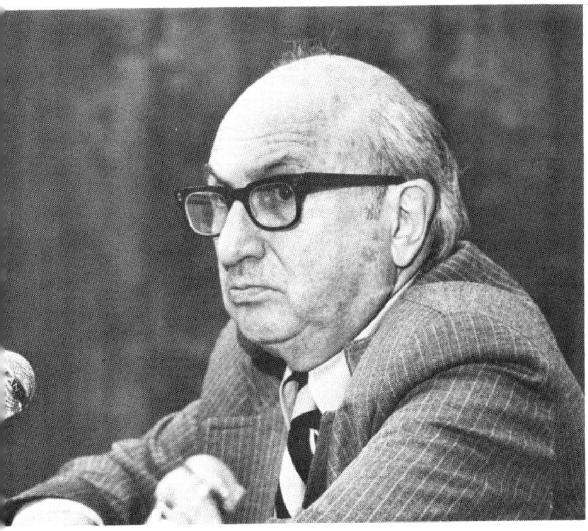

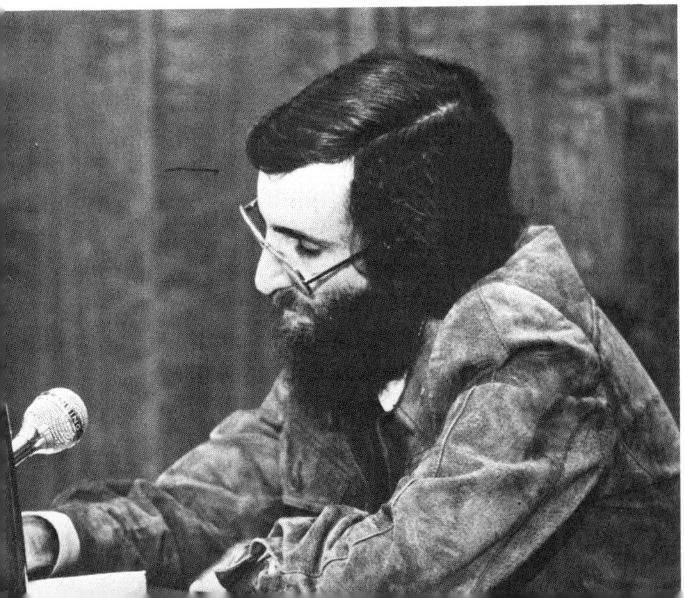

Overview

Bruce Miroff

Bruce Miroff formerly taught at The University of Texas at Austin and is now Assistant Professor of Political Science at the State University of New York, Albany.

I should like to begin by looking at some of the ways in which people have evaluated the conflict between Congress and the President over the past ten years or so. For a good while most political scientists have felt fairly confident that they had a good handle on the relative power of the Presidency and Congress in the twin arenas of domestic and foreign policy.

Ten years ago in a very influential article, Aaron Wildavsky argued that it was necessary to talk about two Presidencies, one being a foreign- and military-policy Presidency and the other a domestic-policy Presidency. Wildavsky looked at presidential success in getting presidential proposals through Congress over a fifteen-year period ending in the mid-1960s. He found that while Presidents got their way about 70 percent of the time in foreign and military matters, they were successful in domestic affairs only 40 percent of the time.

He argued further that this discrepancy could be explained by certain institutional and structural factors. Organized groups, for example, tended to be much weaker when it came to foreign policy than on most domestic policies. And public opinion tended to be more deferential to the President in foreign matters than in domestic matters. The Presidency was very different vis-à-vis Congress in foreign policy from what it was in domestic policy. In foreign policy the Presidency stood out; it towered over other institutions. In domestic policy it clearly did not. This argument has been very influential, and in the past decade it has been very common to argue that presidential power is a very different question in foreign and in domestic policy.

In the aftermath of Watergate many political scientists insisted that we should not overreact to the problems it represented. It was often said that while it might be true that the Presidency had become too powerful in foreign matters and might need certain new restraints placed upon it, that was not true in domestic policy. If anything, the Presidency tended to be too weak in domestic policy. The Wildavsky thesis had become almost a commonplace, even in the great reassessments that followed Watergate.

On the other hand, a number of events of the past decade raised problems in the application of that thesis. It made sense to talk of recurrent presidential frustrations with Congress if one were looking at the Truman record or even at the Kennedy record, but an argument about the President's weakness in relation to Congress scarcely helps explain the remarkable achievements of the Johnson Administration or for that matter President Nixon's very forceful use of weapons like the veto and impoundment.

Or to turn to foreign policy, while it is not difficult to talk about presidential domination over foreign policy in the period from Truman through Lyndon Johnson, can we make the same argument about the Ford and Carter presidencies? Is Congress really that receptive and really that much of a doormat when it comes to foreign policy issues? In other words, is there anything inherent in the structure of the Presidency that dictates a dominance in foreign but not domestic policy, or is that view itself historically conditioned? Moreover, even if we can dispose of that problem, what do we do with the even more tangled one posed when domestic and foreign issues are inextricably intertwined? There are myriads of these; one thinks of energy as being one of the most clear and pertinent examples for these days.

My point is that while most political scientists thought they had arrived at a useful understanding—or perhaps at one of those enduring truths—about the Presidency, events have made it difficult to hold to that accepted explanation any more. We can no longer be content with the simple answer that the Presidency is strong here and weak there. The answers are far more elusive, and the questions must be much more complex. For example, when and how *can* Congress play an effective role in foreign policy? Or under what historical and political conditions do Presidents exercise considerable influence in domestic policy? Under what conditions are they able to bring about significant kinds of policy innovations? Finally, are both Congress and the Presidency influenced primarily by personal and institutional factors, or are there broader political and economic, cultural and ideological forces that are even more basically determinative?

Congress and the President

The Struggle Over Foreign Policy

Robert A. Divine

Robert A. Divine is Professor of History at The University of Texas at Austin

The 1977-1978 debate over the Panama Canal Treaty is a vivid reminder of the inherent conflict between Congress and the President on foreign policy. Throughout the nation's history, treaties have been a major battleground in the struggle for control between the executive and legislative branches of government. As early as the 1790s, President George Washington and the Senate locked horns over Jay's Treaty—an effort to avoid war with England by sacrificing American rights on the high seas. After stormy debate, Washington prevailed by the narrowest of margins, twenty to ten, the bare two-thirds that the Constitution requires for ratification. A century later, the acquisition of the Philippines in the treaty ending the Spanish-American War was the occasion for an equally heated Senate debate, and again the vote was close, with the McKinley Administration prevailing, fifty-seven to twenty-seven, one more than the necessary two-thirds. And we all recall the momentous debate over the Treaty of Versailles in 1919, when the Battalion of Death, led by William Borah, joined with the more moderate Republicans under Henry Cabot Lodge to reject Wilson's League of Nations. The Great Betrayal, as one historian labeled it, occurred when the treaty failed of approval by a margin of seven votes.[1]

Dramatic as these instances are, they should not obscure the fact that the conflict between the two branches over foreign policy is not confined to the ratification process. In recent American experience, there has been a constant struggle between the Legislature and the Executive for dominance in foreign policy. The President has usually had the upper hand, but at times Congress has been able to impose its will.

In the pages to follow, I wish to examine several major episodes in this continuing tug-of-war, beginning with the period just before the Second World War and coming down to the turbulent decade of the 1960s. This survey should help illuminate such themes as the nature of the struggle, the advantages and liabilities of such conflict, the role of partisanship, and the desirability of bipartisanship in the conduct of foreign policy.

I

The neutrality legislation of the 1930s provides a useful introduction to the story of executive-legislative contest over foreign policy. Here is a case in which Congress played the dominant role—taking the intiative with legislation designed to curb executive authority in the vital area of peace or war.

The neutrality legislation was largely a reaction to the experience of the United States during the First World War. The main source was the isolationists' belief that American participation in the Great War had been a tragic mistake, and they vowed that the nation should never again participate in a general European conflict. They blamed President Woodrow Wilson, claiming that the unneutral trade he permitted with the Allies—the selling of arms and munitions, the granting of loans, the defense of American travel on British ships like the *Lusitania*—had compelled Germany to resort to unrestricted submarine warfare, which in turn led to American entry into the conflict. The isolationists' solution was relatively simple: prevent a future President from practicing such a one-sided neutrality. Led by Senator Gerald Nye of North Dakota, they introduced a series of bills in 1935 prohibiting American citizens from selling arms to belligerents, loaning money to governments at war, or traveling on belligerent passenger ships.

At the same time, internationalists wanted a very different form of neutrality. Advocates of collective security claimed that traditional neutrality was immoral—in future wars, the United States should not stand by impartially, but rather should cooperate with the League of Nations in applying embargoes on aggressor nations. The State Department thus favored neutrality legislation that would grant the Executive wide authority to impose restrictions on trade with countries the League found guilty of aggression. Thus in contrast to the isolationists, who wanted impartial legislation designed to insulate the United States from foreign wars, the internationalists favored broad presidential discretion.

The issue came to a head in August 1935. Senator Nye and his colleagues introduced a series of bills designed to prevent the sale of arms or the granting of loans to any country at war, regardless of the justice of its cause. The State Department countered with draft legislation that would give the President broad discretion and enable him to apply embargoes in a discriminatory fashion. When the Senate Foreign Relations Committee tried to work out a compromise, Senator Nye began a filibuster that threatened a series of important New Deal measures then pending before the Senate. The State Department wanted FDR to fight for its version, but Senator Key Pittman, chairman of the Foreign Relations Committee, warned a presidential aide that if Roosevelt insisted on such a measure, "he will be licked sure as hell." The President quickly gave way, and in late August Congress passed the first neutrality act; the main feature was an impartial embargo on the sale of arms to all belligerents.[2]

Why did Roosevelt give way? The usual explanation is the parliamentary situation. A series of vital domestic measures was awaiting Senate action—FDR needed to end the filibuster that threatened the Second New Deal. Moreover, he could ill afford to antagonize isolationist Senators like Gerald Nye and George Norris who supported many of his progressive domestic measures. Nor did the international situation dictate a negative response. The only war in sight in 1935 was in Africa, where Mussolini was preparing to invade Ethiopia. Since Haile Selassie lacked both the funds and the shipping to import arms from the United States, an impartial arms embargo would not hurt the victim of aggression. And finally, it is worth noting that Roosevelt, unlike the State Department, was not strongly opposed to the idea of impartial neutrality legislation. He felt that Wilson had been too sympathetic to the Allies during the World War and he had in fact encouraged Nye to introduce his measures. The President did want some measure of discretion, but he finally agreed to sign the legislation when its effectiveness was limited to a six-month period.

For the next two years, Congress and the President worked on ironing out their differences on permanent neutrality legislation. Neither side gained all it wanted. Roosevelt kept insisting on a broad grant of authority, but Congress refused to give him the discretionary powers he wanted. Nye and his associates hoped to extend the embargo beyond arms to cover raw materials like cotton, petroleum, and copper which could be as vital as weapons to a belligerent. They talked about limiting wartime trade in such materials to prewar levels, but they could not work out an acceptable formula. What they steadily refused to consider, however, was a total embargo on all trade with belligerents. Such a measure would have been the logical fulfillment of their isolationist philosophy, but it would also have meant an enormous economic sacrifice for the United Sttaes. In the midst of the Depression, even the staunchest isolationists were unwilling to place peace above profits.

The permanent neutrality act, finally adopted in 1937, simply embodied Nye's original prohibitions—an impartial arms embargo, a ban on loans to belligerents, and a ban against Americans' travelling on ships of nations at war. Designed to keep America out of the next war, the act was never given a chance. Two months after the outbreak of the Second World War, the President persuaded the Congress to repeal the arms embargo, and in the remaining two years before Pearl Harbor, the Executive steadily chipped away at the neutrality edifice, evading the loan ban with lend-lease in March 1941, and then even winning congressional approval to send American merchant ships into combat zones in November, only a month before we entered the war.

The traditional view of the neutrality legislation is to assert that it proves the danger of congressional initiative and domination over foreign policy.[3] The assumption behind this interpretation is that without the handicap of the neutrality law the United States could have cooperated with England and France in the 1930s and helped prevent the outbreak of the Second World War. I am not so sure. The neutrality legislation was but a symptom of a deeper public mood of isolation in the 1930s, a mood so pervasive that even Roosevelt shared it, or at least catered to it in public. It was the prevailing feeling that the United States ought to stay clear of

European entanglements, not the neutrality legislation, that blocked any meaningful American effort to prevent the outbreak of the war. When war finally did come, the legislation proved to be a very minor obstacle to cooperation with the Allies. Under Roosevelt's leadership, the United States abandoned rather than followed the guidelines set down by Congress in the mid-1930s. Impartial neutrality was not an experiment that failed—it was never given a fair trial.

Yet I think analysts are right when they point to the neutrality legislation as evidence of the danger in congressional initiative in foreign policy. It marked an attempt by Congress to apply a rigid formula to the conduct of diplomacy, to place the Executive within a straightjacket. The President, as Roosevelt realized, must have discretion in foreign policy; he must be able to respond to a constantly shifting international situation and to reorient American policy accordingly. Congress cannot foresee the future course of world events, and the imposition of congressional guidelines can only hamper the President in his efforts to protect and advance national interests.

II

A very different form of congressional-presidential relations developed during the Second World War and reached its zenith in the early stages of the Cold War—bipartisanship. Instead of conflict between the legislative and executive branches, the emphasis was placed on conciliation and cooperation. Patriotism was the primary motivation for this shift; during and after the war, the threat to national security, first from the Axis powers and then from the Soviet Union, called for an end to party quarrels over foreign policy and for a new spirit of unity between Congress and the Executive. Political realism was uppermost in the growth of bipartisanship. The Democrats were determined to avoid Wilson's fate at the end of the First World War. Secretary of State Cordell Hull began the effort to win over Republican Congressmen and Senators as early as 1942 when he asked GOP Senator Warren Austin to become a member of his Advisory Committee on Postwar Foreign Policy. President Roosevelt was more dubious about the bipartisanship approach, viewing all Republicans with deep suspicion; but Hull's views prevailed. In 1943, Republicans joined with Democrats in supporting the Fulbright and Connally resolutions concerning a future world organization, and a year later Hull worked out an agreement with John Foster Dulles, foreign policy adviser to GOP candidate Thomas Dewey, to keep the issue of the future United Nations out of the 1944 election.[4]

The Republicans cooperated in the bipartisan movement because it was in their political interest to do so. The war caused a massive public rejection of isolationism, and with it, a wholesale defeat for GOP Representatives and Senators associated with the prewar mood. Senator Arthur Vandenberg of Michigan realized the importance of reorienting Republic foreign policy from obstruction to cooperation, and he became the leading GOP figure in the new bipartisanship.[5] In a dramatic speech to the Senate in January 1945, Vandenberg announced his conversion to internationalism (he advocated "maximum American cooperation, consistent with legitimate American self-interest") in a thirty minute address in which he pleaded for "honest candor" no less than ten times. Roosevelt rewarded Vandenberg by appointing him to the American delegation to the San Francisco conference. The high point of the new GOP tactics came six months later when the Senate voted 89 to 2 to ratify the United Nations Charter.[6]

Bipartisanship did not end with the defeat of Germany and Japan. It reached its climax in the late 1940s, when the United States adopted the policy of containment to meet the postwar Soviet challenge in Europe. Once again the leading figures in the GOP were Vandenberg and Dulles. The Michigan Senator, in contrast to Ohio's Robert Taft, cooperated in all the major foreign policy decisions from the Truman Doctrine through the formation of NATO. It was Vandenberg who advised Harry Truman to go public during the Greek crisis of 1947, telling him that he should "scare hell out of the American people," advice that the President followed in the March 12 address to Congress setting forth the Truman Doctrine for the global containment of communism. It was Vandenberg who authored the resolution that laid the groundwork for NATO. His role in the framing of the containment policy was indispensable— without his cooperation, it would have been impossible for the Truman Administration to secure the approval of the Republican 80th Congress for the Truman Doctrine, the Marshall Plan, and the NATO Treaty.[7]

John Foster Dulles played an equally vital role in the bipartisan consensus. In 1948, he served once again as Dewey's foreign policy adviser during a presidential election campaign. At the outset, Dewey indicated a desire to attack the Democrats on foreign policy—for their failure to secure access rights to Berlin, for their wartime concessions to the Soviets at Yalta and Potsdam, and for their weak stance on China. But the Soviet imposition of a total land blockade on Berlin in June 1948 produced a major crisis that led Dewey to reconsider. Under-Secretary of State Robert Lovett met regularly with Dulles in June and July to keep the Republican camp fully informed on the deepening crisis and to urge a policy of restraint. At Dulles's urging, Dewey finally decided not to attack the Administration on the Berlin issue, but instead to stand solidly behind Truman's decision to use the airlift to maintain the Western position in the beleaguered German city. For the next six months, Dewey refrained from attacking the Truman Administration's foreign policy while the Berlin crisis continued unabated. In the fall, Dulles went to Paris with Secretary of State George Marshall to attend a UN meeting on Berlin. He sent back a series of telegrams to Dewey's campaign train, urging the candidate to reaffirm his support for the Administration's stand in Berlin. It was vital, he told Dewey, that the Soviets "not be misled into prolonging the Berlin blockade on the theory that [the] result of [the] election will bring about any weakening of U.S. determination."[8]

Dewey followed Dulles's advice and lost the election. Truman's surprising victory in 1948 has been attributed to many factors—the winner's whistle-stop campaign and give 'em hell oratory, Dewey's complacency and lack of appeal, declining farm prices through the fall, and above all, the enduring strength of the New Deal coalition—but as important as any of these was the Republican failure to challenge the Democrats on foreign policy issues. The Cold War was at its height in 1948. It was the single most important issue confronting the American electorate, yet the Republicans let it go by default to the Democrats. In the agonizing reappraisal that took place afterwards within the GOP, many observers noted this omission. Senator Karl Mundt commented on the failure of the Republicans "to focus attention on the mistakes of Yalta and Potsdam," while Allen Dulles wrote that Dewey's greatest mistake "was the failure to attack the Democrat's record more vigorously."[9] The

Republicans took this lesson to heart: they abandoned bipartisanship after 1948, blaming the Democrats for the loss of China and reciting the litany of Teheran, Yalta, and Potsdam in a bitter attack on Democratic appeasement of the Soviet Union. The GOP, they promised in 1952, would repudiate "the negative, futile and immoral policy of 'containment' which abandons countless human beings to a despotism and godless terrorism," and replace it with a dynamic policy of liberation of the captive peoples of Eastern Europe.[10]

Bipartisanship clearly did not serve the Republicans well. But the more important question is how well it served the nation. The traditional answer has been to praise bipartisanship, to give Vandenberg and Dulles credit for helping Truman, Marshall, and Acheson devise and carry out the policy of containment. No one is more glowing in his praise than Dean Acheson. In *Present at the Creation*, he takes great pride in telling how he manipulated Vandenberg. The Republican Senator would usually oppose a State Department initiative, Acheson recalls. But then when he was permitted to make a change in the proposal, usually a small one of little consequence, Vandenberg would suddenly become the measure's strongest supporter and fight for its adoption in Congress. Thus the trick, according to Acheson, was simply to throw the dog his bone and then watch him go to work. For Acheson, who had utter disdain for Congress ("One can learn its uninformed opinion . . . but to devise a joint approach . . . is not within the range of normally available time and people," he once wrote), bipartisanship was a godsend—a way around the congressional roadblock.[11]

The Truman Administration thus found bipartisan cooperation essential. Yet the larger question remains unanswered. Was it wise for the United States to formulate such vital foreign policy steps as the Truman Doctrine and the Marshall Plan without any vigorous debate? Did it really serve the national interest to raise diplomatic issues above the partisan dialogue? Is it really best to spare the American people the agonizing choices involved in foreign policy during a presidential election, as Dewey did in 1948?

Revisionist historians would answer in the negative. They have lionized such curious figures as Henry Wallace and Robert Taft in their attacks on the containment policy.[12] Although they frequently go overboard in their criticism, they have a valid point. If containment were a wise policy for the nation, surely it would have been best to subject it to the full heat of partisan debate. One virtue of the two-party system is that it encourages a full and free discussion of all major presidential actions. Yet the Congress approved of the Truman Doctrine with all its global implications with hardly a murmur of dissent, and the Senate ratified the NATO treaties without the full political debate such a momentous step required. The bipartisanship that Vandenberg and Dulles championed short-circuited the democratic process and prevented the American people from hearing all the arguments and weighing all the alternatives. It led to the creation of a Cold War consensus; for the next twenty years, there would be little meaningful debate over the goals of foreign policy. Blind dedication to the Cold War objective of halting communist expansion, enshrined in such rhetoric as the free world against the slave, limited the foreign policy debate to minor quarrels over means—whether it was better to rely more on foreign aid than military containment, whether massive retaliation was wiser than flexible response. Not until the debacle of Vietnam did the consensus end and debate, often wild and ill-informed after being bottled up for so long, finally occur. The price the nation paid for unity in the 1940s proved too great; the failure of the Republicans to play their rightful role as the loyal opposition cost both them and the nation dearly.

III

The 1960s provide us with yet a third model of congressional-presidential relations—that of executive domination. Beginning with John F. Kennedy and reaching a climax under Lyndon B. Johnson, the White House systematically ignored the Congress in making major foreign policy decisions in regard to Cuba, the Dominican Republic, and Vietnam. Congressional leaders such as William Fulbright and Richard Russell were informed of, but not consulted about, major steps; Congress was expected to follow presidential leadership in the Cold War without question.

Kennedy set the pattern that would prevail in the 1960s in his first crucial decision, the Bay of Pigs. Inheriting a CIA proposal for American support for an exile invasion of Cuba, JFK ignored Congress as he debated whether or not to go ahead with this ill-fated adventure. When Senator William Fulbright, chairman of the Foreign Relations Committee, learned of the impending invasion, he met with Kennedy to voice his dissent. He warned against the adverse reaction abroad to the naked use of force and tried to place the problem of Castro in perspective, telling the President, "The Castro regime is a thorn in the flesh; but it is not a dagger in the heart." Kennedy listened politely, and he even permitted Fulbright to repeat his dissenting views at a meeting of intimate presidential advisers, but the President joined with his aides in rejecting this congressional plea for restraint.[13]

Eighteen months later, during the Cuban Missile Crisis, Kennedy did not even bother to consult with representatives of Congress in arriving at his decision to quarantine Cuba and force a nuclear confrontation with the Soviet Union. Not a single member of the House or Senate was included in the ad hoc group that Kennedy formed to advise him on how to handle the problem of Soviet missiles in Cuba. During the seven days that Kennedy pondered his response, Congress remained as much in the dark as the American people. Finally, at 5:00 p.m. on Monday, October 22, just two hours before his televised address to the nation, Kennedy met with some twenty congressional leaders to inform them of the situation in Cuba and of the steps he planned to take. Senator Russell objected to the plans for a blockage; he favored an immediate invasion of Cuba, a step the other Senators and Congressmen, including Fulbright, quickly endorsed. The President ignored this congressional advice and went ahead with his predetermined policy.

Despite the favorable outcome, Kennedy's action in the two Cuban confrontations set a dangerous precedent. In both cases, he felt he should embark on risky and dangerous policies without benefit of congressional advice or approval. Unlike President Truman, who faced the necessity of gaining the prior approval of a Republican-controlled Congress, Kennedy enjoyed the luxury of full political support in both houses. Moreover, he had little respect for the opinions of members of Congress. Commenting to Arthur Schlesinger, Jr., after the Cuban Missile Crisis, JFK said that the clamor for invasion did not surprise him. "The trouble is that, when you get a group of Senators together, they are always dominated by the man who takes the boldest and strongest line," the President noted. "That is what happened the other day. After Russell spoke, no one wanted to take issue with him. When you can talk to them individually, they are reasonable."[14]

This cavalier disregard, if not outright contempt, for the views of Congress was an important part of the legacy that Kennedy handed down to Lyndon Johnson. Vietnam would help illuminate the danger of presidential domination in the foreign policy process. At first, it seemed that LBJ would avoid Kennedy's mistake. In the summer of 1964, after the North Vietnamese torpedo-boat attack on American destroyers in the Gulf of Tonkin, Johnson asked William Fulbright to shepherd the Tonkin Gulf Resolution through the Senate. Fulbright agreed to do so despite his personal doubts about the Administration's policy in Vietnam. Fulbright and Johnson had been closely allied in the Senate in the 1950s. Johnson had helped Fulbright become chairman of the Foreign Relations Committee by deposing the aging Theodore Francis Green; in 1960, LBJ had lobbied hard, though unsuccessfully, for Fulbright's appointment as Kennedy's Secretary of State. Now, in the face of an apparently unprovoked attack on American warships, he felt no reluctance in sponsoring an open-ended resolution authorizing the President to retaliate.

In the course of the ensuing Senate debate, Fulbright drew heavily upon his own prestige to carry out Johnson's mandate. He assured a skeptical Wayne Morse that hearings to explore the nature of the congressional commitment contained in the resolution were unnecessary; he admitted to John Sherman Cooper that the President could use the Tonkin Gulf Resolution to wage full-scale war in Vietnam; but he persuaded Gaylord Nelson to drop an amendment expressly forbidding the use of combat troops in Vietnam, asserting on the Senate floor after a private meeting with Johnson that the President had no intention of fighting a land war in Asia.[15]

The adoption of the Tonkin Gulf Resolution proved to be a costly victory for the Johnson Administration. When the President began escalating the war a year later, Fulbright felt betrayed. At first he kept his doubts about LBJ's policy to himself, observing the partisan tradition that the chairman of the Senate Foreign Relations Committee should not criticize his own President. But after the Dominican intervention in 1965, Fulbright broke with tradition and spoke out against Johnson's use of force in the Caribbean. On

September 15, 1965, he charged that the policy followed in the Dominican Republic would "make us the enemy of all revolutions and therefore the ally of all the unpopular and corrupt oligarchies of the hemisphere."[16]

The break between Johnson and Fulbright confirmed the President in his tendency to exclude Congress from the foreign policymaking process. Neither Fulbright nor other representatives of Congress were consulted during the escalation of the Vietnam War in 1965; when criticism began to surface in Congress, the President merely cited the Tonkin Gulf Resolution as full authority for the steps he was taking. The President even ignored the protests of a Senator like Richard Russell, a man he once admired greatly, and went stubbornly ahead with his Vietnam policy.[17]

Cut off from any constructive role in policymaking, Congress turned to the only course open to it—growing opposition to an unpopular war. At first the opposition was minute, Senators Wayne Morse and Ernest Greuning—who had alone voted against the Tonkin Gulf Resolution—voicing their dissatisfaction. But gradually other voices joined in. First Fulbright, then such Democratic stalwarts as Frank Church, Eugene McCarthy, and Vance Hartke swelled the chorus of protest. In early 1966, Fulbright gave the developing antiwar movement a new legitimacy by holding televised hearings before his Foreign Relations Committee. The American people listened to such respected figures as George F. Kennan and General James A. Gavin, instead of disillusioned intellectuals and campus radicals, express their discontent with the conduct of the war in Vietnam. After the six days of hearings, the Foreign Relations Committee received over twenty thousand letters and telegrams, most of them critical of the war. In April, Fulbright voiced his dissent most eloquently in a speech at The Johns Hopkins University, aptly entitled, "The Arrogance of Power." In his remarks, the Arkansas Senator interpreted the war in Vietnam as the result of the overextension of American power in the world and pleaded for a more restrained and realistic policy.[18]

Although the tragedy in Vietnam can be attributed to many factors, the systematic exclusion of Congress from any signficant role in policymaking was surely one of the main causes. If Johnson had been able to win a quick and unambiguous victory in Southeast Asia, the lack of Congressional participation would not have mattered so much. But when the Administration became mired down in Vietnam, Congress became the natural focal point for criticism of the war. Having ignored Congress when he escalated the conflict, LBJ could hardly ask the legislators to share the blame for the bloody stalemate. The President had isolated himself and had no choice but to take full responsibility. His decision in March 1968 not to run for another term was seen as the only way to begin meaningful peace negotiations.

III

What can we learn from these cases about the proper relation between the President and Congress in regard to foreign policy? None gives us a desirable model, but as is so often the case with historical examples, each indicates a pattern of behavior that should be avoided.

Congressional dominance, as seen in the case of neutrality legislation, is clearly unwise. Congress lacks the knowledge and flexibility to take the initiative in foreign policy matters. At best, Congressmen and Senators can only reflect the views of their constituents; they can set the guidelines that embody the attitudes of the American people toward such issues as war and peace. But they cannot develop specific policies toward an ever-changing international arena, nor can they become involved in the actual conduct of diplomacy. The most we can expect of Congress is that it serve as a watchdog, overseeing the President's performance, registering dissent and criticism, and insisting that foreign policy conform to the general mood of the nation.

Nor, as the 1960s demonstrated, should the President alone conduct American foreign policy. The temptation for the Executive to ignore Congress is very great. Congress can be obstructive, its criticism petty, its members ill-informed. But unlike presidential advisers and members of the National Security Council, Senators and Representatives do represent the feelings, ideas, and attitudes of the American people. They are the elected delegates, the men and women chosen to reflect the varied and conflicting interests of the entire electorate. Senator Fulbright put it best in a 1971 speech when he said,

> When all considerations of organizational discipline, expertise, and the occasional need for speedy action are taken into account, congressmen and senators have the one essential qualification for an effective role in the making of foreign policy which cannot be found within the executive branch: the power to speak and act freely from an independent political base, the power, . . . to tell the President to 'go soak his head.'"[19]

The President who excludes Congress from the foreign policy process excludes the American people. And Vietnam will always stand as a reminder that a foreign policy framed by experts, by the best and the brightest, is not only undemocratic, but an invitation to disaster.

Yet even the third example, the bipartisanship of the 1940s, is not ideal. As practiced by Truman and Acheson, bipartisanship was but a disguised form of presidential domination. As Vandenberg once observed, the Republicans were in on the crash landings but not on the takeoffs. The Administration formed its policy independently and then sought congressional cooperation and approval. Bipartisanship became a skillful device for avoiding congressional opposition and ensuring executive control over foreign policy.

The best solution would be to encourage genuine collaboration between the President and Congress on foreign policy. Given the nature of international affairs, the Executive must take the initiative in framing the policy alternatives. But somewhere along the way, a wise Executive will consult with congressional leaders, weigh their advice carefully, and try to incorporate useful suggestions whenever possible. Instead of presenting Representatives and Senators with decisions already reached, the President should give them an opportunity to influence the policy in its formative stages. Then they will be able to do more than simply approve or dissent; they can play a creative and constructive role in the making of the policy. In domestic politics, the disagreement over the ends of policy makes conflict between Congress and the President logical and even desirable; in foreign policy, the common agreement on the goal—to defend and advance the national interest—calls for collaboration rather than antagonism, unity rather than discord. But such cooperation can only be productive when it is genuine, when it reflects mutual respect and good will and not just cynical manipulation. The

III/Making of Policy • 180

search for such a consensus thus becomes the challenge facing both Congress and the President in the realm of foreign policy.

Notes

[1] W. Stull Holt, *Treaties Defeated by the Senate* (Baltimore: Johns Hopkins University Press, 1933); Thomas A. Bailey, *Woodrow Wilson and the Great Betrayal* (New York: Appleton-Century Crofts, 1945).

[2] Robert A. Divine, *The Illusion of Neutrality* (Chicago: University of Chicago Press, 1962), pp. 97-117.

[3] John C. Donovan, "Congressional Isolationists and the Roosevelt Foreign Policy," *World Politics* III (April 1951): 299-316.

[4] Robert A. Divine, *Second Chance: The Triumph of Internationalism in America During World War II* (New York: Atheneum, 1967).

[5] Richard E. Darilek, *A Loyal Opposition in Time of War: The Republican Party and the Politics of Foreign Policy from Pearl Harbor to Yalta* (Westport, Conn.: Greenwood Press, 1976), pp. 182-85.

[6] Divine, *Second Chance*, pp. 262-64, 270-71, 313.

[7] Daryl J. Hudson, "Vandenberg Reconsidered: Senate Resolution 239 and American Foreign Policy," *Diplomatic History* I (Winter 1977): 46-63.

[8] Robert A Divine, *Foreign Policy and U.S. Presidential Elections, 1940-1948* (New York: Franklin Watts, 1974), pp. 221-26, 266-67.

[9] Richard S. Kirkendall, "Election of 1948," in *History of American Presidential Elections, 1789-1968*, ed. Arthur M. Schlesinger, Jr. and Fred L. Israel (New York: Chelsea House, 1971), vol. IV, pp. 3143-44; Robert A. Divine, "The Cold War and the Election of 1948," *Journal of American History* LIX (June 1972): 109.

[10] Robert A. Divine, *Foreign Policy and U.S. Presidential Elections, 1952-1960* (New York: Franklin Watts, 1974), pp. 34-35.

[11] Dean Acheson, *Present at the Creation: My Years in the State Department* (New York: W.W. Norton, 1969), pp. 223, 318.

[12] Thomas G. Paterson, ed., *Cold War Critics: Alternatives to American Foreign Policy in the Truman Years* (Chicago: Quadrangle Publishers, 1971).

[13] Arthur M. Schlesinger, Jr., *A Thousand Days: John F. Kennedy and the White House* (Boston: Houghton-Mifflin Co., 1965), pp. 251-52.

[14] Theodore Sorenson, *Kennedy* (New York: Harper and Row, 1965), pp. 791-92; Schlesinger, *Thousand Days*, p. 812.

[15] David Halberstam, *The Best and the Brightest* (New York: Random House, 1972), pp. 416-19.

[16] Rowland Evans and Robert Novak, *Lyndon B. Johnson: The Exercise of Power* (New York: New American Library, 1966), p. 553.

[17] Halberstam, *Best and Brightest*, p. 528.

[18] Alexander Kendrick, *The Wound Within: America in the Vietnam Years, 1945-1974* (Boston: Little, Brown and Co., 1974), pp. 220-21; William L. O'Neill, *Coming Apart: An Informal History of America in the 1960s* (Chicago: Quadrangle Publishers, 1971), pp. 322-24.

[19] John C. Stennis and J. William Fulbright, *The Role of Congress in Foreign Policy* (Washington, D.C.: American Enterprise Institute for Public Policy Research, 1971), p. 67.

Congress vs. President

The Myth and the Pendulum

Sar A. Levitan

Sar A. Levitan is Research Professor of Economics and Director of the Center for Social Policy Studies at the George Washington University.

Who Is Calling the Shots?

Conventional wisdom would have it that during the first century and a half of this nation the executive and legislative branches of government lived more or less happily together, sharing the responsibilities and burdens of governments. This equal coexistence was shattered during the Great Depression by the New Deal attempt to alleviate the deprivations that accompanied mass unemployment in the 1930s. Under these dire hardship conditions the President took the initiative to ameliorate the critical conditions and in doing so gained the upper hand over the Congress. The four-year war further strengthened the hands of the Executive, and after the war this trend continued in an exponential fashion until Congress had almost entered, in David Brinkley's words, a "state of honored irrelevance."[1]

Brinkley's views were shared by many in Congress who should have known better. Speaker Carl Albert exhorted his troops to "halt the wholesale executive invasions of legislative powers and responsibilities."[2] The concern was shared by Republican Leader John Rhodes, who wrote: "Congress has served as little more than a glorifed echo chamber for the Executive Branch of government— usually content to approve or disapprove, rarely willing to initiate."[3]

In the same vein former Senator Joseph Clark paid his respects to his colleagues in a book which he entitled, *Congress, the Sapless Branch*.

Nixon, however, pulled the pendulum a bit too far. Congress convened in January 1973 in "a fighting mood" and began to reassert itself. The trend toward growing executive power was reversed.

Early interpretations of the present Administration continue to portray a dramatic power struggle between the executive and legislative branches. Carter's personal, fresh style and the varied proposals he has espoused symbolize true leadership, according to some analysts. For others, the fate of Carter's proposals for welfare and tax reform, the Panama Canal, and energy policy proves that Congress has retained its supremacy. The conclusion reached by Martin Tolchin of *The New York Times* was more balanced and to the point, when he observed that experts predict the continued sharing of responsibilities and powers by the executive and legislative branches.[4]

A Needed Reappraisal

A close examination of domestic policy over a longer period supports this balanced assessment. The pendulum of power does not swing frequently or dramatically between Congress and the Executive. In fact, domestic policymaking is influenced by other forces as well—pressure groups, the judiciary, public opinion, bureaucracies—all of which limit the size and direction of the swing in the pendulum of power.

As physics taught us though, it is far easier to estimate the motions of a pendulum which moves between two poles than one which has several directions. Thus, there is a tendency to oversimplify what Stephen K. Bailey calls the "almost unbelievably complex" process of policy formulation.[5] Diverse issues—taxes, social security, energy, welfare reform, to pick a few from current headlines—compete for attention and influence on our daily lives. It is no wonder that many individuals and groups seek a security blanket, or as Richard Neustadt has suggested, they create a fatherly, authoritative image of the Executive to alleviate their anxieties over current political problems.[6]

Domestic policy formulation is actually, then, more like a series of "complex positive feats of cooperation" among several participants.[7] Many scholars have attempted to map out the process in detail. One important distinction should be made between the formal introduction of a bill and the initiation of a proposal long before its final drafting. At the earliest stages, pressure groups may urge Congress to introduce legislation. Or, a decision by the judicial branch will require Congress to propose legislation for implementation of the new law. It should be noted that Congress often wishes to have the President take responsibility for new legislation and has, at times, "coaxed, embarrassed and almost forced presidents to propose legislation by threatening to take the lead if they did not."[8] Frequently, the reverse occurs—presidential "stealing" of congressional initiatives.

After the introduction of a bill, the President wields influence through the veto (or the threat of one), while the Congress wields influence over the President by overriding or rejecting clauses he favors or attaching clauses he opposes—or by introducing its own bill.

After passage, pressure groups continue to express their interests to the executive and legislative branches by influencing rule making, implementation, and oversight measures. The Supreme Court can invalidate a bill completely. Congressional oversight hearings of federal agencies (which often direct the thrust of federal programs) and amendments can alter executive-initiated legislation. And it must be remembered that the federal government's unit of measurement is often in billions of dollars. A subcabinet officer in the Nixon Administration remarked that little did he know when he studied decimals that 0.1 would mean $100 million. Even a so-called "minor change" often involves quite a large sum of money and huge resources.

Program administrators, educators, employers, and community and other groups may actually possess the ultimate tool in domestic policy legislation, namely implementation (or the refusal thereof), for that is the weapon by which they affect social legislation.

The complexity of the process disguises the true balance of power in other ways. It is foolish to play a numbers game comparing the size of congressional staff with the number of employees in the executive branch. That is where "rigorous" statistical analyses can lead to distorted pictures, for at any given moment one branch of government may lack the expertise or capacity to meet a specific problem. A dynamic rather than static analysis reveals a truer picture. The creation of the Congressional Budget Office and the budget committees in both houses, as well as a stronger Congressional Research Service and expanded congressional staffs, were part of that dynamic process.

Knowledge is a powerful tool, and until the explosion of the social legislation in the 1960s, Congress depended upon program administrators in the executive agencies for information about existing programs. This has changed radically during the past decade. In 1967, as part of the overhauling of the Economic Opportunity Act, Congress instructed the General Accounting Office to assess the performance of the antipoverty warriors and on the basis of that evaluation mandated the Comptroller General to recommend changes for the future direction of effort. Beginning with that new orientation, which was accompanied by an expansion of support staffs, Congress enhanced its capacity to gain access to program operations, and in consequence its dependence upon the executive agencies for domestic intelligence about the performance of social agencies has diminished.

It is also misleading to think of Congress as a single body. Many congressional committee chairmen and even subcommittee chairmen achieve congressional power and national reputations that a President can ill afford to ignore and must take into consideration. Possibly the most publicized instance during the 1960s and 1970s was the widely held belief that the President could not get any tax legislation unless it had the blessings of Ways and Means Chairman Wilbur Mills. For example, Representative Richard Bolling stated that President Johnson "understood that we needed it [a tax increase early on during the Vietnam War] but he also knew he could not get it through the Ways and Means Committee, so he did not throw the power of his support behind it."[9]

The proposition that domestic policy is a work-sharing process, and that the checks-and-balances system is in good working order, can be demonstrated both by analysis over time and by specific case studies.

III/ Making of Policy • 186

A Historical Perspective

Analysts have had to consider the various stages of the complex legislative process before granting any participant the credit for policy formulation. On focusing on initiation of proposals, John F. Bibby and Roger H. Davidson saw the President emerging as chief legislator early in this century.[10] Ralph K. Huitt concluded similarly that ever since the Truman years the principal source of legislative proposals has been the executive branch.[11]

When "credit" is defined as prime responsibility for the substance and passage of a bill, the results differ significantly. Examining the fifty-year period ending in 1940, Lawrence Henry Chamberlain found that Congress was highly underrated as an innovator in the American political system. Chamberlain concluded "not that the President is less important than generally supposed but that Congress is more important."[12] During the period of his investigation, he found that the President could be given credit for roughly 20 percent of the major legislation passed; the Congress could be credited for about 40 percent; 30 percent was the product of both the President and the Congress; and less than 10 percent could be credited to external pressure groups. Congress and the Executive are credited with an almost equal quantity of economic, including tariff, legislation. Congress was more active than the President in labor legislation after the 1930s and equally active or dominant in conservation legislation. Not even the New Deal, so often viewed as Roosevelt's creation, proved to be unique. Chamberlain notes that much of the regulatory legislation Roosevelt introduced during the New Deal had its origins in congressional efforts several years earlier. Paul Conkin concurs by concluding that "Congress did not abdicate in the '30s. It was willing and receptive, not prostrate."[13]

Moe and Teel find that the balance has prevailed since 1940. The two branches can be granted fairly equal credit for legislation concerning eocnomic prosperity, transportation, agriculture, urban problems, and conservation. The same was true for tariff policy prior to 1950. And after that date, Congress "voluntarily" chose to relieve itself of the burden of drafting tariff policy, and instead continued "to define the limits of executive discretion" through rate setting and other indirect controls. Since their study was completed, the latest trade act has granted Congress and the President new checks and balances in the field of international trade. The New Deal President's active role in labor legislation was matched by a dominant congressional role in the Taft-Hartley Act of 1947 and the Landrum-Griffin Act of 1959. And although the Executive played the more active role in civil rights legislation, he was actually "a reluctant leader who was pressured by individual committeemen, the Attorney General and public opinion."[14] The antipoverty and manpower legislation stand as strong examples of continued work sharing between the two branches throughout the last decade.

President Nixon, despite his intense efforts to increase executive power, was not able to disturb the balance of power for long. Nixon's drastic budget cuts and impoundment of funds proved to be short-lived exercises in power. Congress quickly retrieved its rights, as witnessed by Nixon's voluntary cancellation of those super-cabinet appointments opposed by Congress, and the newly acquired congressional responsibility for fiscal policy achieved through the Congressional Budget and Impoundment Control Act.

The Ford Administration did not experience any major conflicts or power shifts in its relations with Congress. Carter, however, is clearly more susceptible to the myth of the pendulum because of his varied commitments and his populist style. It would be easy to portray an antagonistic Congress anxious to mar his image by taking control. The true picture, however, seems to be that Carter merely achieved an initial publicity victory, which temporarily obscured the traditional equilibrium between Congress and the President. Economic strategy, unemployment, and energy are several major areas in which both branches are actively formulating policy.

The Judicial Branch

Once the law is passed, its meaning is left up to the courts, and the Supreme Court decides whether the law is to survive. In the last fifty years, the judiciary's role in domestic policy formulation has grown significantly, and in more recent years the courts have shown little timidity in exercising power. The Supreme Court's invalidation of the National Recovery Act in 1935, followed by its similar treatment of parts of the Agricultural Adjustment Act the following year, may be construed as part of the general trend toward a broader participation in policymaking which was taking place at that time. Roosevelt's unsuccessful attempt to pack the Court in 1937 revealed "a struggle in power politics as well as in grand principles of government . . . ."[15] Like Roosevelt, the Justices were testing the limits of their power.

The civil rights decisions of the 1950s expanded the Court's role even further and encouraged a judicial influence in policymaking that was to help shape many aspects of social legislation. Abortion, affirmative action, zoning, and pensions are only some of the newer areas in which judicial review may have far-reaching policy implications.

When so major an institution as the Court effects a change in the balance of power, a widespread concern is inevitable. What Conkin saw as merely a change "backed by a balanced system of government," has been interpreted quite differently by others. Raoul Berger, the constitutional scholar, accused the Supreme Court of violating the Constitution in its school segregation and its "one man, one vote" rulings. Berger also saw the 1970 ruling permitting six-member juries as excessive legislative action.[16]

Pressure Groups and Public Opinion

The Constitution recognizes three branches of government, but the exact role and responsibility of the branches are subject to the whims and tastes of the electorate. The vote is the public's oldest means of influencing policy formulation, and it is a very powerful weapon inasmuch as elected officials almost uniformly hope to retain power and position. The public mood has played a significant role in all major domestic policy developments of this century: social welfare legislation of the New Deal sought to relieve the insecurities of the citizenry; the Senate Special Committee on Unemployment was largely responding to the public concern over the recession of the late 1950s; the War on Poverty was presented when the public mood was ripe for activist social policies.[17]

Pressure-group activity, a crystallization of special interests among the general populace, has mushroomed in this century. Even quite early, "journalists and reformers . . . viewed pressure groups as sinister manipulators who held in thrall scores of Senators and Congressmen."[18] Chamberlain gave pressure groups credit (or blame) for half the major tariff legislation passed between 1890 and 1940. And he found them to be in equal standing with the President and Congress in formulating conservation policies in those years. Agriculture and labor were also major influences early in the 1900s. Moe and Teel found pressure groups to be more powerful than Congress in recent civil rights legislation.

The current array of pressure groups reveals them to be as numerous as they are diverse. Consumerism, cultural identity, private enterprise, social services, and public assistance are only some of the major spheres of activities they have entered.

The pressure groups' tools of influence have been refined dramatically. Even the newer, less affluent groups have quickly learned the value of lobbying, publicity, and public education. The future promises an increasing role for pressure groups in most areas of domestic policy formulation.

Antipoverty and Manpower Policy

The War on Poverty produced the most dramatic, sweeping social legislation since the New Deal. Feeling they were responding to a direct presidential initiative, the designers of the legislation were not noticeably generous in sharing credits, and they paid little heed to checks and balances. No doubt there was good reason to view the War on Poverty, and the manpower legislation closely related to it, as presidential creations, but once again reality speaks differently. Antipoverty efforts were actually an outgrowth of earlier efforts to aid impoverished Americans through manpower policies and other economic programs. Many of the antipoverty components were incubated in Congress, on campuses, and in foundations during the Eisenhower "normalcy" years and the one thousand Kennedy days. As early as 1955, Senator Sparkman was leading the Joint Economic Committee in a study of rural poverty. The jargon of the day was "depressed areas" rather than "War on Poverty," but the consciousness was the same. The Special Senate Subcommittee on Unemployment, formed in 1959 at the urgings of liberal Senators and Majority Leader Lyndon Johnson, reflected similar concerns.

The first Kennedy legislation to deal directly with unemployment, the Area Redevelopment Act of 1961, provides a clear instance of shared responsibility for policymaking. Democrats tried for six years to pass the legislation, but were stymied by two presidential vetoes. It took a new Democratic President to approve the congressionally-initiated ARA.

Congressional studies of unemployment problems and the passage of the ARA set the stage for the Manpower Development and Training Act of 1962. While legislative action is widely given the bulk of the credit for this legislation, the reverse is true for the Economic Opportunity Act of 1964, the cornerstone of the antipoverty efforts. The Executive's program arrived with great fanfare but clearly with a past life as well. It is widely supposed that Johnson was responding to a public mood that was ripe for activist social policies, but civil rights groups had been campaigning for these policies for some time.

The contents of the Economic Opportunity Act revealed substantial congressional influence, despite this branch's exclusion from the drafting process. The antipoverty law included the Job Corps and the Neighborhood Youth Corps programs, which had their origins in the Youth Employment Opportunity bill previously passed in the Senate and deadlocked in the House. As Bibby and Davidson noted, "Not all proposals had such lengthy antecedents, but with one exception, they had all previously undergone some gestation on Capitol Hill."[19]

The drama and suddenness with which the Economic Opportunity Act (EOA) was presented left Congress temporarily stunned. But Congress recovered partially even before the enactment was completed. Republicans actively protested during congressional hearings and several substantial alterations of the bill were made. Some of the most notable were: female eligibility for the Job Corps; greater parochial school participation in EOA educational programs; income deductions for public assistance recipients; stricter loans and grants programs from low-income rural families; a title for adult education. Congress would have done more if it had been better informed and better prepared psychologically.

Time was the source of Congress's renewed strength. The failure of the Executive to share credit for the legislation with congressional chieftains left few supporters in Congress whose reputations were identified with the program. For each of the three years following the enactment of EOA, Congress delayed appropriations and attempted to reduce the authority of the antipoverty agency, the Office of Economic Opportunity. The taxpayers joined Congress in a careful scrutiny of OEO's operations and its appropriations. This skepticism may be linked to subsequent congressional amendments adding new responsibilities to OEO (with an old level of appropriations) and earmarking funds for specific groups.

Pressure groups also played a prominent role in EOA policy changes. Sargent Shriver had ignored the professionals in welfare, vocational education, and other fields during the drafting stage of EOA because he feared they would be too tradition-bound. He came to realize, though, that they could contribute valuable experience, and that they held the tools of implementation through their command of the existing facilities. The New York Civil Liberties Union and American Jewish Congress encouraged safeguards against excessive influence by church groups. The American Bar Association and American Trial Lawyers Association threw their support toward OEO in exchange for more moderate legal and political projects. Only poor residents of poor neighborhoods were eligible to use health service centers, thanks to the American Medical Association. Growers proceeded in the same fashion, and succeeded in deleting any provision of OEO funds for organizing migrant unions.

Pressure groups continued to wield influence after EOA's enactment. Black groups encouraged OEO to place more emphasis on the needs of black communities. Some community groups became so alarmed by Congress's scrutiny of OEO funds that the accused it of harassment. Of course, the press exploited both the scrutiny and harassment issues. Surely the pressure created was an important factor in Congress's extension of OEO shortly thereafter.

In short, EOA was well exposed to the checks and balances system of policymaking. Some of the participants may have been late in starting, but very quickly a great number joined the action in the policymaking arena.

Manpower policies have covered a more narrow, less controversial, scope of issues than did OEO. Thus, the interaction between policymakers was of a more cooperative nature. As already stated, manpower legislation combined a fairly equal share of proposals from both branches. Programs in the later 1960s were created with far fewer struggles than had been the case with EOA. The Work

Incentive Program was quickly introduced and passed by Congress in 1967. The Emergency Employment Act of 1971 was the Executive's acquiescence in congressional efforts to counter the effects of the recession.

As the number of manpower programs proliferated, it became clear to both the Congress and the executive branch that there was a need for rationalization and consolidation of these efforts. Both President Nixon and congressional leaders in 1970 spoke of the creation of a single spigot at the federal level to fund manpower programs. But the Congress and the President had very different approaches and systems in mind.

The federal manpower program was really a *national* rather than a strictly *federal* effort. Washington designed the programs, appropriated the funds, and called the shots; state and local officials danced to the federal tune. Under the Nixon Administration, manpower reform took a new direction. One tenet of the Administration's New Federalism was that locally oriented social programs are best administered by those closest to an area's needs, and that local elected officials can best respond to community desires. Decentralization was presumed to involve the shifting of administrative power out of the hands of the program agents, who belonged to a professional bureaucratic cadre, to elected local government officials.

In 1971, President Nixon singled out manpower—along with urban development, rural efforts, education, transportation, and law enforcement—to be funded under special revenue sharing arrangements, which according to the prevailiang rhetoric, was a strategy to give power back to the people. Decentralization also meant decategorization of the funds allocated to the state and local governments. According to the Nixon Administration, shared revenues were to be made available to state and local governments with few federal guidelines, little oversight, and no federally sponsored programs. Frustrated by congressional opposition to special revenue sharing arrangements for manpower and other social programs, the Administration tried several experiments without the blessing of Congress.

In 1973, with bipartisan backing and active Labor Department cooperation, Congress passed the Comprehensive Employment and Training Act (CETA), consolidating in a single law the separate training and antipoverty manpower programs. CETA was the product of prolonged debate and compromise. It incorporated the principles of a single source of funds, but only for programs under the Manpower Development and Training Act and the Economic Opportunity Act, and it also included a consolidated prime sponsorship system by state and local governments.

Who won the battle? Who took the initiative? CETA has some aspects that resemble the Nixon Adminsitration's objectives, including the pirme sponsorship system. But the CETA system hardly represents the decentralization and decategorization championed by the Nixon Administration. The executive, legislative, and even judicial branches have had an important say in the actual operation of the CETA system.

Pressure groups will always play a vital role in manpower programs, if only because close cooperation with employers and the business community is crucial for both on-the-job training and job placement. This is becoming increasingly true as the labor market tightens. Thus it comes as no surprise that in 1969, the Department of Labor contracted for public-interest groups to serve as liaisons between local governments and policymakers in Washington. Also, employers and unions have made major improvements in the operation of several job-training programs. Federal manpower programs are a prime example of the work-sharing reality in the formation and execution of domestic policy.

Is There a Future for Checks and Balances?

The case has been made for an active checks and balances approach to domestic policy formulation, involving the Executive, Congress, the courts, and pressure groups. The signs seem to point to the continuation of that same pluralism of participation in the future. First of all, pressure groups can be counted on to grow, diversify, and exert substantial influence. Second, Congress seems to have been deeply shocked by Nixon's attempts to usurp power, and tends to move promptly to counter virtually every presidential move.

One final question needs asking: Is the present checks and balances system the most effective approach to domestic policy formulation? Some have questioned whether a process full of deadlocks and delays can serve the needs of the American people. James Sundquist is particularly concerned with issues such as pollution, health care, and fiscal policy—issues for which time is of the essence because the damage of delay may be irreversible. He charges that the American government is "less than fully responsive to the popular mandate."[20]

American policies so often emerge very slowly, speeded only occasionally by tragic or major events such as assassinations, natural disasters, and landslide elections. Yet, perhaps that is the beauty of the system. The case can be made that the public mood must be ripe for changes before changes can be made. If the need must be great before the public is ready, then at least the remedies will be well supported when adopted and implemented. Even Sundquist suggests that "where a problem is real in its impact upon the people, and where a national solution is indicated by the failure of all other solutions, then time is on the side of the activists . . . . The pressure for the national solutions will grow . . . until the president and the program have the force to push past the obstacles in the institutional machinery."[21]

Wider participation in policy formulation yields other benefits as well. It increases the opportunity for creative new legislation. It affords the participants a heightened sense of political efficacy. And above all, it provides a crucial safeguard—foreseen by drafters of the Constitution—against unpopular legislation by tyrannical executivs, or legislators, or judges.

Are the current deadlocks over energy and tax policies to be viewed as symptoms of malfunctioning or rather the benefits of representative democracy? The issue comes down to priorities: quick action versus maximum representation of interest. Those who regret that the Great Society has been delayed because too many cooks were involved in its preparation might also consider that the antipoverty efforts were saved because Congress and the courts prevented their abandonment. Checks and balances have high costs, but their long-run benefits may exceed the costs.

Notes

[1] David Brinkley, "Foreword," in Philip Donham and Robert J. Fahey, *Congress Needs Help* (New York: Random House, 1966), p. vi.

[2] *Congressional Record*, February 5, 1973, pp. 3239-40; cited in James L. Sundquist, "Congress and The President: Enemies or Partners?," *Setting National Priorities—The Next Ten Years*, ed. Henry Owen and Charles L. Schultze (Washington, D.C.: Brookings Institution, 1976), p. 595.

[3] *Washington Post*, January 21, 1974.

[4] *New York Times*, October 9, 1977.

[5] Stephen K. Bailey, *Congress Makes a Law: The Story Behind the Employment Act of 1946* (New York: Columbia University Press, 1950), p. 236.

[6] Richard Neustadt, *Presidential Powers: The Politics of Leadership* (New York: John Wiley and Sons, 1976).

[7] Charles E. Lindblom, *The Policy-Making Process* (Englewood Cliffs, N.J.: Prentice-Hall, 1968), p. 32.

[8] John R. Johannes, "The President Proposes and Congress Disposes—But Not Always: Legislative Initiative on Capitol Hill," *Review of Politics* (July 1974): 359.

[9] Richard Bolling, "A Congress For a New Era," *Improving the Long-Term Performance of the U.S. Economy* (New York: Committee for Economic Development, 1976), p. 15.

[10] John F. Bibby and Roger H. Davidson, *On Capitol Hill: Studies in the Legislative Process*, 2d ed. (Chicago: Dryden Press, 1972), p. 246.

[11] Ralph K. Huitt, "Rationalizing the Policy Process," in *The American Political System*, ed. Brown and Wahlke (Hinsdale, Ill.: Dorsey Press, 1971), p. 238.

[12] Lawrence H. Chamberlain, *The President, Congress and Legislation*, cited in Ronald C. Moe and Steven C. Teel, "Congress as Policy-Maker: A Needed Reappraisal," *Political Science Quarterly* (September 1970): 446.

[13] Paul K. Conkin, *The New Deal* (New York: Crowell, 1967), p. 89.

[14] Moe and Teel, "Congress as Policy-Maker," p. 461.

[15] Conkin, *New Deal*, pp. 92-93.

[16] *The New York Times*, October 31, 1977.

[17] James L. Sundquist, *Politics and Policy: The Eisenhower, Kennedy and Johnson Years* (Washington, D.C.: Brookings Institution, 1968), p. 488.

III/ Making of Policy • 196

[18] Roger H. Davidson, *The Role of the Congressman* (New York: Pegasus, 1969), p. 162.

[19] Bibby and Davidson, *On Capitol Hill*, p. 235.

[20] James L. Sundquist, *Politics and Policy: The Eisenhower, Kennedy and Johnson Years* (Washington, D.C.: Brookings Institution, 1968), p. 511.

[21] Ibid., p. 507.

Discussion

JOHN BRADEMAS: I speak as an elected politician and as a member of the Congress who has served—as the late, great Speaker Sam Rayburn would have put it, and as my friend D.B. Hardeman will remind me—*with* six Presidents of the United States, *under* none, half of them Democrats, half of them Republicans.

I'm almost moved to say something about Professor Levitan's very interesting paper and suggest to him that at least in the eight years under Presidents Nixon and Ford, basic federal policy for education in the United States was overwhelmingly initiated on Capitol Hill, and neither Presidents nor commissioners of education nor secretaries of HEW really had very much to say about it.

But instead my task is to address myself to Dr. Divine's paper on foreign affairs. To begin with I shall remark that there are three major factors which it seems to me distinguish the American political and constitutional system from others, either from authoritarian systems or from parliamentary systems in which the legislative branch must by definition follow what the executive wishes. The first is that we have a separation of powers, or to quote Richard Neustadt, "A system in which separated institutions share powers." I shall here not take time to distinguish between the powers in the field of foreign affairs that the Constitution assigns to Congress and those we know are in the hands of the President, except to observe that the powers assigned to Congress are considerable.

A second factor that distinguishes our system in foreign affairs is that unlike the British and some Western European nations, we do not have disciplined political parties. The present situation in Great Britain is in this respect somewhat anomalous, but by and large in America we have decentralized political parties, and as the Whip of the House, I can assure you that I speak from brutal experience. One need only look at the recent votes on the Foreign Assistance Act or on the B-1 bomber to see the proof of what I mean.

The third distinguishing characteristic is one that I perhaps would not have mentioned had this meeting been held a decade ago. I speak of the new configuration of forces in Congress and particularly in the House. We now clearly see a resurgent Congress, the consequence of several factors. One is the reacton against an aggrandizing Presidency in the post-Watergate and post-Vietnam world. A second is the election to the House of Representatives of new kinds of members, younger, very well-educated, usually with some experience in politics. Third is the democratization in the House of much of what we've been doing. We've spread out power. We have given members a greater opportunity to play a role. This is a phenomenon not confined to our political institutions, but one that we've seen in this country over the last ten years or so in nearly every institution in our society, and so we in Congress are affected by it as well.

Also I think we've seen a decline of party loyalty. If one looks at the first Gallup Poll taken about forty years ago, one sees, as I recall, that only 16 percent of Americans called themselves independents. That figure has doubled in the intervening four decades. In turn this decline in party loyalty is reinforced, in my judgment, by the rise of television as the most powerful mechanism for political communication. All of these factors that I've mentioned mean that it is impossible in these days for Speakers of the House or Presidents to lead by edict or command. Another consideration is that more and more members of the House are asked about foreign policy when they go home, and they feel they have a perfectly legitimate right to insist upon some role in the making of it.

Let me just mention—almost at random—some instances in recent years in which Congress has played a role in foreign policy: the 1973 vote to end money for military involvement in Vietnam; the

War Powers Act in 1973, making it difficult for any President unilaterally to plunge the country into war; in 1974 the rejection by Congress of President Ford's request that we continue to send money for the war in Southeast Asia. Shortly thereafter Congress refused to vote funds for helping in the Angolan civil war. Congress insisted on the Turkish arms embargo after Turkey had invaded Cypress in August of 1974, in violation of agreements entered into with us and of American statutory inhibitions on the use of arms that we supplied.

In mid-1977 Congress was imposing restrictions on U.S. contributions to the World Bank and other multilateral institutions. Congress initiated the Jackson-Vanik Amendment of the Trade Act. Congress has written legislation making clear its right to veto major arms sales abroad. And it was Congress four or five years ago that insisted that greater attention be given to aid for the social and economic development of the poorer countries of the world. I'm not saying I agree with the positions that Congress took in all these respects. That is a different issue. All I'm saying is that Congress was very much involved in these foreign policy measures.

Beyond this kind of involvement, you all know as well as I the importance of congressional committee hearings on foreign policy issues. It wasn't Mr. Carter who invented concern with human rights; it was members of the House of Representatives such as Congressman Don Fraser of Minnesota, who for years has been holding hearings on this issue in his subcommittee.

The trips abroad made by members of Congress have considerable effect. I went with Speaker Albert in 1975 to the Soviet Union, Romania, and Yugoslavia, where we met with Breshnev, Ceausescu, and Tito. We sat in the Kremlin and debated trade and immigration and arms control with the top leaders of the Soviet Union. Representative Jim Wright, leading a congressional delegation, has been talking to Mr. Sadat about important developments in the Middle East. I had the honor of leading a delegation to the People's Republic of China in April 1977, and we talked with some of the top people there. Only a few days ago, I and ten of the ablest young members of the House, the Whips, met for an informal supper with Dr. Brzezinski so we could exchange views on foreign affairs.

I remember very well how in January even before he was sworn in, President-Elect Carter had a meeting at the Smithsonian that went on for seven hours. He had forty-five Senators and Representatives there, and we did an around-the-world tour with his top foreign policy advisers, something that would have been unheard of in the Nixon-Ford-Kissinger years, an acknowledgement on his part of the legitimacy of a role for Congress. It seems to me that in this unique American constitutional system, there must be an acknowledgement of the legitimacy of a role for Congress in foreign affairs.

I remember a meeting at the Library of Congress two or three years ago with several distinguished diplomats, including Ambassador George McGee, who said wistfully to a group of Congressmen, "Well, in the old days all we had to do was call Speaker Rayburn and Tom Connally and that was it." Well, that isn't it anymore.

Another important consideration is that a President can learn from Congress, as regards both substance and politics. As I sat in that room for seven hours with Mr. Carter, I was struck by the extraordinary depth and diversity of the knowledge about foreign affairs that was revealed to the new President. But even if you don't learn anything—and you must be fairly illiterate if you can't—you can still do yourself a lot of good as President if you listen, because it is imperative in our system that if policy is to be accepted it must have support in the Congress of the United States. I think Dr. Divine's paper makes that very clear. You may have heard the remark of a Texas state legislator some years ago who was predicting the legislature's likely reaction to a bill; he said "People are going to be down on what they ain't up on." Well, one can think of the Panama Canal debate in that respect, if I may say so. And, to quote a somewhat more eloquent authority, Averill Harriman, "No foreign policy will stick unless the American people are behind it, and unless Congress understands it the American people aren't going to understand it."

Congressmen and Senators are very skilled at educating the electorate. That is how we get elected; that's how we survive; that's the line of work we're in. We know a lot about it. We know a lot more about it than almost all of the people who are appointed to office in the executive branch, and there are only two of them at the other end of the avenue who are elected.

What should we do? Well, in my judgment we need to give greater attention, not simply to formal mechanisms of encouraging trust and respect, but to informal mechanisms as well. The executive branch must learn—and Mr. Carter has been learning, and I say this to his credit—that in a separation-of-powers system there must be constant, continuous, never-ending bargaining, that what the President does in foreign affairs has an effect on what he gets in domestic affairs, and vice versa, for government is a seamless web.

In conclusion, Mr. Chairman, I warmly applaud Dr. Divine's paper, and I do so on two counts in particular. First, his insistence that foreign policy ought not to be above politics. This is a democracy. Politics is the stuff of democracy, and foreign policy is life-or-death politics. I'm glad to hear him denigrate the false god of bipartisanship which has caused so much trouble in our country. Second, I'm glad to see him assert the proposition that there is a legitimate role for both Congress and the Executive in the shaping and conduct of foreign policy. We will never completely resolve the tension between the two because that tension is built into the system, but we must do better.

WILBUR COHEN: My background and perspective are different from those of most of the participants in this program. I have always been an advocate of social reform and I have always tried to make our political system work effectively to carry out the 1912 political platform of the Bull Moose Party.

That particular platform of 1912 was of very great consequence to my professors at Wisconsin who were essentially populists in the great tradition of the LaFollettes. I grew up on that tradition, and I've spent the last forty years trying to see if I couldn't put that 1912 platform into effect. It did, of course, ultimately proceed—periodically and in cycles—through the Administration of Franklin Roosevelt and the New Deal, and then through the New Frontier and the Great Society, and now that system of social reform and social policy is deeply imbedded in the American political, economic, and social system. It's still uncompleted. There is still much more to do, and I'm sure others will continue to use our political system to try to build upon what we have.

Thus as an advocate, I try to look at the political system as a means of effectuating the social policy that I believe is necessary for a democratic and humanitarian and compassionate society.

I do not look upon the role of Congress as one of conflict or confrontation, but of what I would call creative tension. The whole spirit of checks and balances and separation of powers is important only insofar as it effectuates a desired social result. When you realize that the Constitution of the United States does not confer on Congress the power to deal with anything in the field of health, education, and welfare, you recognize that it is a matter of great creative evolution that we have been able to build a system of health, education, and welfare at the federal-state level even though the Constitution of the United States doesn't explicitly provide for it. And it was our great political leaders like Roosevelt and Truman and Kennedy and Johnson who, in my opinion, made possible the evolution of those essential policies.

I don't see conflict and confrontation as things that make the system work. I see the creative tension and the cooperation between the executive and legislative branches. When I was assistant secretary for legislation for both President Kennedy and President Johnson, if I had suggested that we were involved in a confrontation or a conflict with Congress, both President Kennedy and President Johnson would have, I'm sure, said I was the wrong man for the job. The question was not how to precipitate confrontation or conflict, but how to get an agreement with Congress on creative use of the political forces.

The main point I want to make is that one finds a lot of mythology and a lot of misrepresentation and a lot of simplistic notions in any discussion of these matters. That is caused by the need to use shorthand forms in talking about political science concepts. But when I was trying to effectuate the Great Society programs, for example, working between the Executive and the Congress, I did not even think of Congress as an institution. The idea that there is sort of a unilateral or unified thing called "Congress" is a mistaken notion. The House is different from the Senate. The Senate is different from the House. The Conference Committee is different from both the House and the Senate. And if you are trying to pass legislation, you have to treat them differently. The House Ways and Means Committee is very different from the Senate Committee on Finance. You would never have treated Wilbur Mills the same way you treated Harry Byrd, the Chairman of the Finance Committee, or Byrd the same as you treated Wilbur Mills.

That brings me to another point, namely that you must never overlook the institutional difference among the committees in Congress. John Brademas's Committee on Education operates very differently from the Ways and Means Committee. You cannot treat the Education and Labor Committee the way you treat the Interstate and Foreign Commerce Committee or the Ways and Means Committee. These are all elected officials and they're all in the same body, but there are vast institutional differences in the way the committees operate and in the way they view their roles. I'll even go farther: all committees are equal but some of them are more equal than others. That's the way the Ways and Means Committee and the Senate Finance Committee look upon their roles in the Congress, and any President or any cabinet official who doesn't take that into account is going to be in serious difficulty.

Now I subscribe completely to Sar Levitan's and John Brademas's point that much of the legislation that the public and the newspapers credit to the Executive is originally developed by men and women in Congress, and I can find a lot of other illustrations beyond those offered by Mr. Levitan. Take Medicare: obviously both Kennedy and Johnson proposed Medicare, and they deserve a great deal of credit for advocating it, but they never thought it up. Medicare was introduced in Congress in 1951. From 1951 to 1957, nobody of any political importance endorsed it. Then in 1957 a rather obscure Congressman named Aime Forand introduced it, but he was on the Ways and Means Committee and that was important. Even so, nothing happened until 1960 when Kennedy himself supported it. It was defeated in 1960. It was defeated in Congress again in 1961 and 1962 and 1964. But finally, when President Johnson said, "This is a major part of my legislative program, and I'm going to put my imprimatur on it," and especially after he won the 1964 election, Wilbur Mills changed his view on it because Lyndon Johnson had the votes.

Federal aid to education has been introduced in Congress since 1870. There were bills in the thirties and in the forties and in the fifties. But it only became possible to get the Elementary and Secondary Education Act when a President took the leadership and put his political name and support behind it. That didn't mean it was conceived by the executive branch unilaterally or independently. It was the end product of years of work and thought by a lot of people in Congress who undertook the original sponsorship.

As a young man in 1943 I helped draft a national health insurance bill for Senator Wagner. It later became the Wagner-Murray-Dingell bill, which the AMA opposed. I brought it in to Senator Wagner with my youthful enthusiasm, saying, "Here is the bill," and he went ahead and introduced it without even looking at it. I was shocked, you know, and when I asked him why he did that, he said, "Well, it probably won't become law until twenty-five years from now, so why should I worry about whether one detail or another is correct in the bill?" And he turned out to be right. He had the ability of a great legislator to introduce an idea when it was still foreign to the electorate and to the media, and he accepted that as part of the role of leadership in the Congress. Ultimately Truman and then Kennedy and Johnson supported that idea, and now Carter is supporting it. But to think that any one of those people in the executive branch conceived the idea and sent it up, or that the Executive was thus dominating domestic legislation is really to overlook completely the way social policy ideas are developed.

Social policy in this country evolves as ideas, most of them coming from the academic community. The last thing you want to say in Congress, of course, is that those ideas came from a lot of professors. But many of the ideas for social reform come out of intellectual discussion and are then put into some kind of political package. They are introduced by Congressmen or Senators who have a great deal of independence and are not going to lose their seats immediately when they propose an idea that is foreign, socialistic, communisitic, and unwelcome. That is the way a new idea is initially viewed, and then ultimately it becomes acceptable, and the President or the Administration comes along and supports it.

The other thing that is being overlooked in this discussion is the way commitments are made to particular policies. The commitments are usually made in the campaign. During the Carter campaign I was the National Chairman of Health Volunteers for Carter-Mondale. I spent most of my time trying to get Carter and Mondale committed to national health insurance, part of the 1912 Bull Moose campaign program. I'm still working on it and probably will have to continue working on it, and somebody after me will have to continue working on it until maybe 2012. You know, these ideas don't get adopted quickly or easily in our American system. Carter finally did make such a commitment, but he did not think it up and his acceptance doesn't constitute an executive branch domination over the Congress. It was a commitment that he made in the campaign to the people who were supporting him; it grew out of a national idea and a national consensus in which health volunteers and intellectuals and other people who favor the plan were important.

So I believe that to get a correct impression of how domestic legislation is formulated and enacted, we must avoid simplistic notions of checks and balances, or presidential control of legislation, or presidential initiative, or even confrontation. Those notions are simply inadequate to explain the very complex process by which social legislation is formulated in this country.

DAVID PRICE: I'd like first to register my general agreement with what I take to be the main themes of Mr. Levitan's paper. First, that Congress is indeed a remarkably durable partner in domestic policymaking. Second, that we shouldn't take our checks and balances imagery too literally, for the dominant note of executive-congressional relations is cooperation. And third, that broad generalizations about the congressional role or presidential domination of the legislative branch really get us nowhere. One has to be much more precise in distinguishing among the policymaking roles and much more careful in assessing the division of labor among our institutions.

Let me suggest two sorts of observations about these matters. First, I should like to think a little bit more fully about how one might sort out executive and congressional policy roles, and consider how each institution participates in the policy process. Second, I'd like to look briefly at current congressional roles and think a little about how we may best explain them.

On the first question: how can you differentiate the congressional from the executive role? It seems to me when you're talking about policymaking, you need to be very clear which stage of the process you're talking about. Policymaking is not a single act. It involves floating new ideas; it involves investigating problems and abuses; it involves responding in various ways to different groups and interests in the society; and then finally it involves hammering out a compromise and putting together the political muscle necessary to pass a piece of legislation.

I suggest that we might break the process down in some way such as this and then begin to ask: "In what aspects of that process is Congress especially good, and in what aspects of that process does Congress frequently need help?" I think, for example, of Mr. Levitan's examples of the early floating of poverty proposals, the job corps, and the various kinds of educational work-study programs. Those things were floated in Congress. The initial hearings were held in Congress. The proposals germinated in Congress. Congress is very good at that. It's much easier to get an idea floated in Congress than it is in the executive branch.

Congress perhaps is less good at the later stages of policymaking, particularly on broad national issues that involve deep conflicts. Congress may sometimes need help when it comes to the mobilization of support, or the hammering out of a compromise on a matter like energy. The Congress is extremely good and in fact takes the lead at certain stages of the process.

Another way to address the question is to ask what type of policy we are talking about. It seems to me that Congress is better at some kinds of policies than it is at others. Certain kinds of issues it handles enthusiastically and often well, particularly what Mr. Fisher called distributive policies, those that are firmly based in the constituencies and often are firmly based in the committee system.

I first worked on Capitol Hill in the office of Senator Bob Bartlett from Alaska, and we specialized in those kinds of issues. Alaska needed them. It was an important role for the Senator to play, and no one else in the federal system would have played it. We specialized in merchant-marine bills and fisheries bills, and bills for the benefit of Alaskan natives. Congress tend to specialize in farm price supports, in public works measures, in certain kinds of education and welfare and health measures that benefit constituencies and localities. Congress is very good at that type of policy, that kind of local particularized benefit.

There is a second kind of issue that Congress has increasingly tended to specialize in, the kind that combines high visibility and low conflict. I think of health research, for example, or some of the consumer measures. What I'm saying is that one cannot generalize about policymaking roles in general, for the role is affected by the character of the issues. The characterization of Congress's strength and Congress's inclinations will vary according to the type of issue that comes before it.

Now let us turn to the second question, about the current congressional roles and how to explain them. Nearly all our speakers have agreed that this resurgence or reassertion of policymaking prerogatives has found expression in some of the reforms we've seen enacted in the House and Senate in the last four or five years.

It's been suggested that this resurgence, this policy activism, is in large part a reaction to a presidential assertiveness. No doubt that is part of the explanation, at least in foreign policy. But in domestic policy I don't find that explanation very persuasive, because it seems to me that the antecedents of Congress's present activism in domestic policy really antedate considerably the activist presidential administrations of the sixties. The antecedents rather are seen in the Eisenhower years, mainly in the Senate, as more and more members began to stake out policy roles for themselves—roles as policy activists. They began to press for adequate authority and adequate resources to carry out those activist roles. In many ways Hubert Humphrey is the prototype of the activist Senator, trying to make an imprint on national policy and trying to generate a range of farsighted proposals. He attempted that merely in his role as a Senator, for he had no especially high rank, and he commanded no particularly high resources. His notion was that that kind of role was open to a Senator in this body, and indeed we soon saw that pressures for decentralization and the dispersion of resources and authority were coming from a number of Senators who wanted to carve out that kind of role.

A similar development is taking place now in the House, a little later than in the Senate. One can point to the lead that Mr. Brademas has taken in education legislation, or Bob Eckhardt in consumer affairs, or Paul Rogers in health, right down the line. It is a kind of policy entrepreneurship, an activism on the part of individual members.

It seems to me that that is very poorly explained simply as a reaction against presidential authority. What is the explanation? Well, it is a complicated thing but perhaps part of the explanation has to do with the kind of electoral situation these members increasingly face. It is particularly true of Senators, but increasingly true of House members too, that they are no longer able to rely on party machines to deliver the vote. They're no longer able to rely on the old friends-and-neighbors politics. It is no longer sufficient just to check in with the courthouse crowd or with the important interests that they have served over the years. For one thing, television has arrived, and television creates a radically new kind of campaign situation. In many ways there are pressures on Senators and increasingly on House members to make themselves visible, to come on strong as policy leaders.

At the same time, there has been a rising clamor of policy needs and demands that must be dealt with out there in the society, and the astute Representative or Senator perceives that he can profit politically by responding to them. A beautiful example of this is Senator Magnuson of Washington state who used to be a pork-barrel Senator. He used to worry mainly about dominant home-state interests—fisheries, maritime interests, and the like. In the sixties he suddenly took on a new mantle, that of the consumers' champion, and his commerce committee became transformed from rather sleepy operation which handled a few bills each session, to a rather livewire operation with a young, aggressive staff, which started producing consumer bills by the score. I think the kind of electoral situation that Magnuson came to face, in an increasingly urbanized state, had a lot to do with the change in Senator Magnuson. And I think if we're looking for a root cause, this may be it.

Now, of course, this policy entrepreneurship can be pretty superficial. It can be just a matter of staking out positions and making speeches, but it is to the credit of our Congressmen, I think, that often it is not superficial, that it often is quite substantial. One of the virtues of our much-maligned committee system is that it gives members the wherewithal to perform a meaningful policy role. Indeed, the fact that these members occupy committee positions often gives them incentives to be responsible policymakers, and sometimes pressures them to do so.

It is also worth saying that if this congressional resurgence is rooted in the ambitions and goals of individual members, and if it does antedate the presidential activism of the sixties, then it presumably bears the marks of its origins. And it clearly does bear the marks of its origins in the ambitions of individual members. It has resulted mainly in a tendency toward the dispersion of power and a parceling out of authority and resources, a tendency that is still quite strong in the House and only slightly dampened by the Stevenson Committee reforms in the Senate.

This policy activism has produced a heightened and widespread activity, but it has also created problems of coordination and control. It is most visible and most successful in the early stages of policymaking, to go back to our earlier distinction. But it may actually have made the later stages of policymaking—the hammering out of compromises, and the mobilization of support—more difficult and more problematic. It may have led members into less narrow, more contentious national issues, into different types of policy; but at the same time it may have made it more difficult to reach consensual outcomes.

This new policy activism has prompted a series of countervailing or decentralizing reforms that look toward the dispersal of power, the creation of more subcommittees, the spreading around of power and resources. In many ways these reforms have enlivened Congress, made it a more vital and more vigorous policymaking institution. But in other respects they have created problems, and I think some of the centralizing reforms that were discussed earlier are an attempt to correct for those problems. It seems to me that a vital institution needs both capacities. It needs the capacity to generate, to proliferate proposals, to float ideas. But it also needs the capacity to make hard decisions when the crunch comes.

WALT ROSTOW: In listening to the many wise things that have been said, I'm tempted to pick up this or that observation with which I might have some disagreement. For example, I know my old friend and sparring partner Bill Fulbright would have been vastly amused to hear that he reluctantly broke the bipartisan commitment and took a position in opposition to a President. The shade of Harry Truman or Dwight David Eisenhower would surely recall that Bill Fulbright, as part of the sport of being a Senator, had squared off against those Presidents on many occasions, so it was quite predictable that he would do so again in the sixties.

My intention here, however, is not to comment on things of that sort but to offer what I hope will be a constructive contribution. In a book called *The United States in the World Arena*, published in 1960, I suggested that relations between President and Congress were really triangular. That is, one must always bear in mind the complex linkages of both the President and the Congress with public opinion. That strand runs through a great deal of Professor Divine's paper, but there are times in which I think the triangular checkout is not made, and that leads to a somewhat incomplete view of the situations he is describing.

In one sense my theme could have come from Mr. Levitan's remark that, "The public mood played a significant role in all major domestic policy of this century." I would say the same thing of virtually all the major decisions of foreign policy. Indeed the "public mood" played an oblique role even in such apparently inside decisions as those concerning the Bay of Pigs and the Cuban Missile Crisis.

With that as a theme, let me comment briefly on some of the issues raised by Professor Divine. First, his picture of isolationism in the 1930s, I think, portrays this triangular sense quite sharply. I would add only that it was not a question of isolationist legislation not being given a fair trial or being chipped away. The fact is that if you look at the public opinion polls of 1940, there was a most dramatic shift from the spring when two-thirds of Americans said, "We'll aid the allies but at no risk of war," to the fall when two-thirds said, "Aid the allies even at the risk of war."

There is no mystery as to why that happened. It was not an act of persuasion or rhetoric or advocacy, by the Executive or even by Congressmen. What happened was that Norway fell, France fell, German submarines appeared in the Atlantic, and Britain was beleaguered. You recall Dr. Johnson's famous dictum that, "You can depend on it, sir, when a man knows he is to be hanged in a fortnight it concentrates his mind wonderfully." It took those events—it even took Pearl Harbor—to get the United States to begin to define exactly what its interests were in this war. If public opinion is not given its full weight in appraising the transition of 1939-40, we risk discussing *Hamlet* without the prince.

The same thing can be said of the public mood in 1945-46. It was the overwhelming weight of public opinion that forced the unilateral dismantling of our armed forces, the bringing back of our troops, and consequently a validation for Stalin of what Roosevelt had said in his opening speech at Yalta, namely that Americans "were incapable of keeping forces in Europe for more than two years." I do believe that that illustration of the power of American public opinion was one of the things that really led Stalin into commitments and hopes that made the Cold War inevitable.

Now as for the 1948 problem of the Republicans, I agree with Professor Divine's analysis, but it might have been sharpened by a closer look at the dilemma in a two-party system: should the opposition party oppose a policy for which there is widespread support by a classic kind of public-opinion bipartisanship? About 60 percent of Americans supported wholly the Marshall Plan and the resistance in Berlin. Twenty-five were against and fifteen were kind of out to lunch, which is the normal breakdown of American public opinion when an issue is crystallized and action is possible.

What happened was not merely that the Republicans lost the election of 1948. Something else very big happened in 1949. The Communists took over China. That was a great shock to public opinion, and it was that event and the public reaction to that event that shaped the new stance of the Republicans. That story then merges into the story of the Korean War, which also deserves a word in this analysis because it is also a very vivid exercise in the power of public opinion.

It is true that Mr. Truman did not consult Congress in the decision to send troops to Korea. But I don't think any serious student of the Korean War and the political reactions that attended that war believes that is why public opinion moved against him. It is sometimes forgotten in the recent revival of affection for President Truman that in the polls he fell from something like 69 percent in January of 1950, to 46 percent in July 1950, which on the average was pretty high for him, to 23 percent in November of 1951—23 percent approval for the way he was doing his job! The overwhelming reason for that was what I consider Mr. Truman's error in taking the troops north of the neck of Korea. That got us into a protracted, apparently indecisive war. Public support fell away, and he left office with about as weak a position as one could have.

Now as for President Kennedy, I would simply say that I think a sober view of his relations with the Congress would indicate that the popular image of a man who was arrogant in pursuit of his policies and paid no never-mind to Congress is not correct—and I know this from the testimony of members of Congress.

The Bay of Pigs problem, which he inherited, was a very peculiar one which didn't lend itself to open debate. And the Cuban Missile Crisis was also peculiar because the President had to make a decision to act before the issue could come up in the United Nations. He knew that if it ever went public, the United Nations would try to freeze the United States and we would be negotiating with those missiles down our throat.

Until some of the revisionists came along, I think the general view was that Kennedy was quite considerate of the views of Congress. I know the consultation he had on the Test Ban Treaty, on foreign aid, and on Berlin were very extensive. On domestic legislation he thought he was working to an eight-year rhythm and thought that he would build up support in Congress, get a better mandate in 1964, and then be able to put his legislation through. I believe that the notion that he adopted an arrogant, imperialist style which was then carried on to President Johnson will not stand the test of history.

Now we come to the most important of the issues, namely the issues concerning President Johnson's decisions on Southeast Asia. There are in fact three quite separate issues if one is judging the relations among Congress and the President and public opinion concerning Southeast Asia. One is the Southeast Asia Resolution of the summer of 1964; the second is the decision to put in troops in 1965; and the third is President Johnson's conduct of the war in Southeast Asia.

With respect to 1964, I think there is a full convergence of the triangle. While writing *The Diffusion of Power* I read the debate in the Senate, as well as the Senate documents; I read the document-based account in President Johnson's own book; I read the newspapers of the time, and I read the polls. Now the 1964 Southeast Asia Resolution was not a Tonkin Gulf Resolution—it had nothing to do with sanctioning retaliation. It was a commitment which President Johnson, remembering Harry Truman, thought was necessary in order to get freedom of action in case we should have to use military power, and it was fully understood by the Senate.

John Sherman Cooper observed that no Senator could leave that room without knowing that he or she was making a most solemn decision to give the President powers that could result in war. And Senator Javits stood up and said, "We should be all conscious that we are making a decision that could mean thousands of lives, tens of thousands of lives, hundreds of thousands of lives."

If you look at the polls of the time, and the press, and the actual debate in the Senate—not the later fabrications of how people thought they had voted, but what actually happened—there's no doubt that the debate in the Senate was protracted and solemn. Great pains were taken to emphasize the solemnity of the issues, and the President was backed.

Although there was no formal debate n the Senate, exactly the same is true about putting in the troops in July of 1965. There were very careful consultations, fully documented in President Johnson's book, and reflected in *The New York Times*. There was no secret about what was going on. The issue really was this: should one have a new resolution in the Congress as the troops were put in? Should one declare war?

The reason why no further resolution was adopted in 1965 was not that President Johnson was trying to exploit the Southeast Asia Resolution to put troops in. Putting in troops was the last thing in the world he wanted to do anyhow. The decision not to go for a new resolution was due not to any disdain for the Senate, but to Secretary Rusk's statement that he did not know what formal military ties existed between the government in Hanoi and those in Peking and Moscow, and therefore, we would minimize the risk of a large war if no further formal action was taken.

If you will look at the polls at the time, and the press and the editorials, you will find that President Johnson had public opinion with him, and he had the Congress with him, overwhelmingly.

Now we come to the conduct of the war, where there is indeed a problem that deserves precise treatment. The fact is that even in 1965, approximately 75 percent of the people believed that the decision to go into Vietnam had been correct. That figure fell away until at the end of 1968 the number of people who thought it had been a mistake to send troops in rose above 50 percent.

There is no mystery at all as to why the support for the war fell away, and there is no mystery as to why President Johnson bore the burden of it. The reason is that the majority of Americans were more hawkish about the conduct of the war than President Johnson. To give you a sense of this, let me give you some figures. Those who supported the "present" level of fighting numbered 18 percent in November 1966, 10 percent in October 1967. That was about the degree of support for President Johnson's strategy for fighting the war. Those who wanted stronger use of American military power against North Vietnam numbered 55 percent in November 1966, 53 percent in 1967. Those who wanted to withdraw troops numbered 18 percent in November 1966, rising to 31 percent by October 1967. That group was made up of people who were profoundly dovish and the beginnings of the hawks who said, "Win or get out."

Now the essence of the problem was that President Johnson insisted on keeping U.S. ground forces inside South Vietnam. He did this because he felt that was his duty as Commander-in-Chief in a nuclear age. He felt he had a duty to conduct the war that way, even if the restriction was extremely unpopular, because his overriding duty as Commander-in-Chief in a nuclear age was to take no action that could justify a larger war.

The American people and the Congress took the view that American force should be used to force a quicker end to the war. As it happened, I agreed generally with that view, and I thought I knew what might be done to end the war without risking a larger war. But the critical point here is the constitutional problem, not who was right and who was wrong. I do not think Johnson's was an imperial Presidency. My old friend Arthur Schlesinger has written many admirable things, but I think that he himself will regret his analysis of President Johnson's treatment of Vietnam when he has a chance to consider the facts in the light of history.

The point is, what are the constitutional relations in a nuclear age between the Commander-in-Chief, the Congress, and the public? Although as I say, I didn't always agree, I had no doubt in my mind that President Johnson had been elected by the people to make those decisions. He bore the burden of conducting a war that was more careful and painful and slow than the American people or the Congress wanted. He knew Mr. Truman's polls, he knew the risks he was taking politically. But that is the nature of the problem; it is not some egregious lack of respect for Congress.

I go through this because it was not unlike Mr. Truman's problem in the late stages of the Korean War. Presidents in a nuclear age have felt that they bore a responsibility that cannot be dispersed, and indeed there is some evidence (e.g., its reaction in the Cuban Missile Crisis) that suggests that Congress may be a bit more careless about the dangers of nuclear war than Presidents who live with that black box so close to them.

Now, to come back to the lesson of all this, the only lesson I know, as a historian and from my own experience, is that broad generalizations in this field are not worth much. To understand the extraordinarily complex interactions under our Constitution, one must understand—as Mr. Brademas does—that a real power is allocated in foreign policy to the Congress, that there are vast powers that the President himself must exercise, and that an extraordinarily large role is reserved, as it should be, for public opinion. I would say to both analysts and practitioners: check out all three sides of the triangle.

ROBERT DIVINE: I should like to respond briefly to a couple of Walt's remarks. I agree that Fulbright was quite independent. President Truman first called him "Senator Halfbright," when Fulbright had the temerity to suggest that Truman not run for reelection in 1948. He was not chairman of the Senate Foreign Relations Committee at that time. In the 1950s he had some problems with Eisenhower, but Eisenhower was President of a different party. I think you could check on Fulbright's record as chairman of the Senate Foreign Relations Committee; he was at the outset quite cooperative but gradually he was frozen out.

As for the triangular relation between the President, the Congress, and public opinion, I agree there is an important relationship here, but I don't think it is an even relationship. The President has a great advantage in dealing with public opinion. I think the relation is a very sensitive one, but strong presidential leadership can have a great influence upon the public and in turn upon the Congress. Look at what Woodrow Wilson did in 1919 when he took the great tour of the country. He understood that the way to get to the Senate was to go to the nation. That's exactly what Vandenberg suggested to Truman: "Scare hell out of the American people."

With regard to the Congress I think the President holds the whip hand. The Gulf of Tonkin situation suggests a kind of formula: present the issue dramatically to the American people and the Congress ("an attack on American ships!"); give them very little time to consider the matter; don't hold hearings; have the debate end quickly. The President holds the advantage in this situation. There may be a triangular relation, but it is very complex, and in it the Executive has a good deal more initiative than the Congress does.

JOHN BRADEMAS: I think that what Dr. Divine has said is right. It is particularly difficult when a President can say, "Well, I have the facts and those fellows at the other end of the avenue don't. I'm the one who gets the intelligence reports."

An adroit President can make his own policy stick in a highly contentious and volatile foreign policy situation; and supporting him becomes a matter of whether you're a good loyal American or not. That is a device that both Democratic and Republican Presidents are familiar with, and that's one reason why I so warmly applaud what Dr. Divine said about bipartisanship.

I remember one occasion when Secretary of State Rogers came up to talk off-the-record to a bipartisan group of members of the House. The issue of the secret bombing of Cambodia came up, and I remember getting up and saying, "Mr. Secretary, who told you you could bomb Cambodia on your own? According to the Constitution of the United States, it was always my understanding that Congress has some say in these matters." The reaction I received was very sharp, and I don't mean just from Secretary Rogers, I mean from my own colleagues in the House. Many of them turned and looked upon me as though I were a leper for having said something as rude and as forward as that. Mr. Nixon had made it clear that it was unseemly, and to be blunt about it, unpatriotic, to raise questions of that kind. In my judgment that is a profoundly dangerous situation for the national security of our country. It is imperative that elected members of the House and Senate have the right to say, "On that issue the President has no clothes on," and not be thought disloyal to their country.

Finally, I'd like to go back to a point that is somewhat similar to what Walt Rostow is saying. It is also dangerous when members of Congress get to feeling we can't believe what the executive branch tells us in these matters. If they've cried wolf too often, they will meet doubt and skepticism even in a situation where the national security really is at stake. And then we're all in the soup.

So to the extent that it is humanly possible in these matters, we must build up and maintain respect and above all trust. Trust. We may disagree with each other, but we have to be sure that what we are hearing is the truth. Otherwise, the whole system is going to be in great difficulty.

WILBUR COHEN: I should like to mention a few occasions in my own experience when foreign policy seems to have affected domestic policy.

On several occasions when there was a crucial decision to be made in domestic policy, and a foreign relations crisis arose, it was used by the conservatives to delay action on domestic policy. And that brings up an extremely important point: it is only possible to get far-reaching domestic legislation of an innovative character through if the conservatives are either weak or neutral or uninterested. In 1939 and again in 1950, there was a lot of social legislation under consideration, and on both occasions the conservatives were able to cut back the domestic legislation by saying, "Since we have a foreign relations problem on our hands, we must be more conservative on domestic matters." And the liberals and the neutrals would have to accept the situation, because the people who have been the most vigorous in the use of federal power in the foreign field are the conservatives. Many times they have used that very potent political force as a key point to stop or mitigate the effects of social legislation. Thus, though there are big differences in the way foreign affairs and domestic affairs are handled in both Congress and the executive branch, there are times when they have a very important interrelationship which should not be overlooked.

IV

Johnson and Rayburn: the 1950s/ an Era of Congressional Government

Overview: Clarence G. Lasby
Papers: D.B. Hardeman
R.K. Huitt
Discussion: Alan Bible
Lindy Boggs
Harry McPherson
J. William Theis

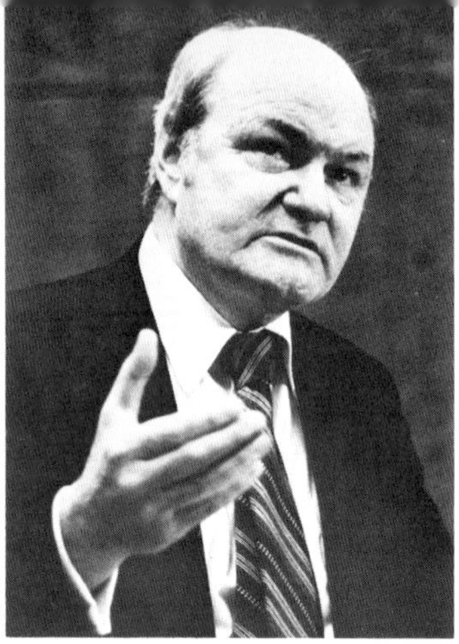
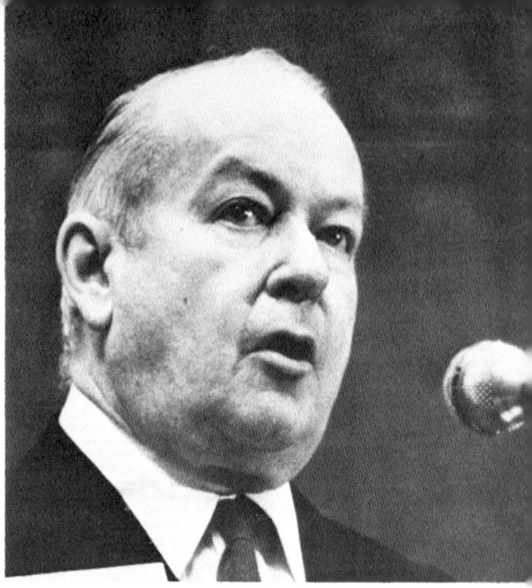
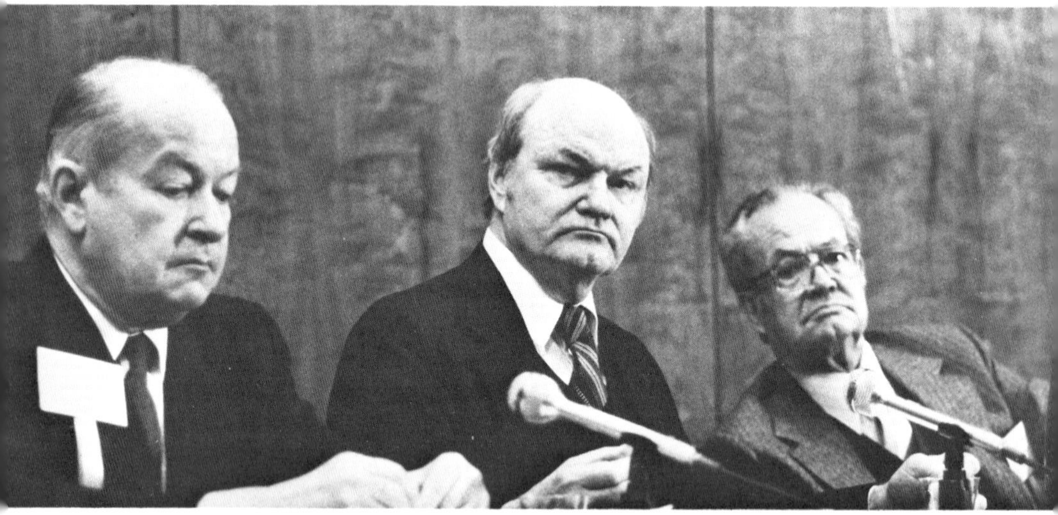
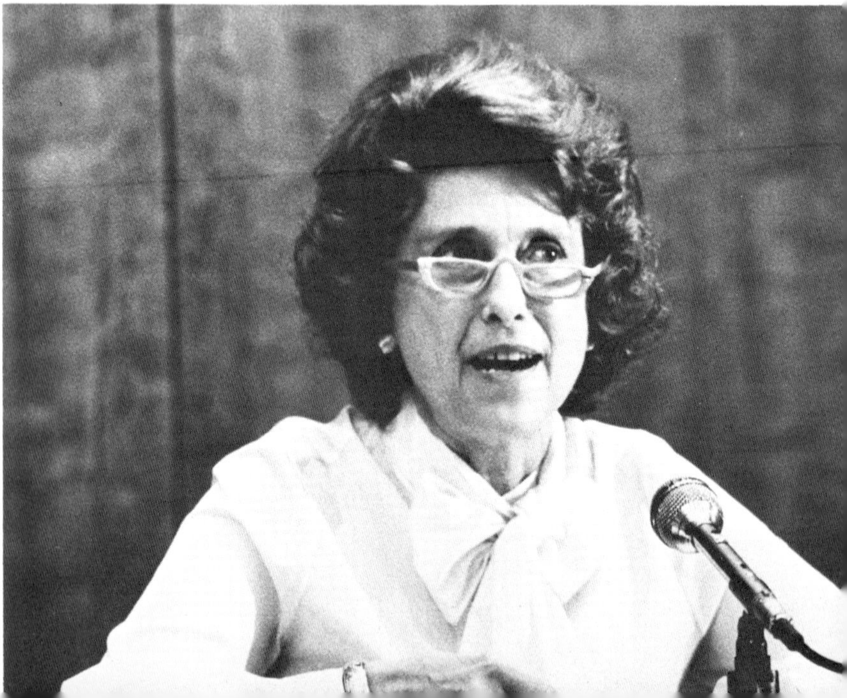

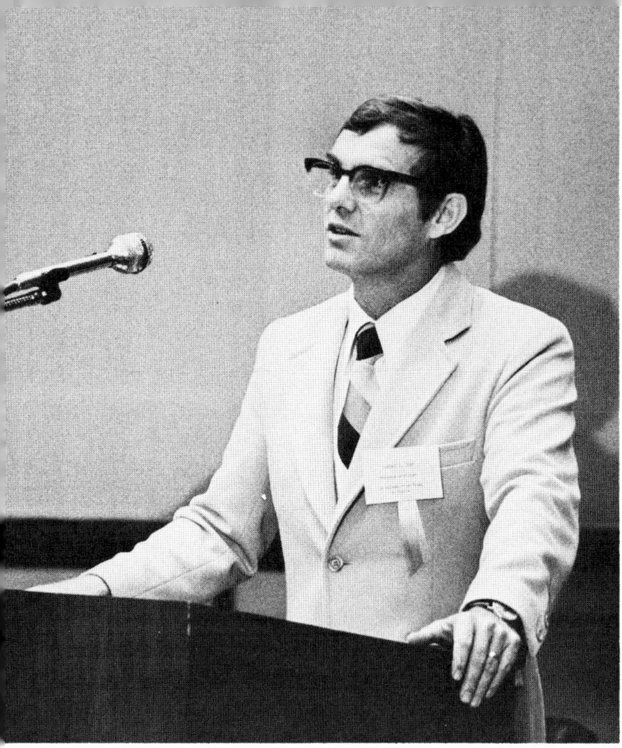

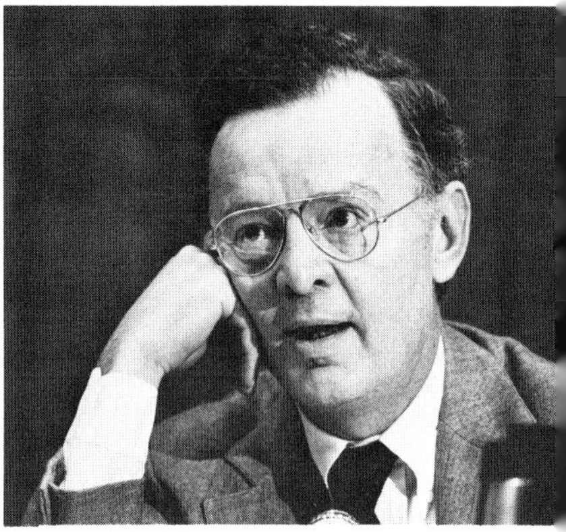

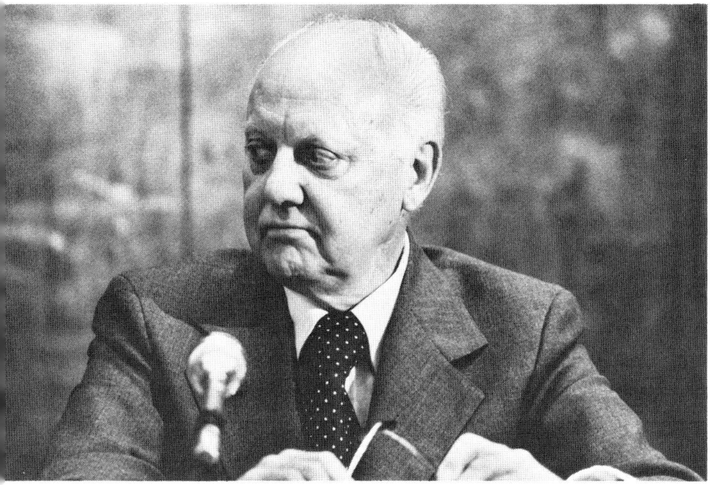

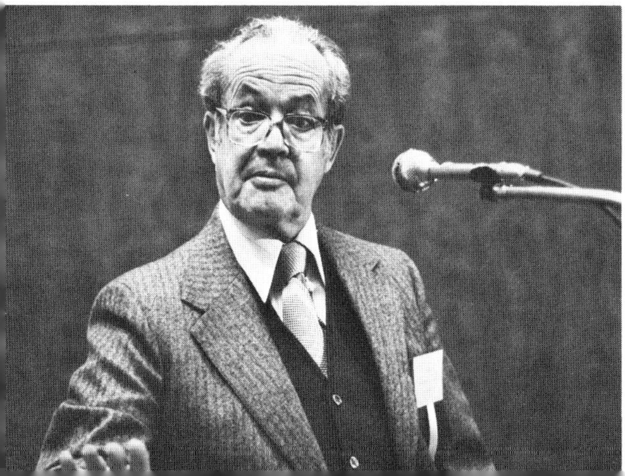

Overview

Clarence G. Lasby

Clarence G. Lasby is Associate Professor of History at The University of Texas at Austin.

In an earlier section Professor Sar Levitan referred in passing to the Eisenhower "normalcy" period. It is a telling phrase with its evocation of the Harding era, reflective of the manner in which liberals and historians—and usually they are one and the same—have viewed the decade of the 1950s. As early as 1958, journalist William Shannon acknowledged that the nation needed Eisenhower, mainly to end the Korean War and to cool the passions aroused by "McCarthyism," but he also observed that his usefulness soon passed.

Thereafter, he would leave office with the country's domestic and foreign policies "about where he found them in 1953," said Shannon. "No national problem will have been advanced importantly toward solution." The Eisenhower years had been the time of the "great postponement."

Ronald Steel added to that by saying that these years were an historical intermission when America stopped off for a snooze while the world turned inconsiderately on.

Other historians and commentators have denounced and decried every aspect of this age and portrayed it as one of blandness, sterility, conformity, alienation, moral cowardice, repression, fear, and greed.

"These were the years," wrote one, "of flabbiness and self-satisfaction and gross materialism. . . . (The) loudest sound in the land had been the 'oink'-and-'grunt' of private 'hoggishness.' It has been the age of the slob."

And Eric Goldman, once a kind of historian-in-residence, said, "Good-by to the 'Fifties—and good riddance!" The era was one wherein "we've grown unbelievably prosperous and we maunder along in a stupor of fat. . . . We live in a heavy, humorless, sanctimonious, stultifying atmosphere. . . . Probably the climate of the late 'Fifties was the dullest and dreariest in all our history."

Some critics would concede that the period was good for home and the family, was good for getting and spending and for cultivating one's own garden, but behind it all—to the liberal critics—were anxiety and the quiet despair whose symbol was the "bomb."

In recent years, I have noticed that historians have shown more understanding toward this decade. That is due, in part, I believe, to the realization that a later generation—however much more committed it was to solving problems than was that of the 1950s—still could not solve all of the nation's problems.

The change is due also to a certain nostalgia among historians, as well as others, that looks more tolerantly upon the period, even if a Republican was in the White House. But it is due as well to the realization—mentioned in the third session by Secretary Cohen—that there were antecedents in the 1950s for the programs of the 1960s, that history did not suddenly have an intermission between the glorious days of the New Deal and Fair Deal and those of the New Frontier and the Great Society.

It is true, nevertheless, that leadership for change did not come from President Eisenhower, however popular and however beloved he was. The President was slow in reacting to "McCarthyism;" the President was slow in his support for civil rights; the President was slow in his sponsorship of social programs; the President was even slow in recognizing the public interest in what came to be known as the "space race." When a member of his Scientific Advisory Council told him that a manned lunar landing was feasible but that it might cost as much as $38 billion, and likened it to the voyage of Columbus, Eisenhower replied, "Well, I am not about to hock my jewels."

This was indeed an era of congressional government and leadership—a very special historical and political situation. And the two most important and powerful among the congressional leaders were Sam Rayburn and Lyndon Johnson, whose powers and styles provide the theme of this section.

Sam Rayburn

and the House of Representatives

D.B. Hardeman

D.B. Hardeman, currently a practicing attorney, served from 1957 to 1961 as research assistant to Speaker Sam Rayburn, who designated him official biographer.

The decade of the 1950s—from January 1, 1951 to December 31, 1960—was one of the busiest of my life. Journalism at home and abroad, four years as a public official, active participation in three presidential campaigns, running a small business, and working for three and one-half years as research assistant to Speaker Sam Rayburn—these kept me hectically busy and usually weary. So my impressions of the 1950s were formed on the fly, with little time to pause and reflect.

In 1951 Sam Rayburn was already a powerful, well-established public official—though scarcely known to the public at large. A man who sought no publicity, he got relatively little outside his own district. Yet he had been in Congress for thirty-eight years—he and Woodrow Wilson came to Washington together. He had been a principal architect of Franklin Roosevelt's New Deal, coauthoring five landmark bills—the Truth in Securities Act, the Public Utilities Holding Company Act, and the bills creating the Securities and Exchange Commission, the Federal Communications Commission, and the Rural Electrification Administration. His bill to break up utility holding companies—which he steered to passage—provoked the greatest legislative battle in the history of the United States Congress. Moreover, through his influence as Speaker, the farm-to-market road program had come into full bloom.

Fifteen years previously Rayburn had been elected Democratic leader in the House of Representatives. Within the month, January 1951, he would break Henry Clay's record for having served longer than any other Speaker. And before his death in 1961, he would have served more than seventeen years as Speaker, doubling Clay's record. Yet to rank-and-file voters—even in most of Texas—Rayburn was all but unknown. That soon would change.

A mighty new force broke loose upon the American scene in the 1950s, transforming many aspects of its national life, not least its politics. Television. Only three cities saw the 1948 national conventions on television; the 1952 conventions were seen nationwide. A new era in American politics had begun.

Rayburn's first national identity came from his television exposure as permanent chairman of the 1952 Democratic Convention. His rich deep voice, his shining bald head, his forbidding scowl, his occasional mirthful laughter, and his tough and skilled control of the teeming mob—which national conventions tend to be—won him a recognition in the national consciousness which he had not had before.

During this period, we stopped in the Fort Worth airport to get his shoes shined. As he paid for the shine, the boy timidly asked, "Aren't you Mr. Rayburn?" Rayburn conceded it, and as we walked away, he muttered with obvious pride, "That boy's got a television."

These were the "golden years" of Rayburn's life. At sixty-eight, his health was still robust, his mind clear and acute as ever, honors and accolades piled up, he was no longer seriously challenged for reelection. His protege, Lyndon Johnson, was orchestrating the United States Senate like an Arturo Toscanini. The Democrats controlled both houses of the Congress for eight of those ten years, including six of Republican Eisenhower's eight years as President.

In that decade it was customary for many of us to think—and to say—that the nation was drifting, that it lacked a sense of purpose, that it was avoiding the really important public problems. Eisenhower, it was said, "reigns but does not rule."

The high drama of the Great Depression and the extraordinary efforts of the federal government during the New Deal and the Second World War were missing, and as I now recall it, many of us felt that the fifties were a paltry, frustrating decade. "The American people are tired of crisis. They want a period of peace and quiet—of inaction. That's why Eisenhower is unbeatable—he's a do-nothing President," we rationalized.

A fresh new look at this period has convinced me that we were simply too close to the trees to see the forest. The fifties were a time of mighty stirrings. The winds of revolution were blowing, but I think few of us understood what was happening. Let me review some of the events of those ten years.

The nuclear age grew into awful maturity as the United States and Russia exploded hydrogen bombs. Before the decade was over, intercontinental missiles to deliver those warheads were under development.

Had we had the vision, we might have sensed the planting of the seeds of Vietnam. As Secretary Dulles bound us to resist Communist aggression in Southeast Asia (the SEATO Pact), Vice-President Nixon advocated armed intervention in Laos—one of the four parts into which French Indo-China had been carved at a conference table. The French expulsion left festering a situation which eventually dragged us into a long and divisive war.

The Middle East was full of portents of trouble. Eisenhower, without consulting Congress, landed Marines in Lebanon to thwart a suspected Soviet move. Egypt nationalized the Suez Canal; Britain, France, and Israel invaded Egypt until a combination of American, Canadian, and Soviet pressures forced them to withdraw.

Although Vice-President Nixon and Premier Khruschev visited each other's countries, and President Eisenhower was invited to visit Russia, the road to peace was dramatic and upsetting. An American spy plane was shot down over Russia, causing Khruschev to break up the Paris summit conference by pounding his shoe as he withdrew Eisenhower's invitiation. And on our doorstep, Communism got an alarming foothold as Fidel Castro's Marxist revolution swept the day in Cuba. The Korean War was ended.

Psychologically, the severest shock during the decade that I can recall was the success of the Russian "sputniks" while our own fell from the sky. Historian Thomas K. Bailey called it "a psychological Pearl Harbor;" *Science News* declared that "the world was changed forever." Speaker Rayburn was deeply grieved. "They tell us we have the greatest engineers in the world and we give the Pentagon tons of money, but something is badly wrong," he said.

Congress for years had wrestled with proposals for federal aid to education. The Russian "sputnik" success opened an angry national debate on the adequacy of American education; Congress responded with the National Defense Education Act, giving scholarships to needy students and lavish grants for teaching sciences and languages. This infusion of federal aid to education broke the door open; in the next decade, federal aid to education became a torrent—often an ill-controlled torrent.

In response to "sputnik," Congress also created the National Aeronautics and Space Administration, and we were on our way to the moon and the planets.

Perhaps the most historic events of the period were those that produced the civil rights revolution. Two Supreme Court decisions mandated the desegration of the public schools and prompted bitter resistance in Little Rock and at the University of Alabama. The Civil Rights Acts of 1957 and 1960 were the opening guns in a revolution of historic world-wide portent.

The first Catholic President was elected.

In Congress itself, many major issues failed of resolution. For a variety of reasons, Truman's popularity was very low during his last two years in office. For six of his eight years as President, Eisenhower wrestled with a Democratic Congress. But important legislation was passed—the St. Lawrence Seaway, the interstate highway program, the Kerr-Mills Medical Aid Act, the tidelands bill, the Griffin-Landrum Labor Reform Act, and the Alaska and Hawaii statehood acts.

The American people were deeply disturbed and divided by many issues in the 1950s—the firing of Douglas MacArthur, Truman's seizure of the steel mills, Estes Kefauver's televised hunt for mobsters, and Joe McCarthy's hunt for subversives.

Perhaps more important, the fifties saw a rise to national power of Dwight Eisenhower, Richard Nixon, Lyndon B. Johnson, John F. Kennedy, and Adlai Stevenson.

So, I now look upon the 1950s, not as a decade of "do-nothingism" or "drifting," but as a decade of great and unnerving events. If the nation did not always see clearly, it often reacted wisely and well. Its response to the civil rights revolution and to sputnik showed a remarkable national resilience. The St. Lawrence Seaway, the interstate highway program, and the admission of Alaska and

Hawaii to statehood were important national improvements.

It was against this backdrop of crises and frustrations that Rayburn lived his "golden years"—the last full decade of his life.

Briefly now, I want to talk about his relations with Presidents Truman and Eisenhower, his long association with Lyndon B. Johnson, and his life with members of the House of Representatives on both sides of the aisle.

Rayburn and Two Presidents

During his Congressional years Sam Rayburn served "*with*, not *under*," eight Presidents. During the 1950s he served with, counseled, criticized, and comforted two—Truman the Democrat and Eisenhower the Republican. Truman was an old, trusted, valued friend; Eisenhower was a newcomer to American politics. On issues such as defense, foreign policy, and reciprocal trade, there was little difference between the two, but on many other issues there was a wide divergence of views. Rayburn's methods of working with the two, of necessity, differed in many respects.

His relation with Truman was close, almost daily, and warmly protective. The Speaker was determined to help his friend in the White House to succeed—for himself, for the Democratic Party, and above all, for the national interest. The interchange of ideas between the two was always frank and cordial, although they were both stubborn men and often argued and acted independently.

Rayburn and Truman had been close friends ever since Truman came to the Senate in 1935. By happenstance, the Missourian was quickly swept into the Rayburn inner circle, and when, sometime in the late 1930s, Rayburn got a private "little room" where he and his friends could go late in the afternoon to drink whiskey and talk politics (the now-famous "Board of Education"), Truman had a standing invitation to join the group.

"Those were ten of the most wonderful years of my life (1935-45)," Truman recalled. "We'd get together and talk things over and compare notes on people, and it didn't take us long to figure out who was an SOB and who wasn't."

Their friendship was no surprise; Rayburn and Truman had much in common. Both were small, stocky men, born into proud but poor Confederate families. Both had dominant mothers. Neither had much formal education, but both loved to read and talk history and politics. Both were simple in their tastes and habits—"We don't put on airs in my family," Rayburn would say.

In politics there were similarities, too. Both were progressives, with a strong streak of populism. They believed that government should work to help the average man—the little man—to get a job, educate his children, own a decent home, and live in safety. The nation should always be militarily strong, and should do its part in world affairs. "You can't be in the world and not be of it," Rayburn would say. Isolationism, they both believed, was the road to ruin.

It was late one April afternoon in 1945 that Truman, walking into Rayburn's "Board of Education," learned the White House was trying to reach him. When he called he was told to come immediately. When he arrived he learned that he was President of the United States.

A few days after Truman was sworn in, Rayburn went to see him.

"The first thing I want to tell you is that I'm not going to call you Harry any longer." Truman protested. "No," the Speaker replied, "I don't call Presidents by their first name. Some day you'll be out of this place and then I'll call you Harry again."

But old habits are hard to break. When Truman came to address a joint session of Congress for the first time, he began speaking without waiting for Rayburn's introduction. As Rayburn leaned over an open microphone, the radio audience heard him say, "Wait a minute, Harry—let me present you."

Like a dutch uncle Rayburn warned him against the worst pitfalls he had observed in White House life for a third of a century. The greatest danger, he said, would lie inside the White House itself; some staffers would try to keep the President from hearing more than one side of an issue. "They'll try to build a wall around you, so you will have to spend much of your time tearing that wall down so you can hear all sides before you make your decisions."

Rayburn had high hopes for his friend. "It is my belief that Mr. Truman is going to make good. He is a good, sound, honest man," he wrote a constituent. Later he wrote a former Congressman: "I think Truman is doing as well as practically anybody could do being catapulted into the position he was without too much training for it. I know he is as honest as any man who ever entered the White House and has a great desire to be of service to the people."

As Truman's fortunes ebbed and flowed—from the peak of his surprising reelection to the lowest rating any President ever scored in a public opinion poll—Rayburn's faith in his old friend never wavered. "Mr. President," he told Truman at the outset, "we are going to stand by you." And Rayburn did, from beginning to end.

Vexed he often was with Truman, for the feisty Missourian, yearning for combat, loved to "shoot from the hip." Rayburn repeatedly warned him against "firing before he saw the whites of their eyes." Truman would reply, "You just wait, Sam, some of those shots are going to take effect." Until the end of the Truman Presidency this dialogue continued.

Truman wanted Rayburn to sit as a member of his Cabinet. Rayburn refused. "My job is to represent the House and relay their views to you, and in turn I must relay your views to the House members. If I start sitting in your Cabinet, pretty soon those fellows will decide that I am your man, not theirs." "Sam was right," Truman later agreed.

Truman and Rayburn differed on burning issues such as civil rights, the return of the tidelands to the states, and the deregulation of natural gas. These were political differences, but such differences never strained their friendship. Once Truman handed Rayburn a bill creating a Fair Employment Practices Commission. The Speaker stuck it in his pocket, where it remained. Later the President chuckled over this. "Sam did that, but I understood. I had to have it introduced in the Senate. Sam knew I had to do that, just as I knew he couldn't do it in the House."

The Speaker's work with Truman fell into two broad categories: the formal weekly meeting of Democratic congressional leaders with the President; and every conceivable type of informal contact. Each week the House and Senate Democratic leaders—the big four—met with the President at the White House to trade notes on the business at hand. Rayburn, having one foot in the Southern conservative camp, often had to play the devil's advocate, and play it he did forcefully. When Rayburn reported that the House would not accept a certain provision of a pending bill, Truman was careful to listen and often he accepted a compromise—unless he wanted to make an issue of the provision.

The more informal contacts took many forms. Truman was an activist President, forever prodding, cajoling, demanding action on his program. He had no hesitancy in telephoning legislative leaders, or writing personal letters or memoranda. White House liaison with Congress was not truly formalized until the Eisenhower years, so communication between the two ends of Pennsylvania Avenue was informal but very active.

Truman and Rayburn did not hesitate to trade advice on legislation and appointments. It was two-way street. The late Justice Tom Clark, seeking appointment to the Supreme Court, asked for Rayburn's help. The Speaker opened his desk drawer, took out a sheet of stationery and wrote the President one sentence, as Clark recalled: "Dear Mr. President: Nothing would make me happier than to see Tom Clark on the Supreme Court." "I think that one note did more to secure my appointment than anything else," Clark said.

Rayburn never ceased not only to defend Truman, but also to defend others in the Administration. When Secretary of State Dean Acheson's standing was at its lowest ebb in the McCarthy period, Rayburn made a public speech in his own congressional district lauding Acheson as one of the all-time great Secretaries of State.

When Truman was gallantly whistle-stopping in 1948, in a campaign that many of his supporters believed was in vain, his train came to Rayburn's hometown of Bonham, Texas, where he spent the night. The Speaker gave him a mammoth reception at his home. When Mrs. Truman and Rayburn's sister Miss Lou left the room, Rayburn sent a secretary upstairs to get a glass of bourbon for the President from a bottle he had hidden from Miss Lou. Both men were afraid of their reigning women.

Rayburn always believed that the tide toward Truman began to turn in 1948 when his campaign train got to Texas. It was a long, warm, trusting friendship that lasted nearly thirty-seven years. "We got to be almost as close as brothers," Truman recalled.

In the decade of the 1950s, Rayburn spent eight years working with President Dwight D. Eisenhower—two years as minority leader (1953-55), and six years as Speaker (1955-61). Eisenhower, in spite of his monumental popularity with the voters—which never seemed to falter—was unable to elect enough Republicans to control either house of the Congress during the last six years of his Administration. That meant divided government, which is agonizingly difficult at best. The temptations to rancorous and wanton political bloodshed are ever-present, and a "deadlock of democracy," to borrow a phrase from James MacGregor Burus, is more than a possibility.

Eisenhower was exceptionally fortunate that during his Presidency the Democratic Party was led in Congress by two non-obstructionist moderates, Sam Rayburn and Lyndon Johnson. Otherwise, his Administration might have been torn to ribbons. For refusing to subscribe to the Robert A. Taft dictum that "the business of the opposition is to oppose," the two Texas Democrats were roundly and continuously criticized, particularly by the liberal wing of the Democratic Party.

Rayburn and Eisenhower had much in common. Eisenhower, eight years younger, was born in Denison, a small town in Rayburn's congressional district, but his family moved when he was a baby. "He was a wonderful baby," Rayburn often chuckled. Both were "middle of the road" in political philosophy; both had a strict sense of national duty; both understood the necessity of compromsie; both were men of kindly goodwill, abhorring venomous, personal attacks.

They stood far apart, however, in their attitude toward politics. Rayburn lived by politics; to Eisenhower, it was "clickety clack." As events developed they differed in other crucial ways as well.

Rayburn's disillusionment with Eisenhower began soon after the new President took office. It came, as Rayburn remembered it, during a meeting between the two in the White House, sometime in January 1953. Anxious to resume the bipartisan approach to foreign policy and national security that had prevailed since 1940, Rayburn told Eisenhower to "just let me know what you want" in the way of defense appropriations, and Democrats would supply the necessary votes. An expression of puzzlement clouded Eisenhower's face. Mistrusting, apparently fearful of a Rayburn trap, he ignored the offer and changed the subject. Rayburn was nonplussed, but he never forgot.

"I told President Eisenhower the other day," Rayburn wrote an El Paso man, "that he should know more about what it took to defend this country than practically anyone and that if he would send up a budget for the amount he thought was necessary to put us in a position to defend ourselves against attack, I would promise him to deliver 95 percent of the Democratic votes in the House of Representatives."

Rayburn felt that there was much rank partisanship on the Republican side of the House. In March 1953, he took the House floor to warn: "If I were the Republican leadership in either the House or the Senate, with the thin majority they have and with as thin ice as they are skating on at this time, I would try to get things done in just as nonpartisan a manner as I possibly could, because there comes a time when partisanship can be practiced on both sides of this House. I know how to cause trouble if I want to."

As 1953 wore on, Rayburn was more and more disillusioned by the Republic performance. On the excess-profits tax extension, Rayburn had to rally Democratic votes to save Eisenhower's bill—Ike couldn't lead his own House Republicans.

"It seems they have been out of power so long that they have lost all ability to lead and be constructive," he wrote one of his political leaders. He told another, "I'm sorry for President Eisenhower. He's not getting any help from Congress or his Cabinet."

By the year's end, Rayburn's patience was near an end. To a constituent he wrote. "He can't find his ass with both hands. He is a good man and wants to do the right thing, but he is in an entirely new field for him. He needs more help than any man who has been President for many years, but he called around him men who never had any political or government experience; not any of them but one has ever held public office or run for public office that I know anything about."

Rayburn and Johnson made a good team from the beginning. Everybody knew it would be a strong team, seeing eye to eye on most issues. "Lyndon is going to be the idea man, and Sam will tell him when it's all right to go ahead," one observer said. As minority leaders they reached an easy agreement on both philosophy and strategy; they would not "obstruct" just for the sake of opposing, particularly on defense and foreign policy. But Rayburn added an "if": he would fight the Eisenhower Administration if it tried to undo "the good thing we Democrats did" in the previous twenty years. "Any jackass can kick a barn down," Rayburn noted, "but it takes a carpenter to build one."

When Eisenhower became President, Rayburn told him: "I'll help you on international affairs and defense, if you can get a majority of your own party to go along." Moreover, Rayburn would help provide the House votes any time Eisenhower sought to extend existing Democratic programs such as reciprocal trade agreements. On other domestic matters, however, especially if Republicans attempted to reverse Democratic policies on public power, reclamation, public housing, taxes, and agriculture, Rayburn reserved the right to oppose. "It is pretty hard for the minority party to have a program (he wrote) because they don't get them considered by the committees, and I have always thought it better for the minority simply to pick to pieces the bad legislation proposed by the majority and try, if possible, to take the bad parts out and put good parts in."

In the early part of the administration, Rayburn had a low opinion of some Eisenhower appointees, especially Sherman Adams, his chief of staff, and Agriculture Secretary Ezra Taft Benson. His special ire was reserved for a presidential secretary named Bernard Shanley, who had been making slashing anti-Democratic speeches. "He made some of the meanest speeches ever made by anybody in the United States," Rayburn wrote John W. Carpenter, a Dallas tycoon, in 1955. "My estimation of him is that he is a 'pip-squeak.' I sent word to him one day that if he made any more speeches like he was making around here, that I would take the floor (of the House) and take his pants off."

Red-baiting McCarthyism reached its peak in this period. Nixon's harsh charges and especially McCarthy's charges of "twenty years of treason" enraged Rayburn. "I have thought all along that McCarthy was the problem of the Republican Party and they would finally have to come to grips with him if they did not allow him to take over the party entirely," he wrote a friend.

Rayburn took the House floor to fling the gauntlet at Eisenhower. "Our backs are getting pretty sore," he said. "The Republican attacks on Democratic patriotism are mean, dastardly, and untrue. They should be stopped by somebody and there is one man in the United States (Eisenhower) that can stop that kind of talk." Eisenhower the next day publicly appealed to his Republican colleagues to "tone down" their criticism of Democrats, but he refused to condemn McCarthy by name.

According to the *Congressional Quarterly*, Rayburn backed Eisenhower on 74 percent of the 1953 "Eisenhower issue" roll calls;

only eight other House members supported the President more frequently. In the first session, *CQ* said, Democrats "saved" Eisenhower bills fifty-eight times when Republicans defected on such issues as aid for drought-stricken farmers, extension of foreign aid, continuation of the reciprocal trade program, and extension of the excess-profits tax. Yet the day-by-day cooperation between Rayburn and Eisenhower required continuous effort and much mutual forbearance. Divided government never works easily. Rayburn placed much of the blame on staff people in the White House, but he also blamed Eisenhower for not keeping them in line. "This administration is the most partisan I have ever seen," Rayburn muttered several times.

A prime example came in 1959 when Eisenhower signed the bill making Hawaii a state. Much of the success of the bill had been due to the personal popularity and untiring efforts of Hawaii's nonvoting Democratic delegate, John Burns. Burns was now the Democratic nominee in the first governor's race. The White House did not want to help his chances of election.

When Rayburn learned that Burns had not been invited to the White House for the signing ceremony, he exploded that he'd be damned if he'd go either. Lyndon Johnson persuaded the irate Rayburn that he must go. When Eisenhower, signing the bill, handed one of the pens to Rayburn, the Speaker dropped it on the desk: "I don't think I want that." The assembled dignitaries stirred anxiously. Then Rayburn changed his mind. Walking back to the President's desk, he said, "I believe I'll take it after all. John Burns might like it."

But Rayburn found it difficult to remain personally angry. Eisenhower was a decent, patriotic, agreeable man. He really was out of place in the White House, Rayburn thought. In 1948, before Eisenhower decided whether he was a Democrat or a Republican, some liberal Democrats, scorning Truman, started a boomlet to nominate Eisenhower as a Democrat. When Rayburn was asked about it, he responded with a very few choice words: "Nope. Good man. Wrong job. Won't do."

But Eisenhower was the only President the country had. He was no isolationist, no medieval reactionary, no corrupt politician. And he needed help—plenty of it. Moreover, to Rayburn, Mamie Eisenhower was a great plus for her husband. Once, at an embassy dinner,

Rayburn told her, "I'm going to say to you, Mrs. Eisenhower, what I have said to many others. As First Lady, you are still the same sweet, unaffected lady you would be if you had been the wife of a corner groceryman or a tenant farmer." "Why, Mr. Sam, that's the nicest thing anybody ever said to me," she replied as she kissed the Speaker on the cheek. The President wheeled around and snapped: "What's going on over there?" Washington heard much gossip about Mamie and her personal problems. Rayburn came fiercely to her defense on every occasion.

After the Democrats recaptured both houses of Congress in 1954, Eisenhower realized that these two Texans held the key to his success or failure. He worked hard at paying court to them. He frequently complimented them in public, and more important he took them into his inner councils. Occasionally he invited them to the White House living quarters for a late afternoon drink and talk. His lobbyists kept in close touch with both leaders. Relations improved, but new disagreements kept cropping up at unexpected times.

Eisenhower was exceptionally fortunate in his choice of congressional lobbyists. Until 1953, White House-Congressional liaison had been rather hit-and-miss. Under Eisenhower the chief burden fell on brilliant, soft-spoken, canny Bryce Harlow, who had worked on Capitol Hill for years. He was trustworthy, truthful, and understanding of the differing problems of the President and the congressional leaders. He had Rayburn's fullest confidence and affection. I always thought the fact that both men were small, terse, truthful, and dynamic strengthened the bond between them. Assisting Harlow was former House member Jack Anderson (R-Calif.), who had been one of Rayburn's fishing partners in previous years. Eisenhower could not have had lobbyists more "simpatico" with Rayburn.

In another important field, foreign affairs, Eisenhower had equally good luck with his lobbyists, though no credit for that is due to the Secretary of State. Eisenhower delegated much of the formulation and execution of foreign policy to his Secretary, John Foster Dulles. But there was a problem—Rayburn held Dulles in "minimum high regard." In 1953 when Rayburn was pushing through the "Truth in Securities" bill to regulate dishonest Wall Street practices, Dulles acted as spokesman for a committee of investment bankers opposing the bill. Rayburn caught Dulles in what he believed to be a deliberate lie; the man from Bonham loathed liars. I cannot vouch for it, but I have been told that while he was Secretary of State, Dulles never set foot in Rayburn's office. Certainly Rayburn viewed him as a narrow-minded, inflexible zealot whose hatred of the Russians was highly detrimental to diplomacy. Once he said, "I sometimes think Dulles hates some of those people so bad he can't talk to them." But again the Eisenhower Administration had good luck. Dulles sent as liaison officers to Rayburn, first Robert Hill, and later William Macomber. The Speaker had great respect for both men, and quickly established a good rapport with them. Both men in fact later had distinguished ambassadorial careers of their own.

So the difficult years passed, and there were considerable accomplishments. The march of civil rights legislation was begun, isolationism was repelled, the United States made an amazing recovery from the shock of the Russian sputnik and began an astounding space program of its own. The nightmare of McCarthyism passed into history, and an atmosphere of good will came back to the country.

As Eisenhower prepared to leave the White House, Bryce Harlow wrote the Speaker, thanking him for all his help. He penned a postscript which, as I recall it, ran like this: "Without you and Lyndon these past eight years, I shudder to think what might have happened."

Rayburn and Johnson

The decade of the 1950s—Rayburn's "golden years"—may also have been the "golden age" of Texas influence in Washington. During the first two years, when they were in the minority, Rayburn and Johnson were the most influential Democratic leaders in both House and Senate. During the final eight years they were the skilled, untiring, dominating forces in the Congress.

The two leaders could not have been more different in appearance or temperament. When the decade began, Rayburn was almost 69, Johnson 43. The Speaker was short (5'6"), while Johnson was tall and powerful. Except for the last four months of his life, the Bonham man enjoyed illness-free, exceptionally robust health. Johnson, for all his extraordinary energy and powerful build, had a variety of illnesses throughout his life. Both were tireless workers, totally immersed in their calling. Their styles were in sharp contrast. Rayburn was quiet, terse, carefully self-disciplined, stingy of time. Johnson had a large measure of theatricality in the way he worked; he seemed to love a crisis and a crash operation. The Speaker said he once told him, "Lyndon, I don't run around and yell and wave my arms half as much as you do, but I think I get just as much done."

Both men possessed a large measure of pride—vanity—which is an attribute of most successful politicians. Rayburn was sensitive about his billiard-ball baldness; he vigorously tried to avoid photographs of his head from the rear. Johnson commanded photographers to shoot his profile from his preferred side. Both men were vainly proud of their jobs, their accomplishments; they liked to talk about them. By Ivy League standards, both men lacked first-rate college educations. That never bothered Rayburn.

Temperamentally they were in sharp contrast. Rayburn was simple, down to earth, old-fashioned; Johnson loved the modern, the grandiose. When dial phones were installed in the Capitol, Rayburn kept his old phone over which he could ask the operator to get a number, while Johnson was one of the first to have a console with a score of buttons to push. Washington laughed at the story that Republican Leader Everett Dirksen was jealous of Johnson's phone in his limousine. So, when Dirksen finally got one, he first dialed the Johnson limousine. Johnson said, "Congratulations, Ev. Wait just a second—the other phone is ringing."

In 1959 Johnson phoned Rayburn at Bonham to tell him that Eisenhower wanted the congressional leaders to come to Washington to be briefed on the President's trip to India.

"I'm not going. He's not gonna tell us anything that hasn't been in the newspapers," the Speaker grumped.

"But you must—I've arranged for General LeMay's plane to take us up and bring us back."

"Well, we can go tourist on Braniff from Dallas for just $69," Rayburn argued.

Rayburn was driven to Carswell Air Base at Fort Worth for the flight. LeMay's plane wasn't there, but waiting were two giant KC-135 tankers.

"Well, I hope *they're* big enough to suit Mr. Johnson," the Speaker chuckled.

In spite of these deep-seated differences in style and temperament, they shared an unyielding mutual devotion and admiration that made the two men almost a father-and-son team. By the start of the 1950s, they had known each other for two decades, beginning in the years when Johnson was a House employee and continuing through his fifteen years in the House and Senate. Furthermore, Rayburn and Sam Johnson, LBJ's father, had served together in the Texas House of Representatives early in the century.

Both men loved politics as if possessed by a demon, and Johnson even outdid Rayburn in the avidity with which he talked politics. As a young man Rayburn loved to read, but by the 1950s, there was little time for book reading. Johnson, like Rayburn, did most of his learning by listening.

Rayburn was terse, almost cryptic, in his speech. His daily press conferences were five minutes long—or less. Johnson was a loquacious, almost compulsive talker. Meeting a friend in the hall, he might talk for an hour. Not Rayburn. Commenting on Johnson's visits to the "Board of Education" for drinks and talk, Rayburn complained that "Lyndon comes over here and tells us every little thing that took place in the Senate that day—a hell of a lot more than we want to hear."

Both were intensely interested in young people, always keeping their eyes open for promising young talent. For example, Rayburn reached down into the House ranks in 1955 and selected Carl Albert as whip and created a new post of deputy whip for Hale Boggs. LBJ once said, in the late 1950s, "If I am not as close to the Speaker as I once was, it is because I'm almost fifty years old. I'm too old for him—did you ever notice—he never has men his age around him—he always associates with people twenty and thirty years younger than himself."

But Johnson had the same disposition. "Ever since I've been in politics, I've been trying to surround myself with talented young people, and I've never been able to assemble as many as I wanted."

In political philosophy the two men were relatively close together—with some basic differences. Both were moderate progressives, with a strong tinge of populism. Both were strong conservationists; both were staunch supporters of education, although Johnson was quicker to accept the necessity for federal aid to schools. Rayburn was more sympathetic to organized labor, but always at arm's length. It seemed to me that Johnson was quicker to sense the need for action on the civil rights front, but in the end Rayburn joined him fully in pushing through the Civil Rights Acts of 1957 and 1960. On foreign policy and national defense, they were as one in combatting isolationism, promoting internationalism and reciprocal trade, and maintaining a strong military posture. On oil and gas legislation, they were Siamese twins.

During their leadership years together the two men had four major goals:

- to lead—or run—the Congress in the national interest;
- to try to keep the warring wings of the national Democratic Party together, with an eye to the next election;
- to seek some common ground on which the embittered Democratic factions in Texas might form a majority; and
- to keep their own political fences up for the next election.

Each man always had to take into account the special qualities of his constituency. Rayburn had a small, compact North Texas district, heavily white Anglo-Saxon Protestant, primarily agricultural, with no cities of great size and no unhappy ethnic groups. Johnson's constituency embraced the largest state in the Union, with variegated and often conflicting economic and social interests, and a true melting pot of ethnic groups. Since the late 1930s the state had moved much to the right from its traditional "brass-collar" Democratic allegiance. Johnson had an excruciatingly volatile and sharply divided constituency, and it was never forgotten that in 1948 he won the Democratic nomination for the Senate by only eighty-seven votes. It is highly doubtful that Sam Rayburn could ever have won a state-wide election.

The Speaker and the Senate Majority Leader not surprisingly had different methods of operating. Some of Rayburn's methods will be discussed later, but it may be said of him here that he was a rather diligent operating engineer, particularly concerned that the trains run on time, while Johnson was the eternal activist, often creating new crises on purpose.

Once, in the late 1950s, I asked Johnson what Rayburn's greatest weaknesses were.

"Two," he answered. "First, he operates his office out of his back-ass pocket. He doesn't know how to use a staff, and in this modern world you have to operate through a staff. Second, he doesn't anticipate crises and try to head them off. He simply waits for them to arrive, and then he deals with them."

Laughing out loud, he related two different conversations he had had with Rayburn in the "Board of Education."

"One night I said, 'Mr. Speaker, that monkey is really on your back.' 'Yup, you're right, Lyndon. But you know what I'm going to do? Tomorrow I'm gonna reach up and take that monkey right off my back,' the Speaker said."

"Another time I thought we were in real trouble. I said, 'Mr. Speaker, this is a bad crisis. This is a real one. You've got to do something!' He jiggled the ice in his whiskey glass and said, 'Well, I've seen damned few of 'em in forty years that I couldn't sit out.'"

One small irritant between the two leaders was Rayburn's view of the United States Senate. Rayburn was unashamedly a "House man," believing that the legislative product of the House, particularly at the committee level, was much better thought out. He scoffed at the Senate as "that place," and referring to the Senate's loose-jointed parliamentary procedure, would say, "Can you imagine a legislative body that tries to operate without rules?" Moreover, the Senate was another world. "We'll have a fine young man here in the House and he gets elected to the Senate, and by God, before he gets to the Rotunda, he starts to strut," Rayburn asserted.

Rayburn had an inflexible rule that he never tried to influence the Senate's actions. After he was elected House majority leader, he never went to the Senate floor—"somebody might think I was lobbying for something." He didn't even like to eat in the Senate restaurant. The Speaker would say, "Lyndon, you run your end of the Capitol and I'll run my end."

Rayburn sometimes suspected that Johnson did not always follow the same rule, although Johnson was always discreet. Johnson maintained close ties with many members of the Texas House delegation and with others. He came to the House side with frequency, always talking politics. When all but three members of the Texas Democratic delegation voted against Rayburn on the crucial test on the Griffin-Landrum labor reform bill, Rayburn and House Parliamentarian Lew Deschler both suspected—but could not prove—that "Lyndon has been talking to some of the boys."

How did Rayburn and Johnson communicate and plan strategy on legislation? Primarily, each went his own way, but communication was frequent and intense—several times a day when an important legislative battle was on. The telephone was the primary means, and calls from either man to the other received top priority. Sometimes a hand-written or dictated note would be delivered across the Capitol by a staff member. Occasionally, a staff member would be dispatched to call either man off the floor to get information in a hurried stand-up conference.

Perhaps most important, there was the "Board of Education" where Johnson came, at least briefly, as often as he could. It might be several nights in a row, or if Johnson was busy, he might not come at all for a week or ten days. (He spurned Rayburn's whiskey, and kept his own Cutty Sark in the Speaker's desk.) There information was exchanged about what was going on in each chamber, or what might take place. The ability and character of members were often evaluated. National or Texas politics had a high priority. Occasionally—but very occasionally—detailed tactics or strategy might be outlined.

As far as they could, Rayburn and Johnson helped each other with political problems. In 1954, Republican Senator Wayne Morse of Oregon switched to an independent status and in 1956 became a Democrat. Morse was up for reelection in 1956 and Rayburn received a call from Johnson.

Rayburn's version:

"Lyndon said, 'Mr. Speaker, Wayne has a rough race for reelection. His vote might be decisive in keeping the Senate under Democratic control. Some House members from Oregon have introduced three bills over there, and if any one gets over to the Senate and Wayne has to vote on them, he's probably a ruined man.'

"So, I got busy and called the subcommittee chairmen who had the bills and they agreed to pigeonhole 'em.

"Well, sir, it wasn't a month until I got another call from Lyndon. 'Mr. Speaker, there are a couple of little bills over there that will ruin Wayne if he has to vote on 'em.' I said, 'Now, listen, Lyndon—there's no way in the world to keep that damned fool out of trouble.' "

So the long years of working together—nearly a quarter of a

century—made of the Rayburn-Johnson friendship a saga of American politics. Rayburn was the Johnsons' closest family friend, sharing their joys and their sorrows. Lady Bird was Rayburn's special love. He had watched her so long, matching her calm, good judgment with her husband's mercurial temperament, her never-failing kindess offsetting the harsher aspects of his nature. "The best thing that boy ever did in his life was to marry that sweet, wonderful girl," Rayburn told many people.

The night Kennedy was assassinated, Johnson came back to Washington as President. When he settled down with a drink, it was reported that he lifted his glass to Rayburn's autographed picture, saying, "Mr. Sam, I wish you were here tonight."

When the Johnsons finally moved to the White House, Lady Bird personally carried this autographed picture. Rayburn knew Johnson like a book, with all his greatness and all his foibles. Frequently exasperated at Johnson, scornful of his judgment at other times, his admiration for—his love for—Johnson never faltered.

During the fifties both men always were conscious of what Rayburn called "Mr. Johnson's vaulting ambition" to be President. It was an ambition which Rayburn shared, and which he would be glad to further—*at the proper time*. But "Lyndon was always in such a hurry."

On April 17, 1959, in a private conversation, Rayburn said that Johnson should be the 1960 Democratic presidential nominee. As the Speaker talked, his listener felt that Johnson's nomination would be rich compensation to Rayburn for never having been nominated himself.

Rayburn, then seventy-seven, ended the conversation: "Lyndon is the ablest man we have for the job. Of course, if I was sixty, I wouldn't say so."

Rayburn

Perhaps the best description ever penned of Sam Rayburn was done by his loyal lieutenant, Congressman Dick Bolling (D-Mo.), in his book, *Power in the House*:

> Short, stocky, erect, and shiny bald, Rayburn exuded strength. He knew more about the ins and outs of the legislative process in the House than any other member. He sucked up information about the

House, its committees, employees, members, and activities like a giant vacuum cleaner. The result was that he knew nearly everything that was going on. He had done ten thousand favors for hundreds of members. When the House was in session, it was his whole life. A childless, unmarried, single-minded man, he devoted twelve to fourteen hours each day to the House, those connected with it and its affairs and then retired early to his lonely, quiet apartment. He was kind and helpful to all new members and to all old members, too, unlike most House seniors. He took a personal interest in their families, their private and public problems, and their careers in the House. He could be remarkably persuasive. He seemed simple but was complex; he seemed open and frank but kept his own counsel to a degree not often comprehended by even his closest associates.

Rayburn was preeminently a leader: he made men want to come together rather than pull apart. Not only was he one of the most successful leaders in the history of the Congress; his leadership in the Democratic Party was perhaps even more successful. During the 1950s the Democratic Party, after its crushing presidential defeats of 1952 and 1956, was a cauldron of seething factions. Rayburn worked tirelessly to promote peace and reunion. *New York Times* analyst James "Scotty" Reston referred to him as the glue that held the Party together.

Why are a few men leaders and the vast majority not? Leadership, like love, defies human analysis. Scholars usually have chosen to plow around this stump rather than confess defeat. Rayburn himself could not analyze leadership. "You can't really say how you lead. You feel your way, receptive to those rolling waves of sentiment. And if a man can't see and hear and feel, why then, of course, he's lost," he once said.

But this man was a national leader for so long that I am going to venture to list some of the qualities which may—*may*—have gone into creating that leadership.

1. *Honesty*—Rayburn was a unique Washington figure in that even his enemies never challenged his honesty. "It's so easy to be honest; so hard to be dishonest," was a favorite saying. Early in his career he bought $1,000 worth of Kirby Petroleum stock; he worried that he might some day find himself in a conflict of interest, so he sold it. After that, he owned only government bonds, Fannin

County farmland, and cattle. His reputation for truthfulness was a great asset. "Tell the truth the first time, then you don't have to remember."

Privately discussing the Supreme Court decision ordering school desegregation, he said, "If you or I had been on that Court, we would have voted like all those justices did—if we were honest men."

He gave Liz Carpenter his recipe for dealing with the media: "First, always be accessible. Those people have a job to do. Second, you don't have to tell them anything—that's your business. But if you do tell them anything, make damned sure it's the truth."

2. *Justice*—"The greatest ambition a man can have is to be a just man—to realize that every other human being has just as much right to be on this earth as you have." This Rayburn dictum implies careful fairness to all with whom you deal.

When it appeared that the seniority system had put Congressman William Dawson (D-Ill.) in line for the chairmanship of the Government Operations Committee—which would make him the first black chairman in Congressional history—a Southern member of the committee complained to Rayburn, "Why if Bill becomes chairman, we'd have to rise when he came in the committee room and we'd have to call him 'Mr. Chairman . . . ' " Rayburn cut him short. "You've got your tenses wrong. Bill *has* become chairman."

Republican Congressman Bruce Alger from Dallas conducted an angry, ill-tempered attack on Rayburn for several years. At the same time, Dallas was pleading for construction of a mammoth federal office building. Rayburn quietly had the subcommittee sit on the bill for several years. One day he told the chairman to bring the bill up for a vote. A friend protested, "Alger and the *Dallas News* and a lot of those fatcats have been so hateful to you for so long that I'd let 'em freeze in hell."

"No," Rayburn replied, "that wouldn't be fair to those people. They really need that building—federal agencies are scattered all over Dallas. I held that bill up so that the Dallas people could finally learn that Alger, for all his talk, couldn't deliver the goods. Now they know that, so they're going to get their building."

In his autobiography, *Outsider in the Senate*, Clinton Anderson (D-N.M.), who had served with Rayburn in the House, wrote:

IV/Johnson and Rayburn • 248

> In his well-organized mind, he (Rayburn) kept accurate accounts on the people he dealt with, rewarding them for political services and punishing them for political slights. Everyone knew he was honest and that when the opportunity arrived for settling a score he would do it fairly and justly.

This policy of fair play was particularly in force in the way in which Rayburn presided over the House. From 1789 forward, Speakers were highly partisan, but after the First World War, a policy of fair play toward the minority party began to operate, and Rayburn in his long tenure greatly strengthened it. Today one of a Speaker's most seriously undertaken duties is the protection of the rights of the minority party under the rules of the House.

Once, when Rayburn was sworn in as Speaker, he said: "I want to tell every member of this House that my door will always be open to you. I stand ready at all times to help any member with any personal problems."

But he also would help Republicans on political problems. One year Republican Leader Charles Halleck told Rayburn: "I'm in a terrible bind. Two of my strongest supporters are fighting over one place on the Judiciary Committee. Either one I choose, I will make a mortal enemy. Would you consider enlarging the committee by two, giving us another seat and giving you another seat?"

"Let me talk to Manny Celler," the Speaker said. Celler was a New York Democrat and chairman of the committee. He was adamant in his refusal. Rayburn countered, "Listen, Manny, we'll let you pick out one of your good northern liberals to go in the new place. We've got to help Charley Halleck out. Sleep on it." The next day, Celler agreed, and Halleck kept both of his friends.

3. *Judgment and Common Sense*—When a soldier goes into battle, he wants his commander to be a man of solid judgment, not a damn fool. So it is with legislators. "Common sense is all the sense there is. You can be highly educated, but if you don't have judgment to go with it, you're still a fool," Rayburn often said. Once Jesse Jones of Houston, Secretary of Commerce under FDR, was asked what Rayburn's greatest quality was. Jones, no great friend of the Speaker, paused and said: "His ability to think clearly." On the morning in 1960 when Rayburn withdrew his strong opposition to LBJ's accepting the vice-presidential nomination, Rayburn clois-

tered himself in a hotel bedroom and thought his problem through.

Coupled with this reasoning capacity was a prodigious memory. Staffers quickly learned always to tell the Speaker the same story, or he would cut them off: "Didn't you tell me awhile back so-and-so?" Late one afternoon in the Rayburn Library in Bonham he saw a copy of Hugo's *Les Miserables*. He began quoting a long, involved description of Napoleon on the field of Waterloo. "He's ad-libbing," I said to myself. When he left, I checked the quotation, which he had last read some forty years before. His memory had not failed him.

Perhaps a part of his common sense was the fact that he was a very cautious and patient man. "About the greatest thing any man ever said was, 'Wait a minute'" was one of his favorite quotations. He would not be rushed into a hasty decision. Several times, when he did not believe conditions were right to send a bill to a committee for consideration, he would simply hold the bill on his desk until the atmosphere changed. One bill he held for forty-one days and a member joked, "Now I know how long Noah's ark was on the waters. Sam kept that bill one day longer."

4. *Knowledge of the Past*—Rayburn had a great love of American history, which gave him perspective. When he was a young Congressman, Speaker Champ Clark (D-Mo.) gave him a list of biographies covering the period from the American Revolution onward. Rayburn read each of them and retained much of what he read. As a young Congressman he liked to stay around older members to soak up historical lore about Congress.

Having been the boy Speaker of the Texas House, he valued more than most members the importance of a knowledge of the rules of parliamentary procedure. Here lay great power. Over the years Rayburn gained a real mastery of procedure, and throughout his Speakership he had the invaluable help of Lewis Deschler, House parliamentarian for nearly half a century—perhaps the world's greatest expert on legislative procedure.

In addition to his knowledge of American history and parliamentary procedure, his remarkable memory absorbed an incredible amount of information about most of the congressional districts in the nation—their political complexion, their economic interests, their ethnic makeup, and more important, what a member could and could not vote for if he wanted to be reelected.

Once an able young friend wanted to be named to the Ways and Means Committee, which handles tariff legislation. Rayburn worked zealously to keep members off that committee if they were opposed to the reciprocal trade program. He told the young member, "I'll help you get on any other committee, but not Ways and Means. I know you think you'll support reciprocal trade, but I have been watching that district since before you were born. You have some important marginal folks there that demand that their member vote for high tariffs, and you just can't stand that heat."

5. *Modesty*—Rayburn was inordinately proud of his accomplishments. He was even prouder of the House of Representatives and its service to the nation since 1789. He was a fierce defender of the dignity, the power, and the prerogatives of the Speakership, and he made every effort to augment, not detract from, the stature of the office. But he successfully walked the thin line between pride and arrogance. He had walked with the mighty, but he never lost the common touch. The shyest farmer in his district was at ease with him.

Once he told Dwight Dorough, his first biographer in *Mr. Sam*, that he believed the real test of a man was the way he carried success. A person who became conceited and arrogant when promoted to a big job was not big enough for that job.

Yet Rayburn did not always follow his own formula in judging other men. He was a great admirer of Secretary of State Dean Acheson, one of the most arrogant men of modern times. "Dean Acheson is going down in history as one of the great Secretaries of State, but by God, I wish he had run for sheriff just once."

6. *Ability as a Speaker*—A useful tool of leadership is the ability to communicate clearly. Rayburn was an excellent speaker, particularly when speaking without a manuscript. His deep, rich voice matched his short, clear, "one-cylinder" words. He spoke with emotion, deliberation, decisiveness, and clarity.

One of his most powerful and effective speeches was made almost at the end of his life when he successfully led the fight to enlarge the House Rules Committee so the Kennedy program could be considered. The speech bristled with power, drama, and eloquence.

7. *Decisiveness*—Rayburn was slow to make major decisions, but nearly all who worked with him considered him a decisive man.

Once he felt that he had the necessary facts, he would make his decision and stick doggedly by it. He angered President Eisenhower by torpedoing his plan for presidential succession, but he never changed his mind. As a second-term Congressman, he flatly defied Woodrow Wilson to his face over a railroad bill. Wilson tried to defeat him in the next election—without success.

When the House Committee on Un-American Activities televised its hearings in defiance of his adverse ruling, Rayburn ordered the hearings to cease and he excoriated the chairman. In spite of strong pressure from the networks and from many Representatives, he refused to allow the televising of House proceedings. He had made up his mind and his square shoulders could take the heat.

8. *Faith*—The Speaker was a man of many enthusiastic faiths—his country, its Constitution, the Congress, the nation's young people, and people in general. "Most people are mighty good people," he said, "Ninety-eight percent of them will meet you halfway."

At the end of the 1950s, Rayburn was nearing his last birthday—his 79th—but he never succumbed to the cynicism and pessimism that often overtakes old men. He was an optimist to the end. Faith—optimism—is contagious, and the fact that Rayburn was a man of great faith made it easy for men to follow him.

As the decade drew to a close in December 1960, Rayburn, had he troubled to do so (which he didn't), would have found more good than bad in its record. He would settle for fifty-one percent any time. The bitterness of the McCarthy period and the Korean War had dissipated; the Democratic Party was no longer charged with "twenty years of treason." The nation had grown in economic strength. The alarm brought on by the Russian sputniks had been replaced by pride in our own astonishing space program. The civil rights revolution was in full swing, and the American people were accepting it with generally good grace.

The Democratic Party, angrily splintered during much of the 1950s, had reunited to elect a President—the first Catholic President in history—with Lyndon Johnson as Vice-President. Texas Democrats—who repeatedly have vindicated Will Roger's declaration that "I am not a member of an organized party; I'm a Democrat"—had come together long enough to carry the Lone Star State for the Kennedy-Johnson ticket, probably salvaging the election thereby. History will not record the "blood, sweat, and tears" that Rayburn and Johnson suffered in order to bring the warring Texas Democrats under one tent.

As 1961 began, the nation would have a dynamic new President. The Democrats once again had full responsibility for governing the country. The nation had made great strides in curbing old prejudices. The world was relatively at peace.

"Yes," Rayburn might well have said, "on the whole, it's been a purty good ten years."

Lyndon B. Johnson
and Senate Leadership

R.K. Huitt

Ralph K. Huitt is currently Executive Director of the National Association of State Universities and Land-Grant Colleges in Washington, D.C., and a Professor of Political Science (on leave) at the University of Wisconsin. He served as Assistant Secretary for Legislation, U.S. Department of Health, Education and Welfare in the Johnson Administration.

Party leadership in the Senate of the United States is not a constitutional position of leadership, but like all political jobs in the United States it is deeply influenced by what *is* written into the Constitution.

The first great constitutional provision that affects it is federalism. Everyone knows, more or less, what federalism is (though college students in an American Government can be warned that a sure question on the final examination will be "What is federalism?" and a third of the class still may miss it). Federalism is a system of government in which power is divided between two levels of government, with some powers assigned to one level (in our case the national government) and the rest reserved to the other (in America, to the states) in a constitutional system which cannot be changed without the participation of both levels.

A federal system is very difficult to operate. Drawing the "line of federalism"—i.e., deciding what powers really belong to each level— is a continuous problem. This problem makes it easy for politicians to confuse and fool people. One remembers a presidential candidate who made much of "law and order," a term which to most Americans at that time meant safe streets, parks, and neighborhoods, over which the government housed in Washington, D.C., has little control. One remembers that the question of what, say, the commerce power really means, has occupied the Supreme Court throughout most of our history.

Why then did the founding fathers choose so difficult a system? Why not a unitary system, with state and local governments directly subordinate to the national? The answer is that the federal system provided in the Constitution was about as strong a central government as the people would accept at that time. It was the states that had prestige and enjoyed the affection of the people. Those who were drafting the Constitution were careful to keep secret from the people what was going on in Philadelphia lest the new nation be stillborn. And when the Constitution was ratified over much bitter protest, the states still had more prestige and the love of the citizenry. Men resigned from high-ranking offices in the new central establishment to take similar jobs in state government. For a long time the people did not travel to Washington to visit the seat of the new government. To Americans today, accustomed to the overweening power exercised by the holder of the "delegated" powers, that may seem unbelievable, but it is true.

The political consequence of federalism is localism. The national politician is and must be the product and servant of a local electorate. Even the President, our most truly national leader, achieves his office by putting together local electorates one by one; only thus can he be nominated and elected. Members of either house of Congress are even more irrevocably committed to the people who elected them. The record is filled with stories of national leaders who have been retired from their glory by people who came to believe that they cared more for the world or the nation than for the "folks back home." Thus a Senate leader, for example, cannot rely on national newspapers or the respect of his colleagues to tell him how he is doing. Three leaders of the Democratic Party in the Senate have been retired by their states in this century—James Worth Kern of Indiana (one term), Scott Lucas of Illinois, and Ernest McFarland of Arizona (each after two years as leader). Party leaders come under criticism from leaders of national wings of the party because they support local interests in the Congress. But if they did not, retribution could be swift and lethal. Needless to say, what a leader can get his party colleagues to do is limited by the same conditions.

The second great basic condition is imposed by the constitutional provision for a separation of powers. That was the principle which Locke and Montesquieu believed existed in the British constitution and to which they, and Blackstone (who was also read by colonial American lawyers), ascribed the freedom from tyranny that marked the English system. The notion of separation of powers also fit the experience of the American colonists, who had dealt with a governor and an upper house which generally belonged to the King, and a lower house which they regarded as their own. So they put the doctrine in their constitution, though they softened it appreciably by "checks and balances."

In practice, the doctrine prevents any person from serving in more than one branch of government at the same time. Actually, the *powers* are commingled; all three branches exercise some part of the legislative, executive, and judicial powers. Separation of powers nevertheless has had an enormous effect on the national government of the United States. It has made impossible the evolution of a parliamentary form of government. The English model, as it has developed, depends absolutely on a ministry which at once provides leadership for both the legislature and the executive. The House of Commons can take guidance and information from the ministry on matters in the executive because the ministry is *their* leadership also. If it deceives or misleads the House, or if it simply ceases to be acceptable, the House may turn it out.

Neither house of the American Congress has, or can have, such relations with the Executive. The response of the houses of Congress to the need to react to legislative proposals was the classic American one; they appointed committees; first, ad hoc committees, then standing committees, and finally committees with specialized jurisdictions. The addition of the seniority principle, generally observed, made the system complete. Neither the President nor the party leader can control either house. A committee of local men, led by a chairman who is a local man, cannot be dominated from outside. And the committees collectively represent a kind of feudal system. The powers of each house are parcelled out to the feudal baronies of the committees. This makes Congress the most powerful legislature in the world, and it imposes upon whoever would lead it in either house the necessity for knowledge of his house and infinite patience, self-discipline, and resourcefulness.

For much of the late nineteenth century and the first half of the twentieth, many American political scientists looked on the American political system as a kind of flawed British system which, with a bit of persuasion, might be made more like the prototype. Plans were put forward for a "more responsible party system." It was generally recognized that "responsibility"—i.e., the ability of the party leadership to make the House of Commons do its will and thus carry out promises made to the electorate—had been purchased at the price of reducing individual members to little voting machines who dutifully walk past the tellers to vote the party line.

At the same time, however, it was understood that democracy in Britain had been preserved through a cabinet whose collective will governed the nation, the prime minister presiding over it as "first among equals." But now the three volumes of Richard Crossman's great "Diaries of a Cabinet Minister" have made it clear that the prime minister is not first among equals, he is just plain first. This assessment is reinforced when we see prime ministers shuffling their cabinets and making replacements; the powers to hire and fire are the sure and certain attributes of a boss. Many members of Parliament, who enjoy prestige and status as MPs, long for some of the actual power enjoyed by members of Congress whose prestige is not as high. A number of British politicians and political scientists, seeing correctly that the source of individual Congressmen's power is the committee system, have suggested that committees be grafted onto the parliamentary system. No doubt that would enhance the power of the MP, but those who are dedicated to parliamentary institutions understand that the central element of responsibility is the concentration of power, and hence they are unwilling to allow committees to share in legislative control.

It must be remembered that the leader of a party in the Senate is neither a national officer (as the Speaker also is not) nor an officer of the chamber in which he sits (which the Speaker is). He is only the elected leader of his own party in his own house. The division of labor in each house between the party leaders and the committee chairmen seems to be that the chairmen work legislation through their committees, and then the leadership accepts the responsibility of passing it through the house.

The leader faces this task with very few formal powers. He must put together "fragments of power," as David Truman states it, combining them with his tactical skill and his knowledge of his colleagues. He has the "power of recognition," which means he must be recognized for the floor first when he pleases, which is a parliamentary advantage. If he is a Democrat, he is chairman of two party committees which strengthen his hand; through the Policy Committee the scheduling of legislation on the floor can be controlled; through the Steering Committee the membership of standing committees can be influenced. The leader in the Senate has the advantage of knowing more than other Senators because he is the center of the party communication network in his chamber, and even if he is in the minority, he will have superior access to the President. The power to share or withhold information certainly augments his influence. Added to these are small favors he can extend which make life better for individual Senators. It is not true that he has "no more power than any other Senator," as Mike Mansfield once put it, but this modest array of tools certainly does not equip him to be boss.

Some elements of the leader's power potential are both crucial and variable. Perhaps the most important among them is the situational element. The most productive bursts of legislative output in this century came in the early years of the Administrations of Woodrow Wilson, Franklin Roosevelt, and Lyndon Johnson. The Senate leader, in each case, had a President of his own party who came into office with a landslide victory, accompanied by eager legions in Congress who were passionately ready to carry out initiatives for which a majority of the people had long been ready. James Worth Kern, Wilson's floor leader, was a freshman, but progressives like himself dominated the Democrats in the Senate. Joseph Robinson and Mike Mansfield, leaders respectively for Roosevelt and Johnson, had no problem getting support for their Presidents' programs. Johnson, on the other hand, began as a minority leader with Eisenhower as President, and never during his tenure as leader did he have a Democrat in the White House. That may indeed have been a help rather than a hindrance inasmuch as he enjoyed a freedom not vouchsafed to others to fight where and on what terms he chose.

The major problem of Johnson's two years as minority leader came from the situational aspects of two of his immediate predecessors in the leadership post, Scott Lucas and Ernest McFarland. Each had a President (Truman) who was aggressive and program-minded but was unable to get adequate congressional support for his program. Truman won reelection to office on what he considered to be a public mandate for his civil rights program. Lucas knew how divisive and controversial civil rights issues were among Senate Democrats. Therefore he urged Truman to enact legislation favored by all Democrats early in the session and to save the explosive civil rights questions for later. Truman insisted on civil rights first. The Senate party was shattered. Lucas was defeated for reelection. McFarland was picked for the leadership, mainly because he was liked by almost everybody; the Senate party would probably have been unwilling to have as leader a senator who was strong-minded and clearly identified.

Johnson's first two years as leader thus must be viewed in light of that situation: the membership included forty-eight Republicans, forty-seven Democrats and one Wayne Morse. Morse tried to dignify his lonely isolation by dubbing himself the Independent Party of the United States of America and making long oral reports to the people for that party on Friday afternoons. Both the Democrats and Republicans declined to return him to his old Republican committee assignments at the cost of excluding one of their own members, but the Democrats could usually depend on his vote. That was not Johnson's concern, however; the luxury of not having to win was too valuable to sacrifice. Johnson's supreme goal in that interregnum was to restore unity to a fragmented Democratic Senate party.

The strategy was to make them think as Democrats and Senators, not as liberals or conservatives. No opportunity was too small to seize upon. One happy event was the floor vote on the contested election of Dennis Chavez, a Democratic Senator from New Mexico. There was no ideological dimension that could be introduced. The general value that all elections should be as clean as possible was uniformly accepted; beyond that, it was only human nature to help a friend and colleague hold onto his job. But Johnson made it a party issue just the same, rallying a solid block on the floor consisting of every Democratic member. The exercise was bracing and good for the soul. A Johnson letter thanked each member for his loyalty and reminded him how good it felt to be a Democrat.

Senatorial pride was also used as cement. At one time a presidential appointment of a business man to the National Labor Relations

Board was about to go through Senate approval unscathed. The charge that he was a conservative picked for his biases caused not a flurry; the NLRB was notorious for its political appointees. But a Johnson staffer discovered that the man had made contradictory statements to a Senate committee, an occurrence hardly unique in Senate history. But oh—that was different: playing fast and loose with the United States Senate! The present generation must, as an act of faith, believe that there were old Senate moguls then who would and did respond to that charge. The appointment was stopped and a variegated combination of political types were brought together again.

One more homely illustration should suffice to drive home the point. In the post-Truman session, some Republican leaders filled the paper with cries that the Democrats (not Truman) were corrupt. The Southerners were not moved; they knew the slander was aimed at Truman. Johnson carried daily a cleanly typed page putting side-by-side the Nixon and Dewey statements with the "bloody-shirt" statements of the post-Civil War era. The old lions got the point: this was the way Republicans had always talked about "us Democrats."

Another variable is how leaders have viewed their role in relation to the President. In many instances the Senate leader has considered himself the Senate's man, that is, a delegate from the Senate to the President. Some others have regarded themselves as the President's man in the Senate.

Johnson never did serve with a Democratic President, of course, and there's little point in speculating on what his attitude would have been had he done so. My guess is that he would have considered himself a partner of the President, as Bob Taft clearly did when he was the Republican leader. Nevertheless, I think that along with his deep abiding knowledge of and concern for the Congress, Lyndon Johnson also had a great respect for the Presidency of the United States.

Toward the end of his leadership there was much dissatisfaction with him on the part of some liberals who thought that he ought to be making issues—in other words, opposing Eisenhower, showing up Eisenhower if he could, trying to make issues on which the Democratic Party could win in 1960. The chief editorial writer of the *Milwaukee Journal* once asked for fifteen minutes with Lyndon.

Johnson wanted to see him because he wanted to tell the midwestern liberals what he was up to. So, he brought the writer in and gave him forty-five minutes of the "treatment." The editor was a bit punchy when he left. But the writer was a Lyndon Johnson man after that forty-five minutes, and he went back to Wisconsin as one of the friends Johnson had there. Johnson did not have many friends among the party leaders and not many friends on the faculty at the University of Wisconsin. But friends could be found among people in filling stations and people who sold insurance and the like. They knew what he was up to, they liked him and they admired him, and they supported him.

In regard to the matter of forcing issues with President Eisenhower, Johnson told the present writer that he tought the Presidency of the United States was the one great office in the system and that in his opinion to attack the President inevitably was to attack the Presidency. So, he said, he was not going to pull Eisenhower down, even if he could, just in order to create issues with him and make him look bad so the Democrats could win in 1960. He said, "We tell old Ike what to do and if he does it, we give him a twenty-one-gun salute!" That was the kind of support he gave the President.

In regard to making issues, he also was very much afraid of letting the Democrats, who were not in the White House, begin thinking from a minority viewpoint. That has happened to the minority party several times. It happened to the Democrats before Roosevelt won; they were out so long that they got to be simply "obstructionists." And of course that also happened to the Republicans when they were out so long. How terrible for a party to get in such a shape that quibbling and haggling and crying is the only thing they can do. Johnson was absolutely determined that the Democrats would not get in that frame of mind, so he treated them and made them treat themselves as a majority party all the time that Eisenhower was in the White House.

The Johnson achievement in the Senate suggests, nevertheless, that the most important variable in the leader's performance may be his own perception of his role and the requirements he imposes on himself.

There were two very revealing interviews in the *U.S. News and World Report* that light up this subject. One was with Johnson about a year before he completed his tenure as Democratic leader; the other was with Senator Mansfield about two years after he assumed that job. Johnson insisted that the only power he had was the power to persuade. That is not unlike saying "the only wind we have around here is hurricanes." When Johnson decided to persuade somebody he turned it all on. He knew the man he was talking to and what was needed to win him over—a small reminder of past favors and a hint of favors to come, and a dark suggestion of how unhappy people could be who weren't Lyndon's friends. All of this, put together and used separately, and delivered with an urgency hard to resist, made his "only" power quite enough by itself.

Mansfield said in the interview (and at other times) that Johnson was the greatest leader the Senate ever had—but that he did not wish to be like Johnson. He was not an unsuccessful Johnson. He was a successful Mike Mansfield, which was quite a different thing. He said that he was just "one among peers," and he meant it. He often said that as leader he wanted only to help all the Democratic Senators to achieve as much of what they individually wanted as he could. He did not round up votes or hold long sessions in order to pressure Senators to reach compromises and pass bills. In effect, he did not set out to lead Democrats in the Senate. It is probable that the Senate Democrats admired and respected Johnson more, but liked Mansfield's leadership better because they liked the freedom he gave them to do what they pleased.

In philosophy and approach, Johnson was a legislative pragmatist. What he wanted was accomplishments. He would work with the committees, but he would not tell the committees what to put in a bill. He would say, "We want a bill, and we want a good bill."

There was a time when he and Eisenhower did have a little public confrontation. Eisenhower vetoed a farm bill and went on television and told the country why he vetoed it. Johnson asked for equal time and got it, and he produced his little charts and showed why the bill should have been signed. He referred to that several times later on, always with regret and with a little bit of disgust. He would say, "Ike got his time on TV and I got my time on TV, and the farmers didn't get a bill." And that was his concern. "Let's get a bill, let's turn out something, let's get houses, let's get farm prices, let's get whatever it is we are trying to get and not score cheap points where nothing is accomplished."

He worked with the Policy Committee, with the Conference, with the Steering Committee—a collaboration made much easier by the fact that in the Democratic Party, the majority leader is the chairman of each of those committees. But it was his power of persuasion, his personal involvement, his mastery of detail, that gave him his great influence.

Now a word about Bobby Baker. Bobby Baker, whose title was that of Secretary to the Democratic Party in the Senate—not a very important-sounding title—was a great tool in a fine hand. Bobby Baker did not get in trouble while he worked for Lyndon Johnson; he never had time to. When would he have done it? After midnight—or two o'clock in the morning or something like that? His energy was apparently inexhaustible. He was a person who was great at the head count. He would find out who was likely to vote which way—and that is the heart of the matter in a body where a majority wins.

The great art of the politician is to know how to divide any number by two and add one, and if he can do that, he has the basic skill. That is what Baker helped the leader do. He moved around with tidbits of information, going up to a Senator and telling him something useful and picking up information in return. He was very helpful in that way. And he was an old Senate man, in the sense that he had all of the biases and values of the Senate.

As leader, Johnson was careful to keep his role straight. He was a Senator from Texas and he was also the leader. When he was merely a Senator from Texas, he had not hesitated to fight for the oil industry, which is after all one of Texas's great interests. But when he assumed the leadership role he ceased playing the champion of local interests; he had to take a broader view and assume a broader responsibility in order to lead a party which was divided on oil issues.

He made great use of the "Democratic bench"; he understood what the talents of each Democratic Senator were and he pulled the right man out at the right time. He used some of them as "umbrellas." He knew, for instance, that if Senator George could be got to say something in favor of the position that Johnson wanted, all the southerners could be counted on to take that position, too, because when they went home they could say, "I voted just like Mr. George." The same thing was true of the liberals with Humphrey. If he could get Humphrey to take a stand, then the liberals could all go home and say, "I voted just like Hubert."

He knew how to put together a majority. If there was a controversy over a bill, he would get the people on all sides together behind the scenes and they would work until they could get a compromise which all could support. Then they would all come back to the floor and beat down every amendment to the bill and pass what they'd agreed upon.

While the negotiations were going on, the Senate was put in stall, kept in session by Senators making speeches on various subjects. It was a dramatic moment when the center doors in the back flew open and Johnson stode in, flanked by the negotiators—who often were very dissimilar in ideology. The speeches stopped and the bill was called. Another strategy was to keep the Senate in session very late. People who work long hours reduce their speeches and objections and finally are ready to make concessions. In calm periods Johnson let the members go early. When big issues were to be resolved, the lights burned late, the treaty-makers beat down all amendments, and the job was done. Part of the agreement often was that later on the leadership would bring up issues the negotiators had agreed to delay.

* * *

It must be said finally that the remarkable achievement of Lyndon Johnson's leadership in the Senate cannot be explained merely by the attributes of the job or the tactics of the leaders. The heart of the matter is Lyndon Johnson himself. Horace Busby once said that "Lyndon Johnson was a very unusual child—he dominated the family from the day he was born." And I have heard a cabinet member say that "Johnson could run any organization in the world—the Ford Motor Company, the Soviet government, anything."

So this was a remarkable and different kind of man. I should confess that I do not know the secret of why that was so. I have read accounts of his childhood and upbringing which purported to account for the special qualities in the man. But speaking as a contemporary of Johnson and a Texan, it seems to me that his childhood and upbringing were about the same as those of about half the boys of Texas in that time. And the same, I am told by friends, as boys in many other states. Needless to say, very few of those boys became President, and it is safe to say, not many had a Johnson personality. An analogy can be found in the lives of many great men. Napoleon was taunted and rejected by snobbish French cadets at a French military school. But so were many other Corsican lads, no one of whom became a Napoleon. The notion of the unique person cannot be rejected out of hand.

As somebody said when I first went to work in his office, "He's like a force of nature," and I think that's not too extravagant. He was a "do it now" man. One of the reasons why he got so much done was that if he knew at twelve o'clock at night that something needed to be done, he didn't wait to start it the first thing in the morning. He started it then.

For instance, when the word came over the television and radio in 1952 that McFarland had lost in Arizona, the Senate liberals began musing on what they would do when they got back to Washington and whom they were going to support. But long before they ever got around to doing anything about it, Johnson had the job nailed down. He and Russell—on the telephone all night long—decided the issue. He was willing to exercise self-discipline and make the personal sacrifices that were necessary in order to get done what he wanted to do.

I remember going one night to a dinner party in Washington where I met a very nice woman who worked in the Johnson Senate office. She told me she worked so hard for a while that her health broke down and she had to be out for several months. I said, "Then why are you working there now? Are you crazy? Do you want to die?"

She said, "No, I work there because I have a sense of a force, a current, a power in the office that passes through me too, and it's exciting to feel as though I've got hold of a high-charge wire."

I believe that all of us who worked for him felt that way. When he died a force went from our lives. The hill country brought forth a giant. I think we shall not see his like again in our time.

Discussion

ALAN BIBLE: I first met Harry Truman in 1948 during his railroad whistle-stop campaign against Tom Dewey. Pat McCarran introduced me to him. He said, "Bible, Bible—that's the best damn political name I ever heard." And that is true.

I first met Lyndon Baines Johnson when he came to the Silver Slipper in Las Vegas, Nevada, during my first campaign. He was out plugging for the ticket, as he always did. He looked at me; he shook his head three or four times, and I don't blame him. He figured, "Good God, is this the best we have to offer?" But notwithstanding that, he said a few kind words. I was elected and served in the U.S. Senate for some twenty years—the remaining two years of Pat McCarran's term, and then three of my own. Then I retired voluntarily and I did it because I was tired and worn out; I thought I had been there long enough.

Lyndon Johnson was a big brother to me. He always felt he had me in his hip pocket when he needed a vote, and the strange part of it is he usually did have. When you go up against a 6'3" Texan with those long arms enfolding you—first, flattering you, then cajoling you, and then finally battering you, it's hard to resist. "Let's see, you have a bill up here that you would like, wouldn't you, for Nevada? Now, if you think you're going to get that unless you vote right, you are wrong." Then he would go back to the majority leader's office and check off all those votes.

Another thing for which I am grateful to Lyndon Johnson was that he put me on the District of Columbia Committee. Most Senators think the D.C. committee is the end of the earth, but he put me on there anyway. I only wanted to be on for one term, but right behind me was a fellow named Wayne Morse, and there were always some differences of opinion between Wayne Morse and Lyndon Johnson. At that time Wayne Morse was a Republican and Johnson was a little fearful that if Wayne Morse were chairman of the D.C. Committee, we would have had reforms starting in every aspect of government, using the District of Columbia as the experimental laboratory. He probably was right.

In those days Bill Knowland was the majority leader and Lyndon was the minority leader. The election of 1956 was coming along and Lyndon wanted me to run. I had said that after serving the unexpired term of Pat McCarran I was going to go back to Nevada where things weren't quite as hectic and I understood most of the problems a little better. Lyndon Johnson told me that whatever I wanted to do was all right—that I was free to make up my own mind—that he enjoyed having me there, but if I wanted to retire, that was all right. What he didn't tell me was that he had primed about every other person he knew to twist my arm, and it almost broke. I finally agreed to run and maybe it was just as well that I did. The Democrats won the Senate by a margin of 48-47 with one Independent. That was the beginning of President Eisenhower's second term, and if I had not run I am told the leadership would have remained with the Republicans, because the man they were running against me in Nevada was the strongest man they had.

These were congressional years in every sense of the word. Mr. Sam and Lyndon Johnson were the two leaders and unquestionably were the greatest team that Congress ever had—not only through the father-son relation between them—which, by the way, I think is an accurate description—but because of the varied abilities of each man. They were something to behold.

I remember time after time when Lyndon Johnson said, "Well, it's about tea time and I've got to go over and see my very dear sponsor, Mr. Sam." It was always "tea time," and I never quite understood that, but, nevertheless, he would go over and counsel with Mr. Sam. I know that he got great, sound advice from him. They were really two great men at an interesting period of time and a time when the Congress was very much in command.

He put me on the Steering Committee, where I served for a long time. That Steering Committee was founded and perpetuated by Majority Leader Johnson to ratify and legitimize his suggestions for committee assignments. Everybody wanted appointment to some particular committee. Number one was Appropriations. Number two, if you were going to run for office, was Foreign Relations. You could go to the history of the Steering Committee and discover that every man who asked to be put on the Foreign Relations Committee was going to be running for President in a couple of years.

I had no aspirations. After all, all I wanted to do was go back to the sagebrush and "God's country." So I didn't ask for those, but as a reward for having stayed on that D.C. Committee and frustrated Wayne Morse's ambitions for so many years, Johnson put me on the Appropriations Committee.

We had a warm fellowship. He came out and campaigned for me several times. One time in Ely, which is a hard-bitten mining camp, he got up and made an impassioned speech, telling them what a great fellow I was. I sounded good to me, but everybody else in the audience kind of shook his head. And then toward the end, he said, "This poor fellow Bible is having a lot of problems. Now, down in Texas where we howdy and shake"—another expression of his—howdy and shake—he said, "we'd pass the hat." He had one of those ten-gallon hats on, and he took it out right through the audience, aisle by aisle, and collected $295 for my campaign. That's a true story; it embarrassed me—but I used the money.

LINDY BOGGS: Sam Rayburn and Lyndon Johnson were at the head of the Congress during what an earlier session called an "era of Congressional dominance," and it was the nation's good fortune to have them there. Let me just review some of their accomplishments.

In housing they incorporated a broad slum-clearance program into a public housing bill. It declared a goal of a decent home and suitable living environment for every American. It authorized a billion-dollar loan fund for slum clearance and community development, extended FHA, authorized 810,000 units of low-income housing, including some subsidized rents. Sounds very modern, doesn't it?

In defense they produced NATO in 1949, and SEATO in 1955. In a bipartisan spirit, both organizations were ratified by the Democratic Congresses.

In international trade their achievements were equally impressive. They passed a trade act in 1951 which extended the President's authority to negotiate trade agreements and provided import relief by an escape clause so as to avoid serious injury to any person or business. In 1955 there was another trade act, further extending for a full three years the President's authority to negotiate trade agreements. And that was followed by another act in 1958. These became very important because after 1957 we had to adjust to the new reality of the European Common Market and after 1958 to the European Free Trade Association. Then in 1960 the OECD, the Organization of Economic Cooperation and Development, was established, which was the Johnson-Rayburn collaboration's final product in world trade.

In nuclear development, President Truman announced in 1950 the plan to develop the hydrogen bomb. In 1953 came Atoms for Peace and the International Atomic Energy Agency. In 1954 the Nautilus was launched. In 1956, the Peace Ship was authorized by the Democratic Congress, on a suggestion by the Republican President. And Lyndon Johnson and Sam Rayburn's Congress cooperated in all these ventures.

Sputnik affected Johnson and Rayburn as much as anybody else. The minute the Explorer was successfully launched in January 1958, they moved to establish NASA, insuring civilian control over space exploration. And as Mr. Hardeman has said, they also pushed through the National Defense Education Act to promote education in the sciences.

In civil rights, though there were some difficulties and disagreements, the Johnson-Rayburn Congress did pass the 1957 Civil Rights Act, the primary feature of which was the provisions empowering the Attorney General to seek court injunctions against obstruction or deprivation of voting rights. It led the way to the great landmark 1960 Civil Rights Act.

Those are some of the solid accomplishments, very exciting

accomplishments, of the Lyndon Johnson-Sam Rayburn Congress in the congressional era of the 1950s.

Mr. Sam recognized the importance of the office of Speaker. He loved the institution of the House of Representatives, and he had a perception of his role there in relation to the President and to the other body. He had a strong loyalty to the individual members of the House of Representatives, and he served them in all sorts of ways. He had a delicate sense of the House, of its moods and tolerances, but he also had solid attendance counts and in the old days when you walked through the teller lines, the whips were there noticing who walked through which line on which amendment. He had a shrewd sense of timing; he knew when things were ready and when they weren't, and he would "put off voting" sometimes until a consensus had been reached. He understood the differences among districts and he understood that all Congressmen have several constituencies—not only their district constituencies but their constituencies in the House and in the committees and among the staff. He recognized Bryce Harlow as a first-rate White House liaison officer. One time when he was a staff member in Congress, Bryce told me, on one committee report, he had written the committee report, the minority views, and the "additional" views, all for the same committee. Mr. Rayburn liked a man who understood the House that way.

Mr. Rayburn was very fond of young people. He used to say that the only thing worse than an "old fogey" was a "young fogey," and he loved to have young people around him. They inspired him and stimulated him. We found that out very early. Mr. Hardeman has told you that Mr. Rayburn reached down into the ranks of young members and made Hale a deputy whip, actually created the job for him. But earlier, when he first came to Congress, Hale was assigned to the Committee on Government Operations. Not for long, because Mr. Rayburn recognized his potential for leadership, promoted him to deputy whip and fostered him from then on. He met with young people whenever he was asked, and he used to tell them that they were the "best generation this nation has ever produced." "After all," he would say, "in my day I could only get into as much trouble as my horse could carry me to."

We've said a great deal about both these men. There's one thing we haven't said, however, that I think was really a hallmark of both of their careers, and that was their belief in the abilities of women. They not only believed in the women in their own families—with good cause—they also had tremendous confidence in their women staff members. Both were promoters and supporters of the WACS and WAVES and SPARS and WASPS during the war and afterwards.

They were confident of the women who served in the President's cabinet, and they were confident of the abilities of congressional wives. In 1956 the Democratic congressional wives were asked to go into the "iffy" districts and try to get a Democratic majority. We put on dinners and arranged for speakers and sold tickets and every time Johnson and Rayburn were there.

That confidence was demonstrated in many ways—in Vice-President Johnson's insistence on extending the Commission on the Status of Women, and in upgrading women in all sorts of appointive offices. Shortly after he took office President Johnson said he wanted fifty women in top government posts immediately. And when six weeks had passed by and there were only seventy, he wondered what on earth was wrong!

Thank goodness for the impatience of Lyndon Johnson in the cause of women.

HARRY McPHERSON: I should like to talk about some of the things back in the 1950s that provided a political and legislative setting quite different from today's. In the first place, in the Senate in the 1950s, out of the thirteen principal standing committees, ten were chaired by southerners. That was a situation that a majority leader, if he was going to be successful, had to think about all the time. Senator Johnson used to say that his principal effort—and his principal purpose in life—was to keep Dick Russell from walking across the aisle and embracing Everett Dirksen. What he meant, of course, was that he had to keep the southern Democratic-Republican coalition from hardening and making it impossible to produce the majorities necessary to support the Democratic program. So that was his first objective. That was just simply in the Senate.

The major event of the 1950s, in my view, was the decision by the United States Supreme Court in the Brown Case in 1954. That was a nation-shaking event. It changed everything. The pressure was on the Congress to do something, to reflect that new attitude toward race in some way. Johnson knew and Rayburn knew that if they pushed too hard they would be in real trouble because they would solidify that Republican-Southern Democratic coalition, once they started putting on the heat in behalf of civil rights.

At the same time, they were aware—Johnson, as D.B. said, more than the Speaker—that the Republicans had a great opportunity. If Eisenhower wished to, he could capture the black vote for the first time since Al Smith. We think of the black vote—at least I think of it in my time—as a Democratic vote, but throughout the 19th century it was a Republican vote—right up until Al Smith and Roosevelt.

And now with Eisenhower's own appointee, the Republican Earl Warren, as Chief Justice, there was a chance for the Republicans to capture that black vote. There was a great deal of pressure among the Republicans to seize that opportunity. At the same time, there was a deep personal and political tie between those conservative Republicans and the southerners—neither one wanted to rock the boat. "You go with us on economic issues, and we'll go with you on the racial issue." So they did not exploit it as they might have done.

Incidentally, one of the fellows who was pressing for the Republicans to exploit it was Richard Nixon, the Vice-President. But Eisenhower was not prepared to make the effort because he had very little personal commitment. You recall he said that one of the unhappiest things about his own eight years in office was that Brown decision. He thought he had made a terrible mistake in appointing Earl Warren because Warren had come out as he did. One would think this would have given the Democrats a great opportunity to seize the mantle that Eisenhower was dropping, but Adlai Stevenson did not care very much about the issue either. Johnson was extremely sensitive throughout this period to the popularity of Dwight Eisenhower. He did not want to be caught attacking Eisenhower. Eisenhower was enormously popular, more popular than any Democrat could be.

In 1958 there occurred what was probably the most significant political event—or at least electoral event—of our time. But to explain it I must go back and talk about some earlier elections.

You will recall that in 1946 the first Republican Congress since the New Deal was elected. It was mostly elected because people were sick and tired of war, New Deal controls, and so on. Fifteen Democrats in the Senate were defeated; fifteen Republicans, mostly conservative, won. They had a majority for the first time in years. I think it is written somewhere in the Constitution—probably in Article I—that the Congress is supposed to be controlled by the Democrats. But this 1946 class came in and broke the constitutional rule. They were conservative Republicans and they were the backbone of McCarthy's support; they were supporters of Taft and Bricker; they were the people who gave Truman so many fits. That was the Congress that Truman campaigned against as a "do-nothing" Congress. They were not strong people—most of them—and they should have been defeated in 1952 when their term was up. But 1952 was the year of Ike's first election; they rode on Ike's coattails, and he carried them in.

They came up again six years later in 1958. Eisenhower was now in the middle of his second term. He had had a heart attack; he was still very popular, but there was a huge recession—the biggest one of the 1950s—and lots of people were out of work. Eisenhower and his fiscal policy were extremely conservative. He was saying, "Let's don't spend; let's don't cut taxes; let's balance the budget," while a lot of people were out of work.

It was a situation tailor-made for a Democratic victory, and what happened? All fifteen of those seats were Democratic, and they went to people like Philip Hart and Edmund Muskie and Eugene McCarthy. A liberal tide swept into the United States Senate. That was the group that was reelected in 1964, in the Johnson landslide, and that was the group that provided the horsepower for the Great Society. They were a great help to President Johnson in 1964, but they were often a pain in the neck to Majority Leader Johnson in 1958. His great genius was in managing a very close Democratic majority. For one thing, you could keep all the Democrats together. You could say, "We have to stay together because we are only a majority of one or two." So everybody would kind of "hunker-up" and vote together. But suddenly when you had a majority of about fifteen in the Senate, the liberals—the people who were most determined to change the Eisenhower policies—were putting on terrific heat to take strong stands. "Now we are in control, we've got a big majority. Let's do it, let's show what we can do." They not only wanted to make issues for the 1960 election, they wanted to pass some legislation.

Johnson knew that the more liberal his party became, the more likely it was that those Southern Democratic Chairmen, the Russells and the rest, would go over and embrace Everett Dirksen. Every time the Democratic Party pushes toward the liberal side, the moderate or conservative part of it starts looking with longing eyes at the Republicans. The same thing with the Republicans. When they go off to the right, their moderates start looking at Democrats with interest. So it's a real problem for a leader when his policy begins to move even moderately toward the extreme. Moreover, even with a majority of something like 62-38, as happened after Alaska and Hawaii were added in 1959, Johnson couldn't be sure of controlling the result. When you take eighteen southern Democrats who are going to vote to sustain a conservative President's vetoes— Eisenhower's vetoes—and you add the Republicans to that (all except Case and Javits and a few other liberals), you've got no problem at all in sustaining vetoes. It's impossible to override one, so it's futile just to pass a bunch of liberal legislation, and get it vetoed. And that was the situation Johnson was in.

The one benefit that situation conferred on the Democrats was to provide an agenda for John F. Kennedy in 1961. We never got the stuff through in 1959 and 1960, but we did have an agenda. Everything Ike had vetoed was now going to be the Democratic program.

Lyndon Johnson was first of all a "can-do" man, and the country likes that. The country, in my judgment, is happiest when the Congress and the President are working together, when they are really producing things.

Senator Johnson and Speaker Rayburn gave the country the feeling that they wanted to help Eisenhower do things, and the country thought well of them for that. If they had attacked him— even if he hadn't been so popular—I think the country would have thought less of them for being narrow and partisan.

Interestingly, the highest rating Congress has received in our times when the Gallup Poll asks, "How do you feel about the Congress?" was in 1965 when the 89th Congress was passing everything that wasn't nailed down. I don't think it was because the country was so hot for all that liberal legislation. It was because Congress was working, and working with the President, and showing that the system would work.

There were two things that nobody did in the 1950s that we

should have done. One was to pay some real attention to the largest in-country migration that ever occurred in any country. It took place in our country between 1942 and 1960. The blacks and the poor whites of Appalachia were moving to the cities—southern cities and northern cities—overwhelming them with social needs, for which they were woefully unprepared. The failure to see that happening and to respond to it has been a source of grief for a long time. The second was the failure to dissociate our interests in Indo-China from French interests. Had those two things been done by the Congress and the President, we would have been spared a lot of grief in the decade to come. But as Mr. Hardeman said at the beginning, many things happened in the 1950s; it was not the period of quiescence that it's been described as being. The presence of Johnson and Rayburn and many others—Russell and Kerr and Clinton Anderson, "whales," as Johnson once called them, distinctive, powerful people; colorful idiosyncratic people—the presence of these people made it a memorable decade and in many ways a more interesting one than the present.

WILLIAM THEIS: I must agree with those who have said that Mr. Eisenhower was lucky that the congressional Democrats were led by a team of "nonobstructionist moderates," as Mr. Hardeman has called Mr. Rayburn and Mr. Johnson. And Eisenhower was lucky that they were savvy politicians, a breed he never quite understood. As astute politicians, Johnson and Rayburn had a very finely honed ability to measure the mood of Congress. They were interested, Ike learned, in achieving results, not in going into a battle that they knew was not going to be won. This was particularly true of the Senate leader. Reporters always learned pretty quickly that Mr. Johnson would rarely put an issue to a floor test or a vote until he knew he had the strength to win, and that's just good common sense.

Newsmen, I think, typically look for flaws in politicians—ethical, political, moral, personality flaws. And they should. But I think in the case of Mr. Johnson the cosmetic or social flaws too often got reported in a way that tended to obscure the real strengths of the man. "How" he did everything—the so-called "Johnson treatment"—often became in print as being as important as the "what" that it produced. And that was unfortunate because many of the "whats" were pretty important legislative landmarks. We know that better now than we did at that time.

I should like to refer back briefly to the McCarthy situation because, looking back, I recall I saw a flaw in the failure of the Senate establishment—and I don't mean Mr. Johnson himself—to control or stop earlier the Senate-debasing tactics of Joe McCarthy. True, the Senator from Wisconsin was a Republican whose party controlled the White House and barely controlled Congress during 1953 and 1954. It was easy to look upon this reckless demogogue as a Republican problem, which he was, of course, primarily.

With such notable exceptions as Margaret Smith, who is remembered for her early anti-McCarthy "declaration of conscience," politicians such as Bill Fulbright, Ralph Landers, Bill Benton all feared tangling with Joe, and at that time with very good reason. Senator Taft, "Mr. Integrity" of the GOP but a stern partisan, encouraged rather than discouraged McCarthy's campaign in its early stages. It wasn't until McCarthy had spun into his own final self-destruction, denouncing some of the Senate's most respected members, that the Senate in 1954 finally voted "condemnation" of him. Even then, the more formal censure formula was modified to say "condemned."

I remember traveling abroad in those years—particularly in Europe after the Cohn and Schine expeditions—and finding it impossible to explain to foreigners how an entire government could be held in trembling shame for so long by this single demogogue. The unfunny part of it was that Joe McCarthy thought it was all a "big, fat joke." He laughed at the Senate's impotence. He knew he was getting away with murder.

As a wire-service reporter covering that story, I understood the reasons for the inaction of the leadership, but I must confess that at the time, I felt that the Senate's inner club—the Dick Russells, the Walter Georges, not Mr. Johnson because he was not yet a veteran of the Senate—might have moved sooner to defend the institution that they all loved so much.

You might ask, "How would Mr. Rayburn have handled McCarthy?" I suspect it would have been just about the same if he had been in Johnson's position, because Mr. Sam and his Senate protege operated on pretty much the same wavelength. But the question is really fruitless because Sam Rayburn would never have been in the Senate; he was a House man to the end.

There was a minor flaw in the LBJ makeup, a by-product of his tenet that a man's judgment is only as good as his information. I thought he wasted too much of his valuable time watching the newspapers and trying to be, in addition to a floor leader or president, something between a rewrite man and an editor, or a TV program director. He was hypersensitive about the turn of phrase of the editorial analysis of a situation that he was involved in, and he would be on the phone to you in a matter of minutes telling you about it. The cost of that habit in time and attention increased when he became President, but he never shook the habit. It was something that was built in, and everybody understood it.

A few other thoughts. Mr. Hardeman says it's highly doubtful that Sam Rayburn could ever have won a statewide election. Now, that's easier for a native Texan to understand than for one who saw him daily as a truly national figure. When I first covered the White House in the summer of 1942, I was awed by the office and by its occupant, FDR, but I must also tell you that I was impressed also by Mr. Rayburn and the aura of respect he drew to his office. There was a great war on, but when he took the floor in his own right to speak, it was a commanding presence.

Speaking as a newspaperman, I might recall some of the liaison men and staffers who were useful sources of information. Bryce Harlow has been mentioned, and I think mention might also be made of the late Jerry Persons, General Wilton B. Persons, Ike's former military aide, who handled Pentagon contacts on the Hill. Then on the Democratic side, there was the late Leslie Biffle, Secretary of the Senate and a Truman confidant, his successor Skeeter Johnson, and of course Bobby Baker. All were key sources for newsmen covering the Senate or the White House. Little of importance happened downtown that was not known shortly thereafter in the Senate, and when legislative maneuvering was at a fast pace, these leadership aides were in constant use and they were enormously helpful to us reporters.

RALPH HUITT: Awhile ago I said something about Johnson's influence on the House from the Senate side. I'd like to add a word of explanation. One of the things that I tried to impress on students for years was that the great disability of going to the House of

Representatives was that you had to spend ten years doing nothing, saying nothing, living in a closet, before they would begin to let you talk.

I heard a story the other day about a House member from Arizona who was a taciturn man anyway, so for four or five years he had no trouble keeping quiet. Then one day there was a bill on the floor that deeply affected Arizona. So he went down to the well and took one minute and he told the House why Arizona was so interested in this bill. When he went back and sat down, one of the old moguls leaned over to him and said, "Just had to talk, didn't you?"

Well, the House was that way, but in 1953 the famous Johnson Rule was established by which he made it the practice in the Senate that every Democratic Senator would get at least one good committee. That was warmly received; it was just like liberating people.

The House did not change, but the Johnson Rule for years was the specter at the banquet. And now the House has adopted something like it and my friend and former student, Dave Obie, came in from Wisconsin and was given the Appropriations Committee in his first year in the House—his first appointment. And now, with six years in the House, he is chairman of the Commission on Administrative Review and a member of the Budget Committee as well. My point is that all this power—intellectual and otherwise—of the young people in the Congress has been liberated by this one great move of Johnson's in 1953.

FROM THE AUDIENCE: I should like to direct this to both Hardeman and Huitt. I am interested in understanding how electoral politics in Texas in the 1950s, both in Mr. Sam's district and statewide, might have affected their national role in Congress and also how Mr. Hardeman would explain the statement that "Mr. Sam could not have won a statewide election."

D.B. HARDEMAN: In his old age Mr. Rayburn thought he had never had any senatorial ambition. I think that was true enough, but there is a letter to his family in the Rayburn files in 1922 in which he was despairing of the fact that he had a serious opponent every two years up in that fourth district. He had just been elected, he said, to the number two spot in Congress (I wouldn't quite agree with that— he was elected head of the Democratic caucus after four terms in the

House), and only one small paper in Texas even noticed it. Of course, the paper didn't know what the chairman of the caucus was. But he felt frustrated, he said he was being urged to run for the Senate, and you can tell that he is smelling the possibility. That is the only evidence I have found of any senatorial ambition.

From my experience in Texas politics I don't believe he was ever sufficiently in tune with popular opinion in the state to have run, unless it was in the very earliest years when he didn't have the resources. Remember that 1922, when he was thinking about running, was the year Texas elected a member of the Ku Klux Klan to the United States Senate. He said, "My God, that year the rye was high; three out of every four men in my district belonged to the Klan," including some of his own family. He was never a Klan member. But I can't think of a time when I believe he could ever have got the financial support to make a statewide campaign or one when he would have had the necessary broad appeal, unless there was a time during the New Deal.

The trouble was he wasn't known outside the district. He sought no publicity. One time Cecil Dixon, with the INS, said, "Mr. Speaker, *The New York Times* really played up your statement on the front page." Mr. Rayburn said, "I don't give a damn about that. What did the Bonham paper do to me?"

V

An Era of Presidential Government: the 1960s

Overview: Horace Busby
Paper: Barefoot Sanders
Discussion: Wilbur Cohen
　　　　　　Henry B. Gonzales
　　　　　　Harry McPherson
　　　　　　J.J. Pickle
　　　　　　Margaret Chase Smith

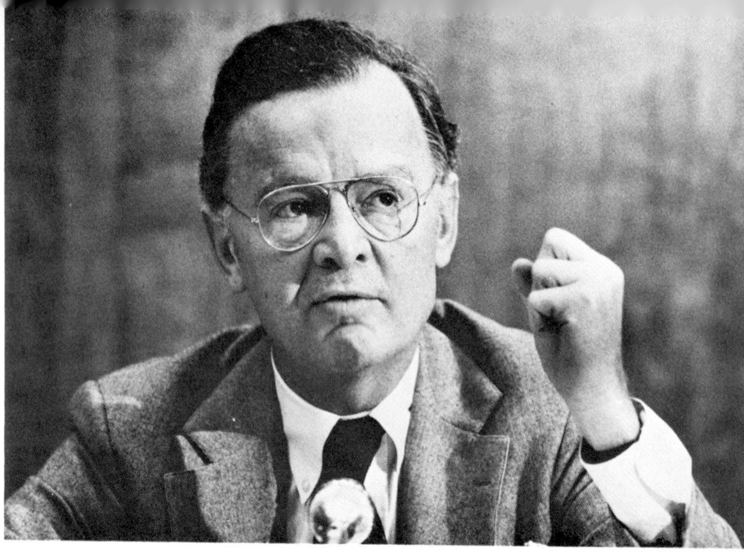

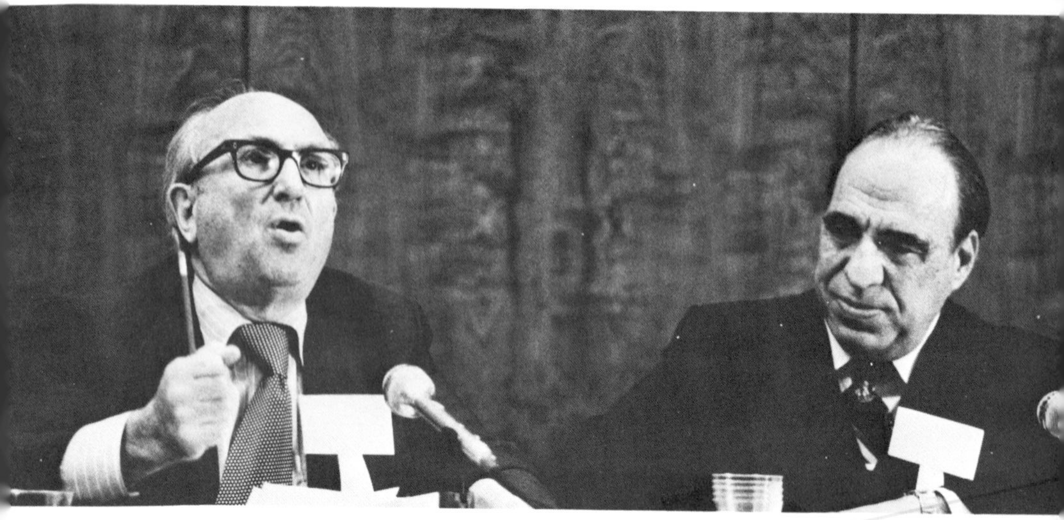

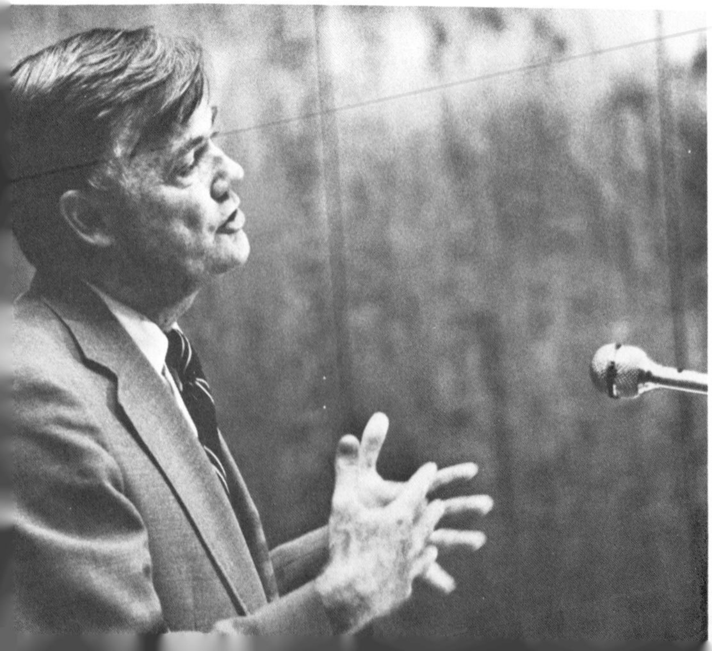

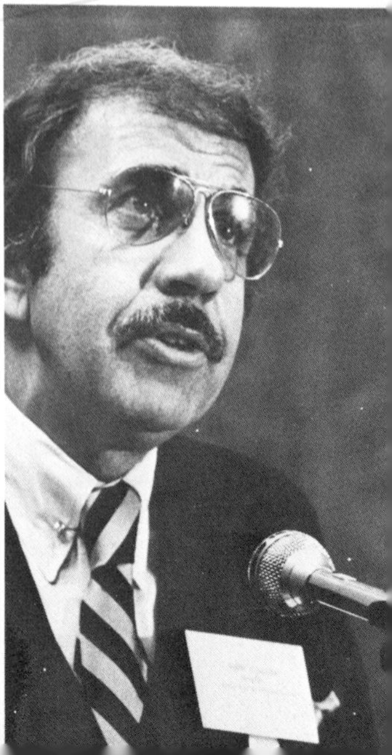

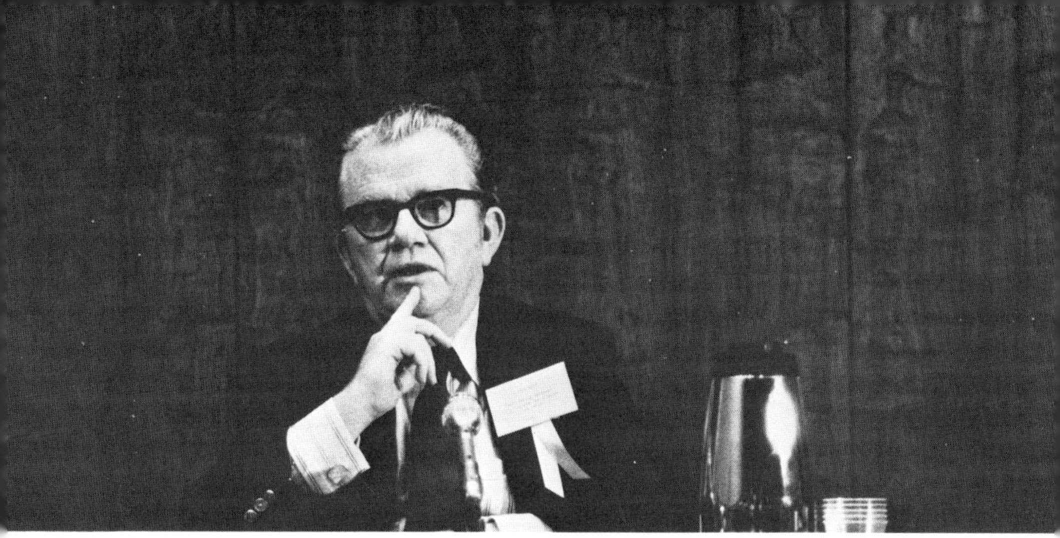

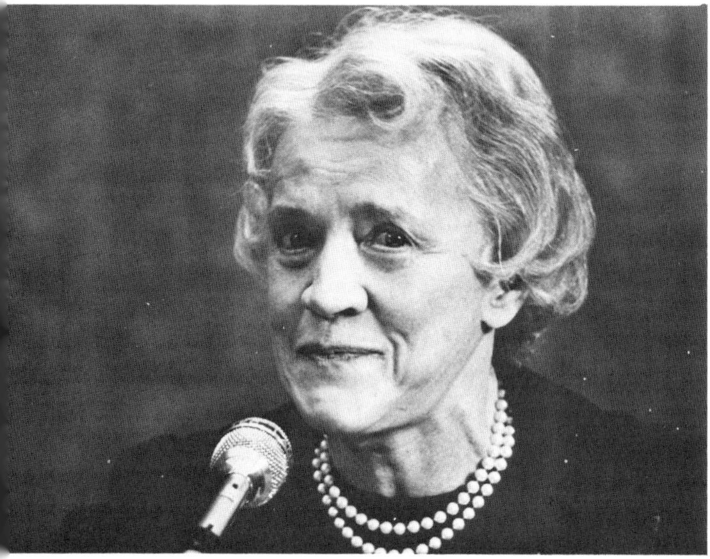

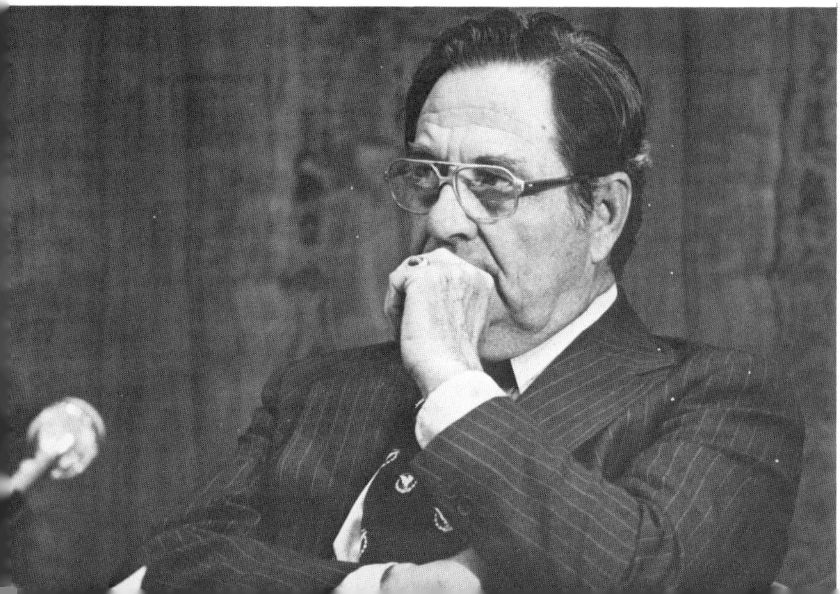

Overview

Horace Busby

Horace Busby was Special Assistant to the President during the Johnson Administration. He has since been a corresondent, journalist, and editor of **Texas Businessman**.

Thirty years ago Congress was coming to an end of what was the longest peacetime session in its history. Serving in the House of Representatives at that time as Congressman from this 10th District of Texas was Lyndon Johnson. He was reflecting upon his future; after all, he was thirty-nine years old. He believed quite sincerely that when a man reached forty, it was all over. He was going to be forty in 1948 and as he looked back over his career in Congress there was no bill ever passed that bore his name. He had done very little, he felt, with his life. He thought he probably should get out of Congress and get into some steady line of work.

So he came back to Austin in December and met with some of his friends, including Mr. Pickle and Mr. Connally. He told them that he had thought this all through and he had reached a decision. He was going to retire from public life. He might come down here and manage a radio station or go back to teaching school, or something like that. Now you must understand that his friends and assistants expected at least once a year to go through one of these sessions in which he was going to quit public life. The best way to handle it was to say, "Yes, sir. We think that's fine. That's right." So the group that gathered around said, "Congressman, that's really the best decision. You don't have any future in Texas politics. Roosevelt's dead. You couldn't get elected to anything any more. You ought to

V/Presidential Government • 284

step aside and let us put forward a younger man." You know, at the age of thirty-nine, he really thought his problem was geriatrics.

He said, "Well, who did you have in mind?" They said, "Well, we're going to run John Connally for your seat; so if you'll just step on aside, we'll start running John." He said, "Now, wait just a minute. Let me think about this a little bit." He invoked the "Rayburn Rule" and thought about it for a minute and decided that maybe this was not exactly the time for John Connally to become Congressman from the 10th District.

The previous section focused on the 1950s as an era of congressional government. This portion will focus on the 1960s as an era of presidential government. The thing that more than anything else marked national politics in the 1950s was the remarkable convergence of two men, Sam Rayburn and Lyndon Johnson, who became the supreme figures of the Congress. That association was warm, unique, and significant. The link between the Lyndon Johnson of the 1950s and the Lyndon Johnson of the 1960s is illuminated by an episode, one that I personally observed in 1963.

Lyndon Johnson began the day in Fort Worth as Vice-President and he returned to Washington that evening at six o'clock as President of the United States. He was flown from Andrews Air Force Base to the White House lawn in a Marine helicopter. A handful of responsible government officers were there, waiting for him and expecting to gather with him in the Oval Office to discuss matters. But he had a remarkable sense of propriety. He did not go into the Oval Office. He did not enter the White House. He went to his vice-presidential office in the Executive Office Building. He met with military leaders and such Cabinet officials as were present.

Then about nine o'clock that night, he went to his residence in northwest Washington, the Elms. I was there with my wife and also with Dr. Willis Hearst, his physician. The three of us were waiting in a little sitting room off the foyer. Mrs. Johnson greeted him and when I stepped out to speak to him, he said, "Buz, turn on the television." He said, "Nobody in the United States knows less about what's happened today than I do. I'd like to see some of it."

We walked back into the sitting room and as he started to sit down his eyes fixed on a photograph, the one photograph on the walls of that very small room. It was a very silent moment. He stood there and a smile came over his face. He threw a salute at the photograph and said "Old friend, how I wish you were here tonight." Well, the photograph, as you may have suspected, was of Speaker Sam Rayburn.

Soon the President began to speak about the evening as he really had not done before, and he made a memorable observation. He said, "You know Buz, when I went into that office tonight and they came in and started briefing me on what I have to do," he said, "do you realize that every issue that is on my desk tonight was on my desk when I came to Congress in 1937?" Civil rights, insurance, health insurance for the elderly, federal aid to education. He went on down a list of eight or nine topics. In my view, those topics formed the basic agenda for the presidential leadership that will be discussed in this section.

Congressional-Executive Relations

During the 1960s

Barefoot Sanders

Barefoot Sanders, a recent nominee to the federal judiciary, is a former United States Attorney and Assistant Attorney General in the Department of Justice. From 1967 to 1969, he was Legislative Counsel to President Lyndon Johnson.

The character of congressional-executive relations varies greatly according to the personalities involved, the temper of the times, and above all according to the importance assigned to them by the President. During the years 1961-69 these factors were all in tune, and the result I believe was a rather effective liaison system. Its special character, however, was shaped by several particular factors.

In the first place, Presidents Kennedy and Johnson both had congressional backgrounds and an understanding of Capitol Hill and the Hill point of view. Both had substantial legislative programs, drawn from the unfinished agenda of the Democratic Party and from their own campaign proposals. Congressional support for these programs was essential. Both Presidents, moreover, believed that the public and the Congress, with proper preparation and leadership, would support the presidential legislative programs. As it turned out, that perception of the public and the congressional mood was correct.

During their Administrations the Democratic Party controlled the Congress, and the leadership of the Congress was supportive and progressive. Beyond the question of party, however, the members of Congress were generally inclined to support the leadership and the President. And both Kennedy and Johnson believed it important to have congressional support for executive policies other than legislation. Finally the President and the leadership knew that to enact an ambitious legislative program, constant communication and good relations (liaison) between the Congress and the Executive were essential.

Speaking more generally, one can say of nearly any liaison system—at least any one that is serious about its business—that it has several continuing and demanding purposes or objectives. By far the most important is that it be able to secure enactment of the President's legislative proposals without destructive amendments, and to obtain support for the President's executive (nonlegislative) policies, such as the general conduct of foreign policy, meeting particular foreign crises, or handling domestic emergencies such as the riots at Watts or Detroit. On a longer-range basis it must maintain a system of open communications and cultivate good will for the President and the Administration with the Congress. At the same time it must do its best to hold congressional criticism of the President and his policies to a minimum, and keep any such criticism from becoming personal or acrimonious.

Now let me turn to the participating elements in a congressional-executive liaison system. It will be seen that there are several of them and that all are important, but there is no question that the most important of all is the President himself.

The President

The emphasis that the President places on good relations with Congress is the most important element in determining the effectiveness of the liaison system. In the Kennedy-Johnson years it was quite clear to all that the President gave a very high priority to good congressional relations. Both Presidents not only believed in the importance of good relations but were willing to provide the necessary time and attention to the subject—and insisted that their staffs do the same. Both had an understanding and "feel" for the congressional system and process—in both the formal and the informal aspects. Along with this they recognized the necessity for constant communication and warm relations with the leadership, committee chairmen, ranking members (both Democratic and Republican) and key staff members.

Personal friendships with individual Senators and Congressmen, which had evolved over a period of years, were quite important in smoothing the liaison process. The President was willing to take time to maintain those friendships and to cultivate new ones, by political as well as social means. The President and his staff were always accessible to the members, and the members knew it.

President Johnson, in particular, had "grown up" on Capitol Hill; he knew the Hill; he knew and liked most of the people there, and he knew how to talk with the members and how to help with their problems. Throughout the executive branch there was emphasis on constant communications and good will with the Congress. This emphasis was continuously projected by the President to his cabinet and subcabinet members, to his staff, and to the Congress.

Communication with Congress is a two-way street. The Executive must be perceived by the Congress as saying to the Congress: "We value your opinion as well as your vote. We need you and you need us."

Whenever possible (and it was frequent) there was a policy of consultation in advance with key members of the Congress in formulating legislation and in timing its submission. The same policy was also carried into consultation and briefing with respect to nonlegislative policies (foreign crises, domestic riots, and so on). Prior to submitting major legislation, the leadership and the committee to which the legislation was to be referred were briefed on its contents. The old axiom was honored and oft repeated: "Bring us in on the takeoffs if you want us in on the landings."

Both Presidents were well aware of the tools available to the Executive in dealing with the Congress. There were many of these, and they were always forward in the minds of the liaison staff: the power of the President to preempt the news and to focus public attention on issues of his choosing—a power more effective and more commonly used in the 1960s than in the 1970s. The President has the ability to build the prestige of members of Congress by public recognition; by invitations to the White House; by careful attention to requests for small favors; and by consultation with respect to federal appointments, not only those requiring Senate confirmation, but also those not requiring any kind of congressional approval. All these the President wanted used and used regularly.

The obverse of these techniques was to avoid ruffling congressional feelings. Threats were to be avoided; persuasion was to be gentle; public criticism of Congress or Congressmen was frowned upon; and above all the use of the veto or the threat of a veto was a weapon to be used carefully, reluctantly, and rarely—and even then, of course, only with presidential knowledge and approval. And finally, there was constant and painstaking attention to details, whether in working out the content of legislative proposals or dealing with the needs, desires, and limitations of Congressmen.

The Congress

The situation in Congress, of course, is also of fundamental importance in shaping the effectiveness of the liaison system. In 1961-69 the alignment in Congress was workable, and the situation was thus conducive to strong and effective relations. Perhaps the most important aspect of that situation was that the Democrats controlled the Congress. Indeed in 1965-66 (89th Congress) that control was quite substantial. In the 90th Congress (1967-68) the margin of control was much less owing to the loss of forty-seven House seats in the 1966 elections.

The congressional leadership, in general, favored President Johnson's legislative proposals and shared his ambitions to enact a substantial legislative program. Between the President and the congressional leadership there were ties of friendship, party loyalty, and common purposes. "The President proposes and Congress disposes" was an accepted principle, though one with qualifications—at the White House as well as on the Hill.

Congress needs legislation to work on just as dogs need bones. If the President does not submit and push a legislative program, Congress is not likely to adopt a legislative program of its own; instead it is likely to involve itself—both through committees and through individual members—in executive branch business, which it has a tendency to do periodically anyway.

Although Congress was always aware of the tools available to it in its dealings with the Executive, an effective congressional liaison operation made it unnecessary and hence undesirable for Congress to utilize them. In addition to the obvious power to vote down Administration proposals, the Congress has other methods available for registering disapproval or hostility toward the Administration.

Those other methods derive from a variety of power-oriented relations, among which one would include the influence of each individual member within his committee and on the floor, as well as with his home constituency; the power of ranking members to accelerate or decelerate legislation; the control over committee staff, which can have considerable influence on the substance of legislation; the availability (or nonavailability) of members to presidential aides; and of course the power over appropriations.

The White House recognized that the constituencies of the members (state or district in character) were different from the President's national constituency, and that this difference placed practical limits on the extent to which the Congressmen could cooperate with the President. As much as possible the function of congressional liaison was to "harmonize" the constituencies, not to browbeat the Congressmen.

It should not be supposed, however, that the influence of Presidents Kennedy and Johnson was exclusively, or even mainly, a party influence. The Republicans in Congress were not unified against most Administration programs, especially in the Johnson years. President Johnson spent considerable time pursuing and persuading Republicans, and his relations with many of the Republican leaders (especially Senator Dirksen) were very close. In fact, Republican votes often provided the margin of passage for many Administration proposals—for example, in the civil rights legislation of 1964, 1965, and 1968 and in the hard-fought tax bill of 1968. On the other hand, on some legislative matters—for example, the essentially meaningless but politically sensitive periodic increase of the debt limit—the Republicans would line up unanimously against the Administration.

Departmental Liaison Staffs

Both President Johnson and President Kennedy continuously stressed to the executive departments the importance of good and responsive relations with Congress. Each department had a congressional liaison staff of its own. The effectiveness of those staffs, however, varied according to the caliber of the people involved and the emphasis the department head placed on congressional liaison. He was supposed to emphasize it strongly, but some did and some didn't.

The members of the cabinet were expected by the President to be knowledgeable about legislation involving their departments, and to be involved actively in its passage. Each department had the primary responsibility for steering through committee the legislation which it would administer or in which it had particular concern or expertise.

Cabinet members and their congressional liaison people were expected to cultivate warm relations with the members and staffs of any committees that were handling legislation relating to their departments. For example, the Attorney General and the Department of Justice were responsible for the Senate and House Judiciary Committees; the State Department for the Foreign Relations Committee in the Senate and the Foreign Affairs Committee in the House; the Treasury Department for the House Ways and Means Committee and the Senate Finance Committee, and so on. Cabinet members and their liaison staffs were expected to be available, as the occasion required, to assist in passing other legislation also, even if it did not affect their own departments directly. Given the size of President Johnson's legislative program, all these expectations and requirements amounted to a considerable demand on the departmental liaison staffs. For instance, on the 1968 tax bill—a major presidential proposal for over a year prior to passage—all departments assisted in communicating with and counting the members. This was coordinated by White House congressional liaison staff and sometimes by the President himself.

A report on the status of the Administration's legislative program was on the agenda of nearly every cabinet meeting. That in itself served to emphasize the importance that the President attached to congressional relations and to the success of his legislative program. The executive departments reported in writing to the White House congressional liaison staff weekly (and, when necessary, more often) on the status of all legislation with which each department was concerned. Included in those reports were requests for White House assistance, if needed, and readings on the attitudes of members of Congress with whom the departments were dealing.

The White House Congressional Liaison Staff

The White House congressional liaison staff had the daily responsibility of providing information to the President about the Congress, and of providing information to the Congress about the Administration's views and interests. The information relayed by the staff to the President related not only to the legislative program, but to a range of matters. In particular it included reports on any expressions of attitudes and interests by individual members of either house.

To accomplish these tasks the White House congressional liaison staff was expected to work in certain established patterns. Staff members had some important powers and privileges, but they also suffered under some limitations, and they certainly had many demanding responsibilities. In the first place there was direct access to the President—in person, by telephone, and by memo. That was essential. Indeed President Johnson wasn't just accessible to his liaison staff; if he didn't hear from his liaison people daily when Congress was in session, he wanted to know why. The staff was expected to provide the President—and that meant directly and promptly—with recommendations as to legislative timing and strategy, and "readings" regarding the attitudes, interests, and suggestions of the members.

The staff was supposed to have a sound working knowledge of House and Senate rules and customs and was expected to work very hard to establish firm if not intimate relations of trust, confidence, and friendship with the members and their staffs. This kind of relation made it far easier to communicate to the Hill information about Administration programs and the Administration point of view, and also much easier to gather information from Congressmen, committee staffs, and party officials.

The staff could assist members, particularly those who were supportive, in a number of useful and interesting ways. They could convey Congressmen's requests to the President, to other White House staff members, and (when necessary) to the executive departments. They could occasionally provide limited access to the President for meetings with members or groups from members' constituencies. They could suggest which members should be invited to the White House for formal and informal social functions, for signing ceremonies, or for meetings concerning the Administration's legislative program and policies. They could help with members' requests for visits of high Administration officials to their states or districts. They regularly arranged to give advance notice to supportive members of federal grants awarded to recipients within their states or districts. They could provide White House tours for constituents on a VIP basis. They regularly acknowledged members' support for the Administration by arranging for letters and phone calls from the President, cabinet members, and White House staff, and they could suggest that the President be available for pictures with members. They might even provide information to members to assist them in preparing speeches. These tactics and devices were warmly appreciated by members and they were an essential part of an effective liaison operation. Liaison was not merely a matter of telephoning and arm twisting, though there was a great deal of the former and a little bit of the latter. All this depended on the staff's having direct and continuous access to the President, but it also depended on a widespread understanding throughout the presidential establishment that the President himself considered the liaison operation to be of first importance.

The White House congressional liaison staff under President Johnson was not large. It included five full-time people and four part-time people, with others available as needed and called upon. When Congress was in session, the staff held weekly White House meetings—occasionally attended by President Johnson or Vice-President Humphrey—with the congressional liaison people from the several departments. Those meetings accomplished several purposes. Each department had an opportunity to report on the progress of its legislative program and to be informed about legislative programs and problems of other departments. They enhanced the prestige of the liaison staffs throughout the Administration and at the same time helped develop a most useful esprit de corps among them. Finally, the meetings enabled White House staff members to spot particularly effective liaison people for use on legislation outside their own departments.

The White House congressional liaison office provided a written weekly report to the President summarizing the status of all Administration legislation. That report was compiled from the staff's contacts with the congressional leadership and committee chairmen, from reports from executive departments, and from the Bureau of the Budget. The staff also regularly reported on legislative progress at cabinet meetings.

When Congress was in session, the President met weekly—usually at breakfast—at the White House with the Democratic leadership. The liaison staff prepared an agenda for the President, who chaired the meeting, but quite frequently the discussion centered on topics brought up by the leadership. The White House congressional liaison people were in constant contact with the Democratic congressional leaders, obtaining their suggestions as to the timing of submission of legislation, making suggestions when appropriate concerning the scheduling of legislation for floor action, conveying the leaders' requests and suggestions to the President, and so on. At least annually, the President met at the White House with the congressional committee chairmen, separate meetings being held for House and Senate chairmen.

While Congress was in session the President expected White House liaison staff to furnish him daily a summary of congressional contacts. On any given day White House congressional staff might be in touch with sixty to seventy-five members, and sometimes more. The President received summaries of these conversations running to two or three sentences—no more. These summaries enabled the President to stay abreast of the current congressional mood. For example, if over a period of several days, conversations questioning the Administration's Vietnam policy predominated, that was significant, and the absence of criticism of Vietnam policy was equally significant. For those summaries to be meaningful, however, it was obviously important that they represent contacts with a broad spectrum of members and points of view; so the staff had to make sure not only that the reports were ample but that they came from diverse sources.

One of the most important functions of the White House congressional liaison staff was to obtain a vote count of Democrats prior to floor action on major Administration legislation. This count could only be made by some sort of communication with each member. It was important that it be accurate to within a very few votes, and it usually was. In making the count, the White House liaison staff worked with the congressional leadership, with the liaison people from the department responsible for the legislation, and with various outside groups. Basically the vote count was necessary in order to determine whether a particular bill was enough support to be scheduled for floor action. A good count would show not only who was for or against, but who might be absent and who was undecided. With an accurate vote count, the White House and the congressional leadership knew where to focus their efforts to obtain additional support.

We could usually get an accurate count (say within five votes on the Democrats) on most legislation within three or four days. Sometimes it took longer. The vote count on the 1968 tax legislation lasted over a year. We began by putting members in five categories: for, leaning for, undecided, leaning against, and definitely against. We began with about thirty-four members classified as "for." The continuing count enabled us to know which members to concentrate on, which ones it was useless to see, and which ones needed no further contact.

Three other aspects of the vote count are worth noting. First, only Democrats were counted. That was simply a realistic recognition that Republicans usually marched to a different drummer. Second, we conducted the count by asking the member what his intention was, if he knew at that time. We did not assume that we could project his current vote from his past voting record. It was very rare for a member to say he would vote one way and, in the event, vote the opposite, so we felt we could pretty well rely on the information we put together. But it takes some knowledge and practice to know how to seek a commitment from a member, and then to judge with confidence when the commitment is firm. Finally, at the end of each session the White House congressional liaison office compiled a voting record on each member, using his votes on those matters considered critical to the Administration's legislative program. That compilation was never published; it was prepared merely for the use of the President and the staff in determining the support that members had provided to the Administration's legislative program. It provided important information later on when a member sought White House assistance or a favor of some kind.

Although only Democrats were counted during the preparations on particular bills, the White House congressional liaison staff maintained contact with the Republican leadership and with ranking Republican committee members. On any given bill, contacts were made with Republicans who might be helpful and their support was often requested. The purpose of these contacts, however, went beyond the possibility of obtaining additional support on any given legislation; it was also important to the White House to maintain friendly relations with the Republicans whenever possible, and to keep down personal hostility toward the Executive, despite political differences. It ought to be added that the task of maintaining good relations and open communications with Congress was not exclusively that of the liaison office. The entire White House staff was expected by the President to be available to members of Congress, and to be prepared to consult with members about legislation when requested to do so by the President or by the congressional liaison staff.

There were certain important and practical limitations on the conduct of congressional liaison that served as guides to the staff; taken all together, they constituted something like a code of conduct. Here are some major examples:

- Avoid trading for votes.
- Do not attempt to influence government contracts or the Department of Justice.
- Stay out of internal procedural matters of the Congress, unless requested by the leadership to participate, and even then proceed very carefully.
- Do not threaten members or gossip about them, for Washington is a town of no secrets.
- Do not get mad about a member's vote and don't try to "get even," for there will always be another day and another vote.
- Do not speak directly for the President unless directly authorized to do so.
- Do not agree to or make commitments about changes in Administration legislation without consultation with the department concerned and the key congressional supporters—and with the President if necessary.
- And above all, appear reasonable: do not expect a member to make a politically suicidal vote.

A congressional liaison staff is essential, beneficial, and sometimes effective, but there are certain general limitations on what it can accomplish. No matter how effective it is, a liaison operation cannot marshal or supplant, and is not a substitute for, public opinion over a period of time. Of course, legislative success in itself helps to form favorable public opinion, and indeed if the liaison staff can persuade members of the Congress to speak out in behalf of Administration positions, it can be said to have had some effect on public opinion. But the plain truth is that the members' constituencies have much greater persuasive power on major issues than any congressional liaison operation. It is both possible and common for members to play an important role in forming and leading public opinion in their constituencies; indeed from time to time they can cast votes that are unpopular at home; but no Congressman can safely ignore clearly delineated constituency opinion, and the liaison staff must always be sensitive to that restraint. A Congressman cannot be expected consistently to defy the majority opinion of his constituency.

The Role of Private Groups

The Johnson Administration aggressively sought and often successfully enlisted the support of nongovernment groups for help with legislation. Many examples could be cited. Organized labor was very effective in behalf of most New Frontier and Great Society proposals; church and civil rights groups, together with labor, coordinated their efforts with the White House in behalf of civil rights legislation; the White House (with help from the Treasury) enlisted business support in behalf of the 1968 tax bill.

Activity on Capitol Hill by outside groups in behalf of legislation served a number of purposes. It demonstrated that there was enthusiastic and organized support, outside of the Administration and outside of Washington, for the legislation at issue. Moreover, if properly orchestrated, private groups could provide some assistance in making the vote count, although the effectiveness of that assistance depended on the expertise of the outside group. The groups could sometimes furnish manpower and time that were not available within the Administration to make the contacts with and attempt to persuade members. And finally, they frequently helped to marshal public opinion in behalf of the legislation and to obtain press attention for it.

The White House was conscious of the contributions of these

groups and regularly attempted to recognize their efforts. That recognition took the form of invitations to signing ceremonies and giving out signing pens, letters from the President and members of the White House staff, and invitations to the White House for meetings or social functions. It was understood very well in the liaison office that if outside groups could be prompted to lobby for the Administration's bills, the task of persuading Congressmen would be much easier.

The press, too, played a role in congressional liaison. The activities of the President, and those of other people at the White House or visiting it, regularly commanded the attention of the media. But in addition to ordinary news stories, White House press coverage—of press conferences, speeches by the President and cabinet members, signing ceremonies, congressional messages, and so on—gave the President a forum and an opportunity to shape public opinion, to prod the Congress to act, to praise the Congress for enacting Administration programs, and to focus public attention on particular issues.

Ten Years Later: The Carter Administration

The basic elements and structure of congressional relations in the Carter years remain much the same as in the Kennedy-Johnson years, but success appears more elusive. Conditions have changed substantially. The character of congressional structure and leadership are significantly different. It is far more difficult now for the Executive to rely primarily on the leadership and the committee chairmen. The centers of power have been multiplied and many more bases need to be checked now—the Democratic Study Group, the freshman caucus, the black caucus, the Wednesday Group, and various other groups of members—to which one must add that there are more individual members with their own individual power bases nowadays. The changes are twofold: the House reforms have diffused power, and the aftermath of Watergate has reduced reliance on, if not confidence in, the Executive. Members appear more independent and less likely to follow either the leadership or the President.

The problems confronting the Congress have also changed. There is no substantial backlog of specific legislative solutions for specific social and economic problems as there was in the 1960s. Medicare, federal aid to education, civil rights, etc., were legislative solutions to specific problems, and it was perceived that important problems could be addressed and solved by concrete measures embodied in one or a few statutes. Now the Congress is asked to legislate with respect to problems that are (legislatively speaking) more general and more complex than the problems of the 1960s—for example, inflation, unemployment, energy, and welfare reform. Problems such as these are not susceptible to solely legislative solutions, or at least it is clear that they cannot be solved by the enactment of one or two bills. The breadth and complexity of these more recent problems make it difficult for the President to marshal and focus public opinion and pressure-group support for particular legislative proposals.

Still another change of importance is in public attitudes. The public appears skeptical, if not cynical, about the ability of government to solve problems, and particularly skeptical of legislative solutions to public problems. That same attitude is reflected in the Congress, which is accordingly more difficult to mobilize in support of Administration bills addressed to those problems. In the final analysis, public support for legislation is essential. But the public is passive. It is difficult for the President to lead or bestir the current "me generation." That skepticism and passivity contrast sharply with, and may be a consequence of, the fervor and activity of the 1960s, of Vietnam, and of Watergate.

The press now views both the President and the Congress with a more critical eye and is more ready to find fault. Intense media coverage makes it difficult for the President and the Congress to communicate outside of public channels, and, indeed, makes it tempting for each to send messages to the other through those public channels. That practice clearly imperils the maintenance of the close relations which are basic to effective executive-congressional relations.

In view of Congress's new assertiveness, and in view of the fact that President Carter's previous political experience has been outside of Washington, it is obviously taking a long time for the White House to establish a *modus operandi* with the Congress.

Discussion

WILBUR COHEN: I imagine a lot of you wonder how a Jewish boy from Milwaukee got in with the Texas Mafia among a lot of Protestants and Southern Baptists. One evening after President Johnson had sent up my nomination to be a member of the Cabinet, my wife and I paid a call on Mrs. Johnson and the President. Before I could say anything, the President said, "Wilbur, I completely forgot when I sent up your nomination that your wife was from Texas." I said, "Mr. President, I thought that was the only reason I got the job." He laughed but he didn't say I was wrong—and that's the reason I'm here today.

I am going to give you a few vignettes which I hope will reflect and interpret the relation between me and the President during this memorable, remarkable period. First, about ten days after the President was inaugurated in 1965, he called together all of the legislative liaison people in the White House and gave us a good sales talk about what we had to do.

We were just about through with the regular agenda of the meeting when the President said in effect, "I want you to get all of my legislative proposals during this session, now!" Well, all of us there had already been working hard for the President for a year, and when he said, "I want you to get it all now," we thought "now" meant during his term of office. That isn't what he meant at all.

When he said "now," he meant between February first and Easter! He proceeded to say in about seventeen different ways, to get the point through our thick skulls, that he meant that legislative program ought to be adopted *now*!

Well, that was understandable, but then the President launched into a discourse that I consider one of the most remarkable experiences I've ever had. He took a half an hour to trace the history of the Presidency from Woodrow Wilson through Harry Truman. In the course of it, he said, "Every day that I am in office, I lose part of my power. Every day that I use that power, I have less power left. You must get this legislation through immediately. I want you to go out and work! I want you to bowl with those Congressmen. I want you to talk to those Congressmen. I want you to sleep with those Congressmen if you have to. I want you to get this legislation through now—while I still have that power." And he proceeded in one of the most dramatic appraisals of the Presidency that I have ever heard to explain how the President loses power as he uses it.

I came home that evening and said to my wife, "I've heard the most remarkable thing I've ever heard so far." She said, "What is it?" And I said, "President Johnson conceives of himself as only a one-term President." She said, "How do you know that?" I said, "Well, that's the only conclusion I could draw from the whole historical summary. He said use up *all* of his power and authority to get the legislative program through *now*." I said, "It's so remarkable, I'd like you to take it down." My wife did take it down in shorthand and we put it away. The next time we recalled it was on March 31, 1968.

Now I'd like to come back to the question of why President Johnson appointed me. I think it was mainly because I had my origins in legislative work with Franklin D. Roosevelt and the social security program. The President was a great admirer of Franklin D. Roosevelt and a great believer in the importance of the social security program upon which the Medicare program was later based. I believe he felt that if I had worked for Franklin D. Roosevelt and social security, I couldn't be all bad even though I came from the state of Michigan, whose delegation had opposed him for both Vice-President and President.

I'll tell you one little story about presidential leadership in terms of my many direct contacts with him on social security. He would press me from time to time. He would say, "Don't you have another good idea, Wilbur, about what we could do for old people?" So I came to him one time and I said, "Mr. President, I have worked out very carefully a wonderful plan for you to announce a ten percent increase in social security." I had probably spent weeks working out that proposal with my assistants and colleagues. Now, that was a sizable increase, but the President said, "Ten percent? You can do better than that, Wilbur." I said, "Well, Mr. President, if I go beyond ten percent, I've got a lot of financial problems and I've got to take into account the effect on the economy and employment and investment. Ten percent is about the best I can do right now." He said, "You go back home and do your homework."

So I went back and I went to work. I consulted with my actuaries and my statisticians and economists and I came back very proudly in about ten days and I said, "Yes, Mr. President, you were right. I got it up to twelve percent." He said, "Twelve percent? Pretty good but not good enough." He said, "Can't you do better than that?" I said, "Well, I've done the best I can." He said, "No. I have confidence in you. You go back."

I went back and for another week or ten days I worked, and I finally got it up to thirteen percent, which is what President Johnson sent up to Congress, a thirteen percent increase. And it was adopted by Congress that year.

I think that story tells a great deal about presidential leadership and presidential intervention. He was a strong proponent of social security, and he knew how to use people like me to get more juice out of the orange than I had originally thought it contained. He was a master at knowing how to use people to get the results he wanted.

There are two other Great Society programs for which President Johnson has never been given the full credit that is due him. The literature of the past ten years has virtually ignored what I think are two remarkable achievements. The first one concerned the Family Planning Program. It was President Johnson who turned the attitude of the whole country around on this question and convinced people that federal legislation and federal policies could be used to give people information on family planning.

That may not seem very radical today, but it did to lots of people in 1965. Under his leadership, we developed legislation and developed policy, both international and national, to provide that the federal government would use funds and use its policies to give both women and men information on what we then called birth control and now call family planning. That is accepted today as a rational, intelligent way to use resources, but at that time it was very important and very innovative. My great contribution on family planning was to meet with the Catholic Bishops to persuade them to be neutral on our attempt to use federal funds.

The second of President Johnson's achievements had to do with the disability insurance program. That occurred while he was majority leader back in 1956. President Eisenhower was opposed to disability insurance legislation, as was his Secretary of HEW. It had passed the House, and had gone over to the Senate where ultimately, with the support of Senator George and Senator Kerr, it came up on the floor.

In the end it passed by a vote of 46 to 44. Vice-President Nixon was in the chair ready to cast his vote against it if it should turn out to be a tie. As the vote was recorded the majority leader was there keeping a tally. As he watched it get to 40 to 40, and 41 to 41, and 42 to 42, then 43 to 42, and 44 to 43, back and forth—all of which took some time—he was holding Senator Earle Clements in the Democratic Cloak Room. Senator Clements was actually opposed to the legislation, but he had told the majority leader that if he needed his vote, he would vote for it. And since he was from the State of Tennessee where the tobacco and other interests were allied with the American Medical Association in opposition to the legislation, it was a key vote for Senator Clements.

The vote finally got to something like 45 to 44, and then there was a long pause. Various Senators got up and asked, "How am I recorded as voting?" which was a technique to stall for time. Pretty soon Mr. Johnson could see that he needed one extra vote, and after about five minutes of his jockeying back and forth, he brought out Earle Clements out of the Cloak Room. His was the forty-sixth vote. There was no tie, so Nixon was not able to cast his vote against it. So it passed the Senate. Today, there are about three million people in the United States who get disability benefits under Social Security because of this kind of majority leadership that Lyndon Johnson showed. It was a remarkable display of legislative skill.

I'd like to conclude my observations by suggesting something for the scholars here to think about. I have developed what I would call a Richter-type scale to measure the legislative effectiveness of various Democratic Presidents. You may not agree with my results, but I think you may be interested in my observations. They are based on forty years of watching the legislative liaison process.

If LBJ is given a rating of 9.8 on the Richter Scale of 10, I'd say FDR was about 6.7, Kennedy was about 5.1, Truman was about 5.0, and Mr. Carter so far is about 2.4. As you see, I am saying that the quality and quantity and effectiveness of the legislative liaison system was particularly outstanding in the Johnson Administration. And I think it will be a long time before anybody can equal it—not in number of laws passed but in the effectiveness of the legislative liaison that carries out the President's program.

People often say I talk a great deal about the successes of the Great Society, and that's true. But now and then I am asked, what were its failures in the legislative process? There were some, all right, and I'll mention four. The first was in the Community Action Program, where in order to meet the political situation, we extended community action and the poverty program to 1,100 communities instead of to a hundred. We had to do that in response to congressional demand. I believe that was a big mistake. We tried to do too much in too many places at the same time. We expanded beyond our limited resources, and Community Action was a much less successful venture than we hoped it would be.

The second failure was international education. We passed an International Education Act, but because of the opposition of Mr. Mahon, we were never able to get a single dollar of appropriations for international education—although the President was very enthusiastic in support of it. So, that was failure number two.

Failure number three was in the Medicare program. We had to make concessions to the radiologists and pathologists and anesthesiologists and so on to allow them to charge whatever they wanted because Mr. Mills had made an agreement with the radiologists to allow them to contract out of the program. The President was very upset about it and directed me to negotiate a compromise on it. I was never able to do it and it has remained one of the sources of heavy increased costs in the Medicare program.

The fourth failure in our legislative efforts concerned a program that I still hope can be achieved. It was President Johnson's recommendation that there be a "kiddy-care" program, that is, at the opposite end of the demographic scale from Medicare. It was to deal with children. We had to start with the aged, not because that was the most important area from the standpoint of social needs, but because the aged vote and the kiddies don't. But President Johnson was very concerned about the next step, which would provide much the same kind of help for children under the age of six. It is a source of great regret to me that we were never able to achieve that, and I hope Mr. Carter will succeed where we didn't in achieving President Johnson's dream of compassionate, intelligent medical care for children.

MARGARET CHASE SMITH: It was a great privilege for me when I came into the House in 1940. It was a privilege to find myself associated with such people as Lyndon Johnson and Sam Rayburn and others. It was a great privilege when I was given the assignment on the House Naval Affairs Committee, of which Carl Vinson was chairman. Carl Vinson was a great, great teacher and so was Lyndon Johnson. Carl Vinson didn't lecture quite as much as Lyndon Johnson, but I benefited greatly from both of them.

The one principal issue that Lyndon Johnson and I always agreed on was the defense program. He was from the southwestern part of this country, and I was from the northeastern part, but both our states were very conscious of the need for defense. We went down the line time and time again. There were issues that we didn't agree on, but we could disagree agreeably because there seemed to be an understanding between us. It was one of the experiences that I shall always cherish through my life, my association with Lyndon Johnson.

When the two of us went over to the Senate in 1948, I found myself on the very same committees that Lyndon Johnson was on: Appropriations, Armed Services, and later the Space Committee. In fact, it was Lyndon Johnson, Richard Russell, John Stennis and Margaret Smith who were listed on each one of those committees and all of the subcommittees. So, you can imagine that I'm pretty nearly a southerner from that experience.

Lyndon Johnson was a tremendous majority leader. Whether you liked him or not, whether you approved of his methods, whether you approved of his positions, he was a tremendous leader. I am sure that his leadership in association with that of Everett Dirksen, the Republican leader at the time, made life very much easier for President Eisenhower. Things would have been much more difficult without Lyndon Johnson's ability to lead that Senate and help get the legislation through that was necessary at the time. I think the Senate became very much weaker after he left, perhaps just by contrast between Johnson and the subsequent leaders. I thought too that the seniority system was weakened a bit when he brought in freshman Senators and gave them major committees. After he left the Senate, absenteeism increased and became one of the Senate's palpable weaknesses.

Lyndon Johnson knew people. He liked people. He worked with people, and if you didn't want to work with him, you had better think twice because there were other ways he could deal with you. But you couldn't disapprove of everything he did or said because you knew from his experience and his background that he was often going to be right. Think of the training he had from Speaker Sam Rayburn.

In my opinion, he was a great President, more so than President Kennedy and President Nixon because they had been loners in the House and the Senate. They had not made the friends there that Lyndon Johnson had made. Lyndon Johnson went into the Presidency with many, many IOUs and he called them only when it was necessary to do what he thought was necessary and right.

I commend to you a book called *Big Story*, sponsored and underwritten by Freedom House, of which I have been chairman. It was written by Peter Braestrup, who was with the *Washington Post* and *The New York Times* and who was in Vietnam during those very, very difficult days. He tells the true story of Vietnam and of the disservice rendered to the United States and to Lyndon Johnson by the news media's misrepresenting the Tet Offensive as a success of the Viet Cong and North Vietnamese when it was actually a great defeat for them and a victory for us. I recommend it to every one of you. If that history is properly written, it will show clearly that we smashed the Tet Offensive, and that LBJ would not only have been a candidate again but would have won overwhelmingly and gone down not only as a great President but as one of the greatest Presidents of all.

HARRY McPHERSON: I should like to go over a few things that struck me as important about presidential-congressional relations in the sixties. First of all, obviously Johnson wasn't in the Senate and neither were a lot of the whales. That term "whales," by the way, was his.

One time when he was Vice-President, I went up and was sitting next to him while he was presiding over the Senate. President Kennedy had just sent a bill down. I forget what it was, but it was a major piece of legislation from his Administration. A young Senator was out there speaking for it. I said, "Any chance of getting that bill through?" He said, "No, because we don't have any of the whales. We've got some minnows like that," pointing at the Senator who was speaking, "but we don't have any of the whales." Well, the whales were Kerr, Russell, Clinton Anderson, Lister Hill, Dirksen, and so on. He didn't have those people behind the Kennedy program, which made it particularly difficult to get anything through. There were some whales still around. Kerr had died, but Senator Russell, though aging, was still there, and so were Clinton Anderson and Lister Hill.

Johnson himself, the great expert in the legislative process, was almost completely unused by the Kennedy Administration. There was a real reluctance to ask him to do anything in the Congress. No doubt there were a lot of mixed reasons for that, but the main one surely was that every Administration wants to have its own legislative program and wants to be responsible for it and get the glory for it. You don't want your Vice-President, who comes from a different side of the party from yours, up there running *your* legislative program. So, Larry O'Brien and the others did not lean on or get the benefit of Vice-President Johnson as a legislative leader.

To a considerable extent, moreover, his Democratic colleagues were relieved that this arm-twisting dynamo was now no longer their leader. On the one hand, they loved the results his leadership produced in passing legislation, but on the other hand, it was much nicer to go home at 5:30, take a month off in the summer, and not work so hard. Things had changed. Senator Mansfield, as someone said, was not a second-rate Lyndon Johnson. He was a first-rate Mike Mansfield. But they were very different and the wheels simply didn't turn from 1961 through 1963.

Johnson as President had three obvious assets. They have already been described: first, an unparalleled understanding of Congress— no President ever understood Congress as he did; second, a superb sense of the uses and limits of presidential power; and third, he had agents. Let me elaborate on the third.

A few weeks ago I was talking to a senior Republican House member, someone I respect a great deal, who had just come back from the White House. He and his committee had spent an hour and a half with President Carter. Carter had been talking about the energy program. I asked him how well he had done. He said, "Superbly. The first time I've ever seen him stay in the room and not turn it over to Schlesinger or someone else to explain the bill. He really stayed there, knows it well, went through it. It was most impressive." I said, "Will he get it through?" He said, "I don't know, really. You know, he doesn't have any agents up here." That was the first time I had heard that word or really thought about it. "Agents" are people like Jake Pickle and Henry Gonzales who care whether the President's program get through, who are willing to go bow their necks to push something through a committee.

Now Johnson had a number of such agents, quite a number, built up over twenty or twenty-five years. Mrs. Smith says he had "IOUs," and that is correct; but this went beyond IOUs. These were deep, personal friendships he had developed that made people want to do things for him. Friends like that are indispensable, and I hope that President Carter, for the sake of his program and for the sake of the country, develops some agents. He comes from the outside and doesn't have the benefit of that long experience in Congress, and of course he campaigned in part against Congress, which is a real problem for him. During one of those debates with Ford, when Ford started criticizing the Congress, Carter said, "Well, if he's going to tie the Congress around my neck, I'm going to tie Watergate around his." Now, if I had been a Congressman, it would have struck me as a bit unusual to compare me with Watergate. A Congressman might have been a little touchy about that.

Another thing Johnson had going for him, of course, was the tremendous contribution Barry Goldwater made to the public weal, by agreeing to run for the Presidency in 1964. That, along with a few other things, resulted in a gigantic Democratic landslide and brought in the 89th Congress, which passed a lot of things that never had got through before.

Finally, there was a lot of legislation coming along in which clear moral issues seemed to be involved. Medicare was waiting to be passed after twenty-five years. Civil rights was an idea, Senator Dirksen said, "whose time has come." Aid to education was a ripe idea. It didn't seem like it then, but looking back, it appears as if all the white hats were over here and the black hats were over here. You had to be for Bull Connor to be against civil rights, and you had to be for uneducated children to be against aid to education, and you had to oppose medical help for sick, elderly people without the means to pay to oppose Medicare. So, you had strong national will behind the President's program, and you had a big Congress coming in.

There is another anecdote that illustrates President Johnson's conception of the diminishing power of a President and his consequent sense of urgency about using it. Toward the end of that first year of his own term, 1965, when he had pushed through all that major legislation, Katherine Graham and some other people from the *Washington Post* came over and asked Johnson to make a real run for home rule for the District of Columbia. That had been around for sixty years and had never been achieved. Well, he agreed and he really made a run for it. Every one of us must have made forty or fifty calls to Congressmen and did all we could to get a rule on that bill. It took a two-thirds vote of the House to get the bill up and we missed it by two or three votes, just a handful. And the *Post*, to my astonishment, wrote an editorial saying, "Well, Johnson drove the Congress too hard. He kept them in too long and he never should have brought that up because it was at the end of the session." Well, I thought he would be ready to tear a hole through the *Post* and I asked him about it. He said, "No. They're right. I really shouldn't have brought it up. Everybody is tired. This is November. They've been working until ten o'clock at night for most of the year." But then he said, "But you know, I've only got one year. In the second year, they all want to put a little distance between themselves and you. Congressmen don't want to be rubber stamps."

"In the third year," he said, "you lose a lot of seats. We've got a lot of our boys in seats that they never should be in. They are Republican seats and we'll lose them, so I won't have as much of a majority in the third year and the fourth years. So it doesn't matter what kind of mandate you come in with; you only have one year when you can really make a run at it." And he did.

The results of congressional-executive relations in the sixties are hard to assess with any finality. In fact, I don't think you can ever assess such things with finality. In my judgment, there is a pendulum effect in most power relations, and at any moment, you may be in the last part of the swing one way and about to go back the other. Our country seems to swing from liberal to conservative and back to liberal.

In 1940 FDR told Jim Rowe, another Washington lawyer, that he wasn't going to run for a third term. He said, "Liberalism in our country only has an eight-year term and then it swings back the other way. I've had my eight years."

There is a pendulum swing between strong leadership and permissiveness, from a desire for a Johnson in the majority leadership to a desire for a Mansfield. The same swing occurs between a demand for a strong President and a demand for a strong Congress. The same people who, in the fifties, were saying, "We've got to have powerful executive leadership; we've got to have more Jacksons and Lincolns and FDRs, and no more Eisenhowers and Hoovers and Coolidges," and who were elated when Kennedy came in promising strong leadership, and even more elated when Lyndon Johnson got all that legislation through in the mid-sixties—those same people by the end of the sixties were saying "Imperial Presidency!" and calling on Congress to exert itself far more. Congress has done so, but we will have a swing back in time. The nation somehow senses that the Presidency, for all its dangers as we saw them in Watergate and in the overweening power of the Nixon Administration, is a necessary institution. Its power and its authority are necessary because it is ultimately the only office in the land that speaks for all the people.

HENRY GONZALES: President Johnson was blessed by a vast array of personal and political strength which he exploited with supreme skill. The more I think about President Johnson's skill, the more convinced I am that he was an absolute master of the legislative politics of his time. And what's more, he would have been formidable in any political arena at any time and under any circumstances.

Johnson did enjoy certain advantages. First, the economy was in a stable condition and that gave the country a sense of basic confidence. Perhaps more important, it also made it possible for the government to undertake major new commitments because there was fiscal flexibility available. Second, there were widely perceived injustices that the President could focus on, and he had a consummate skill in marshalling the moral resources of the country. Because he himself had a genuine commitment to remedying those injustices, he was able to communicate very effectively. Third, he understood that the country wanted to move ahead and he was making it possible for the country to do so. His unique blessing was that he understood what he and the country wanted to do, needed to do, and could do. Here was the right man, in the right place, at the right time, because above all he knew how to get things done.

To those of us in the House who had no special power or position of importance, the President always made us feel important, and wanted, and needed. We were part of the team, and he would remind us that he could do nothing without us. "I'm always thinking about you, Henry," he would say, "and I always ask these Cabinet boys what their ideas will do for Henry and his folks in San Antonio."

That might not have been the literal truth, but the fact remains that President Johnson did care about the effect of programs, and we had confidence that he understood our needs, our capabilities, and the political limitations that we faced. We knew that he would do whatever he could for us as long as we were working with him.

Nobody but Lyndon Johnson would have helicoptered in to help me celebrate an anniversary in office—but he did. Nobody but Johnson would have remembered to write birthday greetings, to send pictures, to send invitations, in short, to do anything possible to help the most junior member of Congress feel recognized, wanted, cared for, and cared about.

Johnson made congressional relations into a high art. He made sure that the executive agencies were responsive. They answered their congressional mail, they worked hard, and they understood that President Johnson watched every move they made. The agencies were part of the White House team, and they worked under his skilled direction to assist members of the Congress in every conceivable way. Agencies knew that he watched them closely and expected them to conform to his program and promote it, and to make friends for his Administration. He was a tremendous administrator, and I don't know of anybody that I can recall who could be compared to him.

Johnson made congressional relations a matter of highest priority. He knew how to work with Congress, and more importantly he wanted to do it. His skill, his commitment, and his determination created a cooperative spirit and a tremendously productive enterprise. His success was astonishing and I think unparalleled in all our history.

His task would surely be a lot harder if he were President today. Congressional centers of power are no longer what they were in 1964. Committee chairmen no longer have any power to speak of and the House leadership has little power. The dispersion of power is so complete now that even getting a good vote count is a major problem. I am one of the zone whips and have been for about four years, and I can tell you that even getting a count on an issue today is a major problem.

This is quite unlike the situation in President Johnson's years, when he could predict a vote within a four- or five-vote margin—as Mr. Sanders explained. Today, by contrast, the House leadership almost never seeks support. The most it does is politely ask what a member might do, not recommend what he should do.

In the House today, there is not much sense of institutional integrity. Members must fend for themselves, there being very little sense of cohesion or common concern. Where the powers of leadership once resided, today we have an incredible variety of caucuses, study groups, and regional organizations. These groups form into passing coalitions that the leadership cannot effectively control because it is effectively excluded from participation in them.

To compound this, regionalism or sectionalism has emerged, probably stronger than at any time since the Civil War. These regional divisions affect everything—energy, housing, tax structure, any issue of national substance. Kennedy saw this only in a nascent form, as when the Area Redevelopment Act was drawn to preclude loans to clothing manufacturers who were fleeing the unionized North for the non-union South. President Johnson probably saw a little more regional influence, but certainly nothing like the situation that exists today, where regionalism is an absolute and is reinforced by formal regional organizations in the Congress, complete with staffs. The northeast-midwest coalition, for example, claims control of 204 votes and doesn't hesitate to use that clout on any matter affecting the economic interests of the area.

Current presidential-congressional relations are characterized by a President who has a modest and ill-defined program and who, up until now, has placed a somewhat low priority on relations with the Hill. To President Carter's credit, he is beginning to see the importance of congressional relations, but he is severely limited by a staff both in his own office and in cabinet agencies that lack skill and experience, and have an inadequate understanding of the importance of that task.

Congressmen's letters today don't get rapid attention—in fact, I have a couple that haven't been replied to at all. Cabinet officers are not always readily available and subcabinet officers not infrequently are reluctant to cultivate good relations with the Hill. There are happy exceptions to this, but the contrast between conditions today and in President Johnson's time are startling indeed.

The President's situation, let it be said, is complicated by the post-Watergate era, which vastly reduces the President's clout. The office has lost much of its mystique because it is now clear that the occupant of the Oval Office doesn't necessarily grow into the job. Further, while the President's authority is diminished, Congress, in attempting to fill the vacuum, is without effective leadership because the reform movement has stripped the leadership of any effective levers of power.

Aside from the institutional limitations of a collective body like the Congress, there is simply no machinery within Congress today to create an effective consensus. Members have no mechanism they can turn to, except a series of competing organizations and interests all of which pose threats of various kinds. You can learn to use a threat or take advantage of a passing situation, but true leadership and true leadership sources simply do not exist. No member has a place he or she can turn to for help simply because the tools have been taken away from the leadership. It may well be true that the leadership can't punish anyone any more, but disastrously, they can't help anybody either.

If the President is limited and Congress is limited by the current shape of politics, it is also true that they are both limited by an extremely unhappy economic outlook which leaves no room for making new commitments. There just isn't money to start new programs now, and there is not much prospect of it either, because the economy is growing slowly and appears likely to do so for quite some time. The deficit is intolerably high, and existing commitments—such as counter-cyclical aid to cities—are built-in and not easily withdrawn, so that even rearranging programs is going to be a major political task.

In other words, whereas President Johnson was in a position to do many things and make many commitments, President Carter faces very close limitations on what he can do, even if by way of rearranging programs. And he isn't helped by the continuing lack of real cohesion and program definition within his Administration.

President Johnson had the advantage of inheriting a settled administration, which saved him a great deal of time, and he was wise enough to keep it. Carter had to go through the process of settling his Administration, and the frustration he faces may compare with some of those that Kennedy faced, for no matter how bright the New Frontiersmen were, they still had to learn how to run a government.

I don't think comparisons can be drawn satisfactorily between different men working in different times and different circumstances, but I would say that President Johnson, with his clearly defined program, his absolute commitment, his consummate skill, and his aggressive determination, accomplished more than anyone could have believed possible. To say that President Johnson played the congressional game with skill is to understate the case most awfully. He was skillful beyond description and effective beyond comparison. There will never be another like him.

J.J. PICKLE: First, I want to talk a bit about Mr. Johnson, who was my mentor and my legislative guide, almost a father to me. Most of what I know about dealing with the public, I learned from him.

He had some special techniques besides just knowing people and knowing how to get things done. One weapon he seemed to use as much as anything was the telephone. He used that telephone like no man who has ever been in Congress, the Senate, or the White House. He could reach you whenever he had something to say to you, and it didn't make any difference where or what hour or under what circumstances. The one exception, I might add, was Henry

Gonzales; he could never reach Henry. He used to say, "I can get a call through to the Pope three times before I can reach you, Henry Gonzales." And he said, "Where can I reach you?" Henry never would tell him and didn't tell him until the very end.

I remember he called me one morning about 2:30 a.m., just to compliment me because I had voted for a civil rights bill. I wasn't going to return the call, but the switchboard operator in my apartment said, "Please call the White House. They've called eight times the last three hours. We told them you weren't going to call back but he said if you don't, we won't get any rest all night." So I called, and sure enough the President was waiting.

Wayne Hays told us one time that the President called him about three o'clock one morning and said, "Wayne, I hope I didn't wake you up." He said, "No, Mr. President, I have just been lying here hoping that you would call."

Warren Woodward told of the time he had worked for two years straight without any vacation. He finally went on a deer hunt way up in the Davis Mountains. He crawled up in the top of a blind way up in a canyon about 4:30 in the morning to settle down to wait for the sun to come up. Just before dawn, he heard an old car come chugging up the canyon and a man started hollering for him. He said, "Senator Johnson wants you on the telephone." Woody said, "I just gave up then and came on back and quit hunting."

Senator Dirksen, when he was minority leader, was uneasy because he felt that Senator Johnson was getting ahead of him. Johnson was majority leader and he put a mobile telephone in that big black limousine. When he started to work in the morning he would call Senator Dirksen. He said, "This is Senator Johnson. I'm calling from my mobile unit and I want to talk to you about some legislation." That went on a few times and Senator Dirksen just couldn't stand it. He figured he was minority leader and he had to have one, too. So, he ordered one, and told them, "I want one, but I want it a little bit bigger and a little bit stronger than you've got in Senator Johnson's car." They put it in, so when Senator Dirksen started to work that morning he called on the mobile unit and said he wanted to speak to Senator Johnson. The voice came back and said, "Just a moment, he's on the other phone."

Well, the phone was his instrument and he could get you anywhere, any time, any part of the country. That was true also about letters. I was a part of his staff the first part of the War. We were still answering letters of people in 1937 who had voted for him; he was thanking them and they were thanking him and back and forth. It never ended. He literally had a love affair with his constituents by way of the letter. He was on the phone and writing letters morning, noon, and night. I am sure that President Johnson made more personal phone calls from the White House with respect to legislation than any dozen Presidents over a period of thirty years. I also think he had more people at the White House for various functions— groups, conferences, dinners, swims, and domino games—than any other man we have had in the White House within twenty-five years. That has to have a payoff.

He had more people on his White House staff working on Congress than any President ever had. Now we may have needed legislation just as a dog needs to chew on a bone, as Mr. Sanders said, but there was certainly a swarm of White house aides up there. It was just like fleas on a dog. They were there everywhere because he had them spread out to get things done.

I suppose it can also be said that he had more bills signed at the White House. He knew who had worked on the bill, and even if you hadn't done very much work, he'd make you feel as though you were responsible for it. We had more bills signed and more pictures made at the White House and at other places than any other President we have ever had. Well, that has to pay off.

President Johnson was the most productive and the most effective President that we have had in at least the last twenty-five years, so far as legislation is concerned. The 88th and the 89th Congresses were probably the most productive two Congresses this county has had in the last hundred years. Some would say that they were too productive, but they were productive because President Johnson was effective.

A lot of people may think because of his phone calling, that he would bully his friends. Not really, he was very discreet. President Johnson never once called me personally and asked me to vote for a bill. I always thought that rather odd, but he knew that I knew this district as well as he did and the problems we had. And he tended to say, "Let the man alone because he'll make the right decision." And he never called me personally and insisted.

Now, his staff weren't so easy-going. Barefoot Sanders and Busby and Christian and Larry Temple—they were constantly talking to me "to get the feel," so I knew he was getting a report. But he never once said, "I want you to do this." I thought that was very considerate of him.

It is quite clear that the sixties was an era of strong Presidents. President Kennedy was a strong person, young and vigorous. The country was asking him to get the country moving again. He came in with a lot of ideas and proposals and though history won't say he was productive, surely he would have been had he stayed in office. I've just talked about how effective President Johnson was. And the first two years of the Nixon Administration were a continuation of the direct power of the Presidency. It was a period, the sixties, of ascending presidential power.

Now, I agree with Harry McPherson that there is a pendulum in these things. What happened in the sixties has happened before. We have strong Presidents when we have weak leadership in the Congress. We have weak Presidents, so to speak, when we have strong leadership in the Congress. And it goes back and forth; it is inevitable and I think the President and the Congress simply adjust to their times. But primarily it is up to the person in the White House to determine what does take place.

For the safety of this country, I'm glad this pendulum exists. The Congress is resurgent now, through three primary means: first, the Congressional Budget Act, which is the first effort by Congress in modern times to do something about checking the power of the President; second, the War Powers Act; and third is the power of the veto with respect to administrative rules and regulations.

VI

The Reorganization of Congress and the Executive

Overview: Emmette S. Redford
Papers: Alan K. Campbell
Roger H. Davidson
Discussion: Lawrence C. Dodd
Herbert Kaufman
Bruce I. Oppenheimer
Harold Seidman

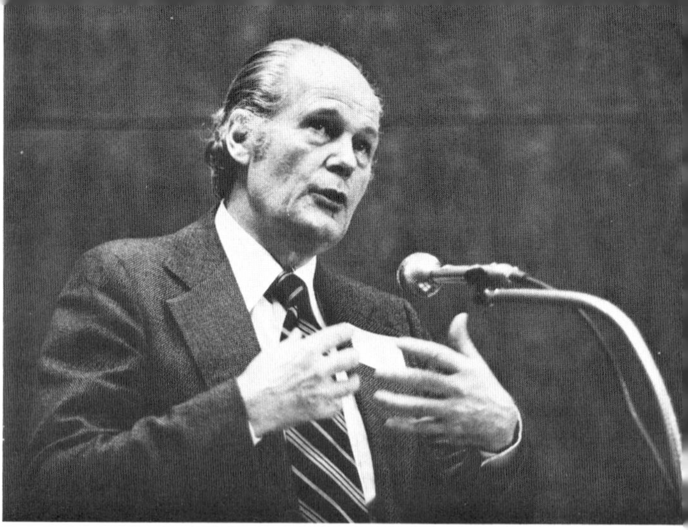

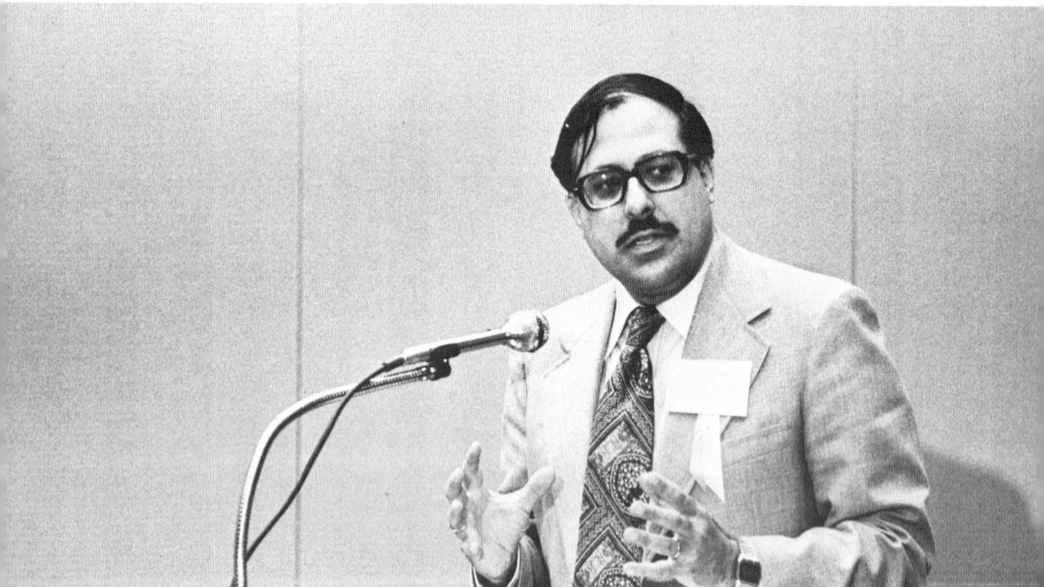

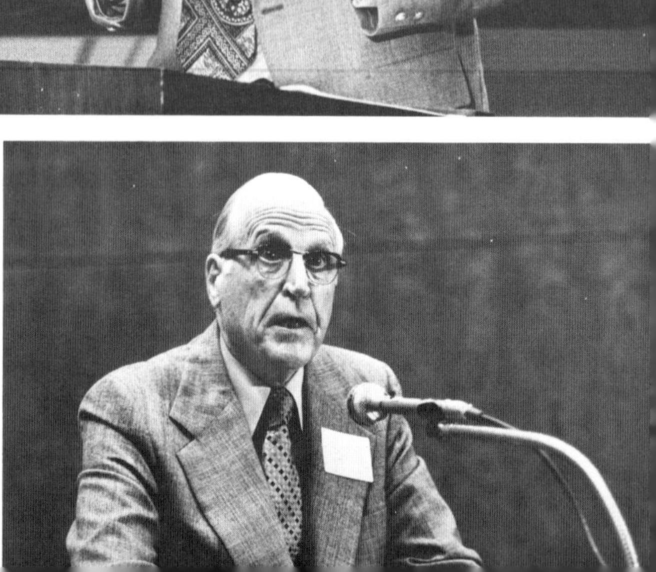

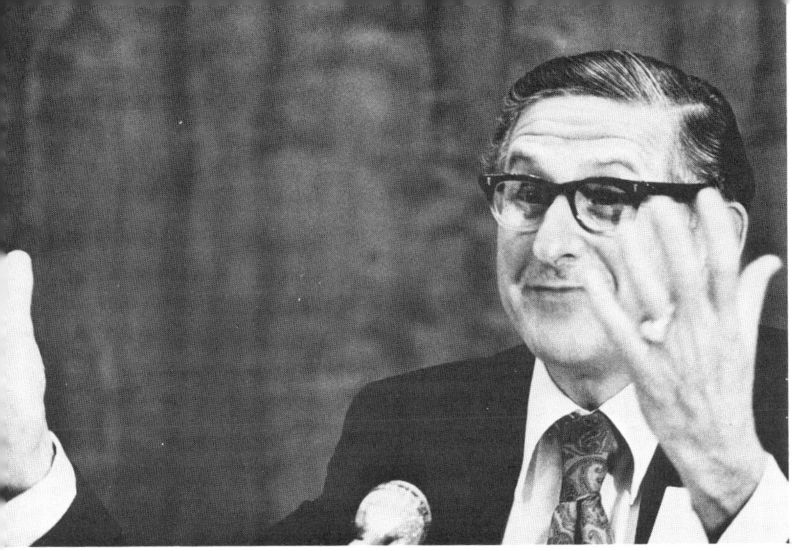

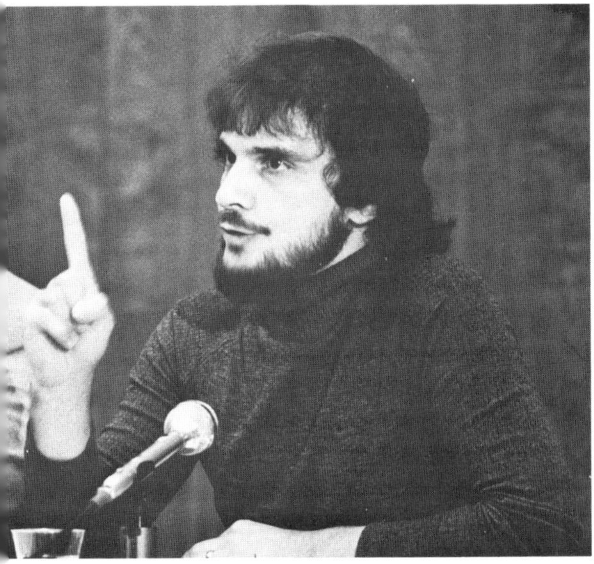

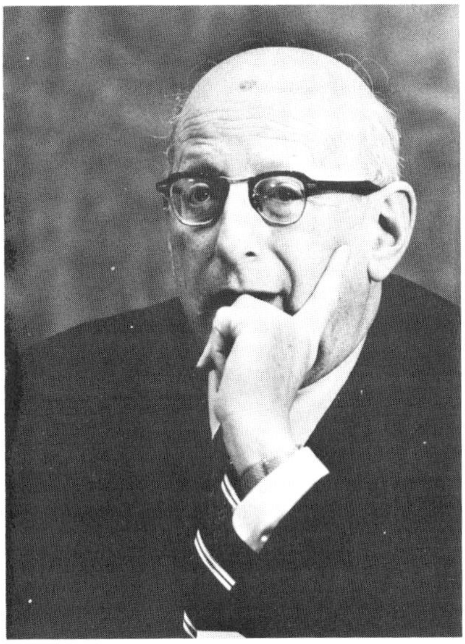

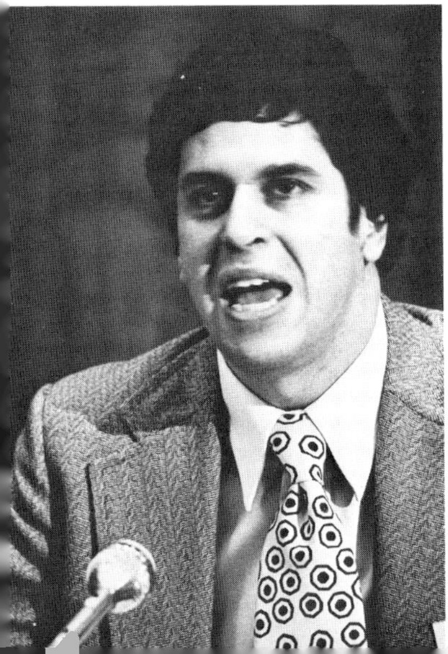

Overview

Emmette S. Redford

Emmette S. Redford is Ashbel Smith Professor of Government and Public Affairs at the Lyndon B. Johnson School of Public Affairs, The University of Texas at Austin.

Congressman Pickle said in the introduction to this volume that presidential and congressional participation in government must be explained, to a very large extent, in terms of the individual actors. The interceding sections have shown just how much truth there is in that statement. Others in the course of these discussions have placed emphasis upon the institutional constraints on the actors in government. In this section we shall deal with the institutions of government and their influence upon the actors.

One paper deals with reorganization in the executive branch, and another on reform or reorganization of the structure of the Congress. The discussion will reveal that there is some connection between the two. One element that is brought out and examined is the contest betwen centripetal and centrifugal forces and how that contest in one branch affects the other.

Our Constitution says nothing about the organization of the executive branch except in terms of the President himself. In the first Congress, it was assumed by the leaders that the function of defining the organization of the executive branch was one for Congress. In more recent years, Congress has delegated some responsibility to the President for reorganization of the executive branch. Hence today the initiatives in reorganization come from the Executive, but they are subject to veto by resolution of either house of Congress, and of course some changes, such as the creation of new departments, require legislation.

There is inevitably conflict between the two branches because of their necessarily different perspectives toward reorganization. Those within the executive branch who plan for reorganizations talk in terms of good management, integration, coordination, unified planning of policy, and presidential leadership. Congressmen, however, may think in terms of protection of legislative programs, maintenance of existing channels of influence of Congress over administration, and the protection of agencies that can offer benefits to their constituents. These differences in perspective mean that some conflict between the two branches is unavoidable.

Some discussions here have been centered around checks and balances, while others have pointed to the complementary contribution of the two branches to the making of government policy. Both concepts will reappear in the following section with reference to the issues underlying reorganization. The process of legislative reorganization is quite different from that of executive reorganization. Each house can reorganize itself without consent of the other and without consent of the Executive; but the way Congress structures itself, the way the separate houses structure themselves, whether in terms of integration of powers in the leadership or through dispersion of powers to committees and subcommittees, has a material influence on the executive branch. This influence, too, will be considered and the interrelation between the two branches will be illustrated in the discussions not only of executive reorganization, but of congressional reform as well.

Management as a Priority

in Executive Branch Reorganization

Alan K. Campbell

Alan K. Campbell is Director of the U.S. Office of Personnel Management (formerly the U.S. Civil Service Commission).

Whatever the reasons that lead Presidents to seek to reorganize the federal government, their intent is a complex set of considerations that almost always includes a desire to clarify the role, priorities, and managerial expectations of their administrative departments. "Virtually every President since Teddy Roosevelt has established a committee to study the organization of the executive branch [and] to recommend ways and means to improve performance and accountability."[1] One can easily assume that any new President will enter that office with a set of organizational objectives—often commitments made during a presidential campaign. Typically, a President's objectives range from doing cheaper or better what is already being done (i.e., more economically or more effectively), to doing something new.

New presidential initiatives and reorganizations aimed at saving tax dollars have frequently been characterized by additions or deletions on the organizational chart. The assumption generally has been that a new structure will provide the mechanism for accomplishing goals at least cost. At the extreme, this approach has led to the view that "there was some one series of corrections which was 'right' and which would return government to its proper place."[2] Short of that extreme, Presidents have found structural reform a means of giving visibility to their interests. New departments like

HUD under Johnson and Energy under Carter are examples of presidential priorities stated in terms of organizational structure.

But presidential objectives can also be stated in terms of procedure. Here the objectives are frequently related to the effective supervision, that is, to organizational management. The adoption of an executive budget and later the use of planning programming budgetry and more recently of zero-based budgeting are procedural manifestations of supervisory objectives. The history of reorganization from the Keep Commission in 1905 to the Brownlow Committee in 1936 was a history of the slow emergence of the primacy of executive management over executive structure.[3]

The categories that are used to discuss reorganization of government are imprecise: policy vs. program; procedure vs. structure; management vs. operation. Rarely, however, does a reorganization fit only one of these categories. In fact, distinctions such as procedure and structure are almost always considered in tandem by those bent on reorganizations. Eisenhower, Kennedy, and Nixon all expressed indignation about reshuffling boxes as a way to accomplish reorganization; yet much of what they recommended was precisely that. The intermixing of structural and procedural reform is a fact, however difficult it makes the analysis of reorganization. An analysis, however, usually indicates that a particular reorganization effort stresses either procedure or structure.

The primacy of management concerns that emerged through 1937 has been neither consistent nor especially successful in generating congressional support. Roosevelt discovered that economizing was a goal more appealing to the legislative branch than was organizational and managerial effectiveness. The American electorate has long been disposed to associate inexpensive government with efficient government.

What Roosevelt came to understand was that the level of government expenditures may be largely independent of the level of program effectiveness. In fact, most of the reorganization for which it was claimed that economies would result have not saved money. It is also doubtful whether, given their focus, they have done a great deal to improve program delivery. And some such economizing reorganizations have done very little to strengthen the hand of the President in managing the bureaucracy. For Congress, the fear of a strong Executive has often been greater than the fear of inefficiency.

In 1936 when Louis Brownlow chaired President Roosevelt's Reorganization Committee, the chief concern was coordination and management. The Committee drew heavily from the experiences of government employees. Brownlow was convinced that the basic problem was administrative management and that it could be solved only by equipping the President with the means of controlling and directing the Administration. Brownlow viewed previous reorganizations as failing because of their lack of attention to process and their myopic concern for structure. He wrote in his diary: "essentially the problem is how to implement (sic) the President with simple but effective machinery which will enable him to exercise managerial direction and control appropriate to the burden of responsibility imposed upon him by the Constitution."[4] The recommendations of the Brownlow Committee are among the most respected tenets of reorganization. But virtually none were adopted. The Brownlow Committee, like numerous other reorganization studies, was a victim of what Frederick Mosher has called bad timing.[5] The report was issued at a time when Congress was unwilling to follow Roosevelt's lead on almost any matter.

The experiences of political leaders since Brownlow with ever-larger organizational units have demonstrated that centralization of organizational power does not in and of itself resolve the problem of coordination and management. As Mayor of New York, John Lindsay created umbrella agencies which resulted in no real improvement in services. Five years after that reorganization, the former budget director for New York City testified before the House Government Operations Subcommittee on Legislation that consolidation in New York City had produced an increase rather than a decrease in administrative overhead.[6] But the failure to improve services he attributed to an unwillingness to expend the time, money, and energy necessary to realize benefits. Reorganization, in his words, was not "self-executing." Furthermore the layering-over of positions which at one time were highly visible made it difficult to attract top talent to the subcommittees (once cabinet-level units) within the new super departments. A similar fate might well have followed from President Nixon's attempt to create a few super-departments, had he been successful.

Centralization of the federal bureaucracy has probably run its course for now. While functional reorganizations will be periodically necessary, the overarching concern today in the executive branch is again on policymaking and administration. From the managerial perspective there are no hard and fast rules as to what level of centralization or decentralization is best. One decentralizes where it makes sense: where incentives deriving from delegation of authority produce the best delivery of services; where coordination between similar functions is maintained while coupling managerial flexibility with accountability; where people closer to the problem save time, reduce red tape, and better understand the difficulties.

The current concern for process stands in contrast to the reorganization interests of the commissions chaired by former President Hoover in 1947 and 1953. The first Hoover Commission's objective was to remove roadblocks to more effective organization and to reduce expenditures. The controlling principles of that commission were that agencies should be grouped functionally, that purpose should dictate manner of organization, and that principles of business management should be applied to public agencies. It was intended to give practical application to the Brownlow Committee recommendations of ten years earlier. Hoover personally rewrote much of the report after Truman's surprise victory over Dewey, which perhaps explains the view of some that the intent of the report was to restrain the President.[7]

The Second Hoover Commission, established by President Eisenhower, went farther in management matters than did Hoover I. For example, Hoover II recommended a Senior Civil Service with rank in person rather than in position. The concerns of Hoover II, however, fell outside the control of the executive branch by virtue of the independent status conferred by the charter establishing the commission. Reorganizations controlled by a group external to government pose considerable risks to the President's public posture.

Eisenhower went to great lengths to justify his rejection of Hoover's recommendations. "Once reorganization is on the public agenda, and you have a commission of that type appointed, it puts the burden of proof on the President to explain why he is not going to do what is recommended."[8] It is not surprising, then, that not a single permanent program resulting from years of depression, recovery, war, and reform was abolished as a result of the Hoover inquiry. Presidents with a strong sense of their overall reorganization objectives will not permit themselves to be caught in this situation. President Carter, to the extent that his management focus has been revealed through the Federal Personnel Management Project, has wisely chosen an internal staffing route. Tyrus Fain, in *Federal Reorganization: The Executive Branch*, notes:

> Executive reorganization became popular as a concept and an activity during what has been described as the Administrative Management period, roughly from 1920 to 1970. The principal administrative goal of the intellectual groups dominant during that period was to reinforce the institutionalized Presidency as the administrative chief of the executive branch. The Presidency was to be strengthened by the unified executive budget required under the Budget and Accounting Act of 1921, the establishment of the Executive Office of the President, and the passage of legislation enabling the President to submit reorganization plans to Congress, the latter two events occurring in 1939.
>
> In the twentieth century, the Congress and the President have vied for preeminence in executive reorganization. While the President has, on balance, been the dominant force, the Congress has made major contributions in the field. Congressional strength in reorganization rests upon a constitutional base; namely, that Congress must establish all new departments, and that agencies cannot exist without appropriations approved by Congress.[9]

Restraints which legitimately should be placed on the President are those against violating congressional programmatic intent, disregarding individual rights, and misusing public funds. But these controls are not strengthened by impeding the President's managerial responsibility. Moreover, one must be careful not to burden the Executive with restraints that impede effective management. To argue that tying the President's hands is the best way to insure a virtuous administration is to misunderstand the problem of government in our time. Louis Brownlow and Charles Merriam understood the problem all too well: that we must provide an alternative in a practical and efficient democracy to the strain in western societies toward arbitrary leadership.[10] Two underpinnings to their "practical efficient democracy" were that Presidents should have power to manage and that Presidents should be persons of outstanding caliber.

Process and Structure

The distinction drawn thus far between process and structure is not precise. In fact, a change in one frequently entails some alteration in the other. Changes in either stem from the policy objectives of reformers. The choice of a structural or a procedural approach to achieve a policy goal may or may not be dictated by the nature of the policy. For example, a decision to end the inefficiencies entailed in disaggregated space acquisition and maintenance dictated the establishment of the General Services Administration. But one can also imagine procedural remedies for the same inefficiencies short of establishing a new organization. Why a President chooses to move in one direction and not another is not altogether clear. Why a President chooses to see one set of problems as central and not another set is not clear either. It is a complex mix of political considerations and personal ideology, though some rules seem to operate.

Public attention in this century has focused largely on structural reform—combining overlapping functions, reducing the span of control, clearing lines of authority from top to bottom, creating new departments for new policy interests, establishing new executive offices for oversight. What we should have learned from this history of reform is first that overlap is inevitable and second that "no amount of clarification and precision in redrawing [jurisdictional lines] will. . .harness the energies required for managing large-scale interdepartmental programs."[11] Rufus Miles recently argued that: "the most difficult task of public management is *not* deciding how the functions of government should be divided among organizational units, but how the functions can and should be effectively coordinated after they have been divided. All government is a complex set of matrices; if work is divided on one set of principles or axes, it must be coordinated on another."[12]

Presidents for whom the central issues have been coordination and management have been less occupied with reshuffling boxes. Their attention has been on the need for information, incentives, budgeting, planning, and the like.

These coordinating functions rest heavily in agencies such as the Office of Management and Budget, the General Services Administration, the Civil Service Commission, the President's staff, and the interagency commissions. Nevertheless, these may cover only a fraction of the overlapping concerns of the federal administrative bureaucracy. Even if these coordinating bodies should cover the universe of interagency issues, they would fail, no doubt, to provide clarity on each such issue for the simple reason that present bureaucratic complexities reflect the competing interests that have been accommodated through time.

Administrative procedure and organizational structure are the media through which policies are acted out. While it is true that good policies can fail if they are badly administered, it is not always true conversely that cumbersome, unwieldy procedures and organization are simply the result of bad administration. Complex procedural requirements and organization often reflect complex policy concerns. Abstruse regulations and organizational duplication are often an attempt to mediate between conflicting policy interests and competing needs. Achieving reform beyond cosmetic box-reshuffling in such situations ultimately means attempting to change policy direction, rather than simply modifying policy execution.

The approach of the various project teams carrying out separate aspects of President Carter's government-wide reorganization has been neither wholly structural nor wholly procedural. By and large, project teams are attempting to deal with particular problems, and to integrate the President's desire for an open government into their actual operation plans. This can be clearly seen in the Federal Personnel Management Project study of the civil service system. The majority of the slightly over one hundred people who worked on the personnel management study were federal personnel specialists who understood the basis for the recommendations. Each of the task forces studying separate aspects of the personnel system developed option papers which discussed the problems and presented a wide range of alternatives. These were circulated to over seven hundred individuals and groups in and out of government, including consumer groups, veterans organizations, organizations representing minorities and women, employee unions, state and local governments, and members of the academic community. The comments drawn from all these efforts were weighed in formulating the final recommendations. Thus the effort, both in terms of the kinds of people actually carrying out the project and in terms of contributions to the final decisionmaking process, was actually a bottom-up undertaking: those who were to carry out and be affected by the policies had a major role in their determination.

Conflicting interests and needs make reform difficult in nearly all large complex organizations, private as well as public. Procedural reform, however, especially that aimed at giving managers greater authority and flexibility to manage, is particularly difficult in the public sector because of the conflicts inherent in government's obligation to safeguard the "public interest."

Every citizen, for example, has a right to demand that the federal employee reviewing his or her tax return, evaluating his or her bid for government contracts, or in other ways directly affecting his or her life, is carrying out the law uniformly, without regard to party allegiance or other partisan considerations. Thus, it is essential to insure that there are sufficient safeguards to protect federal employees from political pressures and reprisals in order to make clear to all that they are servants of the people rather than servants of a particular political party or constituency.

Conversely, while the protection of a career service is important to government, the public also has a right to demand effective government. Safeguards established to protect career employees against politically motivated demotions and separations should not also provide a refuge for the incompetent and unmotivated, as some feel has occurred. Government must be staffed with managers of the highest ability who can manage public resources and serve the public interest efficiently and economically. Those who do not meet these high standards should not be permitted to manage public programs and thus risk failure to achieve public goals.

Federal managerial positions belong neither to the incumbents of those positions nor to their department heads. They belong to the public as a whole, and the people are entitled to have qualified managers filling those positions. If federal agencies are to respond to the mandates of a new administration pledged to significant changes and to new and different goals, then political officials must have adequate flexibility and freedom to select, motivate, manage, and when necessary to remove, those federal employees through whom they must work in order to reach those goals.

This tension between the need for managers to have flexibility, to act quickly, and to move without obstruction toward policy goals, and the need for safeguards to protect the career service from partisan influence or reprisal affects a variety of issues. It also illustrates the underlying forces that make procedural reform difficult. For example, when it comes to firing incompetents, the reviews and appeals which managers find so frustrating and burdensome are the very same procedural safeguards placed in the system to protect career employees. Attempts to streamline the process by limiting the issues that are appealable, shortening the time for filing, or prohibiting appeals to higher management levels, while technically changes in procedure, may be seen as involving incursions into employee rights. Such changes therefore may be opposed by employee unions, and that opposition would become a major factor in settling the question whether the change is to occur, especially if legislation is required to establish the new procedures.

A similar tension exists in the roles assigned to the Civil Service Commission. The commission is assigned responsibility both for providing personnel policy leadership in the executive branch, and for acting as the "watchdog" of the merit system and the final court for administrative adjudication of statutory personnel appeals. Employees, especially employee unions, tend to regard the commission as an arm of management; in their eyes that undermines the neutrality of the commission's adjudicatory role. Similarly the commission, as a separate, semi-independent body with divided constituencies, has an awkward role in advising management. The present system denies the President the strong, proximate instrument of personnel management that is available to industrial managers, military commanders, and subordinate federal executives.

The five organizational options recently circulated for comment by the Federal Personnel Management Project suggested a division between the commission's management functions and its responsibility for hearing merit system appeals. Four of the five options called for the creation of a wholly separate organization—a Merit Protection Board—to guard the merit system and hear appeals.

Viewed solely from the perspective of achieving reform by applying "better" management techniques, a splitting of functions and the possible creation of a new organization runs counter to the often-stated Administration objective of simplifying government by reducing the number of agencies. Nevertheless, while it is "more complex," the proposed split more accurately addresses the problems growing out of the underlying conflict in interests. In this sense it is in fact a step toward better management, whatever the structural consequences.

Some observers say the commission's responsibilities regarding affirmative action have disclosed similar role problems. Title V of the United States Code gives the Civil Service Commission responsibility for overseeing the merit system. This has been the traditional *raison d'etre* of the commission—to assure selection, advancement, and tenure based on individual ability to perform the job without regard to political affiliation, race, creed, color, sex, or any other factor. As a corrective to the nineteenth-century spoils system in which selection, promotion, and separation were politically motivated, the merit principle has served public interests rather well. There is no mass exodus with a change in administrations. Even in times of great national political uncertainty, such as the Watergate period, the day-to-day business of government continues without disruption. Title VII of the Civil Rights Act, however, also assigns the commission responsibility for equal employment opportunity and affirmative action in federal employment. Of equal and growing public concern are the widespread demands for greater progress toward achieving affirmative action goals.

There has been significant improvement in the development of equal employment opportunity since the passage of the civil rights legislation in the mid-1960s. Nonetheless, minorities and women are still substantially underrepresented in upper-level positions in both the public and private sectors; and the federal government's policies on affirmative action are different from those of the private sector. The job of changing past patterns is still far from complete. Many groups within society are seriously questioning whether so-called "color-blind" merit-selection policies will allow the attainment of affirmative action goals within an acceptable length of time. They also question whether it can be done at all if we continue our current candidate-screening devices. For example, a new set of test guidelines for the federal system, known as the Federal Executive Agency Guidelines, require very rigorous validation for any selection instrument that adversely affects any minorities or women being evaluated.

On the one hand, the present Civil Service Commission is charged with its traditional responsibility for assuring selection without regard to factors such as race, creed, color, sex, etc., while on the other hand it also has primary responsibility within the federal sector to take positive steps to assure that more women and minorities are selected and advanced. While these roles are not necessarily conflicting (e.g., affirmative action can be accomplished through better recruiting, better internal training, etc.), certainly they are at times competing. Whether one judges the Civil Service Commission's record on equal employment opportunity to be adequate or not, a consideration of the success or failure of the program must take into account the difficulties inherent in this duality of purposes.

Achieving reforms through legislative action is often very difficult, especially when the barriers to reform involve competing needs of vocal special interest groups. This is clear, for example, in efforts to reform the federal staffing program.

Among the most commonly heard complaints regarding the federal personnel system is that the procedures for hiring employees are cumbersome, complicated, and needlessly time-consuming. On the surface, reorganizing the system to bring better management into play is simply a question of revising the existing processes for recruiting and examining (certifying) the credentials of new employees. In studying the recruiting process, however, Federal Personnel Project task forces found that the most onerous of the restraints on flexibility in hiring stem directly from the legislatively mandated preference for veterans. The rule of three, for instance, restricts managers to selecting one of the first three names on a civil service rank-ordered register of candidates, regardless of how many others had identical or substantially equal rating scores. Within these three names managers are prohibited from passing over a veteran to select a nonveteran unless they file a formal objection, which must be approved by the Civil Service Commission.

It is because these procedures so severely limit a manager's discretion in selecting anyone but a veteran, that they are so successful. Removing or significantly modifying them to give managers greater ability to exercise their personal judgment would also reduce the great preference that veterans now enjoy. Congress, then, in deciding whether or not to change the law, must weigh the obligation of the government to provide preference to veterans, against the greater flexibility that federal managers would gain and the potential for greater efficiency if veterans' preference were modified or abolished. The fact that veterans' preference has withstood the countless attempts to change it over the years attests to the fact that the promise of "better management" has not been sufficient to tip the balance in this conflict of purposes.

Reform, or at least change, does become possible when the public opinion supporting a particular policy begins to shift. This is now occurring with veterans' preference. Preference for one group can only be given at the expense of others or no real preference is conferred. Veterans can only receive preference at the expense of nonveterans; thus veterans' preference adversely affects other emerging high-priority goals such as affirmative action. This dramatically alters the nature of the conflict in objectives. Where previously the conflict was between the country's obligation to veterans and the potential for greater efficiency, it now becomes a conflict between the obligation to veterans and the need to achieve greater progress in bringing other groups, particularly women, into the federal work force. The chances for amending veterans' preference are better than they have been for many years.

Efforts at procedural reform are frequently simply attempts to modify or abolish systems and procedures instituted in previous attempts to achieve "better management." Sometimes, too, the reform effort is prompted by differing perceptions of what constitutes "better management."

One of the messages that came through quite clearly in Personnel Management Project meetings with key people around the country was that although supervisors often feel they have real opportunity to exercise personal judgment and discretion, in essence they have little real opportunity to manage. Agency heads and first-line supervisors alike have to work with the limits set by numerous laws, and central-agency (e.g., Office of Management and Budget, Civil Service Commission, etc.) regulations or policies that govern how they may allocate and manage their dollar and people resources. Some are expressly designed to limit the size, cost, etc. of the federal work force. All are intended to promote efficient, effective, fair management.

Unfortunately, many of these centralized management controls are developed separately, deal with only a single aspect of operations, and are imposed without a full appreciation of their cumulative effect on managers' abilities to achieve their program objectives. As a consequence, many central controls and policies designed to achieve "good management" are in fact themselves serious obstacles to efficiency and economy at the working level and impair the ability of managers and employees to deliver services to the public. Ceilings on positions, limits on the number of people an agency may employ, and limitations on the average grade levels of employees are the most often criticized of these controls.

Agencies are assigned ceiling quotas by the Office of Management and Budget in conjunction with the budget process. The ceilings are part of an overall effort to control government-wide employment. Regardless of determinations by the agency head of the number of people needed to do the job, regardless of the availability of savings from increased efficiency which could be used to fund extra positions, agencies must be within the arbitrary personnel ceiling on the last day of the fiscal year.

Positions ceilings and OMB restraints on the average salary-grade levels for employees are major barriers to effective management. In order to accomplish essential funded work and still remain within the ceiling, managers are forced to contract out, use overtime and temporaries, and hire small numbers of professionals in lieu of larger number of clerks or technicians even when such practices are counterproductive. Average-grade controls force other distortions in the balance of the work force and conflict with number-of-employees limitations. The two, singly and together, conflict with effective work-force planning, position management, and achieving EEO and similar goals.

The case against ceiling controls in particular has been documented in study after study. Most recently, the General Accounting Office recommended that ceiling controls be dropped in favor of other control mechanisms. The Personnel Management Project studied several options, including controls on personnel dollars rather than on number of positions. This would allow managers to use their personnel budgets in ways they see as most effective rather than as centralized controls dictate. Nonetheless, ceiling controls have persisted.

The failure to eliminate ceiling controls is not a failure in technique: more suitable management control systems are readily available. The fact is that successive Presidents have felt that the public perceived attempts to limit the number of government employees as a worthy "good management" objective in and of itself. Failure to eliminate controls is a failure of policy, a failure to counterbalance presidential concern over the public's perception of a burgeoning bureaucracy with a persuasive statement of the true costs of ceilings in inefficiency and poor morale at the working level.

The Paradox of Reorganization

The history that we have traced, and also the example of the current Federal Personnel Management Project, point to the difficulty of achieving change in the public sector. The track record of those attempting reorganization of the executive branch is one of frequent failure. Even with Louis Brownlow the failures outnumbered the successes. One may well ask what makes the attempt to change government's structure and procedures worth the effort.

A principal impulse of reorganization in a stable and enduring government like that of the United States derives paradoxically from the very characteristic that makes the effort so frustrating and so frequently futile: the permanence of the system. Few people want to invest great energy creating something that may not last. Reformers seek to change institutions because those institutions are likely to survive, not because they are ephemeral. The staff of the Personnel Management Project describe in graphic terms the resistance and intransigence they have encountered among those reviewing their proposals, and yet not of those working on the project would have put much concern into those proposals had they not supposed that their suggestions and work would last. It is a simple truth that we only are seriously concerned about changing those things that, having accommodated our changes, will endure.

What makes change endure is its ability to take root, to become in effect part of the established order. There is nothing particularly startling about that. What it does tell us, though, is that attempts to achieve changes that are merely cosmetic may not generate much political support or sacrifice; people will not work all that hard to achieve them. And changes that lack the appeal or capacity to become part of the established order will probably not survive a serious challenge. Some of the social programs of the sixties met that fate: there was inadequate time and support, and quite possibly there were inadequate structural safeguards, to prevent their being easily uprooted. But those who designed such programs and brought them along assumed that they were creating a new order which would not pass away so easily. Else there would not have been so much energy expended. One should view a struggle like that of advocating the Equal Rights Amendment in the same light: the difficulty of passing it is precisely what makes it worth working for passage—the chances of reversal are slim.

It is for this reason, then, that structural changes in the system sometimes seem so unexciting: many though not all of them are seen as unrooted; they express the changing priorities of a passing moment, and they may not last. There have been major exceptions. Lyndon Johnson created the Department of Transportation, and one can assume that it will remain for some time. But by and large the flimsiness of much reorganization is traceable to the fact that structural reorganizations are sometimes ends in themselves rather than means for achieving political and programmatic goals. Harold Seidman tells the story of being called to the Nixon White House and told, "Tell us what to reorganize. We want to have a reorganization program."

The symbolic value of reorganization may be sufficiently great to override the tendency to give scant attention to things that will not last. The country may need assurance, as in the case of NASA, that the government is giving adequate emphasis to a new national goal. But not all symbolic changes are worth the political sacrifice required to achieve them.

Earlier we noted that although many of the recommendations of Louis Brownlow were fundamentally sound, those recommendations went nowhere at the time. And yet many are now in effect. Others resurface periodically, as they have in some of President Carter's proposals. The reason they reemerge is related both to the difficulty of achieving important changes—that is, the likelihood that proposals for major overhauls will at first be unacceptable—and to the worth and appeal of changes that go to the roots of the system and could become themselves entrenched. Fritz Mosher thinks two decades is not too long to wait. That may be hard news to some, but it should not particularly discourage the present Administration. So many of the proposals being advanced by groups such as the Federal Personnel Management Project are ideas that have reemerged from the past; they are considered to be worth fighting for because they will probably endure. They are not symbolic structural reforms, but go to the heart of the government's management process.

Notes

[1] Tyrus Fain, ed., *Federal Reorganization: The Executive Branch* (New York: R. R. Bowker Co., 1977), p. xvii.

[2] Barry Karl, *Executive Reorganization and Reform in the New Deal* (Cambridge, Mass.: Harvard University Press, 1963), p. 191.

[3] Ibid., p. 195.

[4] Louis Brownlow, *A Passion for Anonymity* (Chicago: University of Chicago Press, 1958), p. 337.

[5] Frederick Mosher, "Reorganizing the Federal Government: Some Observations Based on History," mimeographed (Lecture delivered at the Maxwell Graduate School of Citizenship and Public Affairs, Syracuse University, April 29, 1977).

[6] Fain, *Federal Reorganization*, p. 18.

[7] Mosher, "Reorganizing the Federal Government."

[8] Harold Seidman, "Reorganizing the Federal Government: Politics and Strategy," (Lecture at the Maxwell Graduate School of Citizenship and Public Affairs, Syracuse University, March 3, 1977).

[9] Fain, *Federal Reorganization*, pp. xxiii-xxv.

[10] Karl, *Executive Reorganization*, p. 225.

[11] Harvey C. Mansfield, "Federal Executive Reorganization: Thirty Years of Experience," *Public Administration Review* 29, no. 4 (August 1969): 342.

[12] Rufus Miles, "Considerations for a President Bent on Reorganization," *Public Administration Review* 37, no. 2 (April 1977): 160.

Our Changing Congress

the Inside (and Outside) Story

Roger H. Davidson

Roger H. Davidson is Professor of Political Science and Chairman of the Political Science Department at the University of California, Santa Barbara.

Among the regular recipients of congressional subsidies are the nation's pundits, cartoonists, and humorists. Our national legislature has provided a seemingly inexhaustible source of material for our collective amusement—from Mr. Dooley to Johnny Carson, from Thomas Nast to Pat Oliphant. The other branches of government have nothing that quite matches the image of Senator Snort, the florid and incompetent windbag. And during the 1977 Senate filibuster on natural gas deregulation, when cots were set up in Senate cloakrooms, the pundits and humorists were off and running again. Nor are we likely to see much abatement of the Congress-baiting industry: the comedic possibilities inherent even in, say, the Koreans' pathetic "Operation Ice Mountain" will doubtless prove irresistible.

The view of Congress held by serious commentators—among whom I count seasoned journalists, scholars and old Washington hands—has often been scarcely more flattering than the public image. Thomas E. Cronin has persuasively argued that we have long been mesmerized by the awesome image of the omnicompetent "textbook President," a combination of Superman and secular saint. If so, we are equally plagued by a stereotype of the "textbook Congress": an irresponsible and slightly sleazy body of (mostly elderly) men who approach Woodrow Wilson's caustic description of the House of Representatives as " a disintegrated mass of jarring elements." Even among the most serious and sympathetic commentators, the characteristics of disorderliness, irresponsibility, and inertia are often mentioned. Legislators themselves contribute to this shabby image, often portraying themselves to their constituents as gallant warriors against the dragons back on Capitol Hill: as Richard F. Fenno, Jr. notes, they "run *for* Congress by running *against* Congress."

Criticisms of Congress, of course, shift with the political winds. During much of the post-Roosevelt era, the Presidency stood for progressive interventionism in domestic affairs and internationalism in foreign policy. True to their electoral base in the pivotal urban states, Presidents were more attuned than their congressional counterparts to the forces of urbanism, minority rights, and the social-welfare state. In the meantime, malapportionment and seniority lent Congress a more conservative atmosphere, often redolent of magnolia blossoms and honeysuckle. Hence, liberals were the President's natural allies, deploring the parochialism and obstinacy of the legislative branch, characterized by one journalist as that "obstacle course on Capitol Hill."

The winds shifted radically in the late 1960s. The Nixon Presidency dedicated itself to playing out the Vietnam tragedy, while struggling on the home front to contain liberal social programs. Meanwhile, on Capitol Hill the factional balance was tilting leftward. The moderate-to-liberal wing of the Democratic Party was ascendant, gradually loosening the conservative coalition's grasp on congressional leadership posts. By the early 1970s, loyalty to domestic social programs and opposition to foreign adventurism became the orthodox position of Hill Democrats, who took up—at first hesitantly, but with growing confidence—the challenges laid down by the Nixon Administration. Those same liberals who had championed presidential leadership a generation earlier now spoke darkly of the evils of the "imperial Presidency." No less a reformer than Ralph Nader proclaimed that "nothing compares with Congress as the hope for America." For their part, conservatives discovered new virtues in vigorous White House leadership.

The turbulent events of the past decade have not left Congress untouched. Indeed, notwithstanding its reputation for inertia, it is arguable that Congress has been altered more fundamentally than any other governmental institution. The changes have touched virtually every nook and cranny on Capitol Hill—membership, structures, procedures, folkways, and staffs. If Sam Rayburn or Lyndon Johnson were to return to visit the chambers they served with such distinction, they would doubtless be astounded at the transformations that have been wrought—even though both men had a hand in bringing about those transformations.

If we are to assay the present state and future development of our national legislature, we must try to comprehend the meaning of the past few years' changes. This is no simple task. Although they were produced by forces built up over a generation or more, the innovations themselves occurred rather swiftly; and, I must confess, we Congress-watchers have not always predicted them accurately. They have rendered obsolete much of what scholars and journalists have written (and sometimes still write) about the House and Senate. Nor are the changes of a whole cloth; they are rather fragments of puzzling patchwork. Piecing together this patchwork is the assignment I have set for myself here, albeit in a preliminary, tentative form.

The Outside and Inside Routes to Change

In analyzing innovations such as those experienced on Capitol Hill, I should like to advance a simple theory borrowed from the study of formal organizations. A large body of literature has accumulated about innovation in large-scale organizations, mainly business corporations. Naturally Congress, as a legislative body, is a unique sort of organization; in many ways it is very different from, say, an automobile factory, or a hospital, or a fire department. Yet Congress shares many basic attributes with other organizations. It encounters demands from its outside environment, it has a measurable workload, and it manifests all the qualities of a large body of interacting human beings—leadership, communication, networks of power and influence, and various types of traditions and folkways.

From Woodrow Wilson to the present day, commentators have agreed that Congress is a relatively nonhierarchical organization whose prevailing mode of decisionmaking is bargaining. This central attribute flows from unique organizational traits, and suggests that innovation is probably a more complicated and subtle process than in more hierarchical organizations.

Let us start from a simple premise: that Congress, like all organizations, strives to preserve itself and, if possible, expand its span of influence. For many organizations, like the proverbial Mom-and-Pop store, survival is a literal day-by-day challenge, in which keeping the doors open for business is often a triumph. For Congress, the imperative is more subtle but no less real: whether it can preserve or perhaps enhance its independence and its sphere of influence. In our constitutional framework of blended powers, which the late Edward S. Corwin called "an invitation to struggle," Congress competes with many other institutions, including the White House, executive agencies, the courts, and even private bodies.

To survive, an organization must do two things. It must adjust to *external demands*, and it must cope with *internal stresses*. These constitute the outside and inside pressures for innovation—what we might call the demand-pull and cost-push of organization equilibrium—which alone or in tandem can challenge the organization to reassess its traditional ways of doing things. Congress has faced problems of both types, and has responded to each with distinctive sorts of innovations, though to what effect it is too early to tell.

Our age has been called antiparliamentary, and if that is so, it is surely caused by the staggering and ever-shifting challenges emanating from the external environment. These may take the form of rising public expectations, fast-moving events, competing institutions, or simply an exploding workload. In country after country, parliamentary forms have been supplanted by military dictatorships or bureaucratic regimes when the parliamentary systems proved incapable of coping with fast-changing events and escalating political demands. Our Congress is more nearly a legislature in the strict sense of the word than is any national assembly in the world. Yet many people question whether Congress can realistically continue to exert meaningful control over the government's activities, given the complex, technical, and highly interdependent character of current problems. The "imperial Presidency," let us not forget, is one seriously proposed solution to this challenge.

Another set of pressures for change emanates from forces within the organization—primarily from membership turnover, factional shifts, and changing norms. The members of an organization—Senators and Representatives, in this case—make their own claims upon the institution, and these claims must be satisfied in the long run if the organization is to attract high-level talent, provide a workplace where this talent can be exploited, and command loyalty from the participants.

Individual legislators harbor a variety of goals. All members, or virtually all of them, want to get reelected; some members have no other interest. But political men and women do not live by reelection alone; legislators want a chance to contribute, to shape public policy, to see their ideas become reality, and to work in dignity. In a body of 535 politicians, such needs are bound to generate friction. Other internal stresses are ricochet effects from external demands— as when a ballooning workload (external pull) produces a personal or committee scramble for jurisdiction (internal push).

Any organization, from the Mom-and-Pop store to the United States Congress, must hold these external demands and internal stresses in check, if it is to survive. For Congress, this means that it must strive to respond to the expectations held for it by others— Presidents, administrators, lobbyists, the press corps, and general and specialized publics—or in some way shape or modify those expectations into more manageable dimensions. At the same time, it must provide its participants—primarily members and their staffs—with outlets for meeting *their* goals, which include not only reelection but also dignity, sanity, and meaningful participation.

The two types of pressures for change, outside and inside, produce distinctive types of innovation. I call these *adaptation* and *consolidation*. Adaptation refers to shifts in practices or work habits designed to adapt to external pressures. Consolidation refers to adjustments in procedures or power relations designed to relieve internal tensions. These two types of innovation, I shall argue, have different sources and produce divergent effects upon the organization. Moreover, the organization itself may adopt a particular pattern of innovation—primarily adaptive, primarily consolidative, or some in-between combination—that gives the organization a special style, or fingerprint, in handling problems thrust upon it.

The real problem of organizational survival is that innovations must ultimately maintain an equilibrium between outside and inside forces. There are happy circumstances—how frequent, I don't know— in which an innovation helps the organization cope with *both* outside and inside pressures at the same time. Everyone is happy, so to speak. But just as often, outside and inside pressures pull in opposite directions, forcing the institution to make difficult and costly choices. An organization may adapt well to outside demands, but only at painful human cost to its participants; or it may handle its internal affairs effectively, only to be more and more anomalous within its larger environment.

Pressures may be left unattended, building up for years or even generations; but sooner or later they must be dealt with, by gradual adjustment or by cataclysmic rejection of old ways of doing things. The changes that swept Capitol Hill between 1971 and 1976 constitute relatively extensive efforts to release tensions that had been mounting for two generations or more.

I now wish to apply this little theory of innovation to congressional changes of the 1971-76 period. To indicate the course of the argument, it will be my contention that during that period Congress experienced relatively severe pressures, both outside and inside; that two relatively distinct clusters of innovations were attempted in coping with these pressures; that, because of Congress's nature, its inside (consolidative) innovations were more extensive and successful than its outside (adaptive) innovations; and finally, that certain of these inside changes erect for Congress new obstacles for resolving outside pressures.

Outside Pull: The Crisis of Adaptation

Congress, like most of the world's legislative bodies, confronts a prolonged crisis of adaptation. On this point most analysts are agreed, although they may differ over the exact causes and outlines of the crisis. Some students trace the crisis to the downfall of Speaker Cannon early in this century, others to the rise of big government in the New Deal era. The crisis is typified by executive ascendancy, as Congress relies increasingly on the President and the bureaucratic apparatus for its legislative agenda and delegates ever-larger chunks of discretionary authority to bureaucrats. Whatever the ultimate sources of the crisis, it is acutely felt on Capitol Hill, as it stretches legislative structures and procedures to their limits, and sometimes beyond.

By the early 1970s, this adaptive crisis had been under way for a long time. It may be instructive to recount briefly the major factors in Congress's external environment that contributed to the crisis.

1. Government, and Congress in turn, is asked to resolve more problems than ever before. The House and Senate workload, in absolute terms, is enormous and rapidly growing. Popular, journalistic images of idleness on Capitol Hill are simply false. In the past twenty years, for example, House committee and subcommittee meetings have more than doubled, as have the number of hours in session.

2. Today's problems do not come in familiar packages or admit of traditional solutions. Many of them transcend traditional categories and jurisdictions, not to mention two-year legislative time clocks. President Carter's energy package embraced some 113 separate legislative initiatives, which were referred to five different House committees plus one ad hoc body. Nearly every House and Senate committee handles some phase of energy policy. And what is true of energy is equally true of other broad-gauged issues—health, welfare, and international economics.

3. Relative to these demands, resources for resolving them in politically attractive ways have dwindled. It is vexing enough to shape policies for an affluent society, a "people of plenty"; in an era of limits, the task is excruciating. Rather than distributing benefits, politicians find themselves having to assign costs. (In political scientists' terminology, this represents a shift from distributive to redistributive politics—a discouraging prospect for policymakers.) This is a prime reason why we are passing more laws but enjoying them less, and why today's policymakers seem so ineffectual.

4. The advance of the executive establishment causes acute stresses on Capitol Hill. On the one hand, legislators expect sure-handed White House leadership and grumble when it is not forthcoming; on the other hand, they chafe under vigorous leadership, sensing a threat to legislative initiative and control. The Nixon Administration represented a critical period in the constitutional struggle between White House and Capitol Hill, with the President's challenges in impoundment, executive privilege, the war powers, dismantling of federal programs, and even the abuse

of the pocket veto. Nixon's actions left the Democratically controlled Congress in a compromising position, politically, for the President could, and did, argue that he was acting in the public's behalf to curb legislative lassitude or irresponsibility.

5. Public support for Congress as an institution is notoriously low. From its modern-day high in the mid-1960s (the 89th Congress), public approval of congressional performance has dropped to disturbing levels, surging upward only briefly at the time of the Nixon resignation. In the Harris survey of January 1977, 65 percent of the respondents gave Congress a negative rating, while only 22 percent gave it a positive rating.

6. House and Senate leaders sense that, although they are publicly held responsible for congressional performance, they lack adequate power to coordinate or schedule the legislative program. This is why virtually every leader since Sam Rayburn has supported reforms that promised to increase his leverage upon the legislative process.

In the wake of these shifts in its external environment, Congress has resorted to a variety of adaptive tactics, principally to adjust its own workload so as to restrict the scope of its decisionmaking. It has done this mainly by delegating more decisions to executive agents, and shifting its own role to one of monitor, vetoer, and overseer. The proliferation of reporting requirements, not to mention oversight activities, is testimony to this strategic shift. Sometimes, as in the 1973 War Powers Act, the innovation takes the form of lending formal recognition to *de facto* shifts in the constitutional blend of powers. In searching out changes, students of politics often fail to look beyond formal innovations such as reorganization; yet these more subtle shifts in workload structure are of equal or greater importance.

Heightened dependence upon executive initiatives has not occurred without resistance from conscientious legislators, or simply those opposed to the drift of legislation. In Neustadt's suggestive phrase, Congress counters by "reaching for control" that it senses has been lost. Today, in the wake of the Watergate and Vietnam crises, we are witnessing a vigorously reactive phase, in which legislators of all persuasions proclaim their fealty to the principle of oversight, and some even put the principle into practice. Predictably, cries of congressional "meddling" are heard from the nether reaches of Pennsylvania Avenue. The emphasis on this critical but seemingly unrewarding function is laudable. However, some of the more ambitious oversight schemes, such as "sunset" legislation, may so badly overload Congress's institutional capacities that the inevitable result will be failure followed by renewed waves of disillusionment.

Another adaptive tactic is the decision to equip itself with staff to cope with the workload and compete with executive expertise. The most lasting legacy of the 1946 Legislative Reorganization Act, this decision has also wrought the most visible transformations of Capitol Hill. No visitor to the Hill these days can fail to be impressed by hordes of people who work there. There are now some 10,000 staff aides (and another 20,000 in supporting agencies); simply housing them is a major logistical problem.

The congressional bureaucracy has grown in ways that betray the character of Congress. As a nonhierarchical institution, Congress has begotten not a single bureaucracy but a series of discrete bureaucracies clustered about the centers of power and in a sense defining those centers. Efforts to impose a common framework upon the staff apparatus have thus far been resisted. In the wake of the Elizabeth Ray scandal, it was at least plausible to assume that the resulting House Commission on Administrative Review (the Obey Commission) would devise certain broad job descriptions (for example, what is or is not permissible to ask a congressional employee to do), minimal hiring and pay standards (for example, comparable pay for comparable service), and at least a rudimentary grievance mechanism. The commission ventured only gingerly into this domain, and at that its report was rejected. In these ways, congressional staffs reflect the institution's feudal structure.

Congress has been least successful in adapting to the challenges of large, interdependent, long-range policy problems. Reform politics has centered around three major issues: the budgetary process, committee jurisdictions, and central leadership.

The scattered fiscal processes have stubbornly resisted coordination. The edifice proposed by the 1946 Legislative Reorganization Act crumbled before it was even erected. Finally, prodded by President Nixon's budgetary thrusts, Congress enacted the Budget and Impoundment Control Act of 1974. A precarious compromise between competing committee interests in the two houses, the new budget process is a controversial set of innovations whose eventual fate cannot yet be predicted.

Neither the House nor the Senate has succeeded in recasting its work groups in conformity with the altered shape of public problems. As everyone knows, the 1946 Act "streamlined" the committees, paring eighty-one panels down to thirty-four. The shift was mainly cosmetic. Subjects were consolidated but not actually restructured, and subcommittees quickly sprang up where many of the "abolished" committees once stood. A wide-ranging House committee realignment proposed in 1974 by the Bolling Committee fell victim to intense lobbying by committee leaders who opposed curbs on their jurisdictions, and by those alliances known as "iron triangles" (composed of committee members and staffs, lobby groups, and executive agencies), which feared that structural shifts would unwire their mutually beneficial alliances. The Bolling plan was ambushed by a reverse-lobbying process, in which committee members and staffs, seeking to preserve their positions, mobilized support from groups that had benefited from past committee decisions. The Obey Commission's 1977 bid to revive the committee-realignment issue was struck down, for essentially the same reasons.

The Senate was markedly more successful when a 1977 realignment package (proposed by the Stevenson Committee) was accepted, with modifications. Like the 1946 realignment, the Stevenson package left jurisdictional lines pretty much untouched, concentrating instead on consolidating several obsolete committees. The scheme was accepted because, by limiting assignments and leadership posts, it succeeded in spreading the workload more equitably among the Senate's more junior members.

Another tactic for achieving coordination of policymaking is stronger central leadership. Most outside commentators, not to mention Capitol Hill reorganization panels, have urged innovations looking in that direction. Yet the ghosts of "Uncle Joe" Cannon still stalk the Hill, for legislators are reluctant to entrust too much power in their leaders. Leaders themselves are sometimes equally reluctant to accept new prerogatives, preferring to rely on informal powers like those that formed the base of Sam Rayburn's and Lyndon Johnson's strong leadership.

Today's leaders are nonetheless stronger, at least on paper, than any of their recent predecessors, even the legendary Rayburn and Johnson. That tireless mechanic of the Senate, Senator Robert Byrd, has parlayed procedural mastery and meticulous attention to detail into unprecedented controls over floor procedure; new Senate rules also give the majority leader leverage over committee scheduling and coordination. In the House of Representatives, the Speaker now chairs the Steering and Policy Committee, nominates all Democrats to the Rules Committee, and has the power to appoint ad hoc committees and make split, joint, and sequential referrals of bills.

Still, central leadership on Capitol Hill is suspect, and on the whole, centralizing tendencies have been outweighed by decentralizing forces. In our recent book, *Congress Against Itself* (1977), Walter Oleszek and I spoke of congressional history as "a struggle of the general versus the particular, in which the particular seems the most powerful force." Although significant centralizing innovations have taken place, I submit that this is still a fair appraisal. Senate leaders have held back from implementing the bolder administrative powers recommended by the Stevenson Committee and the Culver Commission (the Commission on the Organization of the Senate). Among the Bolling Committee's rejected proposals were those dealing with administrative management and the jurisdictional review mechanism which would have been vested in the Rules Committee. Three years later, when the Obey Commission proposed administrative management for the House, it was summarily turned down.

For an institution reputed to be slow and tradition-bound, Congress has launched a surprisingly large number of adaptive efforts in the past generation. There have been two joint committee investigations (1945, 1965), two major committee reform efforts (the Bolling and Stevenson committees), two administrative review bodies (the Culver and Obey commissions), and a major budgetary reform. Still, the agenda of innovations is lengthy, and pressures for further adaptive innovation are going to persist. This is the most eloquent testimony to the continuing nature of Congress's adaptive crisis.

Inside Push: The Task of Consolidation

Along with its prolonged adaptive crisis, Congress is subject to *internal* stresses and strains. These are hardly surprising for a conflict-laden institution like Congress, whose members are independent political entrepreneurs of relatively equal formal power and who represent diverse constituencies and viewpoints. Many congressional procedures and folkways are merely consolidative tactics for keeping conflict within healthy bounds, so that the institution will not fly apart.

Other stresses are caused by specific factors not endemic to the institution. Some of these emanate from external demands made upon legislators as individuals rather than on the institution as a whole. Constituency expectations fall into this category. Other tensions are outgrowths of shifts in personnel, factional balances, and member attitudes. These conflicts have surfaced in recurrent bickering over members' perquisites, committee jurisdictions, the House Rules Committee, Senate filibustering, scheduling, seniority, and aspects of budgetary decisionmaking. Again without attempting to be exhaustive, I will recount several leading consolidative challenges faced by the two houses:

1. The most important consolidative challenges over the past generation have been shifts in the partisan and factional structure of the House and Senate. The Democratic Party is approaching the status of a permanent government on Capitol Hill. Within the party, dramatic changes have taken place: in both House and Senate, the Mason-Dixon Line has become blurred, and the party's councils are coming to be dominated by the progressive wing. The old coalition of conservative Democrats and Republicans has dissipated.

2. Long-standing trench warfare has been waged between authorizing committees and the taxing-spending committees over federal spending levels. Although partly a by-product of external stresses—particularly criticism from the Nixon White House—this conflict also stems from a clash of committee norms.

3. Jurisdictional competition among committees has become endemic, resulting in member complaints about the need for

coordinating deliberations and scheduling. The advent of pressing issues that cross traditional jurisdictional lines has often resulted in unseemly scrambles for advantage, sometimes breaking into open conflict, more frequently simply escalating decisionmaking costs by necessitating complicated informal agreements or awkward partitioning of issues.

4. Raising constituency demands have inundated individual legislators and their staffs. The average state now numbers some four million people, the average congressional district over half a million. Educational levels have risen. Public opinion surveys show unmistakably that voters expect legislators to "bring home the bacon" in terms of federal largess and services, and to communicate frequently with the home folks. Last year, the House Post Office logged fifty-three million pieces of incoming mail—three and a half times the 1970 figure. Surveys suggest that future constituency demands will, if anything, be greater.

5. After 1969, a tide of new members came to Capitol Hill, following two decades of uncommonly low turnover levels. When the 95th Congress convened in 1977, no less than 54 percent of Senators and 60 percent of House members had been first elected in 1970 or later.

The most widely publicized controversies over reform have in fact been responses to internal shifts of personnel, factions, or norms. In the House, debate initially swirled around the House Rules Committee's obstructionism. As that body grew less obstreperous, attention shifted to the seniority system and the powers of committtee chairmen.

The war over the "seniority system" is too prolonged to be recounted here. But several of its features ought to be recalled. First, it was essentially an ideological and generational dispute within the Democratic ranks. One attribute of seniority is that it records a *past generation's* electoral triumphs, rewarding a party's centers of strength as they existed twenty-five or more years earlier. If the party's factional balance is shifting, the seniority system distorts the leadership ranks, causing a generational gap between leaders and backbenchers. Such a gap—in region, district type, ideology, and even age—lay at the heart of the Democrats' seniority struggles. Historically southern-dominated, the Democratic party was formed into a truly national coalition by the Roosevelt revolution. The transformation did not take place overnight, but in stages. By the late 1960s the internal contradictions within the congressional party were too glaring to continue, and they were resolved inevitably in favor of youth and liberalism. In the House, the revolts were spasmodic and occasionally bloody, punctuated by a series of intracommittee revolts against recalcitrant chairmen, by the dispersion of power among the subcommittees (1971 and 1973), and finally by the overthrow of several unpopular committee chairmen (1975). In the Senate the transformation was more gradual and peaceful, hastened by the "Johnson rule" and the benign leadership of Mike Mansfield.

Republicans experienced similar tensions, although they were more generational than ideological. For the GOP, however, seniority has never been the burning issue it has been among Democrats. Because of the GOP's prolonged minority status, its seniority posts are simply less valuable than those of the Democrats. And, lacking the incentive of chairmanships, senior GOP members have been more willing to retire, producing a surprisingly rapid generational turnover.

A second feature of the seniority reforms is that they have by no means eliminated seniority. Far from it. Seniority has been preserved, if that is the word, by circumscribing seniority leaders' powers and by spreading seniority benefits to more and more members. At latest count (the numbers are constantly changing), fifty-seven Democratic Senators and 156 Representatives were committee or subcommittee chairmen. That adds up to 92 percent of all Senate Democrats and 54 percent of House Democrats. Thus there are more seniority leaders in the House and Senate than ever before. Within House committees, the seniority principle has in a sense been extended to apply to subcommittee posts, in a final effort to circumscribe capricious chairmen.

A final point about the seniority revolution is that, at least in the short run, it has aided the centrifugal forces in Congress. If seniority reforms have succeeded in taming committee leaders and democratizing the two houses, they have not resolved the problems caused by the underlying fragmentation of the committee system itself. Indeed to the extent that they have further institutionalized the subcommittees, the reforms have actually underscored the latter's autonomy. "Subcommittee government" is now the order of the day over much of Capitol Hill, compounding the perennial dilemma of congressional leadership.

One other development, prompted by pressure felt by legislators as individuals, has wrought a profound change in the linkage between individual members and the institution of Congress. This is the impressive growth in members' constituency service activities.

Legislators, and especially House members, have always been expected to run errands for constituents. Yet in an era of limited government, there were few errands to run. As one turn-of-the-century Congressman recalled, constituency mail in those days was pretty much confined to rural mail routes, Spanish War pensions, free seed, and very occasionally a legislative matter. A single clerk was sufficient to handle correspondence.

The constituency service role has been quantitatively, and I think qualitatively, transformed within the past generation. In responding to perceived constituency demands, Senators and Representatives have set up veritable cottage industries for communicating with voters, responding to constituents' requests, and even generating these requests through newsletters, targeted mailings, and hot lines. Staff and office allowances have grown, district offices have sprouted over the landscape, and recesses are now called "district work periods." This apparatus extends the legislators' ability to communicate with their constituents, and it provides badly needed ombudsman services for citizens for whom coping with the federal bureaucracy can be a bewildering and frightening experience.

We may ask which came first, the congressional apparatus for performing constituency service functions, or the public's expectations that such functions should be performed. This is the subject of a lively scholarly controversy, which cannot be fully explored here. Legislators, I think, are responding to what they perceive are strongly held and legitimate voter expectations. There is no question that voters *do* expect legislators to "bring home the bacon" and to communicate with the home folks, and that they give less attention to the legislators' stewardship in Washington. And many legislators, perhaps a majority, have mixed feelings about their heavy involvement in constituency service, no matter how necessary they consider this role to be. Whatever their feelings, legislators have profited from their investment. Indeed, constituent activity is a key ingredient in the advantage which incumbents enjoy in popular assessments and in electoral fortunes.

Less obvious is the effect of constituency activities upon the institutional life of Congress. It is at least arguable that ever more demanding ombudsman functions have helped to erode the legislative and institutional folkways identified by observers in the 1950s and early 1960s—especially the folkways of specialization, apprenticeship, and institutional loyalty. At the very least, it has placed an added squeeze on members' time and energies. To be sure, most ombudsman activities are actually carried out by staff aides rather than by Representatives or Senators themselves. Yet inescapably they put additional demands on the members' own schedules. Large staffs, while helping members extend their reach of involvement, require supervision and have a way of generating needs of their own. And with high (and apparently still rising) constituent expectations, there are inescapably a large number of symbolic functions that cannot be delegated to staffs, situations that require members' face-to-face presence or their personal intervention.

Internal stresses and strains—among committees, between leaders and backbenchers, and between senior and junior members—have not disappeared. In a fundamental sense, they are endemic in a body of political entrepreneurs whose job is to maximize their leverage over policymaking. On the whole, Congress has responded well, if sometimes tardily, to these internal tensions. And that is to be expected, when one recalls Congress's central characteristics: its decentralization, its lack of hierarchical leadership, and its propensity to engage in bargaining to reach decisions.

Yet in one respect—the tension between members' legislative and constituency functions—the internal problems of Congress have not been resolved, and in fact may be more acute than they were a generation ago. The heavy investment individual members have made in performing constituency tasks is quite understandable, and in any event has yielded measurable benefits for both constituents and incumbent members. The price paid by the institution is, however, another matter. Have members overextended themselves, in terms of their energies and their schedules? Has Congress as an institution suffered in this build-up of individual members' constituency activities and career goals? These questions are open to debate, and have yet to be answered satisfactorily.

Conclusion: The Incomplete Revolution

The innovations in congressional organization and procedure that have come to a head in the last half-decade or so are impressive. They represent the most dramatic changes on Capitol Hill since the revolt against "Uncle Joe" Cannon early in the century.

Yet there lingers an aura of incompleteness, a sense that these innovations, albeit impressive, have not resolved the problems faced by Congress as an organization. Some concrete bits of evidence support this intuition. First, we cannot ignore the persistence of discouragingly low levels of public support for Congress as an institution. In a survey taken early in 1977 only 22 percent of the respondents gave Congress a positive report card. Though it may be argued that such judgments are uninformed and unfair, they are still important, for they constitute a significant threat to the legitimacy of Congress as a decisionmaker.

An equally telling clue to Congress's continuing problems is that surprisingly large numbers of Senators and Representatives evidence weariness and alienation from their jobs. In a survey of House Members in the mid-1960s, my coresearchers and I found a generally high level of satisfaction with the institution's performance—an attitude characterized as "a vote of aye—with reservations." A survey conducted a decade later yielded not even so tempered an optimism. The second study, which focused on foreign policy, disclosed widespread discontent among members of both houses. Dissatisfaction was expressed by four-fifths of the legislators and extended to all groups and factions on Capitol Hill. In a more recent survey of House members, conducted by the House Commission on Administrative Review (the Obey Commission), only 12 percent of the Representatives thought the House was "very effective" in performing its principal functions.

This attitude has had another manifestation, and an interesting one at that. Once they have tasted Washington life, Congressmen, it used to be said, "never go back to Pocatello." Apparently that is no longer true; in unusually high numbers, members are in fact electing to retire from Congress or seek other jobs. The number of voluntary retirements has risen every election year since 1966. In 1976, fully 10 percent of Congress's membership, forty-seven Representatives and eight Senators, voluntarily elected to retire—a thirty-year peak. A number were mid-career retirements, by members who could look forward to years of service on Capitol Hill. Particularly fascinating is what appears to be an outbreak of what I call "kamikaze runs" by Representatives for other offices which are, at best, long-shot chances. In 1976 this category of retirees included, according to my estimate, about a third of those Representatives who ran for other offices—none of whom were successful in their bids.

Now, congressional retirements are by no means a bad thing. Indeed, turnover during the past generation has been uncommonly low and, in view of the lack of meaningful competition in many states and a great majority of House districts, voluntary retirements may be the principal means of achieving turnover. Nonetheless, the number of voluntary retirements suggests that congressional life may not be as satisfying as it once was.

Why does this discontent persist? Why have the extensive innovations failed to resolve the problems which buffet our national legislature, hampering its ability to cope with its workload and endangering its legitimacy and even self-respect? I believe that the little scheme I have advanced to help us comprehend Congress's recent innovations also points to the answer to this question.

Any organization that wishes to survive and remain effective, let us remember, must cope with both the tug of outside pressures and the internal tensions of people striving to achieve their individual goals. In the case of Congress, this means meeting the expectations of others—Presidents, lobbyists, the press, and the general public, among others—while providing working conditions that preserve the careers, not to mention the dignity and sanity, of individual members and their staffs. If Congress cannot adapt to the nation's needs, it risks being shunted aside in favor of institutions that can do so, or at least appear to do so. If it fails to facilitate its members' achievement of their individual goals, it may fail to attract the ablest contenders for congressional office, or it may lose the institutional loyalty of those who have already been elected.

The problem lies in the potential incompatibility of these goals. If Congress adapts to outside pressure, it may curtail its members' ability to pursue their individual career interests. If it arranges its internal affairs for the comfort and convenience of its members, on the other hand, it may cripple its ability to respond to outside demands. Moreover, responding to one sort of outside demand may preclude responding to others. Something of this sort has happened to Congress.

Congress has been markedly more successful at responding to internal pressures than in adapting to external demands. Its most spectacular successes have been: (a) democratizing the chambers by curbing committee leaders' powers and by distributing committee assignments and leadership posts more generously; and (b) nurturing the resources of individual members, by building perquisites, personal staffs, and committee staffs assigned to particular members. Heightened activity and broadened participation are hallmarks of today's House and Senate. These developments have made Congress a more democratic place. They have given more of its members the resources to pursue their careers successfully, and to contribute to policymaking.

Yet what members have gained as individuals may have come at the price of the institution's capacity to deal with institutional problems in a coherent fashion. In other words, Senators and Representatives may have fought valiantly to gain a larger piece of a shrinking pie. Their constituency activities have cushioned their efforts at reelection to a job that is increasingly unrewarding. Their numerous committee assignments and leadership posts give them more control over ever smaller slices of policy.

The most conspicuous adaptive failures of reorganization have been in *central leadership* and *committee realignment*. Many critics argue—and I have reluctantly come to agree—that stronger central leadership is going to be required to orchestrate the activities of the scattered committees and subcommittees, schedule consideration of measures, and provide more efficient central services. Vigorous central leadership might also help Congress solve its image problem, by giving the media and the public a handle for identifying what is to most people a confusing and faceless institution. There are heartening developments on both sides of Capitol Hill, but the developments have been painfully slow. And because a majority of members in both houses now have immediate stakes in preserving decentralization, further steps in the direction of strengthening party leaders may be inhibited. The recent rejection of the Obey Commission's administrative proposals, not to mention the reaction against Senator Byrd's role in ending the recent Senate filibuster, indicate once again the limited congressional tolerance of strong leadership.

Reorganization efforts have also failed to recast House or Senate committees to dovetail with contemporary categories of public problems. The House rejected even the Bolling Committee's modest moves in this direction and summarily dismissed the Obey Commission's proposal to take another look at the problem. In the Senate, the Stevenson Committee was more successful, partly because it concentrated on consolidating committees rather than recasting jurisdictional categories.

Not only are jurisdictions sliced too thinly to give members a meaningful grip on problems, but time is fragmented as well. On the average, House members now have 6.1 committee and subcommittee assignments. Virtually any day the House is in session, a large majority of members face meeting conflicts. Members are tempted to committee-hop, quorums are harder to maintain, and deliberation suffers. While Senators early in 1977 decided to cut their committee assignments by about one-third, they are still spread thinly—with an average of twelve assignments apiece. The norms of committee specialization and apprenticeship have been diluted, casting doubt on the committees' continued ability to give in-depth consideration to detailed measures that come before them.

Committee-system modernization is politically the roughest reorganization challenge. It severely upsets the institution's internal balance, for it threatens not only individual legislators' committee careers but also their mutually supportive relations with potent outside clientele groups. The present committee structure fits badly with present and future categories of public problems, but it is buttressed by the "iron triangles," those mutually beneficial ties that bind congressional committees, executive agencies, and lobby groups. In this respect, the hurdles that face committee reformers on Capitol Hill are identical to those faced by executive reorganizers.

And yet, Senators and Representatives profess to be profoundly dissatisfied with the present committee system. In a survey of 101 House and Senate members conducted during the 93rd Congress, the Murphy Commission (Commission on the Organization of the

Government for the Conduct of Foreign Policy) discovered that 81 percent of the legislators were dissatisfied with "committee jurisdictions and the way they are defined in Congress." Only one percent of the legislators were "very dissatisfied." In the House study conducted recently by the Obey Commission, committee structure was the most frequently mentioned "obstacle" preventing the House from doing its job effectively. "Scheduling" and "institutional inertia" were next in line. In short, legislators are fully aware of the committee system's disarray, but they shrink from paying the price of remedying the problem.

The most effective levers for encouraging congressional innovation lie not in a lessening of outside pressures, but rather in intensified pressures directed to Congress's collective performance. Two such pressures are *presidential leadership*, and *public (and media) expectations* for performance. Like all political bodies, our national legislature responds to pressure, and is unlikely to produce innovations without it.

The President is in a unique position to focus public attention on broad public problems and mobilize support for resolving them. The challenges of the Nixon Administration, however inconsistent and excessive they were, at times nonetheless forced the Democratic Congress to recast its budgetary and war-power procedures, among others. That Administration's political suicide over Watergate relieved that source of pressure, not altogether to the benefit of congressional innovation. President Carter's activity on behalf of his energy package has forced Congress to coordinate its committees in innovative ways and to consider the question in a more coherent fashion. That is not to argue that either Nixon or Carter has been necessarily "right" in his policy orientations, but only that the President, among our political actors, has the ability to focus public expectations and force Congress to coordinate its scattered work groups in resolving problems.

Generalized public attitudes toward Congress could also induce it to undertake innovations, but here the picture is not hopeful. The problem is that public attitudes toward Congress are bifurcated. Citizens have a fuzzy conception of Congress as a whole, and they judge it primarily on generalized policy grounds. Citizens have a clearer view of their own elected representatives, who are judged overwhelmingly on the basis of constituent service rather than institutional stewardship. What would be needed to stimulate adaptive innovation would be a public alert to their legislators' stewardship toward the institution, its committees, its deliberations, and its processes. That public awareness should go beyond merely testing members' ethical purity, or recording their faithfulness in attending floor votes. However, neither the general public nor the communications media evidence much interest in those aspects of members' performance. The consequence is a divided incentive system for members, in which constituency relations aid in reelection while institutional contributions count for little. Thus, members have little incentive to mesh their career goals with the needs of the institution as a whole.

In the final analysis, we must face the possibility that the innovations Congress is likely to introduce will simply prove insufficient to preserve the organization's autonomy and scope of operation, given the acute and prolonged demands from without and within. Whether the contemporary Congress faces such a predicament is, of course, an issue over which observers sharply disagree. Predictions of Congress's demise are premature. In the past our national legislature has shown an impressive resiliency and a startling capacity for innovative behavior. It is the most powerful legislative body in the world, certainly one of a small handful that dares to *make* policies rather than simply ratify them. Yet concern over its performance—not merely from professional pundits, but from attentive publics and from members themselves—is strong and genuine, and cannot be summarily dismissed. Discontent is widespread, both on Capitol Hill and elsewhere; what is lacking is a palpable sense of crisis.

Discussion

HERBERT KAUFMAN: Commenting on papers by a pair of experts like this is a little like being the heckler of Al Smith. Al was delivering one of his successful campaign speeches one day and a heckler from the back row yelled, "Attaboy, Al. Tell them everything you know." Al shot back, "I'll tell them everything we both know. It won't take any longer." I'm afraid it will take a little longer, but you won't know any more.

I'm a kind of congenital skeptic about reform. I may be a lapsed true believer. I don't know whether it's simply age and fatigue or whether it's a learning process. I can't deny either the age or the fatigue, but I'll claim a little bit of learning, whether it is deserved or not.

I was reared in an era when we believed a lot in reform, and in those days the orthodox doctrine was to believe in the executive. We needed executive leadership so we had formulas for strengthening Presidents; we had formulas for strengthening governors; we strengthened mayors; we built city managers. We learned how to make budgeting and personnel and planning the tools of the executive. We knew what needed to be done. I inhaled all this as a student and I believed it and I repeated it and to my surprise, some jurisdictions actually did these things, which is not something an academic ordinarily expects. It's a terrible responsibility. I don't know how Scotty Campbell lives up to it.

What I also learned was that in the jurisdictions that accepted the reforms, frequently nothing changed of any significance. One prime example is New York City, where over the years we did strengthen the mayor and ultimately we developed a great super administration and then the city got into great troubles, to put it mildly.

If nothing happened in some cases, unexpected results followed in others. We said we ought to make the executive stronger and we did. And one of the consequences turned out to be Watergate. I don't mean the scandal itself but the revelations that showed the perversion of some of the agencies by some of the high political officers in government, with, indeed, the active connivance in some cases of some members of the Civil Service Commission.

Our reforms didn't exactly produce the results we had expected. Richard Nathan, a colleague at Brookings, wrote a book in which he referred to that as the plot that failed. Everybody accepted the notion of strengthening the executive until they got an executive they didn't like. It never seemed to occur to them that if you strengthen executives, you are strengthening bad ones as well as good ones.

What's more, in some jurisdictions that were benighted enough not to listen to us, things went pretty well. I was a kind of "hanger on" for a while, an unpaid citizen member of some local municipal boards in New Haven. In those days Richard C. Lee was the mayor of New Haven, and in the sixties New Haven was identified, over Dick Lee's protests, as "America's first slumless city." It wasn't, and he knew it, but everybody had to have something to believe in, and so they believed in that. Well, Dick did some marvelous things in that town in the course of eight terms as mayor, and the interesting thing about it is he did it with what is known by political science standards as a "weak-mayor system." It was a weak-mayor form of government. Well, if he was a weak mayor, then I'm the green giant. The form of government didn't seem to make much difference, so I developed a kind of skepticism about the claims and expectations that develop around administrative reform and also around congressional reform.

I'd like to make two pleas for the character of this discussion. One is that I hope that advocates of reform will play the role of their own critics and tell us about both the pros and cons of their proposals. When you are touting a reform, you always mention its benefits, but you leave it to somebody else to advance a list of the costs.

I thought Scotty Campbell was going to get pretty close to that when he pointed out the contradictory nature of the values we were pursuing in Civil Service reform, but then, he ended with a peroration that was a plea for support of the proposed Civil Service reforms.

It would help, Scotty, if you would also mention some of the costs of trying to reward performance. That's one of my pleas. I hope what we will get is a judge's decision instead of simply a lawyer's brief.

The second plea is that we watch the rhetoric we are using. I notice that Roger Davidson ended his paper on congressional reform with the sentence, "Discontent is pervasive inside and outside of Capitol Hill; what is lacking is a palpable sense of crisis." I think that is right; there is lacking a sense of crisis and one of the reasons may be that there is lacking a crisis.

I somehow have the feeling if we don't rationalize the structure of the congressional committees, the Republic will go on. It will go on staggering from one problem to another and one half-solution to another, with a lot of divisions and sparks flying, but I think it will go on. We live by the skin of our teeth, as Thornton Wilder told us. I agree and I am prepared to do it. So, I hope we can tone down the rhetoric.

In conclusion, I would say that if we listen to both papers carefully, I think we can perceive that if all the recommendations that have been made for congressional and executive reform are adopted, we will have a strong Executive, locked in battle with a strong Congress, and I guess that's what we want in our system, isn't it.

HAROLD SEIDMAN: When I was writing *Politics, Position and Power*, I was often asked for whom I was writing it. I always said I was writing for a very limited audience, mainly for budget directors, Presidents, and the White House staff. That book is what I would have told them if I could ever have got them to sit down and listen, which is a very practical problem. It's not disparaging to say that. To get two or three hours of the time of very busy people in order to explain something like this is very difficult. It's much easier to go back to the cliches of economy and efficiency, organization by major purpose, all the other things that are listed in the Reorganization Act.

I noticed in Scotty Campbell's paper that he moved easily from the word "reorganization" to "reform" and then on to "management and improvement," as if these were somehow causally related. I would suggest that reform is very often in the eye of the beholder and that it is not necessarily something that is accomplished by reorganization; reorganization often has very little to do with management improvement. Indeed, the purpose of macro-reorganization of the federal government is a redistribution of power and that is why it is controversial at the executive branch level. It is the same problem within the Congress, and that is why it is controversial there as well.

I should also like to make a point about Civil Service reform, for I think there is a major gap in our discussion. If Secretary Blumenthal thinks that if there just weren't any Civil Service rules and regulations, he could make appointments within the Treasury Department the same way he could in the Bendix Corporation, he has a lot to learn. He does not have either members of Congress or the White House in the Bendix Corporation suggesting appointments.

In discussing the problem, Scotty Campbell talked of the protection of the senior civil servant, but there is another issue here, and that is the protection of the Secretary in the making of appointments. In the years I served in the federal service, I had many complaints from cabinet officers and subcabinet officers, not about their inability to change their senior civil servants but about the pressures coming from both the White House and the Congress to make appointments of people whom they did not think competent. That is one of the continuing problems in the Civil Service. In fact, it is not unknown for the White House to unload some of its problem children on the departments.

And here is another key problem. It seems to be part of the conventional wisdom that noncareer officials—and I avoid calling them political, because they aren't—are somehow more responsive to direction by their political superiors. Well, in many cases the political superior has nothing to do with an appointment. His loyalties may really go elsewhere within the service, or to the Congressman or Senator or the White House official to whom he feels obligated for his appointment. This is a very practical problem. I can cite an instance in one of the major departments. Both the Budget Bureau and the White House were very anxious that certain programs be decentralized to the field authorities, delegated to the regional offices. The Secretary came in and said, "You just don't know the plain facts of life around here. I'm not about to make delegations to my regional directors because I don't really control their appointments. They are working for somebody else. I can control the people at headquarters to whom I delegate authority. I do not have that same control over the regional administrators, even though some of them are in the Civil Service. Their appointments, the influence over their appointments, lie with someone else."

So, I suggest it is important to protect the administrator who wants to keep his career civil servants. Joe Dodge did this when he became budget director. When the Eisenhower Administration came in, Dodge was immediately subjected to tremendous pressure to replace the career assistant directors in the Budget Bureau who were political appointees. He resisted that pressure, but if this new type of service had been in effect, could he have successfully resisted that pressure to replace people whom he did not want to replace?

It is a difficult problem, and I don't by any means suggest that the present Civil Service does not require change. Actually, I don't think any senior civil servant wants to remain in a position where he does not have the confidence of the people with whom he is working. If he doesn't enjoy that confidence, he ought to move on. But that's another problem.

Now I want to talk a bit about structural reorganization. From what I read and what I am told, there seem to be about five task forces now running around dealing with questions of structural reorganization. In April 1976 I got a call asking whether I would serve on an advisory group to candidate Carter without any commitment to him as a candidate. The advisory group was on government reorganization. I said I'd be glad to serve and the first advice I would give to candidate Carter was to forget it, that it was a no-win political issue. I never heard again about that advisory group. I was never asked for further advice.

The only President I know who had the same views about reorganization as the current President was our last engineer president.

Other speakers during this meeting have drawn the parallel between our two engineer Presidents.

It's more complicated than that. Wilbur Cohen correctly remarked that it was a mistake to send up welfare reform before sending up health insurance. It is an even greater mistake to start out your relations with Congress by sending up three controversial blockbuster reorganization proposals. At least on welfare matters, you might find somebody who had an interest in supporting the reform. It is very rare that you find anybody who has a real commitment or stake in reorganization. There are many people who feel they have something to lose by reorganization.

In any case an administration that deals with reorganization as a first priority has got its priorities wrong. It first needs to identify its program objectives and then look at how structure in the organization can assist or hinder the accomplishment of those objectives; reorganization is not something to be done for its own sake. The question I have always tried to ask is what problems have you identified that are going to be solved by what you are proposing? And I have yet to get an answer.

I don't think any of us here really know what reorganization produces. One of my frustrations during my years in the Budget Bureau was that from time to time I would ask the directors for the White House, "Let me use some of our resources to do some post mortems. Let's find out what happens. We don't know. We keep claiming that reorganizations do certain things. Do they actually do those things or do they do something else?" All I ever got was a kind of Satchel Page advice, "Don't look back. Somebody may be gaining on you."

When I went to the National Academy of Public Administration we undertook three case studies on reorganization: one on the transfer of water pollution control activities to the Interior Department, one on the reorganization of the National Advisory Council on International Monetary Transactions, and the other on the reorganization of Customs. Every one of those reorganizations produced changes and in no instance were the changes the ones intended. A major problem in each case was that as soon as the reorganization plan was completed the White House lost all interest. There was absolutely no follow-through from that point on. Now, whether the result would have been different if there had been some kind of sustained interest, I do not know. This is a wide open area for research and would make a good doctoral dissertation. Just what do reorganizations produce?

BRUCE OPPENHEIMER: Let me start by saying I am on basically common ground with many of the remarks Roger Davidson has made. I too lament the failure of congressional reforms of the 1970s to do more in strengthening leadership and in realigning committee jurisdictions. I'm not as much a skeptic as Roger Davidson. I tend to be perhaps too much an institutional defender, a believer in Congress. My concern with reforms is to ask first how they have affected the ability of Congress to mobilize support, to pass legislation, to enact legislative programs; and second how they have affected the capacity of Congress to compete with other centers of governmental power for control over the exact nature of policy.

I recall a conversation in Washington back in 1975 with Harry McPherson. We were talking about whales and minnows, whales being the term used by Lyndon Johnson to refer to people who had a great capacity in the Senate either to move legislation or to stop it, and minnows being people who had very little capacity in that regard. We were somewhat dismayed to realize that there didn't seem to be many whales around and not very many minnows either. McPherson suggested that what we had were mostly speckled trout. What I should like to talk about tonight is the problems of speckled trout.

It seems to me that the reforms of the seventies—which disperse powers, encourage the growth of subcommittee government, and effect greater equality among members of Congress in both the House and the Senate—have the effect of driving both whales and minnows out of existence. They prevent the absence of power just as they prevent the concentration of power. This development has had some positive implications—many of which Roger Davidson has summarized—in terms of activity, in terms of participation of members, in terms of initiation of new legislation, and in terms of building majorities. And the capacity to get legislation through Congress is the capacity to build majorities.

In the 1950s, it was true that Lyndon Johnson or Sam Rayburn might have had to bargain extensively to move one of the whales, to move a Richard Russell or a Robert Kerr or a Carl Vinson or a Wilbur Mills. But it was equally true that once they were moved, once you got them to go along, they were able to deliver support. They could be relied on for influence within the institution because people identified with them. People deferred to them because of their expertise, because of their seniority, because of their power as committee chairmen. They had rewards and sanctions from which they could build support. And finally, they had the policy and political expertise that came from long experience, both with particular subjects and with congressional mores and procedures.

True, it was a problem and still remains a problem if a whale were against you, for a whale can stop things from happening. But what about the people who now have to play the roles of bill managers which the Russells, the Vinsons, the Kerrs, and the Millses played during the fifties and the early sixties? It seems to me that if you are one of 150 committee or subcommittee chairmen in the House of Representatives, there is no real reason why you should be deferred to, or why people should identify with you. You don't have a large number of rewards and sanctions. You have not necessarily been in Congress a long time and, therefore, do not necessarily have a great deal of political or policy expertise. In fact, instead of deference, what you are likely to find is jurisdictional conflicts.

Moreover, it seems to me that when you disperse power, you are also dispersing the capacity to bargain. If you have people with narrow jurisdictions, you don't leave them a lot to trade with. Let me give you a very quick example.

During the fifties the chairman of the Interstate and Foreign Commerce Committee was a Congressman from Arkansas named Oren Harris. He had control over certain types of health legislation, railroads, certain sorts of power legislation, broadcasting, and a number of other matters that came into the jurisdiction of that committee. Now Harris was a conservative and he stopped a lot of legislation.

Today, if you were to look to the people who had those jurisdictions, you wouldn't go to one person; you'd go to four or five people: Paul Rogers, Fred Rooney, John Dingell, Lionel van Deerlin, just to cover the basic legislative areas. They chair the subcommittees of Commerce, but they only have their own narrow turf to trade with. They cannot say, as Oren Harris could, "All right. I'll give you the rails bill, but I'm not going to push the health bill this year." They don't have the capacity, the counters, with which to bargain.

There is now something of a counter movement to this fragmentation. Certain powers are being given to leadership regarding bill referral, and other powers are being given to the Steering and Policy Committee, and thus to the Speaker, on committee assignments and other things. It's important to note that some of the powers now being exercised by Speaker O'Neill were actually accumulated by Carl Albert though Albert chose not to use them to their fullest, which may have been a very wise decision.

It is clear, however, that the Congress is not yet willing to take firm direct action on the problems created by the dispersion of power. As Roger Davidson so aptly put it, there is a fear of upsetting the benefits which accrue from the greater equality and from the dispersion of power. This can be seen in the defeat of the Bolling Committee proposal on committee reorganization, in the rather modest success of the Stevenson Committee, and in the defeat of the Obey Commission recommendations.

Instead, what we get are relatively short-term solutions to the problems of dispersion in the House and to the problems of overlap. We get ad hoc committees, such as the Ad Hoc Committee on Energy. We get the Rules Committee reporting very complex rules that give everybody with an affected jurisdiction a chance to handle legislation when it reaches the floor. We get the Speaker making the Rules Committee a little tougher in granting rules. But it also means that the leadership in effect has to get the approval of the membership to carry out one of these ad hoc decisions, and sometimes, members will have to say, "We simply can't go with the leadership on this one." Thus we have a continuing tension between the dispersion of power and the ad hoc attempts by the leadership to centralize power.

There is a great deal of activity in Congress nowadays, but it's activity without many results. That is to say, there is plenty of planning and incubation. Legislation is getting introduced. Hearings are being held. The Congress is an activist Congress in these respects, yet it hasn't accomplished much. Note too that both House and Senate are Democratic and the House has a Democratic majority very close to the size of the majority in the 89th Congress. Moreover, this Democratic Congress has a Democratic President to work with. Yet a legislative logjam seems to exist.

Of course, there were logjams in the fifties and sixties caused by people like Judge Smith, Oren Harris, Mendel Rivers, Richard Russell, and Wilbur Mills; but they no longer run the show in Congress. In fact, liberals have moved into positions of power, whatever power is left in those positions. It is actually very hard to find villains in this piece.

Finally, I think it can be said that this directly affects the ability of Congress to bargain with other institutions of government. Where do you go in Congress if you are worried about rails or tax reform or welfare reform? It's hard to pinpoint a single member who can deliver, who has something he can control and thus can use to bargain with.

Of course, there would be some costs in going back to a system of whales, but one should remember that whales displace a good deal of space, they can swim in large bodies of water, and they are capable of delivering when persuaded. The problem with speckled trout is that they like to swim in small ponds, which they are very fond of. They are especially hard to organize and even more difficult to catch.

LAWRENCE DODD: I want to turn our attention to the interface between Congress and the Executive as it is affected by congressional reorganization and executive reorganization. In doing that I shall try to respond to the very instructive comments by Mr. Campbell and Mr. Davidson.

In Mr. Campbell, we have a spokesman for the Carter Administration and perhaps we have the first opportunity of any audience in the country to get an inkling of where the Administration is taking us with regard to government reorganization.

Let's start with congressional reorganization. In the last thirty years, Congress has undergone a significant set of reforms. From around 1947 through 1973, particularly 1970 to 1973, Congress was increasingly decentralized.

Today, at a committee and subcommittee level, we have the most decentralized Congress of American history. Virtually every member of the Democratic Party in the Senate chairs a subcommittee or a committee, and approximately half the Democratic members of the House chair a committee or a subcommittee. It is a very decentralized Congress at its base.

In the last three or four years, we have had overlaid on that decentralization some centralization: a budget committee, some added strength to the Speaker. There has not, however, been any significant centralization of the Government Operations Committee, which is the committee that deals with oversight and reorganization of the executive branch. That committee is still relatively weak. That is what we've seen with regard to congressional reorganization.

Now, what does that reorganization mean? I agree with McPherson and with Oppenheimer that it means we have a lot of speckled trout. We have very few people who can bargain effectively and that has special implications for congressional-executive relations. With respect to oversight of the bureaucracy, power in Congress has been lodged in the committee or subcommittee chairmen. Their power, to a large extent, has derived from their strategic bargaining position, in particular from the number of agencies within their jurisdiction. The more agencies, the more they could play off one agency against another, using different agencies against each other, to avoid being blackmailed.

With decentralization we no longer have a single committee chairman, such as Wilbur Mills, or the chairmen of the powerful authorization committees, dealing with a number of agencies. Instead power resides now with a number of subcommittee chairmen, each dealing with one or two agencies. So, the strategic bargaining position of those who have power has been weakened. Instead of twenty committee chairmen with moderate but significant bargaining power vis-à-vis the agencies within their jurisdiction, we find 150 subcommittee and committee chairmen, each facing a very small number of agencies.

Two things result from this fragmentation: the first is an increasing agency independence. Instead of agencies being dependent upon the committees, committees and subcommittees are increasingly dependent upon the agencies. The agencies are bright enough to realize that the power of the subcommittee chairman depends on the fact that that agency is within the jurisdiction of his subcommittee, and he can't threaten that agency very seriously if one or two agencies are the extent of his real jurisdiction.

The second result is that the subcommittee chairmen are much more dependent on the relatively fewer interest groups in their arena than were the old committee chairmen. The committee chairmen had a number of interest groups interested in the things they were concerned with. Subcommittee chairmen have far fewer interest groups. Thus for electoral benefits, for information, for help—they are more reliant on the interest groups today than were the committee chairmen of the past. Today, it's probably true that the committees need the agencies and interest groups more than the agencies and interest groups need the committees—at least in comparison with the past.

All of this means that oversight is more difficult, for Congress is less able to hold the executive agencies responsible. Consequently, reorganization of the Executive looks very attractive to the country at large and to those who hope for a more responsive bureaucracy. This was a view that was very popular with Carter in the 1976 election, and many of his people began calling for a reorganization of the bureaucracy.

Dean Campbell has drawn a distinction between reorganization as structural change and reorganization as management change. I think it is quite clear that in the last election, Carter meant structural change. He talked of reducing the number of agencies from two thousand to two hundred. He talked in very structural terms. Structural change, however, is difficult at best, and because of the decentralization of Congress in the last twenty years, it has been made still more difficult.

In this decentralized Congress, in which subcommittees are tied to individual agencies, structural reorganization will be seen as a threat because it means abolishing agencies. That will mean abolishing the basis of the subcommittee's jurisdiction. Even if it merely means moving agencies into new departments, the parallel between congressional organization and administrative organization will be confused and the committees and subcommittees will look askance at that. The chairman is likely to say to himself, "If they move those agencies around, they may move them out of my committee jurisdiction, and thus my subcommittee loses its major rationale for being."

So the move to subcommittee government has made structural change very difficult, all the more so because there has been no centralization of power in the Government Operations Committee. That is the one committee that might have supported structural organization of the Executive because it would be the committee most directly involved in the reform.

The Carter Administration has now recognized that difficulty and is seeking a less direct way to reorganize. It is beginning—rather subtly or even deviously—to say that organization means management and that reorganization first of all means management personnel reform. Now that in itself is going to be very difficult, as we have heard already.

The power of subcommittees and committees, even if it is limited, rests on the bargaining positions that are created by the stable relations between individual congressional actors and the agency personnel. Twenty years of a working acquaintance between a committee or a subcommittee chairman and the people in an agency develop attachment and a very considerable informal power relation. To allow the Executive any significant ability to reorder and realign the people in the agencies is going to make people in Congress very unhappy because they may have invested years in building a close, stable relation with an agency man, thinking he was going to be there forever, only to find him moved somewhere else. That development would threaten the committee's power base, so there would be considerable opposition to that kind of reorganization. Even so that is a less direct attack than structural reorganization, and very likely it is more nearly feasible.

If that kind of management change takes place, however, it may make structural change somewhat easier. Roger Davidson wrote an article some time ago pointing out that one of the obstacles to the structural reorganization of Congress is the frequent coalition between interest groups, agency personnel, and certain members of Congress—a coalition that opposes structural reorganization because subsystem politics benefits them all. If some of those agency people are shifted around, they are less able to coalesce with interest groups and with congressional actors. They are also less able to mobilize interest-group opposition within Congress. Thus with the coalition split up and its power shattered, it may be possible to move for structural reorganization, at least of the executive branch, and possibly even of Congress.

Now I think both structural reorganization and management

reform are unlikely, but if they do occur, they will have a direct effect on congressional organization. Government reorganization at the structural level would increase the problems of Congress with Congress structured as it is. It would confuse jurisdictional responsibilities and necessitate considerable reorganization within Congress so as to realign congressional jurisdictions with the new administrative jurisdictions. If congressional reorganization should not occur—and it will be difficult—the chaos in Congress will be great. If personnel management reform takes place, the informal relations will be broken up somewhat, which will imperil the close, long-term, stable relations that abet congressional control of the Executive.

So congressional control of administration would be weakened and Congress would have to seek some way to strengthen it, perhaps by a statute providing personnel controls by Congress similar to those envisioned in the Carter reform proposals for the President.

Where does all this leave us? First, it seems to tell us something about Carter, and perhaps also about a cagey fellow he has advising him with regard to reorganization. It suggests that the administration has recognized that the problems of reorganization are going to be more difficult than they appeared during the campaign. It discloses that a more subtle strategy of reform is developing, or perhaps indeed that there is a sliding away from reform. It may be that within four years, people can be convinced that "reorganization" really meant management change and that since management change has passed, we have already had reorganization.

In any case, I think the shift is subtle. I think, too, that the chances of success of either or both of these reforms are limited. If they are successful, Congress will find that its own problems of organization and of congressional control of the Executive will be exacerbated, unless Congress also does some prompt reforming—resolving jurisdictional confusions, solving personnel control problems, strengthening the Government Operations Committee, and rethinking the whole matter of centralization.

One of the speakers said that perhaps we don't have a crisis after all. I hate to be negative about things like that, but I think that either way, we have problems. If reorganization doesn't pass, we will continue to have an unresponsive bureaucracy. If it does pass, it will confuse things mightily in Congress, and perhaps undermine seriously the power that Congress does possess with regard to administration. I see either one of those as a serious crisis down the road.

ALAN CAMPBELL: The Herb Kaufman thesis that it doesn't really make any difference what you do is rather comforting because it means I can't really do much harm in what we try to accomplish. I appreciate that reassurance, Herb. I would suggest to you, however, that the Dick Lee argument is not an argument against a strong mayor; it's an argument for a strong mayor. Those changes in New Haven were accomplished by devices other than creating a city manager plan. I don't think anyone has suggested that the manager plan is the only way to create a strong executive. One of the weakest mayor systems in the United States, by formal structure, is that of the City of Chicago, and Daley did not find that a hindrance to being an effective mayor. The examples of both Lee and Daley say something about strong executives and accordingly I am concerned by your comment that the Nixon experience somehow demonstrates how that same kind of power can be misused. No one would deny that power can be misused, but it surely doesn't follow that you don't need some concentration of power in order to accomplish something.

In that sense, I am on the side of those who have argued here that there are problems with the current concern about the imperialist president. The move to curb executive power may be giving away the ball game before we need to give away the ball game.

Concerning the comments by Harold Seidman about the problems of high-level appointments in the federal bureaucracy, whether career or noncareer, I suggest that if you are concerned with the willingness of those in high positions to carry out administration policy, there is a problem with both career and noncareer people. Speaking as one who has been a long-time champion and teacher of career people, I have been quite disturbed by the resistance of career people to changes suggested by a new administration. It has been a surprise to me and a tremendous disappointment. I agree there are some problems about noncareer appointees and the kinds of pressures on them from the sources from which they come, which may be individual Congressmen or interest groups, or White House politics. But that should not be used to argue against the notion that the Administration should be able to count on a career service that will be willing to listen and ready to move in new directions as those new directions are suggested by the Administration.

If that is troublesome to you, I can only assure you that it is even more troublesome to me that I found a greater sensitivity to any kind of criticism and a greater opposition to change on the part of the career people with whom I have discussed these things than I have ever found in any other group—with one exception, and that was the faculty members back when I was a dean.

Finally, I agree with the final comments made by Professor Dodd. The Carter approach to reorganization has, from the beginning, been a combination of structural and management changes. The statements that were made during the campaign looked toward efforts to improve the effectiveness of the federal government; whether that is a shift from structure to management, I suppose is a debatable point. But I would point out that a recent poll has shown that the public has always interpreted the President's call for reorganization as management improvement, and of course it is our hope to be responsive to what the public wants.

VII

Conflict and a Search for a New Balance: the 1970s

Overview: Robert L. Hardesty
Discussion: Carl Albert
Graham T. Allison
Bill Moyers
Richard E. Neustadt
Elspeth Rostow
John Tower
Nan Waterman

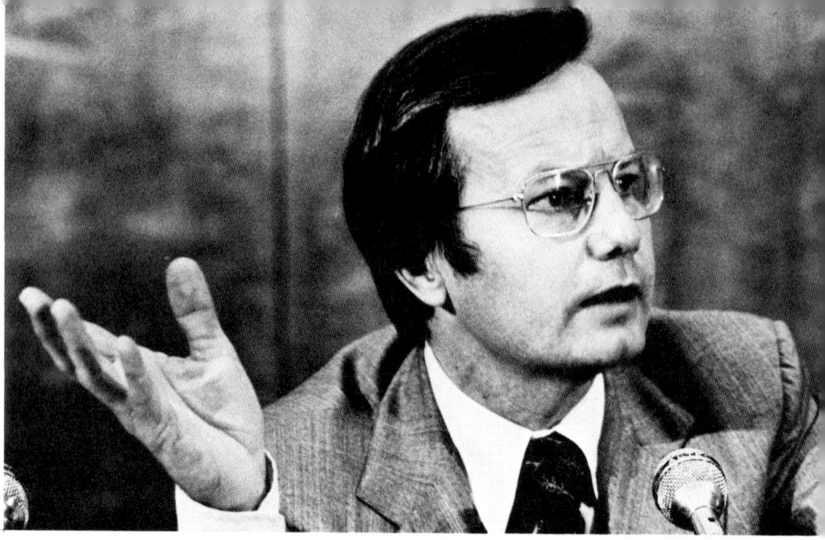

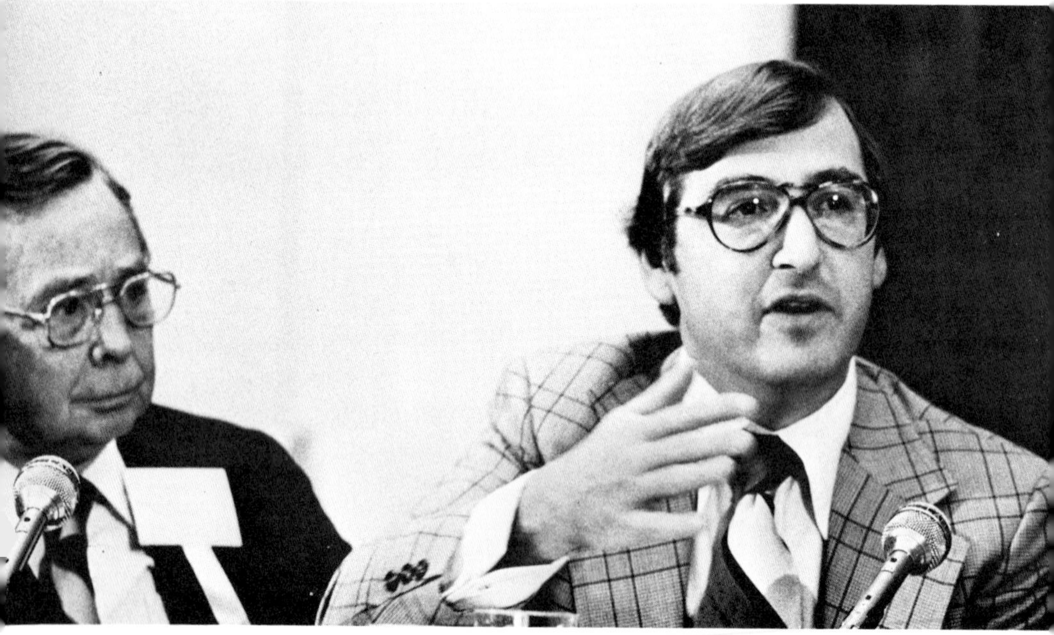

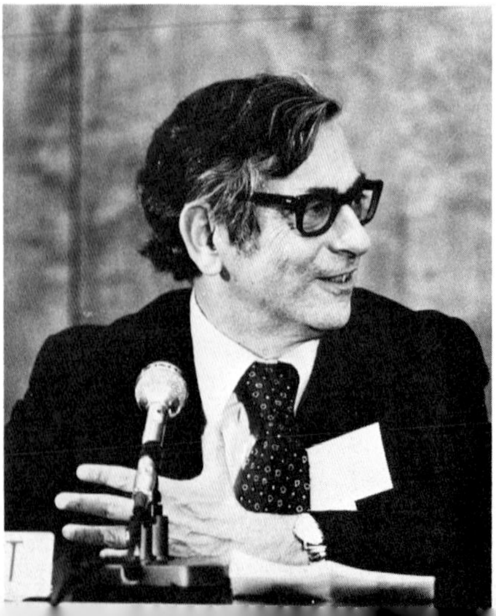

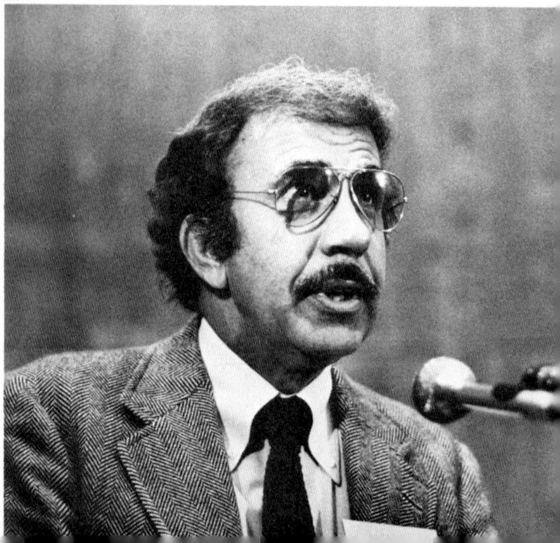

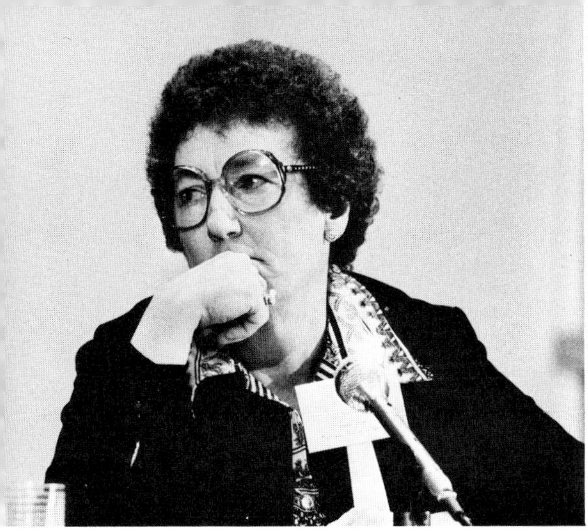

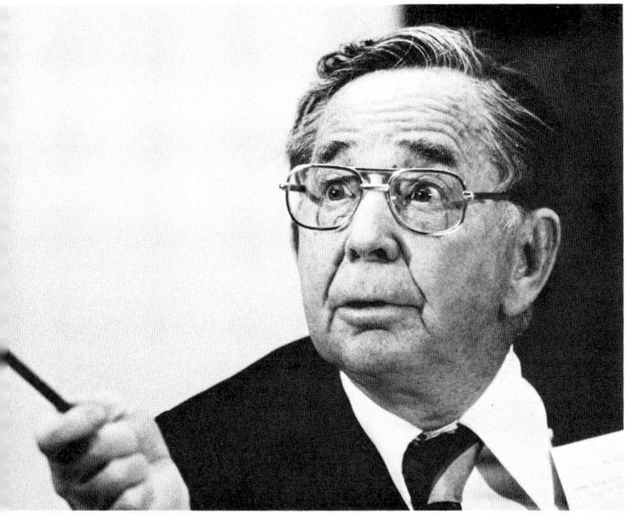

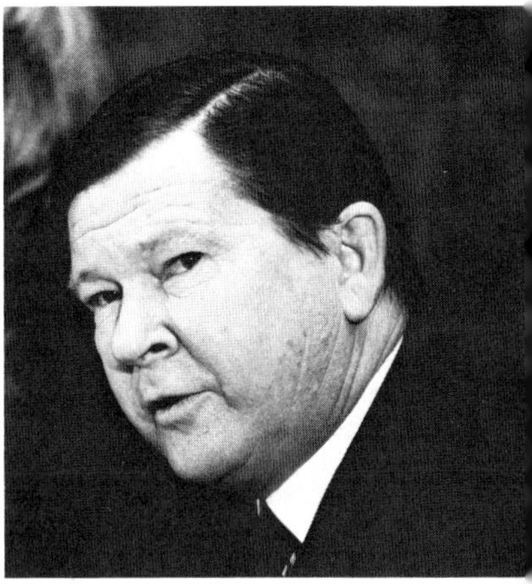

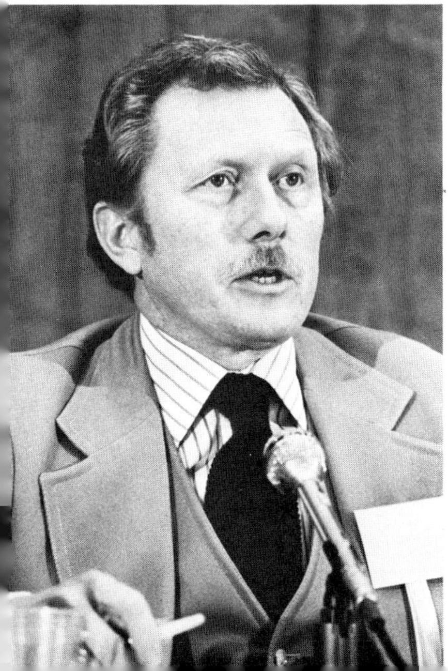

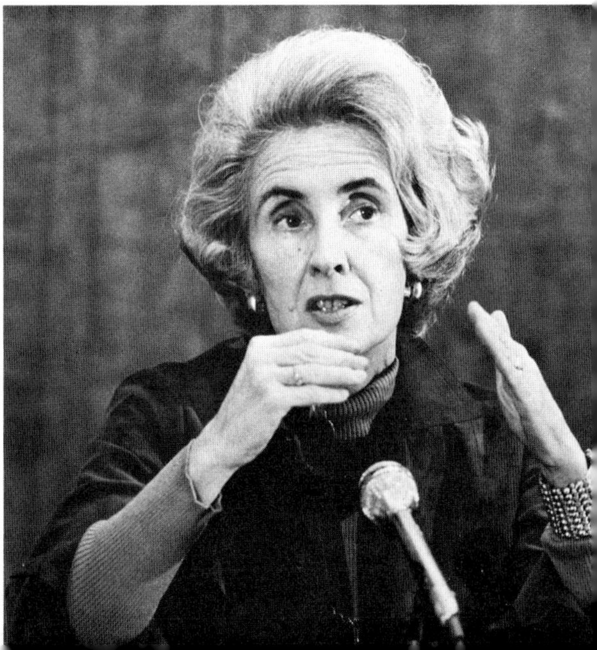

Overview/Discussion

Robert L. Hardesty

Robert L. Hardesty, an assistant to President Lyndon B. Johnson from 1965 to 1969, is Vice Chancellor for Administration of The University of Texas System.

In January 1969, in his final State of the Union Address to the Congress, President Lyndon Johnson was in a mellow mood. He had presided over what may have been the most creative period of progressive legislation in the history of our nation. And while it is generally forgotten today, that legislative accomplishment continued through the last year of his Administration, despite the problems posed by the Vietnam War. The year 1968 alone saw the passage of more major legislation than many other Presidents have passed in a full four years: a major civil rights bill; a monumental anticrime package; a handful of safety and consumer bills, including a truth-in-lending bill that had been languishing in Congress for more than a decade; and several conservation bills, including the first successful attempt to preserve the California redwoods. All that in his final year of office.

And so, facing the Congress on that January evening in 1969, President Johnson felt a sense of affection and shared accomplishment. He told the assembled Senators and Representatives that few Presidents had ever been blessed with so much cooperation from the legislative branch, both Democrats and Republicans. And he concluded: "I hope it may be said, a hundred years from now, that by working together we helped to make our country more just for all of its people, as well as to insure and guarantee the blessings of liberty for all of our posterity. That is what I hope," he said, "but I believe at least it will be said that we tried."

More than half a century earlier, President Theodore Roosevelt said to an aide in the White House that he wished he could turn sixteen lions loose on the Congress. When the aide pointed out that the lions might make a mistake, Roosevelt replied: "Not if they stay there long enough."

A few years later, Woodrow Wilson referred to a group of filibustering Senators as "a little group of willful men, representing no opinion but their own" who had "rendered the government of the United States helpless and contemptible."

And in 1948, campaigning for reelection, President Harry Truman named the 80th Congress "the second worst Congress in the history of the United States."

Obviously, relations between President and Congress are subject to change. The shifting sands of history will allow a former Republican Senator to call Lyndon Johnson one of the greatest Presidents of all time (as Senator Margaret Chase Smith did in an earlier section), and another group of Republican Senators in the 1930s to call FDR "that S.O.B. in the White House"—and they didn't use the initials.

It is that changing relation between the Presidency and the Congress that has brought us together. Our task has been to examine that shifting balance of power and to ask ourselves what it means for our future—to ask what causes it—and to ask how we can influence that change, or if we should. We did come to certain generally accepted conclusions about the relation between the Congress and the Presidency, but one of those conclusions was that we are dealing with a very subtle and complex question—one that does not yield itself to sweeping generalities.

We have all agreed, I think, that there has been a shift of power back to the Congress in the past five, six, or seven years, but we are not agreed on whether it is permanent, whether it is desirable, or even whether it really matters.

In the preceding pages some fascinating theories have been presented. It has been suggested that the modern role of the President as leader of the free world and Commander-in-Chief has created a permanently dominant Presidency, despite temporary shifts in the pendulum.

On the other hand, it has been said that the shifts in the pendulum are inevitable—and while they are influenced by events, there is little we can do to control the events. Still others argued that the balance of power is mainly influenced by the strength of personalities of the principal actors, in both the executive and the legislative branches.

Some have insisted that Congress is more dominant and forceful than most people think; others have said that Congress is incapable of taking the initiative, and that constitutional reform is the only hope of restoring it to its rightful place in the balance of powers.

Some argued that the balance of powers is tragically out of kilter, and that future generations will suffer because of it, while others have argued that there is always tension between the two branches and that such tension is healthy—"creative tension" Wilbur Cohen called it.

It has been claimed that the Congress has *no* power—and that the Congress has the ultimate power; that the country is hungry for strong executive leadership—and that the country is tired of strong executive leadership. In the process, a good deal has been said about Lyndon Johnson—more about him, in fact, than the planners of the conference had intended—but just about enough for those of us who loved him. It was said that the 1950s was the decade of congressional government—and that, of course, was Lyndon Johnson's decade in the Senate. It was also said that the 1960s was the decade of presidential government—and that, of course, was Lyndon Johnson's decade in the Presidency. If the truth were known, I have always felt that if President Johnson had been given the choice of being President of the United States or Senate Majority Leader, he would have chosen both.

More still was said about Lyndon Johnson's congressional-relations techniques (including Barefoot Sander's theory of keeping the Congress supplied with plenty of bones to chew on) and about the cooperation that Johnson and Rayburn gave to President Eisenhower a decade earlier. Others discussed the conflict over the control of the bureaucracy and the conflict over the control of the federal budget. In foreign policy, it has been suggested that bipartisanship is not all it was cracked up to be—especially during the latter part of the Truman years—and may actually have been counterproductive.

But after all the discussion, we are still left with this question: Should we use this period of calm that we are living in today to try to answer some of the basic questions about the balance of power and to look toward the future of that balance? Or should we even worry about it at all? Is it that important?

And finally, can we *do* anything about it? To answer that last question, I shall go to a source no less knowledgeable than the sometime poet, Hilaire Belloc, who wrote at the end of one of his *Cautionary Verses*:

> Oh, let us never doubt
> What we are not sure about.

And so, to get the discussion going, I have prepared a series of questions based on the discussions presented earlier.

1. If we admit that there has been as power shift from the Presidency to the Congress, what has caused it—personality, defense, a swing of the "pendulum?" Has it been pure politics, larger Democratic majorities in the Congress, public opinion, the role of the press in building presidential images and tearing them down, institutional structures, basic issues? We have not arrived at an answer to that question. Maybe we can do so now.

2. Does the change in relative power and influence at either end of Pennsylvania Avenue really matter? Is the result of institutional conflict "creative tension," as Wilbur Cohen said, or is it destructive? Does it impair our ability to get things done?

3. Can Congress be creative even when it is dominant? Can Congress maintain its dominance over any period of time without organizational reform? Will a proper reorganization assure its dominance?

4. Can reorganization in Congress last? If power is centralized, how long can it hold up before it is overthrown—before the reformers grow tired of the reform?

5. What should be the direction of executive reorganization? Is the President too weak in domestic affairs? Should reorganization of the executive take the form of structural

change or personnel management reform?
  6. Are we basically a presidential society? Is there really a yearning to return to a government by strong executive?
  7. Does bipartisanship in foreign affairs really serve the best interests of the American people?
  8. Are interest groups in Washington replacing Congress as a generator of ideas, and thus providing an alternative means of social change?
  9. What sort of balance between Congress and the President is most desirable? Is this balance really out of hand? What can we do about it, if anything?
  10. Would a congressional "security council" similar to the National Security Council help the Congress to balance presidential control over foreign policy?

Now, I should like to address the first question to Dean Rostow. If we assume, as everyone seems to have assumed, Elspeth, that there has been a shift in power from the Presidency to the Congress, to what factors can we attribute that shift?

ELSPETH ROSTOW: Clearly that has been the assumption in a large part of our discussion over the past several days. I wonder, however, to what extent the image of a shift of power may be a by-product of the attention paid in the press to that issue which fixates it—namely, the relationships at the top of the federal pyramid.
  I should like to suggest, for example, that in 1974 when the new post-Watergate Congress came in, it was assumed that it had all the cards it needed to reform itself and to enhance and solidify congressional control over the Executive. In the beginning that seemed to be true. Restraints on the Executive were debated; committee chairmen toppled; the principle of seniority was questioned; and for awhile there seemed to be signs that Congress had taken over.
  Before the end of the calendar year, however, President Ford, coming in as he did under difficult circumstances, had quite a few victories to his credit—even "scalps" on his belt. Though Congress appeared to have so many advantages, the President, with none of the cards in his hand, played a reasonably good game. And now the press, which had heralded a new era but a short time before, began

to say, "What has happened to the Class of 1974?" Why were all the auguries so misleading? And at this stage, the power of the President was at least temporarily exaggerated. I suggest that the notion of a "see-saw," in which the power on one side of the federal balance goes down while the other goes up, is a slight exaggeration.

So my first point is that I am not willing wholly to accept the concept of a power shift. But if we assume that more cards are in the hands of Congress than before, the explanations that have been offered here surely include the attention paid to a President, who in the 1960s as regards Vietnam, appeared increasingly to have been empowered to make independent judgments, without—in the eyes of some commentators—taking Congress sufficiently into his decisionmaking. Second there was Watergate and the reaction to it, which I need not dwell on. So there were two historical circumstances.

A third causal factor that was cited is a kind of "law of cyclical change"—that a shift is inevitable. It was not suggested that it is a product of sunspots, but that there are changes in the tides of politics as in the affairs of men. It is time after a strong President for Congress to try to pull some power back into its hands.

A fourth explanation—aside from the two specific historical circumstances and this theory of the cycles of power—lies in the variations of personality. When a President like FDR is riding high, exerting influence, initiating so much and doing so much, Congress has a hard time being heard above the rhetoric that comes from the White House. On the other hand, when you have a President who is not as powerful, either in his rhetoric or in his grassroots support, Congress takes advantage of a presidential vacuum and moves in. Along these same lines, there may be great heroes in the House or in the Senate who are able to appeal over the President and get themselves not only into the nightly news, but into the minds of the people.

Thus without giving my own answer, I suggest that these are some of the categories of causation that have been suggested in previous sessions.

ROBERT HARDESTY: Senator Tower, having served under three Democratic Presidents and two Republican Presidents, you must have some views on this whole question of the shift of power.

JOHN TOWER: It is my opinion that historically the shift has been cyclical indeed. Whether the cycles will continue in the future I cannot say.

In recent years the shift has been most striking in a field of traditional presidential dominance, namely foreign policy. In my view, that is unfortunate. I don't think it has been nearly as evident in domestic affairs despite the passage of the Congressional Budget and Impoundment Control Act. The fact is that Congress continues to expand the gigantic federal bureaucracy, delegating to it a rule-making power that is tantamount to legislative power. That gives the President an enormous amount of power because he presides over that bureaucracy, and because we cannot exercise adequate legislative oversight over what we have created. Thus the real shift has been in foreign affairs, and that is most clearly manifested by the passage of the War Powers Act—which I vigorously opposed. I think it is unfortunate because we have imposed inhibitions and restrictions on the President that make him less able to deal quickly and effectively with changing situations on the international front.

I think it is unfortunate that Congress chose to institutionalize its disagreement with Lyndon Johnson and Richard Nixon on foreign policy matters—particularly on the war in Vietnam—by the passage of the War Powers Act. I believe that will come back to haunt us.

GRAHAM ALLISON: I think there are two questions here: first, whether there has been a shift, and second, if there has been a shift, what caused it?

I really think the question whether there has been a shift is a difficult question. Elspeth is correct in saying that the press tends to seize upon some particular point in a progression, amplify it greatly, give it a "catchy label," call it a trend, and then either proclaim or bemoan it. It is difficult to distinguish the trends from the "trendy."

Indeed, with apologies to Bill Moyers, let me give you a striking counter-example. It would seem obvious to me that if we are to understand the underlying factors, we should consult the scholars' careful analyses rather than just the views of journalists. But then— listen to this: "The power of Congress has become predominant. Congress has entered more and more into the details of administration until it has virtually taken into its own hands all of the substantial powers of government."

Now, who wrote that? That's Woodrow Wilson in 1885, as a young political scientist. But only five years later Wilson found himself obliged to turn his thesis on its head because events had changed. He now had to recognize what he called, "the greatly increased power and opportunity for constructive statesmanship given to the President"—by the plunge into international politics—and he went on to celebrate the increased power of the Presidency. So I conclude that scholars prove to be about as poor guides in this domain as the journalists.

As to the main question, though, I think there clearly has been a very great shift over the last decade in the relations between President and Congress, in particular—as Senator Tower said—in foreign affairs. The reasons include those that Elspeth Rostow mentioned, but they include a more fundamental feature that has not been mentioned, which is the shifting content of the agenda of foreign affairs.

American foreign policy in the late 1940s and 1950s and even into the 1960s was typically dominated by questions like war and peace, or alliances, or bases abroad. In the 1970s the emphasis is on questions that emerge from the tightening physical and economic interdependence of nations. The agenda today includes issues like oil, or energy, or nuclear power, or food, or international economics, or inflation. These are all issues in which it is very difficult to draw a neat line between domestic policy on the one hand and foreign policy on the other. And each of these issues involves questions like prices and jobs and wages and incomes for Americans—issues in which Congress has always played a major role because they have always been regarded as "bread and butter" issues.

So I think the fundamental reason why there has been so much greater an involvement of Congress in foreign affairs is that the agenda of foreign affairs has changed. Issues like energy and oil and international economics, where the foreign and domestic implications can't be easily distinguished, have come to the forefront. Foreign affairs now have a direct effect on jobs and wages and prices, and consequently they command the attention of Congressmen and congressional committees whereas once they did not.

On that point I think Senator Tower and I are in agreement. Where I disagree with him is on the War Powers Act. In my view the

War Powers Act did not go far enough and did not effectively recapture the constitutional intent, which could not be more clear—that is, that the decision to declare war belongs to Congress. Indeed, I think it would be in the spirit of the Constitution to insure that a decision to *make* war should emerge from the collaborative judgment of both President and Congress.

No doubt technology and modern circumstances have somewhat undermined the original constitutional intent, and I don't think there is any easy way to go back to it. But I think the War Powers Act is less effective in achieving the original intent than its sponsors hoped. And, indeed, I should have preferred an arrangement that was argued about—which I am sure Senator Tower recalls and perhaps favored—whereby the President would consult with the leaders of Congress, perhaps the majority and minority leaders of each house plus the Chairman of the Foreign Relations and Armed Services Committee, before committing the U.S. to military action—as against the more formal mechanism set up by the War Powers Act.

But as to the question whether this involves a congressional encroachment on some rightful presidential prerogative, I don't think either constitutional intent or recent practice support Senator Tower's view. In fact, I think just the opposite.

CARL ALBERT: I think we have a tendency to mix structural changes with changing political issues. There is no question in my mind but that there have been structural changes in the law that have tilted the balance toward the Congress in the last five or six years. The War Powers Act could not have been passed in the particular environment of 1973. It was introduced three years in succession by Clem Zablocki, and it passed the House. It was not passed at all by the Senate one year. The next year the Senate passed a bill also, but the conference report was never agreed to. Finally, both houses passed the same bill. Mr. Nixon was *very* unhappy with that legislation, and he vetoed it. It came back, and we put it on the Speaker's desk, and I just held it there. We decided that we had better not bring it up right then. Well, then came the "Saturday night massacre," and three or four days later, I brought it up.

We had any number of members—both liberal and moderate, and even some conservatives probably—who were sick and tired of

Nixon's using of the veto power as a policy instrument rather than as a method of improving legislation. But it didn't look as though we had the votes to override. When we came to the final vote on the conference report, it seemed doomed to defeat. We had counted every vote in the House of Representatives. I think I had called almost every member on the Democratic side myself.

But when it came up, we knew about five or six young members who were very tired of Nixon's having won eight straight vetoes; Congress had sustained his veto eight straight times. We got six of them to stand by, asking them not to vote until the end of the voting and we knew where we stood. Well, we were obviously two votes behind when the count was about in. We went to them and said, "Now, do you want Nixon to have nine straight, or do you want him to have an imperfect record?" Six members that had voted three times in a row against the War Powers Bill went down and punched the button to override, and we overrode it by four votes. That's how it came about, and that's a good example of procedure by which structural changes sometimes take place in the Congress of the United States. Sometimes you can hardly tell it from politics.

That was definitely a structural change in the war powers of the President. I am not sure it was passed under the best of circumstances. In fact I think that is a poor way to legislate, but we were out to win.

We are going to keep on having cyclical turnovers of power between the President and the Congress, and there will never be a time when any individual Congressman will have the power with the public that the President has. Think of the Joe Cannon era. Cannon was the strongest Speaker in the history of the United States as far as his personal and his institutional power was concerned. He served with Teddy Roosevelt, and I will bet that there are a thousand times as many Americans who know the name of Teddy Roosevelt as know the name of Joe Cannon.

BILL MOYERS: A question to both Senator Tower and Speaker Albert: In this session we are supposed to be thinking about 1980 and 1990. Given all the deliberations that led to the War Powers Act, I wonder if you are prepared to leave to the President the decision about nuclear retaliation in the event—God forbid—that we are attacked. Conceding the very limited time available to the

Chief Executive, are you, the Congress, prepared to let him make that decision?

CARL ALBERT: I think it is the only thing we can do.

JOHN TOWER: That's right. Even the War Powers Act does not deny that to the President. I don't think you would have it any other way. If you have twenty minutes warning, you can't assemble the Congress.

BILL MOYERS: Let's just assume, for the sake of argument, that in that twenty minutes it is apparent to the defense establishment that the United States is about to be heavily damaged, and that all the United States can do is deal a punitive blow to the Soviet Union—too late to be a preventive action.

The President's decision is to retaliate simply for punitive purposes. Are you prepared to let him make that decision?

JOHN TOWER: Are you prepared to announce to the Soviets that because we cannot prevent a first strike we will not retaliate? That, I think, would give the Soviets reasons to suppose that nuclear war was very thinkable indeed.

BILL MOYERS: No, Senator, what I am trying to get at is this. If the War Powers Act was passed as a political message to the White House, then what considerations were given to the substantive concerns to which it would apply, and which prompted it in the first place? And how does the nation debate the issues involved?

JOHN TOWER: To begin with, the War Powers Act was addressed not to some strategic, nuclear war situation, but to more conventional situations—brush-fire wars, police actions, that sort of thing. And I worry whether the War Powers Act inhibits our President from a flexibility of action that he should have in those situations.

I don't entirely disagree with Dr. Allison, but after all, the Congress did acquiesce in the war in Vietnam. The Congress appropriated the money for it. The Congress, at any time, could have provided that no appropriation under this act should be used to prosecute a war in Vietnam, and that would have been the end of it.

NAN WATERMAN: I should like to go back to your original question and talk about the shift in the balance of power, and what brings it about and why.

It seems to me it is a straight political kind of situation. It is cyclical, but the power is always there for either the President or the Congress to use because the Constitution and the federal system and the system of checks and balances establishes that.

When either body—the President or the Congress—perceives too aggressive a power grab by the other side, a reaction sets in and there is an immediate attempt to rebalance the situation.

It probably happens more often than not because you have very strong, aggressive leadership on one side or the other. Basically, however, we need both a strong Presidency and a strong Congress, and the "balance" between them doesn't have to result in stalemate. It is not a zero-sum kind of game, and the more it leads to a kind of healthy tension and conflict, the better off the country is.

ROBERT HARDESTY: Let me jump ahead a little bit and pose this question to Professor Neustadt. Are we, as some have suggested, really a presidential society? Do the people yearn generally for a strong Executive?

RICHARD NEUSTADT: I think in this society there is a deep desire at many levels for what used to be called a "chief magistrate," as a human embodiment of government and of the country.

Now, it is quite a mistake to equate that with "presidential leadership" vis-à-vis Congress. I think it is entirely possible for the electorate to be deeply suspicious of both President and Congress and still deeply desire to have a human embodiment of the country in its government.

You can have periods when a large part of the electorate adores the President and dislikes Congress and another large part feels exactly the other way around. But cutting right across that is this desire for that human embodiment. Henry Ford Jones wrote back in the 1890s that the presidency was a re-creation of the oldest political institution—or at least the second oldest—known to the human race, the elective kingship, the immediate heir of the priest. I think that's very true.

The news media have enhanced this symbolism over time, starting with Teddy Roosevelt's impact on the country through the wire services, which were the new news medium of that day. Nowadays television makes it even more dramatic.

Sure, this is a presidential country in the sense that almost every form of government we know has wanted its human embodiments. But that doesn't have anything to do with presidential leadership as we've been discussing it.

ROBERT HARDESTY: Well, Tom Wicker suggested that the advent of television, coupled with the new role of the President as Commander-in-Chief and leader of the free world, did tilt the balance toward the President on a more or less permanent basis.

RICHARD NEUSTADT: I don't think one can speak of permanent tilting without reference to the issues, as the Speaker said. Or, as Graham Allison was saying, to the particular circumstances in foreign relations. If you are close to war or engaged in hostilities, that Commander-in-Chief role is terribly important—no doubt about it. If you combine that with the televised kingship, you really have something.

But those are circumstantial matters. They don't tell you about tilt in terms of domestic policy, and they don't tell you much about international economics. If you are looking for long-run tilt, I don't think it is either to the President as an elective politician, or to members of Congress as elective politicians. The long-run tilt I see is from them all to a large swirling gooey mass of non-elective officials in the interest groups, in the executive agencies, and now, alas, in Congress itself. If I had to look at the tilting balance in the next generation, I fear I would see that the successors to Senator Tower and Speaker Albert will have sunk virtually out of sight into that large non-elective mass of people in the law firms, the interest groups, the executive agencies, and the congressional subcommittees, who already run almost everything in Washington. That really does trouble me.

BILL MOYERS: But I have an antidote to that. I agree about the growth of nongovernmental agencies operating on our political body, but I suspect one consequence of that growth would be to enhance again the power of the President to perform that role as the embodiment of the nation.

The chief attribute of the office, it seems to me, is that a President is able to act upon the intellectual idea of America in a way that, say, the President of France or the Prime Minister of Britain cannot. I do not think television has been the chief means of developing that capacity, contrary to what I think your implication was. Washington acted upon the intellectual idea of his country without television—so did Jackson, Lincoln, Teddy Roosevelt, and others. If we have this decentralized political process you are talking about, an articulate president will be even better able to act upon the intellectual idea of America. Television can be used to accelerate that. It can be used to trivialize the Presidency, too.

For me, the consequential moment of the Johnson Administration came when President Johnson was asked at a press conference why, after representing the cautious and wary approach to civil rights as a Senator from Texas he had now become a strong supporter of the civil rights movement. The President paused briefly and in an eloquently honest moment said, "All of us recognize that things we do earlier in our lives can be wrong, and when you see the truth, you turn around on it."

He did that on national television, and in that moment by acting upon the intellectual idea of America as a place of equality and progress, Lyndon Johnson—in a way that Congress never could—reached out and turned the nation upward on a new course.

ELSPETH ROSTOW: May I suggest that a modification of the Neustadt-Moyers hypothesis might be that the gooier the mass, the greater the moment of executive opportunity. I don't see how the "gooey mass" theory has much in it for Congress.

I know we are talking about the 1980s, but I do suggest that historians need to recall—and one did in one of our earlier sessions—that over time, if we are to be ornithological, Congress has been much more "hawkish" than Presidents. If you look at the wars or threats of wars in our history, the rhetoric that would have embroiled the country has more often come from Congress than from the White House. Thus, as a bastion of the country against foreign involvement, Congress would have provided us with very poor protection.

The reason that I didn't cite the shifting agenda in foreign affairs as a major cause of the recent power shift is this: It seems to me that the beginning of congressional involvement in these matters was with the Lend-Lease debate. That was an unusual grass-roots discussion of an American position which very markedly committed us to an American interest abroad. Next, I would cite the Marshall Plan and its consequences, which brought in the Senate in its own special way. The Senate had always had a share of the foreign action that the House had not had because of its constitutional mandates.

But once you begin voting annually on expenditures for foreign aid, say from 1947 on, you very much involve Congress in foreign affairs. So, to go back to our chairman's original question, I do not see that the most recent shift is more than another stage in a pattern of increasing concern now a generation old.

Senator Tower said that one thing Congress can do retroactively is to over-respond to presidential actions. He feels that there was such an over-response in the War Powers Act. I would suggest that there was a similar over-response against the many terms of Franklin Roosevelt, one that is embodied in an amendment limiting the President to two terms. The twenty-second amendment will also affect this whole question of presidential versus congressional dominance over the rest of the century.

JOHN TOWER: It's worth noting that now even during this current period of congressional ascendency most significant legislative initiatives still come from the White House, and the Congress either acts positively on those initiatives or reacts and proposes some alternative.

RICHARD NEUSTADT: Let me make one comment on that. I think one has to distinguish between agenda setting and idea creation. The legislative agenda is set in large part by issues the President chooses to put his stamp on and send down. The ideas themselves come from lots of places, and a lot of them germinate in congressional committees for a long, long time.

The other thing I wanted to put to our congressional members here is that somewhere in the "gooey mass" theory there's a tremendous role for somebody in Congress—either the Congressmen themselves or staff directors. If the gooey mass is running the operating programs of the federal government, somebody has to control it, and I don't think the President can do it. Nothing in Bill Moyers's theory about touching the spark of the American intelligence, nothing in setting the legislative agenda, nothing in being an elected king, helps the President one bit to exercise operational control over my "gooey mass." If anybody can control it, it's the people who can really get hold of a piece of it. And that is those subcommittees.

CARL ALBERT: Isn't the Budget Control Act a step in that direction?

RICHARD NEUSTADT: I am not sure it is. It seems to me that pits the houses of Congress against their own subcommittees.

CARL ALBERT: Yes, I think it does, to certain extent.

ROBERT HARDESTY: I should like to know what Common Cause has to say about the "gooey mass" theory.

NAN WATERMAN: Well, it depends on how "gooey" it gets. Public-interest organizations such as Common Cause certainly are proliferating, and some of them are becoming very powerful. If you get the "gooey mass" down far enough to include those groups, I tend to agree. We are also seeing the rise of neighborhood government and neighborhood organizations, which reflects a desire to get some kind of a hold at the local level, the citizen's level. And the Congress has contributed to this—by mandating citizen participation in grant programs, for example.

So we are all probably helping to create this "gooey mass," whatever it is going to be. I think it is important to remember, however, that a lot of the ferment going on right now started in the 1960s, when we first had the OEO, community action programs, urban renewal programs, and so on. That's when we let the genie out of the bottle, and I don't think we are going to be able to put it back in. Your "gooey mass"—public service organizations, citizen organizations, local government bureaucracy—that is probably where we are headed. But I think we are the heirs of something that happened in the 1960s. Where we are going to be in the 1980s is still pretty uncertain.

JOHN TOWER: I think that organizations like Common Cause and Nader's group tend very quickly to become a part of the "gooey mass." Who is going to extricate them from it? We'll probably create yet another organization to do it, and it in turn will also become a part of the "gooey mass."

GRAHAM ALLISON: There's a famous remark by none other than Professor Neustadt, somewhat earlier than his invention of the theory of the "gooey mass," but containing much the same idea. He called for politicians of the world to unite; they have nothing to lose but their emerging bureaucracies.

RICHARD NEUSTADT: That was ten years ago, and I thought I was joking.

ROBERT HARDESTY: Professor Allison, let's shift our focus back to international affairs. The question was posed, "Does and did bipartisanship in the development of foreign policy serve the best interest of the American people, or does it tend to stifle debate when debate is needed?" Would you care to comment on that subject?

GRAHAM ALLISON: For the problems faced in the immediate postwar period, bipartisanship—in the sense of a fundamental agreement on the major purposes to be served by American foreign policy—made sense. With respect to opposition to the Soviet Union and its expansion, to the economic reconstruction of Europe, to the attempt to build democratic regimes in Germany and Japan, to promote the decolonization of empires—with respect to those issues—a very substantial part of the American people were agreed. Not everyone agreed on all those positions, but there was a very substantial consensus. So I think the bipartisanship for that agency in that environment and in those circumstances was a great achievement.

Now, if you look at that bipartisanship when you get to Vietnam—in the mid-sixties or even back at the time of Dien Bien Phu in the mid-fifties—what it really meant was very substantial congressional deference to presidential leadership, even on matters that were not encompassed by the basic national cosensus or the basic objectives of postwar foreign policy. To the extent that Congressmen—of whatever party—follow the President into policies that they really disagree with, bipartisanship becomes very costly.

On the questions of war and peace, we still have bipartisanship, or at least bipartisan acceptance of presidential leadership. To the extent that the agenda of American foreign policy includes the possibility of war with the Soviet Union, the country's unity is manifest. On that I think the points made by Senator Tower and Speaker Albert are correct. The country will line up behind the President, and if he decides it's time to go to war, we'll go.

But as to issues like energy, which are part foreign and part domestic, when the President announces that there's an energy crisis and sets out a bold and imaginative plan for what should be done about it, Congress does not just stand up and salute, because energy affects internal issues that Congressmen believe they are at least as competent to deal with as the President is—and they may well be right. Many of these issues—maybe half the international agenda—directly affect jobs, prices, wages, inflation, the distribution of income, and so on. The proposition that politics should or could stop at the water's edge—because Americans would be likely to agree—denies the "bread and butter" character of politics. What politics domestically is about has been just the issues which are now a very large component of the foreign-policy agenda. The nature of domestic politics is the creative tension of dispute and argument, and on that one wouldn't expect bipartisanship. Indeed, if there were a unanimity or consensus about those matters, one would soon become worried.

JOHN TOWER: I think one of the principal dangers of too much congressional intrusion into foreign policy is that the President's perceptions of the national interest are somewhat more sophisticated and a little clearer than those of the general citizenry who don't have a great sophistication of foreign policy matters.

As a matter of fact, I think there is an appalling lack of sophistication on foreign policy matters in the Congress. Congressional attitudes on foreign policy may be largely shaped by domestic political considerations that are not necessarily consonant with the national interest.

GRAHAM ALLISON: I agree very much with Senator Tower's statement. But let's take an issue like energy, which is a very substantial problem for American foreign policy as it is for domestic policy. The U.S. is today dependent for half of the oil it consumes every day on foreign imported oil. That dependency leaves the U.S. very vulnerable to a situation like the embargo in 1973. To deal with that problem, the President has, as he says, "perceived a national interest and announced an energy policy." Now, would you think that his perception of the national interest, as to the national energy policy, is that much clearer than the perception of the national interest on the part of members of Congress?

JOHN TOWER: No, because I think that is essentially a domestic issue—a domestic problem that has its international implications. As I see it, the President is absolutely correct in saying we have an energy crisis, or at least a very severe problem. And he is correct in some other suggestions, that we must pay the replacement cost of fuel, and so on. He is tragically incorrect in his approach to a solution to the problem. But I am sure he understands the international implications of it. Even though he doesn't support increasing the means of production, and places nearly all his emphasis on conservation, his purpose is to reduce our consumption of foreign fuel, to become less dependent on the external sources. And on that point, I would say his perception and mine are essentially the same.

ELSPETH ROSTOW: I feel that I am acting as a kind of historical ombudsman. In the 1960s I did not sense in many Congressmen any great deference to either of the two Presidents who were in office during those years. On the contrary, when you talk about the degree to which Congress deferred to the President in foreign policy, I suggest that was another element of importance, namely the polls. Congressmen are always reading about opinions back home in their districts, and if you look at the polls on Vietnam, for example, they held up very strongly throughout most of the period.

VII/Conflict and Search • 402

So if you found a Congressman who was reacting in the same way the President was, he might not have been looking down Pennsylvania Avenue at all, but looking to his district and to the views he found there.

ROBERT HARDESTY: Mr. Speaker, may I put a question to you? One of our discussions has dealt with the internal organization of the Congress. Some of the panelists and some of those who presented papers have argued that because of its own organization the Congress is incapable of acting creatively and in many respects is incapable of dealing with the problems of modern times. Indeed Professor Dodd suggested that we need both internal reforms in Congress and some constitutional amendments:

First, to enhance the power of the Speaker and the Senate majority leader by allowing them to nominate committee chairmen.

Second, to amend the Constitution to make it easier for the Congress to override presidential vetoes.

Third, to create a Congressional Security Council to give the Congress more of a voice in foreign affairs. Would you please comment on those proposals?

CARL ALBERT: Yes, sir. As long ago as my first term in office we had a large number of energy bills introduced, and there was not a single one that didn't affect from two to seven committees. So we had a constant fuss with the chairmen of different committees about who should have which bill and then how we would handle them—jointly, consecutively, or what? And we did try all of those methods. You may remember Lew Deschler, the Parliamentarian—a very conservative person but a very bright one—

JOHN TOWER: Carl, if you will yield, I'd like to suggest that the two are not always incompatible.

CARL ALBERT: Conceded. Lew said to me one day, "We've got to have an energy committee." So, I set out to get a congressional energy committee where we could dump all these bills regardless of whether they affected the merchant marine, fisheries, interstate and foreign commerce, ways and means, or what not. I got together with a number of bright young members of the House and discussed the proposition with them, and they agreed. Congress did need to reorganize itself; the 1946 Act had been largely ignored; and we needed to change the structure of the committees.

Well, you could change the name of Arkansas easier than you could change the structure of the committees.

I made Bolling the chairman of a select committee that brought out a bill to change the structure of the committees to try to make their various jurisdictions more suitable to the issues that confronted us. But it was fought by the toughest, strongest, meanest men and women in the House and the ones with the most power; and it was defeated by a vote of about 121-109. More of the young members went along with it because they hadn't yet reached positions of seniority that would give them much influence over the things their committees controlled.

On the next issue, I personally oppose giving the majority leader any constitutional powers. He's a political officer, he's not a constitutional officer; he's not a legislative officer, he's never voted on by the House of Representatives. We don't recognize political parties in the Constitution and I am not ready to start changing the Constitution to give majority leaders and Speakers specific powers.

It would be more logical to prescribe the powers of the Speaker and Vice President, but that would raise problems because the Vice President may be of the opposite party from that of the majority leader who actually sets the policy for the Senate.

I would not change the Constitution to give any additional power to either the Speaker or the majority leader. I might be willing to do it by simple legislation or even by concurrent resolution, but not by amendment.

Now on the matter of overriding vetoes, I am a bit skeptical of making changes. I think the President has a place in legislation. I think you need one person in this country who can keep an eye on the whole nation and who can represent everybody.

I would hate to cut the two-thirds very much; I wouldn't know what to cut it to, so I think we'd better leave it alone. I don't think it would do much good to give, say, 55 or 60 percent of the Congressmen the power to override a veto because you would have exactly the same problem if your party ratio were different.

It really depends on what your ratio is. We have now about 294 Democrats in the House, the rest Republicans. That's a little more than two-thirds. That gives the President, of course, a chance to go with his program, at least when he agrees, as he generally does, with the leadership in the Congress.

Johnson's was a great legislative performance—far greater than Roosevelt's. Roosevelt did perform miracles, and he did give strength and confidence to the people of this country, but he did it during the Depression, when we had millions of people unemployed. Johnson did it at a time when we were at peace and the economy was healthy. He did it because he was a capable legislator. I worked with him day and night, as we passed those seventy-three bills, which are called the Great Society bills. I think Johnson's knowledge of the Senate and the House and his determination—of which he had more than anybody I have ever known—combined to make his program an even more sensational one than the great program of President Roosevelt. Roosevelt has always been an idol of mine, but I must say he had the times helping him far more than Johnson did.

Now you asked whether Congress should create its own national security council. I doubt it. We have foreign affairs and military affairs committees in both houses. Frankly, I don't know what a security council could do that they can't do. They can do just about anything that they want.

JOHN TOWER: I agree with the Speaker in virtually every respect. Most of what you suggest—with the exception of the veto override—we could accomplish by concurrent resolution, or simply by internally changing our rules in either body.

As to a security council, that is a totally unrealistic proposal. You can't have a congressional Secretary of State or a congressional Secretary of Defense or a congressional progressional military section. I don't think it is realistic to institutionalize any kind of foreign-policymaking process in the Congress. It would create widespread distrust and lack of confidence in the ability of the United States to conduct diplomacy all over the world. Moreover, it would sharply increase the tension between White House and Congress on foreign policy matters.

CARL ALBERT: What about changing the constitutional provisions concerning the veto?

Discussion • 405

JOHN TOWER: No, I would not support a constitutional amendment aimed at that. In a sense the presidential veto in its present form does what William S. White said the Senate was supposed to do, and that is "to protect the minority from the precipitate and emotional tyranny of the majority."

NAN WATERMAN: As a representative of an organization that is constantly harassing the Congress to change its ways, I agree with Speaker Albert and Senator Tower. We don't really need the Constitution cluttered up with rules by which the House and the Senate govern themselves. The Senate and the House have instituted a number of very progressive procedural reforms in the last few years, and I don't think people realize exactly how much Congress has done toward making its operations work more effectively.

GRAHAM ALLISON: I should like to expand on one point. I don't really see the advantage of a formal arrangement in Congress providing for a congressional national security committee. Nevertheless, there have been a number of suggestions that reach in that direction. I should like to throw out an idea and see how Senator Tower or Speaker Albert reacts to it.

The standard complaint by people today in the executive branch is that, whereas in the past it was possible to deal with a limited number of committee chairmen, or in the Senate with people who took a position of leadership on one issue or another, today, for a variety of reasons it is necessary to deal with a much greater number of people. The change in the agenda, the growth of congressional staff, the change in the composition of the members of Congress, the general change in the times, some changes in the rules—all these things have contributed to the shift. The Senate is no longer looked on as the "gentlemen's club." That used to mean that a freshman Senator wouldn't pick an issue and start making speeches about it; he would defer to his seniors. But now the new person feels capable of speaking on almost any topic. The result of all this has been a considerable dispersion of influence in both the Senate and the House, to the point that the members of the Executive—even the new members of the Carter Administration who used to argue strongly for increasing Congressional involvement in foreign affairs—bemoan the fact.

A good friend of mine is responsible for administration policy on nuclear proliferation. He and I used to teach a course together in which he generally put the argument for an increasing role for Congress in foreign policy. He's now been consulting in the Senate about the Carter Administration's policies on nuclear proliferation. He says at first it was explained to him there were six Senators who had to agree. So the six discussed the matter, and the six agreed. Then there became sixteen, and now there are sixty—each of whom has a rather independent view on the subject and needs to be consulted.

Indeed, when you put on top of that the tier of staff in both houses, the number of people participating becomes staggering. When Pat Moynihan was elected Senator, he came back to Cambridge and said, "How many staff members do I get to hire as a new Senator from New York?"

What would you guess? The answer is one hundred. One hundred people he was involved in hiring. There are now 17,000 staff people who work on the Hill. Most of them are working on this topic or that topic, and many of them have substantive views.

So, the question on which I should like to hear the views of the Speaker and Senator Tower is whether it would not be possible to recreate some of the strong leadership we used to have. The suggestion of a "national security council" for Congress puts it perhaps in too formalistic terms, but it is a legitimate impulse toward reestablishing in the Senate and in the House some real leadership on major issues. As it is, the people who work on the issue and think about it have to deal with the opinions of most of the 535 Congressmen and also those of several cascades of staff members, each having an independent view. Is there not some way to recapture some of the baronial leadership that was decried only two decades ago, which, as you say, has been carefully eroded by the changes that have taken place?

JOHN TOWER: Let me say first that the growing complexity of government and the increasing number of things we must deal with make it extremely difficult for us to become expert on anything. Usually, in the Senate, the real experts among Senators on certain matters tend to come from the smaller states because they are not spread so thin. I come from a state with a multifarious economy, topography, populace, and everything else, so that makes it somewhat different. I suppose I am excusing myself for not being an expert on anything.

I think one thing that has precipitated the huge congressional staff is the growth of an enormous bureaucracy in the executive branch. We have had to create a comparable bureaucracy on Capitol Hill to deal with it. I should like to see us start dismantling some of the bureaucracy downtown; then I would be perfectly willing to see us begin to dismantle our own. But it really is true that Congress has become a bureaucracy. We have got very far away from the original idea of the founding fathers that members of Congress should be "citizen" legislators. We are no longer citizen legislators; we are full-time professional, legislative bureaucrats—that's what we've become.

ELSPETH ROSTOW: As a Dean of a School of Public Affairs, hoping to place our graduates in positions of strength, I cannot agree with the Senator.

CARL ALBERT: Well, I think I agree with Senator Tower on that. I have been in the leadership for twenty-odd years. I have always had a lot of staff—usually more than I wanted.

Sometimes I have good ones, sometimes bad ones, but you do have to have experts. And we really do have some—people like Maurice Stans, with the Joint Committee on Taxation, Lew Deschler in the House. And I want to say to Bob Hardesty that he was the best speech writer I ever had, too. I am not for ignoring any of these people out there who want to be staff members. I find lots of young people everywhere who want to be a staff member for a Congressman or a committee. I think it is a worthy ambition, but it is true that we may be building up more than we can take care of here.

Professor Neustadt, you know more about this than anybody. You send down more young people to become clerks and staff and administrators than anybody. What do you think about all this?

RICHARD NEUSTADT: I am still thinking about the 1946

reorganization, which was the last formal, big-scale reorganization of committees. I am still puzzling about how that could occur in 1946.

CARL ALBERT: You know why it passed?

RICHARD NEUSTADT: Please enlighten me.

CARL ALBERT: Because they put a congressional pension in the bill. The press was for the 1946 Reorganization Act, and they didn't say anything about the salary. They were afraid of not getting the whole thing; that's why it passed—the only reason it passed.

RICHARD NEUSTADT: Why couldn't you get similar incentives behind Dick Bolling's reorganization scheme?

CARL ALBERT: Well, we should have. We should have had a pay raise with that. I think I'm the only Congressman who never failed to vote himself a pay raise when he got a chance to. My people never did say anything about it. They didn't print it in the papers down there. But I think we probably should have done something like that with the Bolling plan. That probably would have been the right time to do it. We waited until this year when we could have done it that year.

BILL MOYERS: Mr. Speaker, you remind me of the salesman who offered the purchasing agent the gift of a color TV set, and the purchasing agent said, "Oh, I couldn't do that; my conscience wouldn't let me."

The salesman said, "Well, I tell you what I will do. I will sell it to you for five dollars."

The purchasing agent said, "Well, under those circumstances, I'll take two."

CARL ALBERT: The things that helped sell the 1946 Act to the press as much as anything else were the facts that we were creating a professional staff and that it was an effort to cut down the number of committees. Those were the two big things. That was a Republican Congress; it was the Republicans on the House side that wanted a change. They wanted opposition members corresponding to the chairmen of subcommittees, and we gave that to them. And since the chairmen of the subcommittees were getting chiefs-of-staff, we had to give those to the other side, too.

We doubled the number of subcommittes in the House so that a lot of the young members became chairmen of subcommittees. These staffs didn't build up to match a bureaucracy that had been created downtown. They were built up because we had spread the authority in legislative matters to subcommittees and had increased the number of subcommittees in the House. I don't know how it worked in the Senate, but that's the way it worked in the House.

NAN WATERMAN: Mr. Chairman, reorganization is a fine thing, but I don't think it's going to solve all the problems that people seem to be expecting it to solve. I think it would be useful to examine some of the bureaucracies both in Congress and on the executive side. Indeed I am rather fascinated with the idea of a very slow, cautious approach to a sunset law, by which we would try to see if some agencies are no longer performing their original functions. I realize, however, that there is a danger that we might create another whole bureaucracy to do the evaluation of the agencies.

But let's not kid ourselves into thinking that moving boxes and titles and people around and calling them something else is going to achieve the magic kingdom for us.

BILL MOYERS: That enables me to say that we are neglecting one very important element, namely the effect of human personality on policies and bureaucracies and institutions. It is difficult for any of us to figure out where any changes will lead us because the personalities of the men and women in Congress, and particularly the personality of the President, determine so many of these issues.

The strength of Congress gains in proportion to the mediocrity of the President. Strong Presidents have always put Congress on the defensive; weak Presidents have yielded to Congress; and that observation speaks to the President's personality and goes to his perception of his own capacity and that of the Congress.

Richard Nixon was a strong President. Whether you agreed with either his leadership or his character, he was a strong President. So was Lyndon Johnson, and with him Congress was on the defensive.

Jerry Ford was a weak President, and Congress ascended. Jimmy Carter is proving to be weaker than many people expected, at least in the first year or so of his term. And correspondingly Congress is, for the moment, in the ascendancy. But, let the wheel turn, and let a President come into office who has the personality and the perception, and that can change very easily.

Somebody quoted Woodrow Wilson a minute ago. Wilson also said, "I would a great deal rather know what they are talking about around the quiet firesides all over this country than what they are talking about in the cloak rooms of Congress."

Well, Jimmy Carter felt the same way. He is coming to the same grief that Woodrow Wilson came to, in denigrating the institutional and political role of Congress. If your perception is that you don't need Congress, then you can go on and attend all the town meetings in Clinton and Yazoo City you want to. But meanwhile Congress will be emasculating your legislation.

Jimmy Carter walked down Pennsylvania Avenue and failed to remember that Congress sat on the other end and that for the next four years he was going to be going up and down that Hill, that he would always be going to or coming from the Congress. Forgetting that, he denigrated an institution that is absolutely vital to the changing nature of our society.

So, the personality of the President—the strong, the weak, the depraved, the enlightened—his personality and his perceptions of the Congress will probably have more effect on these issues than anything else.

FROM THE FLOOR: A number of the speakers have alluded to the power of the bureaucracy and lamented the inability of the Congress and the President to control or direct policy—the "gooey mass" syndrome. I think blaming everything on the bureaucracy is a little bit easy. Isn't it often used as a political scapegoat? As a student at the LBJ school and as a future bureaucrat, I feel a little beleaguered by some of the conversation. Missing from the panel right now are a couple of bureau chiefs to talk about what it is like to work with a "waffle" in Congress or an uncertain President.

A question to you, Professor Neustadt: How successful do you think the bureaucracy will be in persuading or negotiating with Congress or the President to set specific policies, so that the bureaucracy doesn't end up taking the brunt of the flak from the public?

PROFESSOR NEUSTADT: Sir, I want you to know that my father was a bureaucrat; I was a bureaucrat; my son is now a bureaucrat; I hold bureaucrats in high esteem. It's a good question, but I think you have to ask it program by program, categorical grant by categorical grant. It's a matter of balance among the program managers, the subcommittee staffs, the interest-group representatives.

Ours is a government of subgovernments, more so now than ever, and that's all I meant by "gooey mass"; the numbers involved are so great. The President is not a very important personal participant in these outcomes, and hasn't been for years. Key members of Congress are more important.

So, I don't know how to answer your question. There are bound to be some areas in which perceptions of public need and public opinion are sufficiently focused so that legislative changes actually take effect and are administered by the federal bureaucracy, if you will. But you have to remember that most of that bureaucracy spends most of its time shoveling money out to other bureaucracies at other levels, which actually perform services. If one is going to make the kind of judgments you are calling for, one must ask, "what programs, what time period, what's the state of public opinion, what's the state of perceived crisis or difficulty?"

CARL ALBERT: I think that's right. I think we have a tendency to be governed by slogans and by words that mean one thing in one place and something else somewhere else.

Bureaucracy is bad, but what bureaucracy is bad? Who is the bad bureaucrat? Who is the good bureaucrat? I think some of the people down in some of the departments have contributed immeasurably to the country, and I think some of the staff members on the Hill have, too. I don't think we should jump on bureaucracy. I think the American people should decide what programs it wants and how many people it will take to run them. Listen, the blame everywhere, in the end, is at the ballot box, in my opinion.

NAN WATERMAN: The trouble with that is that, by and large, the closest contact the citizens have with governments tends to be with the bureaucrat, not with their elected officials—except, possibly, at the local level where they know their council or mayor, or whatever form of government the community has. For the most part, American citizens have more contacts with bureaucrats than they do with elected officials.

CARL ALBERT: Their contact with the bureaucrat is through their Congressmen. The Congressman is a representative of the constituency as well as a legislator, and is the only one who knows which bureau is in charge of the program that interests the constituent.

Now, there are a few people who go straight to the bureaucrat and know just exactly what to say, but I don't think that is true across the country.

NAN WATERMAN: Well, I am not just talking about federal bureaucrats and federal agencies. I am talking about what happens at the local level. Now I don't want to put down all bureaucrats, because some of my best friends are bureaucrats, but too many bureaucrats do not perceive that the public is their constituency in the same way that elected officials do. They perceive themselves as working for their superiors in the department, which was created by the next-higher level department, and so on.

CARL ALBERT: Again, I want to invoke the agreement of my good friend, John Tower, with what Alben Barkley said at the Democratic Convention in 1948: "A bureaucrat is a Democrat that's got a job that a Republican wants."

JOHN TOWER: The reason being that the Democrats have destroyed all their opportunities in the private sector.

I should like to comment on what Mrs. Waterman said. I don't frequently find myself in agreement with Common Cause, but I think she is right that the bureaucrats don't see themselves as the servants of people the same as the elected officials do. I think that is one of the problems of the bureaucracy.

Certainly, people do have individual contacts with bureaucrats. When an inspector from the Occupational Safety and Health Administration walks into your small business and starts pushing you around and levying fines on you, you know you have had some contact with the bureaucracy.

I say that all of the failings of the bureaucrat are ultimately the fault of Congress. I don't take it all the way back to the ballot box. I think that we in Congress have very often responded to interest-group pressures by creating programs and then creating agencies to administer them that are not really a result of popular demand, but a result of smaller constituencies that may be well-organized and well-disciplined and have a great deal of political power. So I think the ultimate blame—if indeed blame is to be assigned—lies with the Congress.

FROM THE FLOOR: I have a question for Senator Tower. Earlier you said something to the effect that the President was the head of the bureaucracy or controlled the bureaucracy, but isn't it the Congress that appropriates the funds to keep the bureaucracy alive? My question is: Who has more control over the bureaucracy—the Congress or the President?

JOHN TOWER: Unfortunately neither has enough.

It is very difficult for a President to get a handle on the bureaucracy just as it is difficult for Congress to exercise adequate oversight. But the President does have effective administrative control of it, and he can influence what the bureaucracy does.

His authority is somewhat restricted by the Civil Service system, which was created in 1883 to correct the abuses of the "spoils" system. That was very badly needed at the time, but now I think the system is a little too rigid and doesn't lend itself well enough to responsive control by the President. As for the Congress, I think it has done a poor job of oversight. Yes, we appropriate the money, but we don't know what we are appropriating it for sometimes.

RICHARD NEUSTADT: May I disagree just a little bit?

I am less impressed than you are, Senator, with the amount of oversight that a President can manage on any given operating program, unless he is willing to bring an enormous amount of weight to bear over a considerable period of time. Programs get their funds from Congress; they get their legislative authority from Congress; they get such detailed oversight as they get from Congress and the Office of Management and Budget, and by and large, Congress has much more staff to put on the problem than OMB does.

My impression is that a well-organized and well-staffed subcommittee chairman who has managed to establish effective oversight and who has sufficient influence with the appropriations subcommittees concerned to be of use to the officials, can exercise a very high degree of direct authority over an operating bureau.

FROM THE FLOOR: Last week *The Economist* carried on its cover these bold words, "Guy Fawkes was right." On the inside there was a devastating attack upon the performance of the House of Commons. Now, I am wondering if anybody on the panel would consider that the American Congress is performing significantly better or significantly worse than its counterpart in Great Britain. If there's a possibility that in the future it might perform badly, I am wondering whether the only thing that can forestall that sad possibility might be direct action by an American Guy Fawkes. Perhaps Senator Tower would be prepared to answer that.

CARL ALBERT: Well, we had our Puerto Ricans. . .

JOHN TOWER: I think Carl ought to answer that one.

CARL ALBERT: I have visited the House of Commons several times. It's so different when the whole government is concentrated right there in one body—legislative and executive, and in a sense judicial, authority—as compared with a "check and balance" and "separation of powers" system, such as ours.

I don't think they have a strong Parliament right now, but I think it is just one of those things. Right now the American Congress seems to be performing better than the British Parliament.

JOHN TOWER: May I add one little word to that? Obviously, we cannot perform in the same way as the British Parliament. Ours is organically a different system and must be; the United Kingdom is a small and relatively homogeneous country, with a unitary system. We are a large and relatively heterogeneous country and must have some kind of federal system. They have almost pure party discipline in the House of Commons, which we do not have in the Congress of the United States. The government rises or falls on a vote in the House of Commons; therefore, party discipline is very strong. Over the long run, they can function perhaps more efficiently and responsively than we can, but their system is not adaptable to our situation, nor ours to theirs.

NAN WATERMAN: Senator Tower is right. The debate about the relative merits of the parliamentary system and our presidential system continues, but it won't get anywhere. Common Cause, which I represent, has consistently pushed for institutional reforms and has emphasized accountability and openness in the Congress. We have criticized what we believed to be flaws and abuses. But I believe, and I think I accurately reflect our membership, that the Congress is the most remarkable legislative body in the world. It is precisely because we want it to remain a strong institution that we keep prodding it. It does participate directly in the full governance of the United States; it makes policy; it cooperates with the Administration; it participates in foreign affairs; and over the past few years it has produced some genuine and constructive internal reforms.

We are dealing with a very pluralistic Congress now, especially in the House, in which new members—an interesting group of members—are more independent. They don't believe government can solve everything; they don't observe all the old lines of party loyalty. They don't want to plan society, but they expect better planning, and they are often very realistic. They try to work their way through a myriad of conflicting priorities, which are pressed upon them by their constituents and their peers, and come up with decisions that none of us may love, but most of us can live with comfortably.

There is some lag in the Congress's responsiveness, but that is not all bad. Public opinion changes so quickly now that it may not be a lag at all. There is some value in being a "conservative body," in the sense of being cautious and deliberate. The Congress often has to slow down its processes so that a little more thorough look can be taken at some of the issues.

A certain amount of conflict is inevitable between the two houses and between citizens and their Congress, but I think that's a very healthy kind of tension. We must remember that conflict is not a dirty word; it is one of the ways that we hammer out policy.

So, in spite of the fact that I have heard many times that Congress is dead, it seems to me that it is very much alive—though I must say it is often ponderous, sometimes it's petty, and it always needs its constituents to prod it.

FROM THE FLOOR: Dr. Allison quoted from Wilson's *Congressional Government* of 1885, and then gave another quotation from a work which reminds me of his 1908 *Constitutional Government*, but I believe he said that second quotation was dated 1890. What work was that?

GRAHAM ALLISON: That's the preface to the fifteenth printing of *Congressional Government*, which was in 1890. I suspect it was the Administration of Grover Cleveland that helped him to dissipate his poor view of the Executive.

FROM THE FLOOR: This will be directed to Speaker Albert and Senator Tower. I'm a student and I hear all kinds of theories on what makes Congressmen "tick," things like electoral motiviation and searching for power and great dreams of the American ideal. I just want to ask you: What is it that makes you tick? Why did you do what you did? Why do you do what you do? Why did you become a Congressman? How much of what you do is directed toward just being reelected? I have read books that say everything you do is shaped by that concern.

CARL ALBERT: I really don't know the answer to your question. Let me try to respond by illustration. I don't claim to be the bravest man that ever served in Congress; but in the 1964 Civil Rights Act—which was the act that opened up public accommodations to all races—we counted our letters as running over 37,000 against and 800 for.

I am from the "Little Dixie" part of Oklahoma. Every member of my staff said I would be defeated if I voted for it; I voted for it and didn't even have an opponent in the next election.

I think on the big things the average Congressman will vote for what he thinks is important. On the little things he'll vote for whatever he thinks will help get him reelected. That's been my judgment, and I believe I have known the Congress as well as any human being for a long time. Most members of Congress are good Americans; they are good citizens; they are honest; and they are responsible people. They do do a lot of things that are not very sound; they sometimes vote for things that are rather silly, but I think when it comes to the real "gut" issues of the nation, the average member of Congress will vote for the country.

ROBERT HARDESTY: Mr. Speaker, President Johnson used to say that most Congressmen voted for his program about fifty percent more than was politically healthy for them to do it.

CARL ALBERT: I think that's about right.

FROM THE FLOOR: What about power? I have read another theory that says you are only in it for power.

JOHN TOWER: I think that anybody who seeks political office understands that power and influence go along with it. Obviously, that would be a motivation. Some people are fascinated with the exercise of power. Some, unfortunately, have messianic complexes about how to use it. They are usually defeated, which is fortunate.

As to how a Senator or Congressman votes—in fact, is it not essential to democracy that those sitting in governance over the people reflect the views, the wishes, and the aspirations of the people?

Therefore, if a Senator or a Congressman reflects the popular sentiment in his district or his state, as he should over the long run, then it is likely that he will continue to be elected.

If, however, a Senator or a Congressman is privy to information or has a peculiar insight or understanding into a problem or a situation in which his conscience and his intellect tell him that he should take a position contrary to that of the majority of his constituency, I think he is bound to do it. In good conscience he should do it and then try to explain to his constituency why he did it.

FROM THE FLOOR: I should like to direct my question to Speaker Albert. Senator Tower may wish to comment, but the question is probably more pertinent to the House.

Mr. Speaker, you commented on the great achievements during the Johnson era, and there were many. That was an era in which there were very strong committee chairmen. Since that time, the House has continued to decentralize, to disperse power, and to become democratized. Can the American people continue to want majorities to govern in Congress, but not have strong political parties? If you had your "druthers," what further centralizing tendencies, if any, would you like to see in the House?

CARL ALBERT: Well, I think first of all that Congressmen are not just looking for power, or even for the passage of legislation. Sometimes it's neither necessary nor desirable. Above everything else, they are looking out for the defense of the nation, the protection of the rights of citizens, the economy and well-being of the nation. So we don't always need legislation on everything; we probably didn't need all the bills that were passed during the Johnson Administration. Johnson just happened to be the ex-majority leader of the Senate, and he probably had been the most effective vote-getting leader the Senate had ever had. It was obviously an historical accident that he became President at the time he did.

I can't say that we shouldn't have openness and shouldn't have power dispersed, because power in the hands of too few is pretty dangerous power, and for a long time power in Congress was in the hands of a very few people. The chairmen of the Rules Committee, the Ways and Means Committee, the Appropriations Committee, and a few subcommittees had too much power for the good of the country. We have stripped them of a great deal of that power, but these recent reforms would not have affected Johnson's ability to put his program over. It would be easier to put it over now than it was then.

Do you know what saved Johnson's Great Society program? We had a meeting of the House leadership, and we decided that we were going to pass a twenty-one-day rule. That meant that if the Rules Committee didn't report a bill within twenty-one days, the chairman of the committee involved could get permission of his committee to ask the Speaker to recognize him to call up that bill without a rule. Well, that took a lot of the power away from the chairman of the Rules Committee. But we don't even need that now. The Speaker appoints the members of the Rules Committee, and he can say to the member, "You won't be reappointed if you don't vote for this," if it's that important. The members know that, so what we have done is to help a man like Johnson—rather than to hinder him—put over a program such as the so-called "Great Society" program.

FROM THE FLOOR: Doesn't the dispersal of the power in the House tend to give more power to the Speaker?

CARL ALBERT: Yes, it does. And it also tends to give more power to more people. The Speaker today has more power than any Speaker since Joe Cannon. He has the authority to nominate every member of the Rules Committee. The caucus can turn him down, but he has the authority to nominate somebody else; the caucus does not have that authority.

The Speaker is chairman of the Steering and Policy Committee. The Steering and Policy Committee is an agency of the caucus, but as an agency of the caucus, it represents the last election and not the seniority of the Congress. And, as the committee on committees, it selects the members to serve on various other committees.

For many years that great, strong, able southern group ran the Democratic side of the Congress. It maintained the seniority principle and it kept control of the key positions. The most important were the Rules Committee and the Ways and Means Committee because through them they appointed the kind of people they wanted. But now those decisions are controlled by people who were elected in the last election.

In 1948 in the eighty-first Congress there were enough Democrats in the Congress that Rayburn could really have taken over, if he had wanted to, and gone back to the Cannon rules. But Rayburn was never one for much reform. He would never have stood for all the reform that I have stood for, or that I have helped put in, because he did not like it. He didn't like to change the Rules Committee; he refused to take a man off the Rules Committee just because he hadn't supported the Democratic Party in the election. He didn't like the twenty-one-day rule, and he got rid of it as soon as he could. To be sure, he had eight Democrats and seven Republicans on Ways and Means, and he had to take two Republicans off to get that. He did that, but he did it unwillingly because, as he told me, he would rather have the Congress in a situation where you can't do everything you want to do, but you can do everything that you try hard enough to do. And that was his philosophy. Mr. Rayburn was a great strategist and had terrific wisdom, but he wasn't nearly as liberal on questions like these as John McCormack and some of the others. And he wouldn't like what we have today.

ROBERT HARDESTY: I am going to call on Mr. Moyers now to sum up and to make some sense out of all that's been said.

BILL MOYERS: I might just sum up by saying that I don't consider the question of institutional reform a bogus question, but like the American penny, it probably has more currency than it has value. The more important factors are probably the influence of personality and, as Elspeth Rostow said, the impact of the times.

The secular moods in this country change quite often, and they often affect politics more than politicians do. Lyndon Johnson, with the help of Congress, passed all that legislation. How? Probably the two greatest forces acting on the civil rights era were the fact that so many blacks had moved north where they could vote, and the 1954 Supreme Court decision, which was expressing a kind of national demand not yet fully sensed or articulated by the people. These were the forces that produced the civil rights legislation.

The war in Vietnam wasn't started by legislation, and it wasn't ended by legislation. It was ended when the secular mood of America turned against it, and the politicians followed.

As both a former bureaucrat and a present observer of the scene, I am not much concerned about the issue of "who's up and who's down" because the genius of our system is the great elasticity permitted by the Constitution. That is why I come down on the side of the Speaker and Senator Tower and others who are loathe to tamper lightly with that document.

The basic issues go far deeper than institutional reform. Almost all democratic societies today are in trouble, partly because the great sweep of our times is toward centralization and statism, and we are having a hard time holding our own against a swing of the public tolerance of those forces. But the troubles of democracy in this era are also due to the insistent demands of unleashed expectation. It is almost impossible for a Parliament, a Congress, or a

President to satisfy the demands placed upon it by people who are enjoying more rights, seeking greater expectations with a keener sense of their entitlements, than ever before in the history of the human race.

The democratic system will survive these stresses and strains, I suggest, just to the extent that elasticity is encouraged and the political "give and take" is not institutionalized or rigidified but instead is permitted to express the creative, political, and tumultuous conflicts that arise out of a people trying to govern itself. As someone has said, a people governing itself is the most beautiful sight in the eye of mankind. That's what I subscribe to. The turbulence and strain that we are talking about is the consequence, not of a small elite group of men or women dictating the public consciousness, but of people attempting to find their own way in an exceedingly complex period.

I do not want James Schlesinger and his friends to dictate our energy policy, and I do not want John Tower and his friends to dictate our energy policy. But somewhere in that confrontation and compromise will come out a policy which will not serve any of us as well as each of us would like, but which may well help us negotiate our way into an era in which presently unseen developments will take us onto a new plateau.

So, I like the system. I enjoy my role as a critic of it because that is an affirmation of what I am talking about. The very fact that we love our system but are free to criticize it, is an affirmation, it seems to me, of its essential genius, a genius that survives despite the fact that a lot of fools like us are involved in it.

Participants

Carl Albert
served as Speaker of the U.S. House of Representatives from 1971 through 1977. He represented the Third Congressional District of Oklahoma from 1947 until his retirement in 1977.

Speaker Albert also served as House Majority Whip from the 84th Congress through the first session of the 87th, then as House Majority Leader from January 1962 until he was chosen Speaker. His committee assignments included House Agriculture; Science and Astronautics; Post Office and Civil Service; House Administration; and Education and Labor.

He is currently a Distinguished Visiting Lecturer in the Political Science Department at the University of Oklahoma.

Graham Allison, Jr.,
Professor of Politics at Harvard University, serves as Dean of Harvard's John F. Kennedy School of Government and Chairman of the Public Policy Program.

His government-related activities have included appointments in the U.S. Department of Defense and memberships on the Committee on Defense and Arms Control of the Democratic Policy Council, and the Council on Foreign Relations.

In addition to numerous articles in professional journals, Mr. Allison's published works include *Essence of Decision: Explaining the Cuban*

Participants • 424

Missile Crisis (1971) and *Remaking Foreign Policy: The Organizational Connection*, (with Peter Szanton, 1976).

Alan Bible
is currently Professor of Political Science at the University of Nevada, Reno. A graduate of Georgetown University Law School, Mr. Bible served in the U.S. Senate from 1954 until his retirement in 1974. Senator Bible held a wide array of committee assignments, including the Appropriations and Interior Committees, the District of Columbia Committee, the Joint Committee on Atomic Energy, and the Small Business Committee.

Lorinne C. (Lindy) Boggs
of Louisiana was a member of the 93rd-95th U.S. Congresses. She served on the House Appropriations Committee and was chairperson of the 1976 Democratic Convention.

John Brademas
has been a U.S. Representative from Indiana since 1958. A former Rhodes Scholar, he has served on the Committee on House Administration, the Committee on Education and Labor, on a number of subcommittees, and as House Minority Whip.

Horace Busby,
a graduate of The University of Texas, served on the staff of the Senate Preparedness Subcommittee from 1948 to 1951. During the Johnson Administration, he was Special Assistant to President Johnson. He has since been a correspondent, journalist, and editor of *Texas Businessman*.

Alan K. Campbell
is Director of the U.S. Office of Personnel Management (formerly the U.S. Civil Service Commission). His academic career has included positions at Harvard University, Hofstra University, and Syracuse University, where he was Dean of the Maxwell School of Citizenship and Public Affairs from 1969 to 1977. He is currently Professor of Public Affairs (on leave) at the Lyndon B. Johnson School of Public Affairs, where he was also Dean before his appointment in the Carter Administration.

In addition to articles in scholarly and professional journals, Mr. Campbell has authored *Metropolitan America: Fiscal Patterns and Governmental Systems* (with S. Sacks, 1967), *Financing Equal Educational Opportunity: Alternatives for State Finance* (with Joel Berke and R. Goettel, 1972), *Taxes, Expenditures and Economic Base: The Case of New York City* (with Roy Bahl and David Greytak, 1974), and *The Political*

Economy of State and Local Government Reform (coedited with Roy W. Bahl, 1976).

Wilbur J. Cohen
is Dean of the School of Education and Professor of Public Welfare Administration in the School of Social Work, the University of Michigan, Ann Arbor. He served as Assistant Secretary for Legislation in the Department of Health, Education, and Welfare from 1961 to 1965, and then as Under-Secretary of HEW through 1968. Among his publications are *Retirement Policies Under Social Security* (1957); *Social Security: Programs, Problems and Policies* (1960); and *Income and Welfare in the United States* (co-author).

Thomas E. Cronin
is Professor of Political Science at the University of Delaware. A former White House Fellow, Mr. Cronin's writings include *To Govern the Metropolity* (1968); *The State of the Presidency* (1975); *Government by the People* (coauthor, 1974, 1978); *The Presidency Reappraised* (coeditor, 1974, 1977); and *The Presidential Advisory System* (coeditor, 1969).

Roger H. Davidson
is Professor of Political Science and Chairman of the Political Science Department at the University of California, Santa Barbara. He served as a staff member for the Select Committee on Committees of the U.S. House of Representatives (1973-74), and as special research consultant to the U.S. Senate's Select Committee on Committees (1976-77).

He is author of a number of books on congressional politics, including *Congress in Crisis* (coauthored with David M. Kovenock and Michael K. O'Leary, 1966); *The Role of the Congressman* (1969); *On Capitol Hill: Studies in Legislative Politics* (coauthored with John F. Bibby, 2nd edition 1972); and *Congress Against Itself* (coauthored with Walter J. Olezek, 1977).

Robert A. Divine
is Professor of History at The University of Texas at Austin. In addition to his memberships in numerous professional organizations, he is a member of the nine-member committee that advises the U.S. State Department on its "Foreign Relations" series.

Mr. Divine is the author of a large number of books including *The Illusion of Neutrality* (1962); *The Reluctant Belligerent* (1965); *Second Chance: The Triumph of Internationalism in America during World War II* (1967); and *Foreign Policy and U.S. Presidential Elections, 1940-1960* (two volumes, 1974).

Lawrence C. Dodd
is Associate Professor of Government at The University of Texas at Austin. A former Congressional Fellow, his publications include *Congress and Public Policy* (1974), *Congress Reconsidered* (coedited with Bruce I. Oppenheimer, 1977), and *Congress and the Administrative State* (coauthored with Richard Schott, 1979).

Morris P. Fiorina
is Associate Professor of Political Science at the California Institute of Technology. His publications include *Congress: Keystone to the Washington Establishment* (1977).

Louis Fisher
is a specialist in American national government with the Government Division, Congressional Research Service, Library of Congress. In addition to his many contributions to professional journals, Mr. Fisher has written *President and Congress: Power and Policy* (1972); *Presidential Spending Power* (1975); and *The Constitution Between Friends: Congress, The President, and the Law* (1978).

Henry B. Gonzalez
of San Antonio has been a member of the U.S. House of Representatives since 1961. He has been a member of the Banking and Currency Committee and chairman of its Subcommittee on International Finance; and served as a House delegate to the U.S.-Mexico Interparliamentary Conference.

D.B. Hardeman,
who received his J.D. from The University of Texas, is currently a practicing attorney.

Mr. Hardeman served as a member of the Texas House of Representatives from 1951 to 1953, and from 1955 to 1957. From 1957 to 1961 he was research assistant to Speaker Sam Rayburn, who designated him official biographer, and from 1962 to 1965, he was administrative assistant to Hale Boggs, Democratic Majority Whip.

Robert L. Hardesty
is Vice Chancellor for Administration of The University of Texas System. He also serves as Vice Chairman of the Board of Governors, United States Postal Service. He was an assistant to President Lyndon B. Johnson from 1965 to 1969, and was editor of Mr. Johnson's memoirs, *The Vantage Point* (1971).

Stephen Hess
is a Senior Fellow in Governmental Studies at the Brookings Institution. He has served as Assistant to the Senate Minority Whip, as Staff Assistant to President Eisenhower, and in a number of other advisory posts. Author of a major monthly column, Mr. Hess has authored several books, among them *Organizing the Presidency* (1976); *The Presidential Campaign: An Essay on the Leadership Process After Watergate* (1974); and *Nixon: A Political Portrait* (with Earl Maxo, 1968).

Ralph K. Huitt
is currently Executive Director of the National Association of State Universities and Land-Grant Colleges in Washington, D.C., and a Professor of Political Science (on leave) at the University of Wisconsin. He is a former Assistant Secretary for Legislation, U.S. Department of Health, Education and Welfare (1965-1969). Mr. Huitt is author (with Robert L. Peabody) of *Congress: Two Decades of Analysis* (1969).

Herbert Kaufman
has been a Senior Fellow at the Brookings Institution since 1969. Formerly Professor of Political Science at Yale, he has written, among other works, *The Forest Ranger: A Study in Administrative Behavior* (1960); *Governing New York City* (with Wallace S. Sayre, 1969); *The Limits of Organizational Change* (1971); *Are Government Organizations Immortal?* (1976); and *Red Tape: Its Origins, Uses, and Abuses* (1977).

Clarence G. Lasby
is Associate Professor of History at The University of Texas at Austin. In addition to numerous articles and papers, Mr. Lasby has published *Project Paperclip: German Scientists and the Cold War* (1971).

Sar A. Levitan
is Research Professor of Economics and Director of the Center for Social Policy Studies at the George Washington University, and Chairman of the National Council on Employment Policy. He is a member of the Federal Mediation and Conciliation Service, the Industrial Labor Relations Association, and other organizations, and has authored many books. These include *The Great Society's Poor Law: A New Approach to Poverty* (1969); *Programs in Aid of the Poor for the 1970s* (1973); *The Promise of Greatness* (1976); and *Warriors at Work: The Volunteer Armed Force* (1977).

William Livingston
is Professor of Government and Chairman of the Comparative Studies Program at The University of Texas at Austin. A former editor of the *Journal of Politics*, his publications include *Federalism and Constitutional Change* (1956); *Federalism in the Commonwealth* (1963); and *Australia, New Zealand, and the Pacific Islands Since the First World War* (with Wm. Roger Louis, 1979).

David R. Mayhew
is Professor of Political Science at Yale University. A student of Congress, his writings include *Party Loyalty Among Congressmen* (1966); and *Congress: The Electoral Connection* (1974), which won the *Washington Monthly* Annual Political Book Award in 1974.

Harry McPherson
is a partner with Verner, Liipfert, Bernhard and McPherson, a business consultant firm in Washington, D.C. He is General Counsel for the John F. Kennedy Center for the Performing Arts.

Mr. McPherson has held positions as General Counsel for the U.S. Senate Democratic Policy Committee, as Assistant Secretary of State for Educational and Cultural Affairs, and from 1965 to 1969, as Special Assistant and Special Counsel to President Johnson. He is author of *A Political Education* (1972).

Harry J. Middleton,
Director of the Lyndon Baines Johnson Library in Austin, served as White House Staff Assistant to President Johnson from 1967 to 1969. A former writer and journalist, his publications include *Pax* (1958) and *The Compact History of the Korean War* (1965).

Bruce Miroff
formerly taught at The University of Texas at Austin and is now Assistant Professor of Political Science at the State University of New York, Albany. He is author of *Pragmatic Illusions: The Presidential Politics of John F. Kennedy* (1976).

Bill Moyers,
a native of Texas, has been anchorman and chief reporter for *CBS Reports* since June 1976. His experience in government is extensive, including serving as Deputy Director of the Peace Corps under President Kennedy, and successively as Special Assistant to the President, Administrative Chief of the White House Staff, and Press Secretary for President Johnson.

Richard E. Neustadt
is Professor of Government at Harvard University, where he has also served as Associate Dean of the John F. Kennedy School of Government. His experience in the federal government includes a stint with the Office of Price Administration in World War II, Special Assistant to President Truman, and consultant to Presidents Kennedy and Johnson. Among his books are *Alliance Politics* (1970), and *Presidential Power* (1960, 1976).

Bruce I. Oppenheimer
is Associate Professor of Political Science at the University of Houston. He was formerly an Assistant Professor of Political Science at Brandeis University (1971-1974) and an American Political Science Association Congressional Fellow (1974-1975). His publications include *Oil and the Congressional Process—The Limits of Symbolic Politics* (1974), and *Congress Reconsidered* (coedited with Lawrence C. Dodd, 1977).

J.J. ("Jake") Pickle
has served since 1963 as a member of the U.S. House of Representatives from Texas's Tenth District. He is a member of the Ways and Means Committee. Congressman Pickle was formerly the Director of the Texas Democratic Executive Committee.

David Eugene Price
is an Associate Professor of Political Science and Policy Sciences at Duke University. A former legislative aide to the late Senator E.L. Bartlett of Alaska, Mr. Price has written *Who Makes the Laws? Creativity and Power in Senate Committees* (1972), and *The Commerce Committees: A Study of the House and Senate Commerce Committees* (1975).

Emmette S. Redford
is Ashbel Smith Professor of Goverment and Public Affairs at the Lyndon B. Johnson School of Public Affairs, The University of Texas at Austin. A former president of the American Political Science Association, he has written a large number of books and monographs, including *Administration of National Economic Control* (1952); *Ideal and Practice in Public Administration* (1957); *American Government and the Economy* (1965); and *Democracy in the Administrative State* (1969).

Elspeth D. Rostow
is Professor of Government and Dean of the Lyndon B. Johnson School of Public Affairs at The University of Texas at Austin. Mrs. Rostow has taught at several institutions, including Barnard College, MIT, and Ameri-

can University. She is active on many professional and political boards and organizations. Among her many affiliations and appointments are the President's Advisory Committee for Trade Negotiations and the Executive Council of the National Academy of Public Administration.

Walt W. Rostow
is Professor of Economics and History at The University of Texas at Austin. He served as Counselor and Chairman of the Policy Planning Council, U.S. Department of State, 1961-66; and then as U.S. Representative to the Inter-American Committee of the Alliance for Progress and Special Assistant to the President in the Johnson Administration.

Among his publications are *The United States in the World Arena* (1960) and *The Stages of Economic Growth* (second edition, 1971); *The Diffusion of Power* (1972); and *The World Economy: History and Prospect* (1978).

Francis E. Rourke
is a Professor of Political Sciences at The Johns Hopkins University. Among his publications are *Dilemmas of Democracy* (1961); *Bureaucratic Power in National Politics* (1965, 3rd ed. 1978); and *Retreat from Empire* (with others, 1973).

Barefoot Sanders,
a recent nominee to the federal judiciary, is a former United States Attorney and Assistant Attorney General in the Department of Justice. From 1967 to 1969, he was legislative counsel to Lyndon Johnson, after which he returned to private law practice.

Allen Schick
has been a Senior Fellow at the Brookings Institution, a Senior Specialist with the Congressional Research Service, and a Research Associate with the Urban Institute. His publications include *Budget Innovation in the States* (1971) and numerous articles on the federal budgetary process.

Richard Schott
is Associate Professor of Public Affairs at the Lyndon B. Johnson School of Public Affairs, The University of Texas at Austin. A graduate of the Maxwell School at Syracuse University and former Foreign Service Officer, his publications include *Professionals in Public Service* (1973), *The Bureaucratic State* (1974), and *Congress and the Administrative State* (with Lawrence Dodd, 1979).

Harold Seidman
is Professor of Political Science at the University of Connecticut. He worked with the U.S. Bureau of the Budget for twenty-five years, serving as Assistant Director of Management and Organization during the Johnson Administration.

He is author of *Politics, Position and Power: The Dynamics of Federal Organization* (1970 and 1975).

Margaret Chase Smith
of Maine served in the U.S. House of Representatives from 1940 to 1948 and in the U.S. Senate from 1949 to 1973. She was Chairman of the Republican Conference from 1967 to 1973. Her Senate Committee memberships included the Armed Services Committee, Space Committee, Appropriations Committee, and on the Appropriations Subcommittees on Foreign Relations and Defense. Mrs. Smith served as Chairman of the Board for Freedom House from 1970 to 1977, and has been director of the Lilly Endowment since 1976.

She is the author of *Gallant Women* (1968) and *Declaration of Conscience* (1972).

James L. Sundquist
is a Senior Fellow at the Brookings Institution, where he serves as Director of Governmental Studies. His government positions have included Administrative Analyst in the U.S. Bureau of the Budget and Deputy Under-Secretary of Agriculture. Among his publications are *Making Federalism Work* (1969), *Dynamics of the Party System* (1973), and *Dispersing Population: What America Can Learn from Europe* (1975).

J. William Theis
is Senior Communications Advisor for the American Petroleum Institute in Washington, D.C. He worked for over thirty years with the International News Service and United Press International, serving as Washington correspondent and Chief of the Senate staff from 1945 to 1968. He is author (with Raymond M. Lahr) of *Congress: Power and Purpose on Capitol Hill* (1967).

John G. Tower,
U.S. Senator from Texas, is a former professor of government at Midwestern University, Wichita Falls, Texas. First elected to the Senate in 1961, his committee assignments have included Ethics; Armed Services; and Banking, Housing, and Urban Affairs. He has also served as chairman of the Senate Republican Policy Committee.

Nan Waterman
of Muscatine, Iowa, has served on the National Governing Board of Common Cause since 1972. Since 1975, she has chaired the Organization Committee of the Board. While with Common Cause she has also chaired task forces on criminal justice and state issues. A former vice president of the National League of Women Voters, Ms. Waterman headed the League's human resources department and was a trustee of its Education Fund.

Thomas Grey Wicker
has been a member of the staff of the Washington bureau of *The New York Times* since 1960, and Associate Editor since 1968. In addition to a number of novels, Mr. Wicker has written *Kennedy Without Tears* (1964), *JFK and LBJ: The Influence of Personality Upon Politics* (1968); and *A Time to Die* (1975).

Garry Wills
is Adjunct Professor of Humanities at the Johns Hopkins University and a newspaper columnist for Universal Press Syndicate. He has written eight books, including *Second Civil War* (1968), *Nixon Agonistes* (1970), and *Inventing America* (1978).